The Adams Papers

ROBERT J. TAYLOR, EDITOR IN CHIEF

SERIES I

DIARIES

Diary of John Quincy Adams

Diary of
John Quincy Adams

DAVID GRAYSON ALLEN, *ASSOCIATE EDITOR*
ROBERT J. TAYLOR, *EDITOR*
MARC FRIEDLAENDER, *EDITOR*
CELESTE WALKER, *ASSISTANT EDITOR*

———————— ☆ ————————

Volume 2   *March 1786 – December 1788*

Index

THE BELKNAP PRESS
OF HARVARD UNIVERSITY PRESS
CAMBRIDGE, MASSACHUSETTS
AND LONDON, ENGLAND

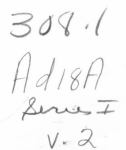

Printed in the United States of America

10 9 8 7 6 5 4 3 2

This book is printed on acid-free paper, and its binding materials have been chosen for strength and durability.

Funds for editing *The Adams Papers* were originally furnished by Time, Inc., on behalf of *Life*, to the Massachusetts Historical Society, under whose supervision the editorial work is being done. Further funds were provided by a grant from the Ford Foundation to the National Archives Trust Fund Board in support of this and four other major documentary publications. In common with these and many other enterprises like them, *The Adams Papers* has continued to benefit from the guidance and cooperation of the National Historical Publications and Records Commission, chaired by the Archivist of the United States, which now also provides this enterprise with its major financial support.

For the first two volumes of the *Diary of John Quincy Adams* additional funds were supplied by the National Endowment for the Humanities, in its continuing effort to promote humanistic studies, and by the Andrew W. Mellon Foundation.

Library of Congress Cataloging in Publication Data

Adams, John Quincy, 1767–1848.
  Diary of John Quincy Adams.

    (The Adams papers. Series I, Diaries; v. 1–)
    Includes bibliographies and indexes.
    Contents: v. 1. November 1779–March 1786—v. 2. March 1786–December 1788.
    1. Adams, John Quincy, 1767–1848. 2. United States—History—1783–1865.
3. United States—Politics and government—1783–1865. 4. United States—Foreign relations—1783–1865. 5. Presidents—United States—Biography. I. Title.
II. Series: Adams papers. Series I, Diaries; v. 1–2.
E377.A185 1981   973.5'5'0924   81-6197
ISBN 0-674-20420-4   AACR2

Contents

Descriptive List of Illustrations

1. JOHN QUINCY ADAMS' ADMITTATUR TO HARVARD, 17 MARCH
   1786   4

   In the late eighteenth century no one was admitted to Harvard unless he could "translate the Greek and Latin Authors in common
   use, such as Tully, Virgil, The New-Testament, Xenophone &c,"
   understood grammar, wrote correct Latin, and had "a good moral
   Character." After an oral and written examination, successful candidates were expected to pay three pounds to the college steward
   "towards defraying their College Charges," and to give bond of two
   hundred ounces of silver for their quarterly college costs ("College
   Laws of 1655, 1692, and 1767 and College Customs 1734/5," Col. Soc.
   Mass., *Pubns.*, 31 [1935]: 347). Sections from the college laws relating
   to admission policy are printed on the third page of the four-page
   document illustrated here. On the second page, otherwise blank,
   the college steward, Caleb Gannett, attested that the candidate,
   Adams, had completed the admission procedure. The admittatur
   was then taken to President Joseph Willard for his signature.
   Adams seems to have been spared the additional task, assigned candidates of the previous generation, of copying out all the college
   laws by hand, its completion also certified by the college president
   in writing.
   From the original in the Adams Papers.

2. JAMES WINTHROP, HARVARD COLLEGE LIBRARIAN   7
   James Winthrop, son of Professor John Winthrop of John Adams'
   student days, served as college librarian from 1772 until 1787, when
   he was eased out of the position. His eccentricities, contentiousness,
   and overbearing manner rendered him intolerable to colleagues and
   students (see entry of 7 July 1787, below). John Quincy Adams was,
   however, quick to perceive the range of Winthrop's intellectual interests, seeing him as the only college official "who for genius and
   learning, would make a figure in any part of Europe." On the other
   hand, he criticized the "old bachelor" for being "without one parti-
   cle of softness, or of anything that can make a man amiable," particularly for his alleged severe remarks "upon the ladies." Once married, Adams added, "He will be more esteemed and beloved than he
   is now, he cannot be less." Winthrop's outside activities in politics
   and the law provided college authorities with the opportunity to rid
   themselves of the brilliant but troublesome and intemperate man. A

vii

succession of judicial posts culminated in the chief justiceship of the Middlesex Court of Common Pleas, but his major concerns remained with learning. He was an original member of the Massachusetts Historical Society. Winthrop willed his library of over three thousand volumes to the fledgling Allegheny College in western Pennsylvania. The portrait used here is one Allegheny's president Timothy Alden repeatedly requested of Winthrop's brother and finally received "to accompany the books" (Sibley-Shipton, *Harvard Graduates*, 17:317–329; JQA to JA, 21 May–14 June 1786, Adams Papers; JQA to AA2, 18 May–17 June 1786, AA2, *Jour. and Corr.*, [3]:116–117; Lawrence Shaw Mayo, *The Winthrop Family in America*, Boston, 1948, p. 251–252).
Courtesy of Allegheny College, Meadville, Pennsylvania.

3. HENRY WARE   8

Henry Ware, Harvard 1785, was John Quincy Adams' first Harvard roommate and a fellow member of Phi Beta Kappa. After graduation Ware taught school in Cambridge while pursuing theological studies, probably under the direction of Timothy Hilliard, Cambridge minister. In August 1787 he declined a tutorship at Harvard to accept a call to Hingham, as successor to the liberal minister Ebenezer Gay. Ware is best known for the controversy generated by his nomination and subsequent election to the Hollis Professorship of Divinity at Harvard in 1805, which precipitated the strife between Unitarians and Trinitarian Congregationalists in New England. His portrait, which now hangs in the Andover-Harvard Divinity School, is a copy by George Fuller of a portrait attributed to a Frothingham, presumably James, the Massachusetts-born artist (Sprague, *Annals Amer. Pulpit*, 8:199–202; Conrad Wright, "The Election of Henry Ware: Two Contemporary Accounts," *Harvard Library Bulletin*, 17:245–261 [July 1969]; George C. Groce and David H. Wallace, *The New-York Historical Society's Dictionary of Artists in America, 1564–1860*, New Haven, 1957).
Courtesy of the Harvard University Portrait Collection. Given to Harvard University in 1879 by Dr. Charles E. Ware.

4. SCIENTIFIC INSTRUMENTS AT HARVARD: THE SMALL MARTIN ORRERY AND THE SET OF WEIGHTS AND PULLEYS   26

Named after Charles Boyle, fourth Earl of Orrery and patron of science, this orrery, or planetarium, was used to show planetary motion in classroom demonstrations given by Samuel Williams, Hollis Professor of Mathematics and Natural Philosophy. Adams attended Williams' classes during his junior and senior years at Harvard. The cylindrical case, mounted on a stand and containing a gear-driven mechanism, has on its top a calendar and the signs of the zodiac. The larger ivory balls, representing the planets, are fastened to rods which are connected to the drive shaft. When the crank is turned the planets revolve around the sun, a centrally placed brass ball. Tiny ivory moons are placed around the Earth, Jupiter, and Saturn. The college purchased this orrery from Benjamin Martin, London scientific-instrument-maker, in 1766, two years after the disastrous fire at Harvard Hall had destroyed the library and scientific instruments in the philosophical chamber.

The set of weights and pulleys, suspended on strings and hooks from a rectangular mahogany frame, was acquired from Martin a year earlier. Until the early part of the present century it was in constant use at Harvard to demonstrate the mechanical properties of pulleys (David P. Wheatland, *The Apparatus of Science at Harvard, 1765–1800,* Cambridge, 1968, p. 48–51, 86–87).

Courtesy of the Collection of Historical Scientific Instruments, Harvard University.

Eliphalet Pearson, Hancock Professor of Hebrew and Other Oriental Languages from 1786, came to Harvard after serving as the first principal of Phillips Academy in Andover. Besides Eastern languages, he taught a course in English grammar to beginning Harvard students. One student found Pearson's "severe criticism" of his work "beyond its legitimate boundaries," but conceded that he was "indulgent to the faults of those who manifested strength of thought, or taste in expressing it, or signs of self-culture." Believing that the man was unduly maligned by student opinion, John Quincy Adams wrote in his Diary that he knew of no official at Harvard who was "so polite to Scholars, or show[ed] so few Airs." Called by students "the Elephant," as much a play on words as a comment on his bulk, Pearson was a dominant force in college politics. Serving briefly as president in 1804, he was forced out in the quarrel attendant upon the election of Henry Ware to the Hollis Professorship of Divinity. After resigning from Harvard, Pearson returned to Andover and established the theological seminary there (Col. Soc. Mass., *Pubns.,* 5 [1897–1898]: 205–206; Sidney Willard, *Memories of Youth and Manhood,* 2 vols., Cambridge, 1855, 1: 268–269, 271; JQA, Diary, 17 Sept. 1786, below; Morison, *Three Centuries of Harvard,* p. 188–190).

Courtesy of Philips Academy, Andover, Massachusetts.

"Mr. Williams is more generally esteemed by the students," John Quincy Adams wrote to his sister shortly after entering Harvard, "than any other member of this government. He is more affable and familiar with the students, and does not affect that ridiculous pomp which is so generally prevalent here." Adams had come to Harvard several weeks earlier than he had expected, because Williams, the Hollis Professor of Mathematics and Natural and Experimental Philosophy, was to begin his series of twenty-four lectures. Adams became so engrossed with the subject, which he had never before studied, that he wrote copious notes on the lectures during and after their presentation. On balance, Adams liked the professor, but was more restrained in his praise of Williams the intellectual, who he thought was "too fond of his ease, and unwilling to make any great efforts for acquiring a perfect knowledge of the branch which he professes." By his senior year, when he again attended Williams' class, Adams noted that his "lectures which were highly entertaining last year, afford me little amusement or instruction at present" because they were repetitious and unvaried. Despite some important scientific work at Harvard and his rapport with students, financial difficulties and the scandal which ensued led Williams to resign a year after Adams graduated. He spent the rest of his life in Rutland, Vt., where he followed various pursuits—legal copyist, historian, and newspaper editor (JQA to AA2, 18 May–17 June 1786, AA2, *Jour. and Corr.*, [3]: 118; JQA to JA, 21 May 1786, JQA, *Writings*, 1:22; JQA, Diary, 5 April 1787, below; Sibley-Shipton, *Harvard Graduates*, 15:134–146).

The engraving of Williams reproduced here was made from a miniature, now lost, and appeared in *New England Magazine*, 12:498 (June 1895).

Courtesy of the Massachusetts Historical Society.

7. A WESTERLY VIEW OF HARVARD COLLEGE, CIRCA 1783–1784   140
This sketch of the college and nearby buildings, drawn by Samuel Griffin shows, from left to right: Apthorp house; the First Church; Wadsworth and Wigglesworth houses, both nearly obscured by the church; the Sewall house; the parsonage; Christ Church; Massachusetts, Harvard, and Hollis halls; and several houses which faced what was later called Holmes Place. Apthorp house, dubbed the "Bishop's Palace," was constructed in 1761 for the Reverend East Apthorp, who was in charge of the Anglican mission in Cambridge. Although unclear in this perspective, the houses in front of the First Church faced Braintree Street (now Massachusetts Avenue). Wadsworth house, at this time the residence of Joseph Willard, served from 1728 as the home of Harvard presidents for well over a hundred years. Wigglesworth house, owned successively by the professors Wigglesworth, became the temporary home of John Quincy Adams and James Bridge during the long, enforced vacation of 1786–1787. Professor Stephen Sewall owned the third house; Thomas Boylston Adams lived there during his freshman year at Harvard (1786–1787). Also along Braintree Street was the parsonage, home of the Reverend Timothy Hilliard during John Quincy Adams' student days at Harvard. The First Church, its thin spire shown in this view, was built in 1756; here students and faculty gathered for the services that were compulsory until the beginning of the following century. Christ Church (Episcopal), shown to the right of the parsonage, was actually across the Common and some distance away from the college buildings. The small structure de-

picted in front of Harvard and Hollis halls was the college brew-house (and perhaps a barn), which was later put to other uses and eventually torn down in the early nineteenth century. Of the three houses on the right-hand side, one was owned by Caleb Gannett, Harvard steward from 1779 to 1818, and another belonged to Professor Eliphalet Pearson.

Massachusetts Hall, built in 1720 and used as a dormitory, contained thirty-two rooms, each with two smaller studies. Harvard Hall, constructed after the fire of 1764, served many purposes. Within it were the chapel and library, a philosophical chamber with lecture room and scientific apparatus, and the kitchen, buttery, and dining hall. Built in 1763, Hollis Hall, in which John Quincy Adams lived, contained thirty-two rooms, each with two small studies or a study and a sleeping closet. During his junior year, Adams shared with Henry Ware a corner room on the third floor on the southeastern side, from which he commanded "a fine Prospect of Charlestown and Boston and the extensive Fields between." He was less fortunate the following year. Because he lived with his brother Charles, a sophomore, he was assigned a room much inferior. The room was in such disarray and disrepair that the brothers spent their first two days repapering their studies (Hamilton Vaughan Bail, *Views of Harvard: A Pictorial Record to 1860,* Cambridge, 1949, p. 61–62, 64–72, 77–80, 32, 54–55, 57; Col. Soc. Mass., *Pubns.,* 20 [1920]: illustration between 146 and 147; Richard Cranch to AA, 5–6 July 1786, Adams Papers; JQA, Diary, 26 July, 16–18 Aug. 1787, below).

Courtesy of the Harvard University Archives.

8. JOHN QUINCY ADAMS' HANDWRITTEN MUSICAL SCORE FOR
FLUTE, 1787   187

These two pages (recto and verso) of John Quincy Adams' hand-copied flute music give evidence of his college pastime. Evidently he copied new tunes on various sheets of paper of different sizes, keeping them in order with page number and a number system for the tunes. Evidence that has come to the attention of the Adams editors suggests that Elizabeth C. Adams, daughter of Thomas Boylston Adams, John Quincy's brother, may have distributed sheets of flute music to friends desiring mementos, just as she did with other manuscript pieces from the family collection. Few pages have come to light, and none have survived among the Adams Papers.

John Quincy Adams began playing the flute shortly after his cousin Billy Cranch bought one for him in Boston in early April 1786. Within weeks he was taking lessons and thought he had "begun to learn." Although he felt accomplished enough within a few months to perform for relatives and young ladies, his main interest was performing with the Musical Society, one of the many extracurricular clubs he joined at Harvard. Still, he complained that the flutes and violins were usually so difficult to tune "that we can seldom play more than three or four times at a meeting" (JQA to

AA2, 15 April–16 May 1786, in AA2, *Jour. and Corr.*, [3]: 106; Mary Smith Cranch to AA, 14–26 July 1786, Adams Papers; JQA, Diary, 17 July 1786, 28 March 1787, below).

When his sister sought to dissuade him from playing because it was "certainly very prejudicial to Health," he reassured her that those whom he had consulted felt no harm would come from "moderate use" of the instrument. Insisting that flute-playing was his "greatest amusement, and the chief relaxation after study," he felt he could not give it up (AA2 to Elizabeth Cranch, 18 July 1786, MHi: Cranch Papers; AA2 to JQA, 22–23 July 1786; JQA to AA2, 14 Jan.–9 Feb. 1787, Adams Papers).

Courtesy of the Essex Institute, Salem, Massachusetts.

9. HARVARD THESES, 1787: THE THESES SHEET   256

10. HARVARD THESES, 1787: DETAIL FROM JOHN QUINCY ADAMS'
    MATHEMATICAL THESES   257

The broadside, measuring approximately 25 by 16 1/2 inches, was a compilation of questions based on subjects studied by members of the class of 1787. All Harvard graduating seniors were assumed to be able to answer these propositions in Latin if an inquiring alumnus posed them. The propositions were compiled by four theses collectors chosen by members of the class at the beginning of the senior year. The four areas assigned were technology, grammar, and rhetoric; logic, metaphysics, ethics, theology, and politics; mathematics; and physics. To his surprise, John Quincy Adams was selected as mathematics collector. He proudly wrote to his father: "Little did I think, when you gave me those Lessons at Auteuil, which you call our suppers, that they would have been productive of this effect. It is a laborious task, and will confine my studies for the ensuing year, much more to the mathematics, than, I should have done if I had been left at my own disposal." John Adams approvingly told his son that "the Same part fell to my Share in the Year 1755" (JQA, Diary, 26 Aug. 1786, below; JQA to JA, 30 Aug. 1786; JA to JQA, 10 Jan. 1787, Adams Papers).

Adams worked on the theses off and on throughout the winter and early spring, occasionally mentioning in his Diary his troubles with "fluxions" (differential calculus). Eventually he passed them on for approval and was later in charge of the publication of the sheet. In later years, Charles Francis Adams or Charles Francis Adams 2d donated a number of these 1787 theses sheets to Harvard. The one reproduced here shows insertions in Adams' more mature hand denoting the names or initials of the theses collectors. Two of the theses (in metaphysics and ethics), printed in bold type, were used as topics for "syllogistic disputations" in the commencement program.

Courtesy of the Harvard University Archives.

Theophilus Parsons, Newburyport lawyer and later chief justice of the Supreme Judicial Court of Massachusetts, was John Quincy Adams' first choice, after his father, for a legal preceptor. As early as August 1786 John Quincy had determined to spend the next three years studying law in a place like Newburyport, "where there might be Society sufficient for relaxation at Times, but not enough to encourage dissipation." As the possibility of his father's return to America before the summer of 1787 became more remote, Dr. Cotton Tufts made arrangements for John Quincy to apprentice with Parsons.

Over the course of years Parsons established a reputation as an outstanding law teacher. He was so popular that the Suffolk Bar voted to limit the number of student apprentices to three for each office because of the disproportionate number that flocked to him. Parsons impressed John Quincy as a human "law-library . . . proficient in every useful branch of science." The Newburyport lawyer's far-flung practice and his interest in politics often kept him away from the office, but when he was there, Adams received the intellectual stimulus denied to so many of his contemporaries: "No student can be more fond of proposing questions than [Parsons] is of solving them. He is never at a loss, and always gives a full and ample account, not only of the subject proposed, but of all matters which have any intimate connection with it."

Parsons' portrait is from a stipple engraving by S. A. Schoff of the unfinished sketch by Gilbert Stuart, which appears as the frontispiece in Theophilus Parsons Jr.'s memoir of his father. According to the son, the sketch was painted from memory almost immediately after the Chief Justice's death (Sibley-Shipton, *Harvard Graduates,* 17:190–207; JQA to JA, 30 Aug. 1786; Cotton Tufts to JA, 30 June 1787, both Adams Papers; JQA to James Bridge, 17 Nov. 1787, owned in 1961 by Richard Hamlen of New York; JQA, Diary, 27 Nov. 1787, below; Theophilus Parsons [Jr.], *Memoir of Theophilus Parsons . . . ,* Boston, 1859, p. 35).

This view of Boston from Dorchester was a familiar sight to John Quincy Adams in traveling between Braintree and Boston, Haverhill, or Cambridge. Drawn by landscape and townscape painter William Pierrie (or Pierie), ca. 1776, it appeared among the numerous coastal charts in Joseph F. W. Des Barres' *The Atlantic Neptune,* London, 1777. Both Des Barres, a Swiss-born naturalized English subject, and Pierrie had served as British officers in America before the Revolution.

In the foreground to the right, the brook flowing into the South Bay then formed the boundary line between Dorchester and Roxbury. Shirley Palace, the large building on the left, now standing as the Shirley-Eustis house, was an elegant country home in the Dutch Palladian style, built in the 1740s by Governor William Shirley and occupied by Governor William Eustis from 1814 to 1825. Beyond the estate, across the Charles River estuary, is Cambridge.

From Shirley Palace the road to Boston turned toward the Shawmut peninsula, which was connected to the Roxbury mainland by a narrow neck of land, soggy at high tide and spray-blown in rough weather. Beyond the neck was the town of Boston, built at the base of three distinct peaks—Mount Vernon, Beacon, and Pemberton hills. From its founding and throughout the eighteenth century, settlement in Boston was concentrated along the road to the neck (now Washington Street), on King Street (now State Street), around Dock Square, and along a number of streets in the North End where merchants and shipbuilders had their dwellings, warehouses, wharfs, and yards in close proximity (George C. Groce and David H. Wallace, *The New-York Historical Society's Dictionary of Artists in America, 1564*–1860, New Haven, 1957; Edith Roelker Curtis, "The Palace That Will Shirley Built," *New-England Galaxy,* 4:21–34 [Spring 1963]; Walter Muir Whitehill, *Boston: A Topographical History,* Cambridge, 1959, p. 1–46 *passim*).

Courtesy of the Boston Athenaeum.

VOLUME 2

Diary 1786–1788

Diary of John Quincy Adams

15TH.

Between 9 and 10 in the morning, I went to the President's, and was there ⟨admitted⟩ examined, before, the President, the four Tutors three Professors, and Librarian. The first book was Horace, where Mr. *James*[1] the Latin Tutor told me to turn to the Carmen saeculare where I construed 3 stanza's, and parsed the word *sylvarum,* but called *potens* a substantive. Mr. Jennison,[2] the greek Tutor then put me to the beginning of the fourth Book of Homer; I construed Lines, but parsed wrong αλληλομς. I had then παραβληδην given me. I was then asked a few questions in Watts's Logic by Mr. Hale,[3] and a considerable number in Locke, on the Understanding, very few of which I was able to answer. The next thing was Geography, where Mr. Read[4] ask'd me what was the figure of the Earth, and several other questions, some of which I answered; and others not. Mr. Williams asked me if I had studied Euclid, and Arithmetic, after which the President conducted me to another Room, and gave me the following piece of English to turn into Latin, from the World.[5] *There cannot certainly be an higher ridicule, than to give an air of Importance, to Amusements, if they are in themselves contemptible and void of taste, but if they are the object and care of the judicious and polite and really deserve that distinction, the conduct of them is certainly of Consequence.* I made it thus. *Nihil profecto risu dignior, potest esse, quam magni aestimare delectamenta, si per se despicienda sunt, atque sine sapore. At si res oblatae atque cura sunt sagacibus et artibus excultis, et revera hanc distinctionem merent, administratio eorum haud dubie utilitatis est.* (I take it from memory only, as no scholar is suffered to take a Copy of the Latin he made at his examination.) The President then took it, was gone about 1/4 of an hour, return'd, and said "you are admitted, Adams," and gave me a paper to carry to the Steward. I had the form of a bond, which is

I

to be signed by two persons, in the presence of two witnesses: this is what every student is obliged to do; and the bondsmen forfeit 200 ounces of silver, if the bills are not paid once a Quarter. Mr. Shaw went to Boston before dinner: I sent by him the form of the bond to Doctor Tufts to fill it. I went with my brother to Mr. Dana's, where we dined, in Company with Harris, of the Senior Class, who boards there. It is against the Laws of the College to call any under-graduate, by any but his Sir-name, and I am told, the President, who is remarkably strict in all those matters, reproved a gentleman at his table, for calling a student Mr., while he was present.

Spent the afternoon, and evening in College. The Sophimore Class had what is called in College, an high-go. They assembled all together in the Chamber, of one of the Class; where some of them got drunk, then sallied out and broke a number of windows for three of the Tutors, and after this sublime manoeuvre stagger'd to their chambers. Such are the great achievements of many of the sons of Harvard, such the delights of many of the students here.

Return'd to Mr. Dana's, and lodged there.

[1] Eleazar James, tutor 1781–1789, was later a lawyer in Barre, Mass. (MH-Ar:Quinquennial File).

[2] Timothy Lindall Jennison, tutor 1785–1788, became a Cambridge physician (*Harvard Quinquennial Cat.*; John A. Vinton, "Memoir of the Lindall Family," *NEHGR*, 7:22 [Jan. 1853]).

[3] John Hale, tutor 1781–1786, became a lawyer in Portsmouth, N.H. (Bell, *Bench and Bar of New Hampshire*, p. 413–414).

[4] Nathan Read, tutor 1783–1787, was later an inventor and served Salem in the congress, 1800–1803 (Essex Inst., *Hist. Colls.*, 24:259–262 [Oct.–Dec. 1887]).

[5] *The World*, No. 171, 8 April 1756.

16TH.

Rain'd, a great part of the day. Walker went to Boston and brought back my bond properly filled. Dined with Mr. Dana. Returned to the College in the afternoon, and lodged with my brother. The Government have been endeavouring to discover the principal actors in the last Night's riot. The Sophimores are very much afraid, that some of them will suffer some public punishment, for it.

17TH.

This morning I finished the business of my admission. I carried the bond to Mr. Gannett the Steward. He then certified that

I had complied with the Law. This certificate I went with to the President's, who thereupon signed an *Admittatur,*[1] which I had to carry again to the Steward, to be filed with the College Papers. The Steward told me then I was to all intents and Purposes, generally, and in all particulars a Member of the University.

I then went to Boston with my Cousin, and *Abbot,* of the Juniors. I paid a number of Visits, and dined at my Uncle Smith's. Walk'd about the Town, with Charles Storer; spent the Evening, and supped, at Deacon Storer's, lodged at my Uncle Smiths.

[1] JQA's certificate of admission (Adams Papers) is described and illustrated in this volume; see the Descriptive List of Illustrations, No. 1.

18TH.

Went with Charles Storer, and heard, the debates in the House of Representatives; and afterwards, the pleadings, at the Supreme Court. Dined at Deacon Storer's with Mr. Jackson. As Dr. Tufts was detained in Town, he let me have his horse, to go out to Braintree with. I set out between 3 and 4, with Mr. Cranch. I stopp'd and drank tea at my Uncle Adams's. Got home, just before dark.

19TH.

Heard Mr. Wibird, preach all day from Romans VIII. 1st. There is therefore now no Condemnation to them that are in Christ Jesus, who walk not after the flesh, but after the Spirit. The Ladies complain'd that it was an old one, which, had been delivered so many Times, that, they had it, almost by heart: indeed it is said Mr. Wibird has written but very few Sermons; and preaches them over and over in a continual succession. I went down to the Library, in the Evening, and got me, some books, which I shall want at College.

20TH.

The whole forenoon, I was with my Cousin, down at our house, packing up, furniture, though many articles, are yet to be got. Mr. Cranch went to Boston in the forenoon, and Mr. Tyler, said he was very much mortified, he was obliged to attend the town meeting, but he should be at home in the Evening. It was

I. JOHN QUINCY ADAMS' ADMITTATUR TO HARVARD, 17 MARCH 1786
See page vii

however so late before he return'd that I could not have the Pleasure of his Company in the Evening.

21ST.

Cold, disagreeable Weather, all the morning. In the afternoon it storm'd. My Aunt and myself, sat out to go and see Mrs. Warren, in Milton, but it began to storm before we got far; so we turn'd about and went down to Uncle Quincy's. We drank tea with him. I believe he would be much happier than he is, if he was married.

22D.

At about 10 o'clock, Lucy and I, set out from Braintree. She came with me to Boston, to purchase, the remainder of the furniture that I shall want. We stopp'd at Milton, and saw Mrs. Warren; she was much affected at the news she lately received, of the Death of her Son Charles, in Spain a few Weeks after his arrival there. Nothing else was to be expected when he sailed from here, but however prepared we may be for the Death of a Friend; the tears of Nature, still must flow from the eye, and the sigh of sympathy from the heart.

As we passed by Milton hall, we saw the Ruins, of the Windows. On the 21st. of March the Junior Sophister Class, cease reciting at 11 in the forenoon; they generally in the Evening have a frolic; yesterday they had it, at Milton-hall, and as they are not by any means at such times remarkable for their Discretion, we saw many fractures, in the Windows of the hall they were in.

We got to Boston at about 1 afternoon; Mr. Cranch, and Dr. Tufts dined out. We dined with Mr. Foster; and soon after dinner, I footed it for Cambridge. When I got here I found all my things had arrived. Immediately after Prayers I went to the President, who said, "Adams, you may live with Sir Ware,[1] a batchelor of Arts." I made a most Respectful Bow, and retired. I was the greatest Part of the Evening, fixing all my things to rights.

[1] Henry Ware, Harvard 1785.

5

23D.

I did not hear the Bell Ring this morning, and was tardy at Prayers. Every time a Student is tardy at prayers he is punished a penny; and there is no eluding that Law, so that a Student must prefer not attending prayers at all; to being 1/2 a minute too Late. After prayers we went in to Mr. James to recite in Terence. The manner of reciting this is, the Persons at the head of the Class, read an whole Scene in the Latin, and then the same into English, and when they have finished the next read another Scene and so on.

Cranch went to Boston in the forenoon. Thursday, is a Day which commonly both Tutors and Students take as a leisure day, and there is seldom, any reciting, except in the morning. After Prayers the President read a Paper to this effect. That on the evening of the 15th. it appeared the Sophimores had assembled at the Chamber of one in the Class, and had behaved in a tumultuous, noisy manner; that at length they sallied out, and were very riotous to the disturbance, and *dishonour* of the University. But as their conduct till then had been such as deserved approbation, and was *submissive* and, as they early shew a proper repentance for their fault having, presented an humble petition to be forgiven. Therefore, it had been voted that no further Notice should be taken of it; but it was hoped the Students, would not abuse, the Lenity of the government, but rather show that they were deserving of it. The Fresh men, who are always, as a Class, at Variance with the Sophimores, thought the government had been partial; and the Consequence was, that Mr. James, the Tutor of the Sophimore Class, and who was supposed, to have favoured them, and to have been the means of saving them from severer punishment; had four squares of glass broken in his Windows. Such was the Effect of the Lenity, which was to induce the Students to do their Duty.

24TH.

No reciting, for any of the Classes, on Fridays, for the whole, Day. I wrote some Problems out of Ward[1] to carry to Mr. Williams, next Monday Morning. After Prayers, I declaim'd, as it is term'd. Two Students every evening Speak from Memory, any Piece they chuse, if it be approved by the President. It was this Evening my turn, with the 2d. Abbot, and I spoke, from *As you*

2. JAMES WINTHROP, HARVARD LIBRARIAN
See pages vii–viii

3. HENRY WARE
See page viii

like it. All the world's a stage &c. When I came to the description of the Justice, in fair round Belly with good Capon lined, Tutors and scholars, all laugh'd, as I myself, truly represented the Character. But the President did not move a feature of his face. And indeed I believe, it is no small matter, that shall extort a smile from him when he is before the College. This Afternoon I took from the Library, Montesquieu's Reflections on the rise and fall of the Romans, and an Anacreon.[2] The two elder Classes have a right, every second friday to take from the Library, each person three volumes, which he must return at the End of a fort'night.

[1] John Ward, *The Young Mathematician's Guide. Being a Plain and Easie Introduction to the Mathematicks . . . with an Appendix of Practical Gauging,* London, 1719, and other editions (Harvard, *Catalogus Bibliothecae,* 1790, p. 92).

[2] *Considérations sur les causes de la grandeur des Romains et de leur décadence,* Amsterdam and Leipzig, 1759; *Works of Anacreon,* transl., with the original Greek, by Joseph Addison, London, 1735, and other editions (*A Catalogue of the Library of Harvard University in Cambridge, Massachusetts,* Cambridge, 1830; Harvard, *Catalogus Bibliothecae,* 1790, p. 12).

25TH.

We had no reciting to day. Saturday mornings commonly the two elder Classes, recite to their own Tutors in Doddridge's Lectures on Divinity;[1] but our Tutor did not hear us. The weather, warm and Pleasant. In the Afternoon Mr. Cranch, and my Cousin, came, and brought me the remainder of my furniture; I did but little to day, because the weather being so fine, we were almost all day walking, about.

[1] *A Course of Lectures on the Principal Subjects in Pneumatology, Ethics and Divinity,* London, 1763, by Philip Doddridge. So essential had the lectures become to the Harvard curriculum that the college treasurer ordered thirty sets of them from London to lend to such of the two senior classes as were unable to buy them (Harvard, *Catalogus Bibliothecae,* 1790, p. 166; MH-Ar:Corporation Records, 3:199).

26TH.

Mr. Patten,[1] a young Clergyman from Rhode Island, preach'd in the forenoon, from Proverbs III. 17. Her ways are ways of pleasantness, and all her paths are Peace. I never felt so disagreeably, in hearing any Preacher. He look'd as if he had already, one foot in the grave, and appeared plainly, to suffer while he spoke. His diction was flowery, but he spoke, in a whining manner, lowering his voice, about an octave, at the last Sylla-ble of every Sentence. I dined at Mr. Dana's. In the afternoon Mr. Everett,[2] a Boston preacher, gave us a discourse, *from II of Corinthians. I. 12.* For our rejoycing is this, the testimony of our conscience, that in simplicity and godly Sincerity, not with fleshly wisdom, but by the grace of God, we have had our Conversation in the world, and more abundantly to you ward [toward you]. The Contrast in the preaching, was as great as that in the men, for Mr. Everett is quite, a large man. He pleased very generally. The weather has been uncomfortably warm all day, and the Evening, has by no means been cool.

[1] Probably William Patten, minister at Newport (*Historical Catalogue of Brown University, 1764–1904,* Providence, 1905).

[2] Oliver Everett, minister of New South Church, Boston, 1782–1792, and father of Edward Everett (Sprague, *Annals Amer. Pulpit,* 1:559).

27TH.

We recited this day in Euclid, to our own Tutor, Mr. Read, as we shall do all the week. We began, at the 4th. Book, and the way of reciting is, to read the Proposition, and then without the book demonstrate it: but it is by no means a popular, book, and many of the Students, will do nothing with it. At 9 we attended Mr. Williams. He gave each of us two or three problems, to draw the Diagrams: this is a more easy, and more pleasant Study than Euclid. After Prayers, the Senior Class, had a Class meeting, in order to check the freshmen, who they suppose have taken of Late too great Liberties. By the Laws, of the College,[1] all freshmen, are obliged to walk in the yard, with their heads uncovered, unless, in stormy Weather, and to go on any errand, that any other Scholar chuses to send them, at a mile distance. But the present freshmen have been indulged very much, with respect to those Laws; and it is said, they have presumed farther than, they ought to have done. The Seniors it is said, have determined to enforce the old Laws, send the Freshmen, and order, their hats off, in the yard.

[1] JQA actually means not laws but the college customs, nearly all of which applied only to freshmen. For the most nearly contemporary extant listing, recorded in 1781, see Josiah Quincy, *The History of Harvard University,* 2 vols., Cambridge, 1840, 2:539–541 (MH-Ar: Faculty Records, 4:257).

28TH.

Mr. Williams, this day, gave us, the first Lecture, upon Experimental Philosophy. It was upon the Properties of Matter, as *Extension, Divisibility, Solidity, Mobility, figure,* and Vis Inertiae. After the Lecture was over, he told us, the Regulations, which were, that the Door should be lock'd at the beginning of the Lectures; that there should be no whispering, nor spitting on the floor, and some others. After prayers *Bancroft,* one, of the Sophimore Class read the Customs to the freshmen, one of whom (McNeal) stood with his hat on, all the Time. He, with three others, were immediately (*hoisted,*) (as the term is,) before a tutor, and punished. There was immediately after, a Class meeting of the Freshmen; who it is said determined they would hoist any scholar of the other Classes, who should be seen with his Hat on, in the yard, when any of the Government are there. After the meeting, several of the Class went and had a high go. In Consequence of which the Librarian,[1] had a number of squares of glass broke, in his windows. Drunkenness is the mother of every Vice.

[1] James Winthrop.

29TH.

This forenoon we had a Lecture from Mr. Wigglesworth,[1] the Professor of Divinity, upon the Question, whether Some Persons, had not carried their Ideas of the Depravity of human Nature, too far? He appeared to reason very coolly, and without prejudice upon it. He supposed that although mankind, are greatly depraved; yet that the Scriptures, show, he is not so, absolutely in capable of doing any thing good. In the afternoon Mr. Cranch, and Dr. Tufts, stop'd here, on their Road to Lincoln.

[1] Edward Wigglesworth, successor to his father as Hollis Professor of Divinity 1765–1791 (Sibley-Shipton, *Harvard Graduates,* 12:507–517).

30TH.

My Trunks, which I have been so long expecting, came, at last this morning, from Haverhill. White, and my Brother, went to Boston; this day our Class finished reciting in Euclid. A Lesson was set us in Gravesande,[1] for next Quarter; when we go, in to Mr. Read. It would have been best to have gone in to Gravesande before Mr. Williams, began his Lectures; but the Class was considerably delayed last year, by Mr. Howard's[2] going away, as he was the mathematical Tutor. Mr. Cranch stopp'd here, on his Return, from Lincoln. Weather fair and pleasant all day. The freshmen, are still very high. Sullivan, one of the Seniors had a Window broke, by one of them this Evening.

[1] Willem Jacob van's Gravesande, *Mathematical Elements of Natural Philosophy, Confirmed by Experiments, Or, An Introduction to Sir Isaac Newton's Philosophy . . .*, transl. John Théophilus Desaguliers, 2 vols., London, 1720–1721. When JQA requested JA to purchase a copy for him in England, he asked for the octavo edition because it was the one "studied here. They are very scarce in this Country, as they can neither be bought,

nor borrowed out of College" (JQA to JA, 21 May – 14 June, Adams Papers).

[2] Bezaleel Howard, Harvard 1781, tutor 1783–1785, had been minister at Springfield, Mass., since 1785 (Heman Howard, *The Howard Genealogy: Descendants of John Howard of Bridgewater, Massachusetts, from 1643 to 1903* [Brockton, Mass.], 1903, p. 54; *Harvard Quinquennial Cat.*).

31ST.

No reciting, this day. I was not in at Prayers, in the morning. Mr. Williams gave us, his second Lecture, upon those Properties of Matter, which though not essential to it, was in a greater or smaller degree common to all. Such were Attraction, which was of 2 kinds, Cohesion, and Repulsion, and Gravitation. The Substance of the Lectures I have taken down on Separate Paper,[1] so that I shall not repeat it here. I attended the Junior tea-Club, and signed the Regulations, as I was admitted to it, Last Evening. A Nephew of the President, by the same Name, was this day examined, and admitted, as a Junior Sophister.

[1] None of JQA's Harvard lecture notes has been found.

SATURDAY APRIL 1ST. 1786.

After having had a month of March uncommonly pleasant, and warm, the Present one begins with a Snow Storm. From about 2 o'clock afternoon it has snow'd, steadily till late in the Evening. Our Class recited this morning in Doddridge, but I was not in. My Chamber is so situated that the College bell, does, not sound with sufficient force to wake me, in the morning, and I have not of late been used to rise, so early as 6, which is here, the hour for prayers.[1]

[1] For a discussion of JQA's physical surroundings at Harvard, see the Descriptive List of Illustrations, No. 8.

2D.

The storm continued all night with unabated violence, and it blew so hard that one of our Windows was burst in. While we were fixing it up again, the bell, rang and toll'd for prayers though neither of us heard it. It continued snowing as much as ever till about noon, and there was no meeting all day. After dinner, I went and spent a couple of hours at Sever's chamber, after which I returned to my own, and wrote something upon surveying.

3D.

We recite this Week, to Dr. Jennison in Greek. Mornings in Homer, and afternoons in the Greek Testament. Willard, first came in to recite; the Dr. ask'd me by what rule λαβων, governed γομνῶν. H: 6: v. 45. I did not know, and said Verbs of Sense &c. No, it was under *that long Rule;* I read the long Rule, there was nothing to be found in it, that would apply. He said there was something very peculiar in it, and I sat down. He is not a very extraordinary greek scholar, but they say, he improves, as it is but of late since, he has taken that department. At 11. We had a Lecture from Mr. Williams, upon Motion; that of elastic, and that of nonelastic bodies. The Lecture was not, to me, so entertaining, as the two former. This evening, there were it is said upwards of 100 Scholars out on the common, armed with Clubs, to fight the People, belonging to the Town. A few evenings since, Lovell, a junior, got quarrelling with a man belonging to the Town, about a girl, two or three other juniors being present took Lovell's part, and a few blows were dealt on both sides. Lovell, has told his Story just as he pleased; and has raised almost all college; for this Society like most others thinks that an insult offered to one member, must be resented by all, and as in a well ordered Republic, although, some of the Classes, have of late, been so much at Variance, yet immediately upon a foreign insult they all United. The only thing wanting, to make the scholars highly praise-worthy in this Case, is a good Cause. It appears plainly that the first insult was from Lovell, and the original Cause of the quarrel an infamous girl. There would probably some very severe blows have past had not the Tutors and Professor Williams, interposed, this Evening. They perswaded both

13

Parties to disperse; but this will perhaps be only a Suspension of arms: I doubt whether the matter will end here.

4TH.

The Seniors this morning, had a forensic disputation, upon the Question, whether a democratical form of Government, is the best of all. The Class in alphabetical order, alternately supported or opposed this Question. I went to Sullivan's chamber. Studied in the 7th. Book of the Iliad. I made tea, for the Club this Evening. They were all here Amory, Beale, Bridge, 3 Chandler's, Cranch, Hammond, Kendall, Little, Lloyd, Mason, Putnam, White, and Williams. After tea, and singing two or three songs, they all retired but Bridge, a very steady, and studious young fellow, who sat and had a couple of hours chat with me.

5TH.

No reciting this morning. Cranch went to Boston, bought me a flute. We had a Lecture from Mr. Williams, upon Motion proceeding from Gravity. Williams, the Professor's son, made tea for the Club; I was a great part of the Evening, taking off, extracts from the morning Lecture.

6TH.

Fast day: I was at meeting all day, as indeed all the Students, must be, by Law, unless, excused by a Tutor. The President preach'd two Sermons from Micah VI. 6, 7, 8. Wherewith shall I come before the Lord, and bow myself before the high God? Shall I come before him with burnt offerings, with calves of a year old. Will the Lord be pleased with thousands of Rams, or with ten thousands of rivers of oil? Shall I give my first born for my transgression, the fruit of my body, for the sin of my soul? He hath shewed thee O man what is good; and what doth the Lord require of thee, but to do justly and to love mercy, and to walk humbly with thy God? It is certainly a most noble Subject, and we had 2 good Sermons upon. That in the afternoon especially, I thought excellent. No flowers of rhetoric, no Eloquence, but plain common Sense, and upon a liberal plan. But the President has by no means a pleasing Delivery. He appears to labour, and struggle very much, and sometimes strains very hard. And making faces, which do not render his harsh countenance, more agreeable.

7TH.

Return'd my books to the Library. We had the 5th. Lecture from Mr. Williams, who informed us, he should not have another till the first Monday in the next Quarter. This was upon projectile Motion, and the central Forces. Deacon Storer pass'd by in a Chaise, and gave me a Letter, from my Sister which was dated December 9th.[1] It was very acceptable, as I have not heard before, since, the beginning of January. White returned to Haverhill, by leave from the President, though the Vacation will not begin till next Wednesday. We had no Prayers.

[1] Letter not found.

8TH.

Dined at Mr. Tracy's, in Company, with Mr. Molyneux, Mr. Price, Dr. Cutting, Mr. Mores an Englishman, Mr. Storer and H. Otis,[1] and Mr. Hughes. There were two sharp wits present, Mr. Hughes and Dr. Cutting; their bons-mots flew about very frequently. After Dinner I went with Mr. Storer, to Mr. Gannetts for a few Minutes. Went very early to Bed.

[1] Harrison Gray (Harry) Otis, who received his master's degree from Harvard in 1786 and shortly thereafter was admitted to the Boston bar (*DAB*).

9TH.

Attended the meeting all day. Mr. Hilliard preached in the forenoon from Job II. 10. What? Shall we receive good at the hand of God, and shall we not receive evil. He inculcated submission to the Divine will both in Prosperity and Adversity: it was occasional, as he lost one of his Children, in the Course of the week. Dined, with Bridge, at Professor Williams's. Mrs. Williams is affable. Miss Jenny, very pretty. Sam: is one of my Classmates. The afternoon Text was from Matthew VI: 33. But seek ye first the kingdom of God, and his righteousness, and all these things, shall be added unto you. We drank tea, and spent the Evening at Bridge's Chamber. I wrote a Letter to my Father.[1]

15

[1] No letter has been found written by JQA to JA between 2 April and 21 May. Internal evidence in the letters written on these two dates indicates that no other letter was written or, at least, sent during the intervening period.

IOTH.

No reciting this Day, because the Government met to examine the reasons of those scholars that are absent, or have been within the two last Quarters. Went over in the Evening with the musical Club, and heard them play a number of tunes, at Mr. Tracy's Summer-house. Spent the Evening with Bridge at his Room.

IITH.

We recited this morning in Locke on the Understanding to Mr. Hale. A number of the scholars first read, the Lesson that has been given, and the others in their turns give an account of particular Sections. At about 10 o'clock 2 horses came from Braintree for my brother and myself to go home upon. Mr. Cranch came a little before 11. At about 11 1/2 the Government and Corporation came and seated themselves, and the President spoke very audibly, expectatur Oratio in Lingua Latina, per Andrews. It was in praise of Literary Societies, and mentioning the advantages derived from them. The next thing was a forensic dispute upon the Question, whether Error could be productive of good to mankind. Sullivan supported, and Taylor opposed it. Their parts were both very well; but Taylor, though I think he had the wrong side of the Question maintained it best. The English Dialogue, between Scipio Africanus, and Julius Caesar,[1] was spoken by Williams, and Waldo, and I thought well. The Greek Oration by Cranch, and the Hebrew by Burge followed, and lastly the Oratio in lingua Vernacula, as the President calls it, by Gardner. It was upon the progress of the Christian Religion; was very well done, and closed with about 20 lines of very pretty, Poetry. The President then called out expectatur Symphonia, and a song was sung, after which, as all the Company was going, the musical Club play'd a number of tunes upon their Instruments which closed the Scene. We soon after went into Commons, and dinner was not quite ready; there was no bread, and there was such a screaming from every part of the Hall, *bread! bread!* that it might be heard I suppose at a mile's distance.

At about 4 o'clock Beale, my brother, and myself set off to return to Braintree. Beale left us about 3 miles from Mr. Cranch's where we arrived just at Sun set. The weather very fine.

¹ This was the highly republican dialogue in George Lyttelton's *Dialogues of the Dead*, 4th edn., London, 1765, p. 353–370 (MH-Ar:Faculty Records, 5:216–217).

12TH.

I went down to our Office,¹ to see if there was a Gravesande, there, but none was to be found;—while we were at dinner my Cousin came in from Boston, where he went last night from Cambridge. In the afternoon Charles, and I went out fowling, but came home, as deeply laden as we went. We went in the Evening, and Cranch play'd to an Echo; it has a very agreeable effect.

¹ That is, JA's law office, a ground-floor room in what is now known as the John Quincy Adams Birthplace.

13TH.

Went down and staid part of the forenoon, at the Office. Drank tea at Mr. Apthorp's. A man of a strange character. I intended when I came from Cambridge to have written, a great deal during this Vacation, but I find there is continually something or other happens to prevent me; so that I begin to fear, I shall do but very little.

14TH.

We went down to General Palmer's at German town. Went to catch fish, forenoon and afternoon, but with little success; It was late before we got home, and I was very much fatigued; I have, not walk'd so much in one day these 6 months.

15TH.

At home all day; wrote to my Sister.¹ Mr. Cranch return'd, in the Evening, and brought a number of English News Papers with him. All, as common, full of nothing.

A Declamation to be spoken on Wednesday June 7th. 1786.

"Varro, the most learned of the Romans, thought, since Nature is the same wherever we go, that this single circumstance was sufficient to remove all objections to change of Place,

taken by itself and stripped of the other inconveniences which attend exile. M. Brutus, thought it enough, that those, who go into banishment cannot be hindered from carrying their Virtue along with them. Now, if any one judge that each of these comforts is in itself insufficient, he must however confess that both of them joined together, are able to remove the terrors of exile. For, what trifles must all we leave behind us be esteemed, in comparison of the two most precious things which men can enjoy, and which we are sure, will follow us wherever we turn our steps, the same Nature, and our proper Virtue? Believe me, the providence of God, has established such an order in the World, that of all which belongs to us the least valuable parts can alone fall under the will of others. Whatever is best is safest; lies out of the reach of human power; can neither be given nor taken away. Such is this great and beautiful work of nature, the world. Such is the mind of man, which contemplates and admires the world whereof it makes the noblest part. These are inseparably ours, and as long as we remain in one we shall enjoy the other. Let us march therefore intrepidly wherever we are led by the course of human accidents. Wherever they lead us, on what coast soever we are thrown by them, we shall not find ourselves absolutely strangers. We shall meet with men and women, creatures of the same figure, endowed with the same faculties, and born under the same laws of nature. We shall see the same Virtues and Vices, flowing from the same general Principles, but varied in a thousand different and contrary modes, according to that infinite variety of laws and customs which is established for the same universal end, the preservation of Society. We shall feel the same revolution of Seasons, and the same Sun and Moon will guide the course of our year. The same azure vault, bespangled with stars will be every where spread over our heads. There is no part of the world from whence we may not admire those planets which roll, like ours, in different orbits round the same central Sun; from whence we may not discover an object still more stupendous, that army of fixed Stars, hung up in the immense Space of the Universe, innumerable Suns, whose beams, enlighten and cherish the unknown worlds which roll around them; and whilst I am ravished by such contemplations as these, whilst my soul is thus raised up to heaven, it imports me little what ground I tread upon."
Bolingbroke, Reflections upon Exile.[2]

[1] Letter not found. One letter, printed in AA2, *Jour. and Corr.*, [3]:106–112, bears the date 15 April – 16 May 1786, but the substance of the letter under the initial date shows that it was begun on 25 April.

[2] Henry St. John, Viscount Bolingbroke, *Letters on the Study and Use of History*, London, 1770, p. 445–448 (MQA).

16TH.

Mr. Weld[1] the Minister in the middle Parish, preached for Mr. Wibirt, and took his text all day from Hebrews IV.11. Let us labour therefore to enter into that rest, lest any man fall after the same example of unbelief. I have not heard a more indifferent prayer, or Sermon, since I came home. Sermon I say, for although I was all day at meeting, yet I did not hear the afternoon one. We went down to our house in the Evening to get some Papers, and books.

[1] Ezra Weld, minister of the First Congregational Church, Braintree, 1762–1816 (Weis, *Colonial Clergy of N.E.*).

17TH.

We went out on a shooting party, and were gone all the morning. The weather quite warm all day. Mr. Tyler return'd, but did not come into the House, till 11. at night. It is the last day before the setting of the Court; so that he had a great deal of Business.

18TH.

My Uncle Cranch, and Mr. Tyler went to Boston in the morning. About noon it began to Storm; at about 5 afternoon, Mr. Tyler came up the yard, with Eliza, just returned from Haverhill and there was nothing, but how do you do? and I am so glad to see you, and when did you come? and how and so on. No news from Haverhill but bad. Mr. Johnny White's wife, after lying in the 6th. of this month, was very well for several days; but caught a cold, which produced a putrid fever, and sent her the night before last to "that Country from whose bourne no Traveller returns."[1] It seems as if misfortunes of the severest kind, were continually the lot of this family.

[1] *Hamlet,* Act III, scene i, lines 79–80.

19

19TH.

Drizzling, misty weather all day. Did not stir out of the house. Amused myself with reading, writing, and taking lessons on the flute; which I have lately begun to learn.

20TH.

The weather continued just the Same, all day. It sets every one yawning, and keeps all within doors. But it is very advantageous for the husbandry, and has already given a great start to the grass.

21ST.

Same Story over again. Chilly, and misty. This is but a poor way of dragging out an existence; I want much to be doing something: here, every minute something turns up to prevent me, from writing. I could do more in two days at Cambridge, than I have in the whole vacation here. Next Wednesday we shall again return to our Business.

22D.

I went to Boston this morning, with a Chaise, for Mr. Cranch to come home. Stop'd at Milton, and bespoke me a writing desk. Dined at Mr. Foster's: and at about 4 o'clock set out again and got to Braintree, just after dark. Convers'd on the road, with Mr. Cranch Who is always entertaining, and always instructive. Continuation of the Storm. The Sun has not appeared this week.

23D.

Heard old Parson Wibird, preach from Luke. XIX. 10. For the Son of man is come to seek and to save that which was lost. Mr. Cranch said he had heard it ten Times before. No one would complain if the Parson would read printed Sermons, But to hear one thing continually repeated over which does not deserve, perhaps, to be said more than once, is very fatiguing.

We had the Pleasure of Mr. Tyler's Company, in the morning, and at noon. It is the first Time I have seen him since I returned to Braintree.

24TH.

It seems as if there is to be no end of this Stormy weather. It does not look more likely to clear up, than it did, a week agone; Charles and myself lodg'd down at our house; it is almost 7 years since I pass'd a night there before this.

25TH.

Weather still the same. Mr. Wibird spent the afternoon at Mr. Cranch's. I went with my brother down, and drank tea at my Uncle Adams's. Had some difficulty to get horses to go to Cambridge with to-morrow. Mr. H. Hayden, died last night of a wound he received by a gun going off, while he was fowling, about 3 weeks agone.

26TH.

The Vacation being at end; Charles and I left Braintree at about 10 o'clock. My Cousin has been unwell, with a bad Cough several days, and therefore intends to stay till Saturday. The weather, for the first Time these ten days was favorable, which was a lucky circumstance to us. We got to College, at about 1. just after Commons. I dined on bread and cheese; there were only 40 scholars, in at Prayers, this afternoon. Put my name in at the Buttery. At the end of each Vacation, every scholar, must go in Person, and give his name to the Butler; any scholar who stays away after the expiration of the Vacancy, unless, he gives good reasons for it, forfeits 1 sh. 6d. every night. Spent the Evening at Mr. Dana's, where I found a Mr. and Mrs. Buckminster, from Portsmouth.

27TH.

A List of the Present, junior Sophister Class[1]

William Lovejoy Abbot.
*Abiel Abbot
*John Quincy Adams.
Jonathan Amory
Samuel Angier
*William Amherst Baron
   [Barron]

*Benjamin Beale
*James Bridge.
*Josiah Burge
John Chandler.
Thomas Chandler
*Gardner Leonard Chandler
Caleb Child

*William Cranch
*Joshua Cushman
Peter Eaton
*Oliver Fiske
John [Murray] Forbes
Bossinger [Bossenger] Foster
**Nathaniel Freeman
Timothy Fuller
Thomas Hammond
*Thaddeus Mason Harris
Walter Hunnowell
  [Hunnewell]
Joseph Jackson
Asa Johnson
Ephraim Kendall
Nathaniel Laurence
  [Lawrence]
Ebenezer Learned
*Moses Little

James Lloyd
James Lovell.
William Mason
Daniel Mayo
Samuel Mead
Ephraim Morton
*Hezekiah Packard
Nathaniel Shepherd
  Prentiss.
Samuel Putnam
Isaac Rand.
John Sever
Solomon Vose
John Jones Waldo
Francis Welch
Leonard White
Richard Whitney
Samuel Willard.
Samuel Williams.

No reciting this day, nor indeed this week. The Scholars that live near Cambridge, commonly come and enter their names in the Buttery, and then go home again, and stay the remainder of the Week. I went down to the President's in the morning to carry a Letter to him. Spent my Time in writing, reading, and playing on the flute. Lodg'd with my brother.

[1] JQA's classmates are identified under the "character sketches" which he included in the diary entries of his senior year. In addition to those listed here, the class of 1787 included three other students—William Samuel Judd, Samuel Kellogg, and John Phelps, who were transfer students from Dartmouth and Yale. They entered Harvard in the months following this entry. The asterisks apparently denote members of the Harvard chapter of Phi Beta Kappa inducted before 11 Dec. 1786. Putnam and White were also members, but their names are unmarked and were presumably missed because the list continues on the verso of the Diary page. The meaning of the double asterisk before Freeman's name is uncertain (MH-Ar:Phi Beta Kappa Records, 1 :*passim*).

28TH.

The weather fine, but rather cool.

Somewhat unwell, and had a bad head ache in the afternoon. My Cousin, and Leonard White, both came. We had been anxious for Leonard, as we heard he was sick: he was so in the beginning of the Week, but, has now pretty well recovered. About half the College, are now here. The bill at prayers, is not kept,[1] till the Friday after the Vacation ends.

[1] That is, bills of absence and tardiness. See entry of 19 Aug., note 1 (below).

29TH.

Went to Mr. Dana's, in the afternoon, upon some business. There were two gentlemen, there, one of which, had a deal of small talk with Miss Almy,[1] upon matrimony. Tea, at 3d Chandler's. Most of the Members were there. Few of the Scholars are now absent. Windy Weather.

[1] Presumably a daughter of Benjamin and Mary (Gould) Almy, of Newport; Mrs. Elizabeth Dana's family, the Ellerys, were intermarried with the Almys (*Vital Record of Rhode Island. 1636–1850. First Se-* *ries. . . .*, ed. James N. Arnold, 20 vols., Providence, 1891–1911, 4:Part II:80; Joris Janssen De Rapaljé, *William Almy, of Portsmouth, Rhode Island, 1630*, Chicago, 1897, p. 35, 82).

30TH.

Heard Mr. Hilliard[1] all day upon Acts. VII. 9. And the patriarchs moved with envy sold Joseph into Egypt: but God was with him. The Sermons were good, but there is such, a sameness in almost all the Sermons, I hear preach'd, that they are Seldom very entertaining to me. Dined at Mr. Dana's, with his brother in Law Mr. Hastings, Captn. Hobby, and two Seniors, Dwight, and Harris. Mrs. Dana, always sociable and contented. Dwight and Harris, have a very good reputation in College; it is supposed they will have good Parts at Commencement, they will be distributed in about a fort'night. Two young fellows from New Haven, offered themselves yesterday, for the Senior Class; but after examination, were not found qualified for admittance; this was surely losing the Substance by grasping at the Shadow; for they have not only failed getting their degree, here, but have lost the opportunity of having one, at their own College.

[1] Timothy Hilliard, minister at the First Church, Cambridge (Sibley-Shipton, *Harvard Graduates*, 16:59–63).

MONDAY MAY IST. 1786.

We recite this Week again to Mr. Jennison. This is a young man: indeed much too young, (as are all the Tutors,) for the Place he occupies. Before he took his second degree, which was last Commencement, he was chosen a Tutor, of mathematics, in which he betray'd his Ignorance often. In hearing the Sophimores recite in Geography, he had occasion to speak, of the alteration of the Style by Pope Gregory. But instead of giving them an account of the fact, and the reasons, for which it was done; he only said (very wittily) I don't know how it happened, but there have been eleven days knocked in the head. Several other Instances equally absurd are told of him. Last fall, he changed departments with Mr. Reed, and took up the Greek. His own Class, the Freshmen, were the first that laugh'd at him in that: for he gave one of them the word γυνη to parse, it was said right, but he was corrected by the Tutor, who said the genitive Case was της γυνης. He has improved since that, but still makes frequent mistakes. It is certainly wrong that the Tutors should so often be changed, and be so young as they are. It would be better to chuse a person immediately after he has taken his degree, than as they do: because, when a youth leaves College, he is obliged to turn his attention to other Studies, and forgets a great deal, of what he studied at College: whereas when he has lately graduated, he has all fresh in his mind. The Dr. affects a great deal of popularity in his Class, and with the help of the late disagreement between the Classes he has pretty well succeeded; but he does not seem to care, what the other Classes think of him.

2D.

Our Tutor, gave us this morning, a most extraordinary, construction of a passage in Homer. Abbot 1st. was beginning to construe, the 181st. line of the 6th Book.

πρόσθε λέων, ὄπισθεν δὲ δράκων, μέσση δέ χίμαιρα[1]

He said, a Lion, before, but the Dr. corrected him, by saying it meant superior to a Lion; Abbot immediately took the hint, and made it, superior to a Lion, inferior to a Dragon, and equal to a wild boar. I confess I should never have had an Idea, of giving such a Translation of this passage, though it always appeared to me a plain, easy one. I was pretty confident too, that comparative adjectives, governed a genitive; but now it is plain that it is no matter what case, a word is in and with this manner, it is much easier to read the ancient authors; because, you may render, any Latin or Greek word, by any English one you chuse.

24

¹ "In front a lion, and behind a serpent, and in the midst [middle] a [she-]goat," a description of a Chimaera, a triple-bodied monster (*The Iliad of Homer, Done into English Prose,* transl. Andrew Lang and others, London, 1925, p. 116).

3D.

Wednesday, and Monday, are our two busiest days in the Week. Every minute is employ'd. This morning at 6. We went into Prayers after which we immediately recited. This took us till 7 1/4. At 7 1/2 we breakfasted, at 10, we had a Lecture on Divinity from Mr. Wigglesworth. It was upon the Wisdom of all God's actions, and justifying those parts of Scripture which some, have reproached, as contrary to Justice. At 11. we had a Philosophical Lecture, from Mr. Williams, upon the mechanical Powers, and particularly, the Lever, and the Pulley. At 12 1/2 Dinner. At 3. an Astronomical public Lecture upon the planet Mercury, a very circumstancial, account of all its transits over the Suns Disk, since the first discovery of it by Kepler, to this day May 3d. 1786. when it will again pass the disk of the Sun, the 15th. Time since its first Discovery. Unfortunately it will pass in the Night so that it cannot be observed in this Country. Mr. Williams told us of all its different periods which are 6 or 7. from 3 years to more than 260. In the Course of this Century, it will pass twice more, in 1789, and in 1799.

At 4. again we recited, and at 5, attended prayers again, after which there are no more exercises for this day, but we are obliged in the evening to Prepare our recitation for to-morrow morning. This I think is quite sufficient employment for one day, but the last three days in the week we have very little to do. Thursdays and Saturdays, reciting only in the morning, and Fridays, a Philosophical Lecture.

⟨4th.⟩ A Cart came this day from Braintree, and brought us some things. We had after Prayers a Class meeting, about making a present to our Tutor. It is customary at the end of the freshman year to make a present to the Tutor of the Class: but it has been delay'd by ours to the present Time, and many would still delay it, and lay it wholly aside. The Custom, I think is a bad, one, because, it creates partialities in a Tutor, because it increases the distinction between the wealthy, and the poor Scholars, because it makes the Tutor in some measure dependent upon his Class, and because to many that Subscribe it is a considerable expence but the Salaries of the Tutors, being so low,

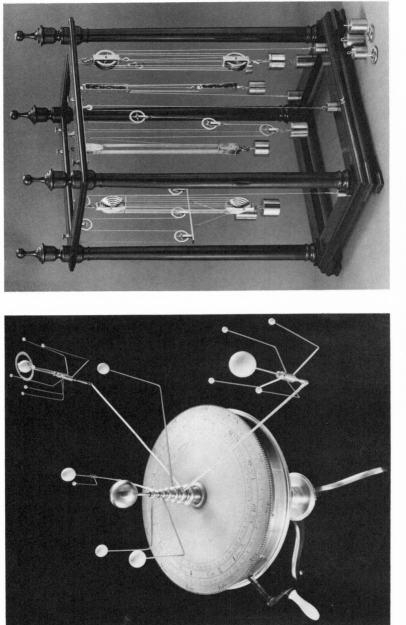

4. SCIENTIFIC INSTRUMENTS AT HARVARD:
THE SMALL MARTIN ORRERY AND THE SET OF WEIGHTS AND PULLEYS
See pages viii–ix

and it having been for many years an universal custom, I am sorry to see our Class so behind hand, and several, who could well afford it, and have really subscribed, meanly endeavouring, to put off the matter from Quarter to Quarter, till they leave College. *Bridge,* was chosen moderator, and it was finally voted that those who chose to give any thing, should deliver it to Kendall, on or before the 20th of this month: and another Class meeting was appointed for the 22d. to consider how the money should be laid out: the meeting was then dissolved.

4TH.

No reciting this morning, on account of the last Nights Class meeting. This is a privelege, that all the Classes, and joy,[1] and I am told there have been in our Class fellows, so lazy, and so foolish, as to call a Class meeting merely for that Purpose.

I went to Boston this morning, with Leonard White. Sauntered about Town; almost all the forenoon. Dined at My Uncle Smith's. In returning, Leonard, and I, were all the Time, disputing, upon Love, and Matrimony. Upon the whole, his System, is the best I believe, though, it might be carried to extremes, that would be very hurtful.

I saw to day in the News Papers, of a duel fought between Mr. Curson, (who is mentioned: p: 115) and a Mr. Burling, in which the former was kill'd.[2] The Circumstances, that caused it, were not honourable, to the Person, that fell, and if ever a duel, was justifiable, it is surely, in such a case as this.

[1] Thus in MS; probably an inadvertence for "enjoy."

[2] JQA had met Samuel Curson, a New York merchant, on 21 July 1785. Burling, from Baltimore, accused Curson of injuring his family, and pursued him to the West Indies, London, and finally back to New York, where he challenged Curson to a duel. Curson agreed to meet him, but refused to fire because he claimed he had done Burling no injury. After an exchange of words, Burling killed him (*Massachusetts Centinel,* 3 May).

5TH.

We had, this morning, a Philosophical Lecture, from Mr. Williams, in which he concluded the Subject of the mechanical powers. This is not so entertaining a subject, as some others but it is a very important one as all the instruments that mankind make use of: of what kind so ever, are upon the principle, of one or more of these Powers. There was a Lecture, at the meeting house in the afternoon; I did not attend: but went, and stay'd at Williams's till about 4 o'clock. Kendall, got quite high. We went to his Chamber with him. I made tea for the Club in the Evening. They stay'd with me, till about 9 o'clock. A number of the Seniors too, got very high this afternoon.

6TH.

Recited in Doddridge's Lectures on divinity. This is an attempt to refute mathematically all the objections, that have been raised against the Christian religion, and the Bible in general; I wish we studied some other book instead of that. A day or two since, Mr. Hale, the Tutor in metaphysics, gave us out a forensic question, to dispute upon, Tuesday, the 16th. of this Month. I employ'd almost all this afternoon, in writing mine, yet have not written, 3 pages full. We have now Stormy weather.

7TH.

Sacrament day. Mr. Hilliard, preach'd in the morning from 1st. of Corinthians. I. 30. But of him are ye, in Christ Jesus, who of God, is made unto us, wisdom, and righteousness, and sanctification and redemption. I do not remember all his arguments; What I did [remember?], was not so pleasing to me, as his afternoon, discourse, which was from Acts. XI. 26. And the disciples, were called Christians, first in Antioch. This was, I thought, a very good one; he recommended to his hearers, to consider themselves, as Christians and not particularly belonging to any sect. He introduced, very properly, an excellent passage from Scripture, against Schisms. I: Cor: III. 4,5. For while one saith, I am of Paul, and another I am of Apollos, are ye not carnal? Who then is Paul; and who is Apollos, but ministers, by whom ye believed, even as the Lord gave to every man? His argument was, if a particular attachment, to such men as Paul, and Apollos, was reproved in the Scriptures, how much then must particular sects at this day, or enthusiasm for the opinions of men, much inferior to Paul or Apollos, be displeasing to God.

8TH.

We recite this week in Terence, and Caesar to Mr. James. This is the tutor of the oldest standing in College. He is very well acquainted with the branch he has undertaken, and Persons, that are not Students, say that he is much of a Gentleman. But it seems almost to be a maxim among the Governors of the College, to treat the Students pretty much like brute Beasts. There is an important air, and a haughty look, that, every Person, belonging to the government, (Mr. Williams excepted) assumes, which indeed it is hard for me to submit to. But it may be of use to me, as it mortifies my Vanity, and if any thing, in the world, can teach me humility, it will be, to see myself subjected to the commands of a Person, that I must despise.

Mr. James is also accused of having many Partialities, and carrying them to very great length and moreover, that those partialities do not arise from any superior talents or Virtues, in the Student, but from closer, and more interested motives. There are some in our Class with whom, he has been peculiarly severe, and some he has shown more favour, than any Tutor ought to show to a Student. I wish not his favour, as he might prize it too high, and I fear not his Severity, which he can never display, if I do my Duty. Mr. Williams, gave us a mathematical Lecture at 9. Still on Surveying. About two thirds, of the Class are behind hand, and the rest are obliged to wait for them till they come up.

9TH.

We had this afternoon a public[1] Lecture upon Divinity. It is a pretty common Custom among the Students, to take their books into the Chapel, and whilst these Lectures are going on they study their next Lessons; those indeed, that do this, are some of the good Scholars of the Class, for there are many, that do not look, into a book, more than once a Quarter, before they go in to recite. Lovell, was punish'd this morning, for carrying to the recitation an English Terence. Was he to punish all, that do so, about 2/3 of each Class would be fined. I was not at reciting this morning, because, the prayer Bell did not wake me. This is only the second Time, that it has happened to me this Quarter, and I hope, I shall soon be so used to early rising, as to be up every morning, a little after five. I find my Time flies away here, as fast as any where. Being engaged now in a multiplicity of Studies, I cannot make, a very rapid progress in any branch. Latin, Greek, Mathematics, natural Philosophy, and Metaphysics, are enough to fill any ones hands at one Time, and I have calculated, that about 6 hours every day are taken up in Prayers, recitings, Lectures &c. which are not to be consider'd, as studies. But mathematics and natural Philosophy, are studies so agreeable, that the Time I devote to them, seems a time of relaxation.

¹ Public lectures were open to the entire college; private lectures, which JQA mentions in later entries, were given to selected classes.

10TH.

We finished the Andria of Terence this morning. The Class began it last Feby. I went through it at Haverhill in 3 Evenings, however it must be said, here they Study it only 1 week in 4, and that week, only 4 mornings, but even in that way, it has taken 12 lessons to go through this one play. At 11. we had a Lecture from Mr. Williams, upon hydrostatics. He keeps exceeding close to Gravesande's. Definitions, experiments; nearly all the same. We recite afternoons, the Latin Week, in Caesar, but I have had nothing to say this Week: the Class is so numerous, that he, cannot hear more than one half of them recite at once, and so he takes turns. Mr. I. Smith and Dr. Welch, were here in the afternoon. There was a Concert, by a number of Performers from Boston; Several of the Ladies and Gentlemen, of the Town were present, as well, as many of the Students, but I did not attend. *Bigelow,* a Senior came, and spent an hour after the Concert. He told me, that his mother,¹ went to school to my father, about 30 years ago.

¹ Timothy Bigelow's mother was Anna Andrews Bigelow, the only daughter and heir of Samuel Andrews of Worcester (Chart, "Pedigree of Lawrence," *NEHGR,* 10:facing 297 [Oct. 1856]). JA had taught school in Worcester while reading law with James Putnam thirty years before.

11TH.

There has been no reciting this day. Cranch, went to Boston, in the morning, and will not probably return this Night. I have been employ'd almost all day in writing off, Mr. Williams's yesterday Lecture; perhaps I spend too much time, at this, but I think it may be of considerable advantage, for the Study of S'Gravesande's; and the whole must be over before the 21st. of June; on that day, the Seniors leave the College. It is Customary, for every Class, as soon as they commence Seniors to choose, among themselves, a person to deliver a Valedictory Oration on the 21st. of June. But by the Intrigues of several of the present Seniors, who wanted to have it, and saw no prospect of obtaining it, the Class, had delay'd hitherto, choosing any one, and it was thought there would be None; but they had this afternoon a Class meeting upon the Subject, and at length chose Fowle, to deliver a Valedictory Poem. The President was inform'd of it by a Committee, who also told him it was the unanimous desire of the Class, that Fowle, might, have another Poem, as a Part, for Commencement. He answered that he approbated their Choice, and would consider upon the other matter.

Was Part of the Evening at Waldo's chamber.

12TH. FRIDAY.

We had a Lecture, this day from Mr. Williams upon Hydraulics. Studied Algebra, in the morning; as I have determined to do, a couple of hours every friday, and Saturday morning. Cranch came back to day; he stay'd to hear the Concert, which was given last Night. The musical Society, took it into their heads to Serenade, the Tutors, and a number of the gentlemen, belonging to the Town; they were out till 3 o'clock in the morning.

13TH.

No reciting, this morning: was employ'd all day in mathematical Studies, of which I begin to grow exceeding fond. After dinner, I had Bridge, Kendall, Little and Sever about an hour at my Chamber. Bridge, and Little are two of the best Scholars in our Class, and moreover very clever fellows. Sever has a strong natural genious, and genuine Wit. But his morals are loose, and he is not by any means fond of studying.

14TH.

Mr. Thatcher of Boston preached in the forenoon from John XX: 13. And they say unto her, Woman, why weepest thou? She saith unto them, Because they have taken away my Lord, and I know not where they have laid him, and in the afternoon, from Ephesians V and 11. And have no fellowship, with the unfruitful works of darkness, but rather, reprove them. This is the best Orator, that I have seen in the Pulpit for a long time—and he has

31

a fine Voice; his Composition is good, but nothing very extraordinary; the excellent manner in which he reads it, sets it off to great advantage. There were some expressions, particularly, in the forenoon Sermon, which I thought favoured too much of Conceit. Such for Instance, was his deducing, a long discourse upon atheism, from the expression they have taken away my Lord. Indeed he appeared to be very anxious about infidelity, and libertinism, all day, and finished his afternoon Sermon, with an address to the debauched infidel, whosoever he was.

15TH.

We recite this week to Mr. Hale, in Locke. This is upon the whole, the most unpopular Tutor in College. He is hated even by his own Class. He is reputed to be, very ill natured, and severe in his Punishments. He proposes leaving College, at Commencement, and I believe, there is not an individual among the Students, who is not very well pleased with it. One of my Class Mates, said the other day, "I do not believe it yet, it is too good news to be true." Such are the Sentiments of all the Students with Respect to him.

16TH.

We had this morning, a forensic dispute, upon the Question, Whether the immortality of the human Soul be probable from natural Reason.[1] My Inclination coincided, with my duty, and I read the following piece in the affirmative.

"That there is in Man, an interior Power, far different, and vastly superior, to that possess'd by any other being, of the animal Creation, no one I believe will deny to be highly probable from natural Reason. Indeed, it is so obvious, and there are such continual proofs of it, that all Nations seem to consider it as a moral certainty, rather than a probability. Our bodies we have in common, with every other being of the animal Creation, and like them we are subjected to pain, disorders, and to final dissolution by Death. It is therefore natural to Conclude, that the faculty, which we alone possess, and which raises the vast distinction between man, and all other animals, is totally independent of the body; and if so, I know not of one reason, why we should suppose, it began with the body, or that it will end with it. The Soul it is true, while it is in Connection, with the Body, has no natural proof of its own immortality. But the supreme Being, in all whose works, an infinite wisdom, is display'd, when he saw that it was best to leave the Soul, thus in Suspense, at the same time has made, all its hopes, all its desires to centre in immortality. We know of no animal in the Creation (man excepted) that has if I may so express myself an Idea of Immortality; man himself neither expects nor wishes, that his body might remain forever; there are indeed frequent instances of his being so weary of it, as to become himself, the willing instrument of its destruction. But, is there a man in Nature, who if he had it in his power, would annihilate his own Soul, unless a consciousness of its crimes, had joined the idea of eternal damnation, to that of eternal existence. For what Reason, can we suppose this abhorrence of a dissolution, and this fond desire for immortality has been implanted in the Soul, if there is no foundation for them?

Perhaps some one may say; if a man had nothing but natural Reason, to assist him in this Enquiry, he would not know, where to draw the line of distinction. There is perhaps a complete gradation of genius from a Newton, to the meanest insect in Creation; where then shall, we stop, or shall we also, grant immortality to the beasts? I answer, that I see not the necessity of this although I confess it will be difficult to distinguish aright. But would it not equally puzzle, the most skilful geometrician, to ascertain the limits between an angle, and a right Line. For although we can make an Angle, verging as near as we please, to a right line, yet a right Line never can be an angle. No two things can be more distinct, than these, yet no one knows where one begins, or where the other ends.

But the most convincing proof of the probability, natural Reason affords, that the human Soul is immortal, is the opinion, of those nations, which having never been favoured with the blessings of a divine Revelation, could have no other standard. The Greeks and Romans, undoubtedly, generally believed in the Soul's immortality: almost all the authors extant in these two Languages, are fully perswaded of it. It may be said, that the opinion of a few, writers, does not in any Country form that of the whole Nation, and that the greatest parts of the Greeks, and Romans, might believe the contrary. Supposing this to be the Case, must we not confess, that men whose Reason was enlightened, and cultivated, were more proper judges of what is probable, than the common herd of mankind, who derive but little advantage, from the Soul, that is given them. But these men, were universally admired; their writings were sought for with the utmost eagerness. Homer and Virgil were considered as Oracles, and in many Places, they went so far even as to deify the Greek Poet. They do not raise a doubt concerning the immortality of the Soul: one book of the Odyssey, and one of the AEneid, are founded entirely upon this belief: there is no reason to think, that, when their Countrymen, consulted those Poems as Oracles, they excluded the 11th. book of the Odyssey, or the 6th. of the AEneid.

But this perswasion of an eternal future State, is not confined to the Greeks, and Romans: if we look among Nations where Reason had made, but little progress, we shall still find the same belief. The northern parts of Europe, were unknown to the Greeks, and to the Romans in the days of their Republic; they had a System of Religion, and gods peculiar to themselves. As they were continually at War, their delight was, to slaughter their fellow creatures, and they believed that after death, their Souls would enjoy an eternal happiness, in drinking the blood of their enemies, from their skulls. Even at this Day, in the west India islands, the enslaved African, bending under the weight of oppression, and scourged by the rod of tyranny, sighs for the Day, when Death, shall put a period to his woes, and his Soul again return to be happy in his native Country.

But to mention all the Nations that believe in the Soul's immortality from natural Reason, would be to enumerate, almost every People, that is or has been known on Earth. Happy the People, who to confirm this Opinion, have been favoured, with a Revelation from above."

At 11 o'clock, when the Bell rung for Mr. Williams's Lecture, several had not read their Parts. Angier and Mason who had done theirs, went and requested leave to retire, and attend the Philosophical Lecture. He[2] flatly denied them; probably, merely for the sake of showing his tyrannical Power. The Class shew how much they were out of humour, by shuffling with their feet, and when he had kept us there about a Quarter of an hour; and at length dismiss'd us. If Mr. Williams had not waited all that Time for us, we must infallibly have lost a great part of as Important a Lecture, as we have yet had upon Pneumatics. After commons as Hale, was going through the alley, an universal hiss, was heard from the juniors. This is almost the only way, that the Students here have, to keep the Tutors within any bounds. With all their pedantic despotism, they affect Popularity, and I believe the fear of hissing, or shuffling often prevents them from being so arbitrary as they would otherwise be. I receiv'd this afternoon Letters from Europe, as late as March 20th.[3]

[1] Questions, varying in quality and interest, were assigned to Adams throughout his junior and senior years by the tutor of logic, metaphysics, and politics (John Hale and, later, Jonathan Burr), who expected his students to write a short essay for delivery in the chapel during the one week each month they studied with the tutor.

[2] Tutor John Hale.

[3] AA to JQA, 20 March, and probably JA to JQA, 19 March (Adams Papers); any other "European" letters remain unidentified.

17TH.

I never was so impatient in my Life, as I am now for other Letters from Europe.[1] Leonard White, went to Boston in the morning, but did not bring back any Letters. Was employ'd great part of the Day in writing off yesterdays Lecture.

[1] JQA's curiosity was aroused after Billy Cranch had received "a hint of a certain Circumstance" in a letter from his mother the previous day, the same day JQA had received AA's letter containing no mention of AA2's impending marriage to WSS (JQA to AA, 15–19 May, Adams Papers). The matter was cleared up the following day when JQA received letters of an earlier date from AA and AA2.

18TH.

This morning I received two very long Letters from my Mamma, and Sister;[1] at length the whole mystery is revealed, and explain'd. We had from Mr. Williams a Lecture of an hour and an half, with which he finished the Subject of air.

[1] One of these letters was AA to JQA, 16 Feb. (Adams Papers), in which he was informed of AA2's engagement. AA2's letter "No. 11," which concluded on 15 Feb. and in which JQA learned on the first page "in the most delicate, manner possible . . . of the Connection," has not been found (JQA to AA, 15–19 May, Adams Papers; JQA to AA2, 18 May – 17 June, AA2, *Jour. and Corr.*, [3]:112–120).

19TH.

I was informed, that Captain   [1] will sail to-morrow for Europe; went to Mr. Reed, and requested to be excused from reciting to-morrow morning, in order to write, to my friends. Studied Algebra, and wrote off part of the Lecture. Sullivan a Senior Sophister, spent an hour with me, in the afternoon. The Class are in the greatest anxiety, and Suspense, concerning the Parts, which are expected to be given out, every hour.

¹ Left blank in MS.

20TH.

Cranch went to Boston this day, and brought me back, another large packet from my Sister, inclosing a Poem written, by Coll. Humphreys, on the happiness of America, addressed to the Citizens of the States.¹ There is a great brilliancy of Imagination, I think display'd in it, and he is somewhat poetical, in describing the happiness, that reigns in this Country; but the poem I take to be a very fine one.

I wrote to my Mamma, and Sister this morning.²

¹ Probably AA2 to JQA, 9–27 Feb. (Adams Papers), and 25–27 Feb. (AA2, *Jour. and Corr.*, [3]:120–127). The copy of David Humphreys' *A Poem, On the Happiness of America; Addressed to the Citizens of the United States*, London, 1786, has not been found in the Adams Papers or Adams libraries.

² Probably JQA to AA, 15–19 May (Adams Papers), and JQA to AA2, 18 May – 17 June (AA2, *Jour. and Corr.*, [3]:112–120). JQA was deeply moved by the news of his sister's forthcoming marriage, and heartily concurred with AA in the "Contrast" between WSS and Royall Tyler. Smith "enjoys a Reputation, which has always commanded my Respect," JQA wrote to AA, and "I wish henceforth to esteem him as a friend, and cherish him as a brother, as Circumstances have prevented me, from enjoying a personal acquaintance with him, his connection, with a Sister, as dear to me, as my Life, and the Opinion of my Parents, will stand in lieu of it. Will you be so kind," he continued, "as to remember me affectionately to him?"

21ST.

We had to day a Doctor Haven,¹ from Portsmouth to preach; to day: he took his text from Psalm XXIII. 1. The Lord is my shepherd, I shall not want: in the forenoon, and in the afternoon, from I Corinthians. I: 18. For the preaching of the Cross is to them that perish; foolishness: but unto us which are saved it is the power of God. I did not by any means like him so well, as I did Mr. Thatcher last Week. He is neither an extraordinary writer, nor speaker. 'Tis said he is an humble imitator of the famous Whitfield;² which does not by any means raise my opinion of him. He talk'd a good deal about shepherds; and the Cross, and those that perish &c. but I heard nothing very edifying to me, in the whole day.

[1] Samuel Haven, minister of the South Congregational Church of Portsmouth, N.H., 1752–1806 (Sibley-Shipton, *Harvard Graduates*, 12:382–390).

[2] George Whitefield, the English evangelical missionary and New Light apostle, who made several trips to America between 1738 and 1769 during the Great Awakening. JQA shared the views of Whitefield that his father had expressed as an undergraduate. Compare JA, *Earliest Diary*, p. 33.

22D.

We recite this week to our own Tutor Mr. Reed, in Gravesande's experimental Philosophy. This gentleman, is not much more Popular, than the rest of the Tutors; he is said to be prejudiced, and very vindictive. He is liked in general by the Class, however; and this may be a Reason why I have not heard, as much said against him, as against the others. We had a Class meeting, this evening about making him a Present: but there had been scarcely anything collected; and it was determined, that it should be put off till next Quarter, and I suppose the Class will go on in this manner, having two or three Class meetings every Quarter, and finally do nothing. We endeavoured to get the Class to recite, to morrow morning, and a number have agreed they would.

23D.

We could not recite this morning, because Mr. Reed, was not in at prayers. This morning a number of the Seniors were sent for, by the President, to go to his House at 8 o'clock. They went, and the parts were distributed thus. *Thompson*[+1] English Oration A:M: *Champlin* Latin Oration A:M: *Fowle* and *Gardner* 2d. each a Poem. *Blake* English and *Andrews*[+] 1st. Latin Oration's P.M. *Harris, Dwight*[+], *Hubbard*[×], and *Parker*[+] a Conference, *Bigelow* and *Crosby*[+], *Lowell* and *Taylor, Loring* and *Sullivan* Forensics. *Lincoln* and *Warland,* a Greek dialogue, *Bradford, Norton, Simpkins*[+], and *Wyeth,* Respondents in Syllogistics, and all the rest opponents to the same. These Syllogistics, are very much despised by the scholars, and no attention seems to be paid to them by the Company at Commencement. The scholars in general think that the Government, in giving them those Parts write on their foreheads DUNCE in capital Letters. Notwithstanding this some of the most learned men, in the Country, had syllogistics, when they graduated here. The good Parts, as they are called, are more numerous this year, than they ever have been.

Before this there has been only one English, and one Latin Oration, and no Poems. It is a doubt, whether they intend, to establish this as a Precedent or whether it is only a distinguished favour, to the present Class who pretend[2] to be the best Class for learning, and genius that ever graduated here. It is said, that the Parts have been exceedingly well distributed; and all the College, are pleased. There is only one person, who is said to have a part he did not deserve×,[3] and one or two are mentioned, as deserving others than Syllogistics. However that may be, the syllogists all got together this Evening, and drank, till not one of them could stand strait, or was sensible of what he did. A little after 9 they sallied out, and for a Quarter of an hour made such a noise, as might be heard, at a mile distant. I was then up in Freeman's chamber, upon a certain affair, he was informing me of. The Tutors went out, and after a short time, perswaded them to disperse. Mr. Reed had two squares of his Windows broke.

[1] Thomas W. Thompson, with whom JQA was to study law in Newburyport the following year, was later a New Hampshire lawyer, U.S. representative, 1805–1807, and senator, 1814–1817 (*Biog. Dir. Cong.*). The names with plus signs, which were placed above the names in the MS, were all members of the A.B. Club (entry for 29 May, below).

[2] Probably "profess" (*OED*).

[3] Dudley Hubbard.

24TH.

It is feared that some bad consequences, will ensue, from the high-go, of the Syllogists last evening. Borland,[1] it seems, was the most active of them all; he collar'd Mr. Reed, and threw an handful of gravel, in his Face, and was rather disrespectful to Mr. James; He went this morning to the former, to make an apology for his Conduct, but was told, it could not be received, as the matter was already laid before the Government. Thus those fellows play the Tyrants here; they have no regard, no allowances for youth, and Circumstances; they go out, when they are almost certain of being insulted, and then bring the scholar, for a crime of which he knew nothing, under public censure. They cannot with any face, say that a scholar ought to be so severely punished for depriving himself of his Senses. For there are here, in College persons, who have seen Mr. Reed, ⟨as much⟩ much intoxicated, as Borland was yesterday; and behaving quite as ill. But Compassion is too great a Virtue, ever to be admitted into the breast of a Tutor, here. It is supposed however that Borland's punishment will not be very severe, because it requires an unanimous Vote among the Governors of the College to punish a Student, and they are said to be at such Variance one with the other, that they can very seldom all agree.

¹ Samuel Borland, son of John Borland, of Boston and Tory Row, Cambridge, the short-lived loyalist (d. 1775) (Edward Doubleday Harris, "The Vassalls of New England," *NEHGR*, 17:120 [April 1863]; Paige, *Hist. of Cambridge, Mass.*, p. 167–169).

25TH.

Government met, and were assembled, almost all this day, to determine what Punishment to inflict upon Borland, he was informed of it in the evening, and the Class petitioned, that it might be mitigated; but probably without much success.

26TH.

This morning after Prayers, Borland, was called out to read an humble Confession, signifying his repentance of his Conduct &c. The President read, the Votes of the Government; the affair was stated, and it was said, that Borland, had insulted in a flagrant manner, two of the Governors of the University, whereupon it was voted, that he read a Confession, and 2dly. that he be degraded to the bottom of his Class, and that he take his place there accordingly. The other Scholars, were warn'd by this example, not to run into such excesses, and to behave respectfully. I wanted I think neither of these warnings, but the event has warn'd me, to alter my Opinion concerning Reed; I thought him, the best of the Tutors, but now, I do not think he is a jot better than the Rest: Reed said, as I have heard that he should not have complained of any other scholar, but Borland, had always treated him disrespectfully. This makes the blame in the Tutor much greater, for it displays, a partiality, which every governor of the University ought to be free from.

27TH.

No reciting this morning. I was employ'd all day in studying mathematics, which are the most pleasing to me, of any of our studies. Spent, a couple of hours at Bridge's chamber after dinner. Rain in the Evening.

5. PROFESSOR ELIPHALET PEARSON,
BY SAMUEL F. B. MORSE, 1817
See page ix

6. PROFESSOR SAMUEL WILLIAMS
See pages ix–x

28TH.

Parson Hilliard preach'd us a Sermon in the morning from Isaiah LIV. 14. In righteousness shalt thou be established; thou shalt be far from oppression; for thou shalt not fear, and from terror; for it shall not come near thee, and in the afternoon, from Galatians IV 27: For it is written, Rejoyce thou barren, that bearest not, break forth, and cry thou that travailest not; for the desolate hath many more children, than she which hath an husband. I have heard the substance of one Sermon, with a Variety of texts ever since I have been, here; it is with him, as with most of the preachers I have heard: there is one favourite point, (often self evident) which they labour, to prove, continually; and beyond which they seldom, have much to say.

29TH.

We recite this week to Doctor Jennison, but he was not in this morning.

Je fus ce soir a l'assemblée, d'une Societé,[1] etablie, depuis deux ans, par quelques jeunes gens de la presente premiere Classe, qui voulaient se perfectionner, le stile, et se donner reciproquement des conseils vrais, et sinceres. Les assemblées ordinaires sont une fois dans trois semaines. Chacun y lit une piece de sa composition, et au bout de chaque phrase, les autres membres font des observations, et lui disent, ce qu'ils en pensent. Les membres de la premiere Classe sont, Andrews 1r. Crosby, Dwight, Parker, Simpkins, et Thompson, qui etait president de la Societé, l'année passée. Ils on quitté la Societé parcequ'ils s'en vont bientôt; Les membres de notre Classe sont, Abbot 2d. Bridge, Burge, Chandler 3me. Cranch, Fiske, Freeman, (president) Harris (qui a été admis, à la derniere assemblee en même tems que moi.) Little et Packard. Le President fit un discours, à l'occasion de son election, qui se fit à la derniere assemblée. Ensuite chaque membre lut sa piece; aprés quoi chacun reçut un sujet, pour la prochaine assemblée ordinaire. Enfin chacun se retira, sur les onze heures.

Rain'd almost all day, we had a mathematical Lecture in the morning from Professor Williams.

¹ This is doubtless the A.B. Club, presumably a code for a secret name, which appears to have been a rival to the more famous Speaking Club, begun as early as 1770, of which JQA was not a member. Unlike the Speaking Club, the A.B. did not require its members to speak from memory, as JQA's entry above indicates (Morison, *Three Centuries of Harvard,* p. 138; MH-Ar:Speaking Club Records).

30TH.

The weather cleared up, in the afternoon. A number of the Class have had leave to be absent till the end of the week, on account of Election day. My Cousin, set off, at about 4 afternoon to go on foot to Braintree, We had a Lecture from Mr. Wigglesworth at three.

31ST.

Election day. This is a day of great festivity throughout the Country. The last Wednesday in May, is appointed, for declaring the choice, of the Governor, Lieutt. Governor &c. It is the only day in the year, in which the Student here is left at his Liberty to do whatever he pleases; and it is most frequently the Case, as it has been this day, that one Party is playing in the yard from 8 in the morning to prayer time in the afternoon: Most of the scholars however go out of Town, on this day. There is a custom among the scholars here, which some of the Classes follow, and others do not. It is choosing a governor and Lieutenant governor, for the Class. They commonly take some rich fellow, who can treat the Class now and then. The Seniors this morning, chose Champlin governor, and Lowell Lieutt. Governor. The Lieutenant Governor treated immediately and they chose their other officers. At commons, they all went into the Hall, in Procession, Thomas, who was appointed sheriff march'd at their head with a Paper cockade, in his hat, and brandishing a Cane, in his hand instead of a sword. He conducted the Governor and Lieutt. Governor to their seats, made his bow, and retired to the other table, for which Jackey Hale, punished him 4 shillings. However he performed his part so well, that the Spectators were much pleased and clap'd their hands. Hale happened to see Baron, the junior, clapping, and sent orders for him to go to him after commons. Baron, not happening to go before 2 o'clock was punished 5 shillings for impudence and 4 for disobedience, that is the way, these modest Tutors tyrannize over us. As there was a little noise in the Hall, Hale, struck the handle of his knife 3 times on the table, to still it, but instead of that, almost every knife in the Hall was struck on the table 3 Times. At last the Tutors rose, and as they were going out, about half a dozen fellows hiss'd them, they were enraged, turn'd round, and look'd as if they would devour, us. But they did not discover one Person; which made them look silly enough. When they turn'd their backs again, there was nothing but hissing, and groaning, and clapping hands, and stomping, heard in the Hall, till they got into the yard where, a few Potatoes were sent out to meet them. Hale was in such a fury, that I don't doubt but in Imitation of Caligula,[1] he wished, that the whole College, had but one head, and that he might chop it off with impunity. He sent for all the waiters after Dinner, and endeavoured to pump something out of them, but he could not succeed.

This evening I happened to be about half an hour, in Company with Dr. Jennison, and if every thing is in Proportion to his small talk, he is as silly a Tutor, as I should ever wish to see. I smiled several Times this Evening, and it was not without difficulty, once or twice, that I restrain'd myself from laughing out.

[1] While at The Hague JQA had translated into French Suetonius' account of the life of Caligula (16 April–22 July 1784, M/JQA/44, Adams Papers, Microfilms, Reel No. 239) and had made a rough, incomplete translation earlier (ca. 1783, same, Reel No. 240).

THURSDAY JUNE IST. 1786.

We had this forenoon a Lecture from Mr. Williams. Upon the reflection and the refraction of light. It is not usual for him to give Lectures on Thursdays, as many of both the Classes, are always absent on that day; as was the Case to day, not above half being present. But he has been so long prevented, by the weather, from giving any, that he is obliged to take the first fair day that happened: he has yet given but fourteen Lectures, it is said he has ten more to give, and must finish before the 21st. of this month. The Lecture was not to me so entertaining as some have been.

2D.

We had another Lecture from Mr. Williams to day, with an explanation of the different optical Instruments, that are most commonly made use of. But there was such, a flocking to see through the microscope, and the magic Lantern, and the camera obscura, that something got broke, and Mr. Williams, shew nothing more after it. Weather very warm, several of us, bath'd in the River this afternoon.

3D.

We had a Lecture this morning upon Electricity; we received two small shocks, which however, gave me such a stroke in the joints at my elbows that I could not write after it; The weather very warm indeed. Fahrenheits' thermometer I am told was at 87: 80 is the common summer heat. We did not recite in Doddridge, this morning.

4TH.

Attended meeting all day. It was very uncomfortable, the weather being so warm, and we are crowded there so thick. The Parson for our Comfort was very short. In the forenoon he preach'd from I Ep: John V. 11. And this is the record, That God, hath given to us eternal Life, and this Life is in his Son, and in the afternoon from, I Corinthians VII. 31. And they that use this world, as not abusing it: for the fashion of this world passeth away.

5TH.

We had a Lecture from Mr. Williams, concerning heat, proper Lecture for the weather. Je fus le soir à l'assemblée de nôtre petite Societé,[1] ou nous eûmes, Burge, Chandler, Harris, et moi une petite dispute impromptue, sur la Question, si l'Europe est plus favorable au genie que l'amerique. Moi, je soutins, le contraire, et je le soutiendrai toujours. Après avoir fait quelques autres petites affaires, chacun se retira.

[1] The A.B. Club. See entry for 29 May (above).

6TH.

Mr. Williams gave us another Lecture upon heat; and introduced a new System of his own. But the heat being increased in the Chamber, by a small fire, which was necessary for making the experiments, and by the breath of an hundred Persons, assembled in it, became almost insupportable, Thompson fainted completely, and was carried away to his chamber.

7TH.

We had this morning a continuation of Mr. Williams's System; by which, he pretends to account for the aurora borealis, in a manner different from any that has yet been started. His Hypothesis appears to be very plausible, and I hope, that if it is not wholly true, it may lead on to further discoveries concerning a Phenomenon, which has not yet been well accounted for.

I declaim'd in the Chapel this afternoon. (See page 318.)[1]

Immediately after prayers, the Parts for exhibition, were given out. *Little,* has the English Oration, *Beale,* the Latin, *Abbot* 1st. and *Burge* the Forensic. It is a matter of surprize, that Beale, should have an Oration as he is not considered, as very extraordinary either as a scholar or, a speaker.

[1] That is, in entry of 15 April (above).

8TH.

A very warm day again. I was in the morning with Mr. Williams, at the Philosophy Chamber. I made tea for the Club this afternoon. We were at Beale's chamber in the afternoon.

9TH.

Quite unwell almost all day. We had a Lecture from Mr. Williams, upon magnetism. The weather has altered so much that it is now very cool.

10TH.

The Course of Philosophical Lectures was closed, with one, giving an explanation of the Orrery, and as an Introduction, to the astronomical Course, which we shall have next Quarter. I went also, and heard a Lecture from Dr. Waterhouse, upon digestion. I have nearly Lost this day; strol'd about with White in the afternoon. Cranch went to Boston. After Tea, we walk'd, half, an hour and then return'd and spent the rest of the Evening at Bridge's Chamber.

Mr. Williams closed his Lectures, with these Verses from Pope

All are but parts of one stupendous whole,
Whose Body, Nature is, and God, the Soul;
That, chang'd through all, and yet in all the same;
Great in the Earth, as in th'aethereal frame;
Warms in the Sun, refreshes in the breeze,
Glows in the stars, and blossoms in the trees,
Lives through all Life, extends through all extent,
Spreads undivided, operates unspent;
To him no high, no low, no great, no small;
He fills, he bounds, connects and equals all.[1]

[1] "An Essay on Man," Epistle I, lines 267–274, 279–280.

11TH.

Mr. Howard[1] a Minister from Boston, preach'd in the forenoon from, Proverbs I. 20. Wisdom crieth without; she uttereth, her voice, in the Streets. 21. She crieth in the chief place of concourse, in the openings of the gates: in the City she uttereth her words saying. 22. How long ye simple ones, will ye love simplicity?, and the scorners delight in their scorning, and fools hate knowledge? And in the afternoon from Luke XII. 48. For unto whomsoever much is given, of him shall be much required. I like the last much the best. There was a liberality of Sentiment, in his System, which is very seldom, found among preachers in this Country. Those of Boston, however are distinguished, in general for this Quality.

[1] Simeon Howard, minister of the West Church, Boston, 1767–1804, and holder of Arian and Arminian views. JQA described another sermon of his as "excellent . . . full of candor, benevolence, and piety, with the most liberal sentiments"; attending the Dudleian lecture given by Howard in Sept. 1787, he found the minister's views "replete with sound sense and a wholesome doctrine, as all the sermons that I ever heard from this gentleman, have been" (Sibley-Shipton, *Harvard Graduates*, 14:279–288; entries for 18 April, 5 Sept. 1787, below).

12TH.

Recite this week to Hale, who was absent this afternoon. Je n'ai rien fait de toute la journée, qu'ecrire pour nôtre Societé, voici une piece, que je finis hier.

A. B. N. 1.[1] "Nil tam difficile, quod non Solertia vincat."

I must inform those of my hearers, that have never studied, the Latin Language, that the meaning of this is "nothing is so difficult, but it may be overcome by Industry."

In a litteral Sense this Proposition is false. There are doubtless certain bounds, which the supreme being has placed to the faculties of man, and beyond which, it must always be impossible for us to penetrate. A man who should endeavour by industry, to live upon air, or to be immortal, would not succeed better, than the monks of a Certain Convent, who having read in Scripture, that faith as big as a grain of mustard seed would be sufficient to remove a mountain, were determined to pray without ceasing, untill a very inconvenient hill, that stood before the Convent should disappear. After they had spent, 3 or 4 days in displaying their faith; they were greatly surprized to see the mountain standing as firm as ever. They consulted together, to know what was the Reason, of their being so unsuccessful; one of them finally said, he imagined there was some mistake in the Translation, and that it ought to be, Faith, as big as a mountain, would be sufficient to remove a grain of mustard seed: But had those monks ever studied the writings of celebrated authors in any Language, they would often have met with this figure of rhetoric.

Nor is this Proposition strictly true, in a moral Sense; for if a man, is born with small abilities, the utmost stretch of Industry, will not enable him to equal one, who, possess'd of more genius, does not cultivate it, with so much assiduity. But when we consider that Industry without genius, is sufficient to carry a man thro' Life, with honour, that Genius without Industry, serves only to increase the fault of the Person, who is possess'd of it, and that they produce such surprizing Effects, when they are united, we must conclude, that the Poet has Reason to say, Industry, can overcome all Things.

If we look into history, we shall find; that this Virtue, has been productive, of greater effects, than any other. Those stupendous works, which struck every beholder with amazement, and which for that Reason were styled the wonders of the world, display'd, and those of them, that are yet extant, still display, the Industry of mankind, in the Infancy of Creation. But, while we admire the Principle, which enabled them, to execute such surprizing undertakings, we must lament their want of judgment for spending so great a portion of their Time, in erecting a Colossus, a mausoleum, and Pyramids, which could afford only a momentary pleasure to the Eye of the beholder, who could acquire neither wisdom nor Virtue from the contemplation of them. It is not necessary to mention, that the republics of Greece, and Rome, owed their grandeur, more to their Industry, and Perseverance, than to any other Cause; but the Republic of Holland, furnishes perhaps, the most striking and most brilliant advantages, produced, by these Virtues. Placed on a small, insignificant portion of the Earth, which is continually subjected to the impetuous attacks of the Ocean, and which cannot produce even the necessaries of Life, for a tenth part of its Inhabitants; they have been enabled by their Industry not only to withstand the encroachments of the Sea, but to rise to the Summit of national glory, and take their Seat among the most powerful Empires on Earth. Such are the benefits, which accrue, from Industry, to nations. Its benign Influence, is not less advantageous to Individuals. It is one of those Virtues, which is equally to be esteemed and admired, in all ages, in all places, and at all Times, and next to Innocence, it is perhaps the most amiable quality, that can adorn the characters of Men.

¹ That is, JQA's first speech before the A.B. Club.

13TH.

No reciting this morning.

This reciting in Locke, is the most ridiculous of all. When the Tutor enquires what is contained in such a section; many of the Scholars repeat the two first Lines in it, which very frequently [say?] nothing to the Purpose, and leave the rest for the Tutor to explain, which he commonly does, by saying over again the words of the author. The only advantage, which can, I think be derived from this, is that it forces some of the Students, whether they will or not, to know, the opinion of the author, whom they are presumed to study: this, may be of some use to the idle, but can be of none, to any youth, who is fond of study.

I began Robertson's History of Scotland,¹ which I took last Friday from the Library.

¹ William Robertson, *The History of Scotland During the Reigns of Queen Mary and of King James VI till his Accession to the Crown of England . . .,* 2 vols., London, 1759.

14TH.

The Freshmen, by their high Spirit of Liberty, have again involved themselves in difficulties. The Sophimores, consider themselves as insulted, by them, and in a Class meeting, last evening determined, to oblige all the Freshmen, to take off their hats in the yard, and to send them [on errands?]. There has been a great deal of business between them to day; Mr. Hale, has had several of them before him. Isaac Adams among the rest, a daring, insolent fellow, who has too much Influence in that Class, and who will not, perhaps, take his degree with them.

15TH.

We did not recite this morning. The struggle between the Freshmen and Sophimores still continues. They have been mutually hoisting one another all day. I went with Andrews 1st and Dwight, and spent, part of the Evening at Mr. Dana's.

16TH.

Warm weather. Nous eûmes une assemblée extraordinaire de nôtre Societé; *Dwight* y fit un discours, au nom de sa Classe, en prenant Congé de la Societé. C'est une Loi que lorsqu'une Classe, quitte l'Université, un membre de la Societé et de cette Classe, fera un discours; on le choisit un an d'avance; mais comme, ce furent les membres de la presente premiere Classe, qui ont institué le Societé, le discours de ce soir, fut le premier dans ce genre. Le Discours fini ces messieurs, se retirerent, et nous fimes Choix, de *Freeman,* pour faire le discours de l'anniversaire, l'année prochaine, et de *Bridge,* pour celui du Congé. Aprés avoir fait quelques autres affaires nous nous retirâmes, chéz nous.

17TH.

This day, the Bridge over Charlestown Ferry was compleated, and as the same day 11 years agone, was mark'd at Charlestown, with dreadful Scenes, of Slaughter and Destruction,[1] the managers, and directors of the Bridge, determined, that this day should be mark'd with Pleasure and festivity. I do not think however that the scheme, was good. A Dinner was provided for 600 People, on Bunker's hill: the havoc of oxen, sheep, and fowls of all kinds, was I suppose as great to day, as that of men upon the former occasion and I dare say, there was as much wine drank now, as there was blood spilt then, and to crown the whole, The head of the table, was I hear placed on the very spot where the immortal Warren fell. I think however, that the ground which had been the scene, of such an awful Day, should [not], be made a scene, of revels, and feasting. What must be the feelings of a man of Sensibility, who, would naturally say to himself "perhaps, I am now seated on the grave of my dearest friend. Perhaps this is the Spot where he drew his last gasp; and I may now be treading down his bones." All this may be called prejudice, but they are feelings natural to the heart, and such as ought not I think to be rooted from it. Three or four Songs were composed upon the occasion, by different persons, in every one of which Charlestown was compared, to a Phoenix, rising from its ashes.² All the Tutors were gone, so that we had no Prayers in the afternoon, and there were not more than 30 persons in to Commons. For my Part, I did nothing all day in Consequence of it. After dinner we bathed in the River.

¹ The Battle of Bunker Hill, which JQA viewed from Braintree, and the death of Dr. Joseph Warren left a vivid impression on JQA which remained throughout his life. As late as 1846, he wrote of the events of that day: "I saw with my own eyes those fires, and heard Britannia's thunders in the Battle of Bunker's hill and witnessed the tears of my mother and mingled with them my own, at the fall of Warren a dear friend of my father, and a beloved Physician to me. He had been our family physician and surgeon, and had saved my fore finger from amputation under a very bad fracture" (*Adams Family Correspondence*, 1:29, 223–224; JQA to Joseph Sturge, March 1846, Dft, Adams Papers).

² For an account of the opening of the Charles River Bridge, which attracted a crowd of 20,000, see the Boston *Independent Chronicle*, 22 June.

18TH.

The Weather extremely warm, all day. I Dined at Mr. Dana's. Parson Hilliard gave us two Sermons, from *Philippians II. 15.* Among whom ye shine as lights in the world. It is customary for the minister to preach an occasional Sermon, to the Senior Class, the Sunday preceding the 21st. of June, and this was such. By changing the indicative mood *ye shine* into the Imperative *shine ye:* he made it quite applicable; in the afternoon he addressed them in particular, and they all rose, as is customary. He paid them many Compliments, and concluded with many good wishes for their welfare. The only fault, I heard found with his address, was that he dwelt too much upon divinity, and too little upon the other Professions.

19TH.

Doctor Waterhouse gave, what he called his Valedictory Lecture containing a comparative view of Reason, and Instinct. I thought it an exceeding good one; and it pleased very generally. We had a meeting of the A B this Evening. Only four members attended. Three of them read their Pieces, I did not, on account of my speaking one next Monday; at one of the last meetings it was enacted, that one member at every meeting should speak an Oration, and two at every occasional meeting, read a forensic disputation. It is to go round alphabetically, and the first Oration fell to me; but by this Law, the person that speaks at the occasional meeting shall be excused from reading a piece the meeting before. The weather being rainy, prevented I suppose, many of the Society from attending.

20TH.

Bridge obtained leave of absence till Commencement. He intends to pass the Summer Vacation here, and supposes he shall be able to Study with much more advantage, when he is not continually called away by the College exercises, than he can now: and I think he is quite right.

21ST.

This day the Seniors leave, College; there is no recitation in the morning, and prayers are deferred till 10 o'clock. The Class then went down in procession two by two, with the Poet at their head, and escorted the President to the Chapel. The President made a very long prayer, in which in addition to what he commonly says he pray'd a great deal for the Seniors: but I think he ought to get his occasional prayers by heart before he delivers them. He bungled always when he endeavoured to go out of the beaten track, and he has no talent at extempore Composition. The Poem was then delivered, by Fowle, who paid most tremendous Compliments to the President but his addresses, to the Professors and Tutors, to the other Students, and to his own Class, were excellent. The Seniors soon after it was over set out, on their party.

In the afternoon I was admitted with *Burge,* and *Cranch* to the $\phi\bar{\iota}\beta\epsilon\tau\alpha$, $\kappa\alpha\pi\pi\alpha$ Society. It is established to promote friendship, and Literature, in several of the Universities of America. The initials of the words φιλοσοφια βιομ κυβερνητης,[1] are on one side of the medal, and on the other S. P. which means Societas Philosophica [Philosophicæ]. They had met in Harris and Dwight's Chamber, and there was in the admission a considerable degree of Solemnity. Mr. Paine,[2] the butler, was present as vice president, Mr. Burr,[3] and Mr. Ware, as members, Andrews, and Harris of the Seniors, and *Bridge, Fiske, Freeman, Little,* and *Packard,* who were admitted some time Since, from our Class.

[1] "Philosophy is the governess, rule or guide of life." Because of the rising criticism of secret societies, JQA was instrumental in 1831, at a time of anti-Masonic feeling, in helping expose the secrets of Phi Beta Kappa to the world (JQA, *Memoirs,* 8:383–387, 389–392, 394–399; Oscar M. Voorhees, *The History of Phi Beta Kappa,* N.Y., 1945, p. 184–191).

[2] Joshua Paine, Harvard 1784, M.A. 1787 (*Harvard Quinquennial Cat.*).

[3] Jonathan Burr, Harvard tutor, 1786–1787 (same).

22D.

White and Cranch went to Braintree this morning, and intend to stay there till Saturday night. Weather cool, and in the afternoon rather disagreeable.

23D.

I made tea, for the Club: only four attended: many of them being out of town. I answered for no absences, this morning. Almost all the Seniors are now gone.

24TH.

My Cousin return'd from Braintree this Evening. We had no reciting this morning. Weather comfortable all day.

25TH.

Mr. Mellen,[1] preach'd here: he was a Tutor two or three years since. His forenoon discourse was from Psalm. c. 3.[2] *Know ye that the Lord, he is God: it is he that hath made us and not we ourselves; we are his People, and the sheep of his Pasture.* The afternoon, from Acts X. 2. *A devout man, and one that feared God with all his house, which gave much alms to the people, and prayed to God alway.*

Mr. Mellen's manner is more affected, than that of any preacher I ever saw. His Sentiments were more liberal than is common, and his composition good; but all is entirely spoilt by his manner of speaking.

[1] John Mellen was minister of the first parish of Barnstable (Sibley-Shipton, *Harvard Graduates,* 17:405–409).

[2] That is, Psalms 100:3.

26TH.

A. B. N 2.[1] (but was spoke first).

Destitute of Abilities which might induce you gentlemen, to overlook my want of experience, and of experience to conceal my want of talents; it is with the utmost Diffidence, that I address a number of Characters so respectable, as those that are now before me. But I have frequently observed, that those Persons, who excel the most in any art or Science, are possessed of the greatest share of Candour, and are the readiest to encourage those who endeavour to follow their example; my greatest fear therefore is that not only your candour, but your Patience also, will be put to trial.

The advantages which are derived from Education is one of the most important subjects that can engage the attention of mankind; a subject on which the welfare of States and Empires, as well as of small Societies, and of individuals in a great measure depends. It has long been an opinion generally received, that the Situation which should afford the greatest degree of happiness to mankind, would be the most eligible; and the Poet appears to be of this Opinion when he says

> "For forms of government let fools contest
> Whate'er is best administer'd is best."[2]

But with due reverence, to the Sentiments of mankind in general, and of a person so celebrated in particular I must beg leave to think otherwise, and to suppose, that happiness, should not be the criterion by which to judge of the excellency of a government or of the Situation of men. I do not know whether I am singular in the Idea; but I believe there is nearly an equal Sum, of felicity, and of unhappiness, as to Individuals, spread all over the Earth; and that whatever difference there may be is in a great measure owing to the difference of dispositions which in some men, are much easier and happier than in others: but that it depends neither upon a good form of Government, nor upon civilization.

We who have had the good fortune to be born under a free government frequently exclaim, with Reason, against despotism. Yet in one of the most despotic monarchies on Earth, I have seen more sprightliness, more cheerfulness, and contentment, than in any other Country in Proportion: because, as they have no Ideas of the blessings of Freedom, they can neither desire to possess it, nor lament their being deprived of it, and I am perswaded that a man perfectly in a State of Nature, would enjoy as much, and perhaps more real happiness, than another with all the learning of a Newton. Ideas of happiness appear always to be local, and always adapted to the Situations of men. The inhabitants of the East naturally of warm Constitutions, place the Summit of felicity in being forever buried in the Embraces of perpetual Virgins, without ever finding their Vigour impaired. The North american Savage, whose Life is one continued Scene, of slaughter and destruction, considers it, as his supreme delight to prolong the Torments of a Captive enemy, and his pleasure is always increased in proportion to the Pain which he Causes. The original inhabitants of the West India Islands, placed their chief happiness, in being stretch'd from morning to night, under the shadows of their Trees, and enjoying a Perpetual and undisturb'd repose. In short it appears plain that what would be the Summit of bliss to one man, would make another very wretched.

Civilization is to a State what Education is to an Individual. When men become civilized they alter their Ideas of happiness, their object is more noble, more exalted, and more reasonable; but desires remain, and as they are more refined, and have their Source in the mind, they are not so easily gratified, as the desires of Sense and thus in the progress of human Life. The youth despises the Pursuits of the Child; the man slights the desires of the youth; and he whose forehead is furrow'd by the brazen finger of Time, and whose head is sprinkled with the Snow of the winter of Life, looks to his God, as the object of his happiness, and concludes with Solomon, that all else is but vanity and Vexation of Spirit. May we not therefore conclude, that civilization does not increase the Sum of happiness among Men? And if this is to be the Standard by which we must judge, it appears to me Clear that education can be of little or no Service to mankind, and that it were better to be a beast of the Fields than the Lord of the Creation.

But Nations and Individuals, are I think to be esteemed and

admired, according as they fulfill the Purpose of the Deity in creating them; according as their Virtues are great and numerous, and their Vices small and few. And here we shall find that all depends entirely upon civilization and Education: for it is I suppose beyond all doubt, that the progress of every virtue, and of every amiable Quality in a Nation, or an individual, is always in Proportion to the progress of civilization. If we take a view of Man, merely as nature forms him, what a despicable figure will he make, in comparison with man in a State of civilization. Endowed by nature with abilities greater than those of any other animal, he soon extends his Empire over them all: his ingenuity furnishes him, with arms to destroy them, and by this means he accustoms himself to view with indifference, the agonies of Death in another. Bound to his fellow Creatures by no tie of Society, whenever his Interest or his Passion prompts he is as ready to kill a man as any other animal. Violent in his Passions as all men naturally are, and never having been taught that it was his Duty to restrain them, the least irritation hurries him on to the highest pitch of Fury, and he commits the greatest outrages, without being troubled with a Conscience which might reproach him, when his Passion subsides. Society first lays him under restraints, and in Proportion as he advances in that he learns the Duties which he owes to those that surround him, and his heart improves with his understanding.

I have neither Time, nor a Capacity sufficient to trace the progress of civilization, to the pitch, at which it has arrived in most parts of the Earth at present. The advantages of Education are so well known that they need not to be mentioned: nor is it necessary to observe that youth is the Time for the improvement of the heart, and of the understanding. At that time of Life the mind, like wax readily receives every impression that is applied to it: A Good Education inspires the Soul with those exalted, and divine Sentiments, which form, the Patriot and the Sage; which warm the breast of the Hero, cause him to spurn every Idea of fear, and to think with the Roman Poet, "Dulce et decorum est pro patria mori,"[3] which raise the voice of the Orator to speak in thunder, for the Cause of his Country, and which shew Man, at the highest degree of Perfection, to which the supreme being is pleased he should arrive. Or as it has been beautifully expressed in Verse.

In the pure mind at those ambiguous Years,
Or Vice, rank weed! first strikes her poisonous Root
Or haply, Virtue's opening bud appears,
By just degrees, fair bloom, of fairest Fruit.
For if on youth's untainted thought imprest,
The generous Purpose still, shall warm the manly breast.

Finis

Besides this we had an extempore disputation on the Question; whether a public Education, was more advantageous, than a private one?

We had this morning a mathematical Lecture from Mr. Williams, and a public one from Mr. Pearson, in the afternoon, on the origin of Language.

[1] In the speech which follows, JQA's second before the A.B. Club, paragraphing has been editorially supplied.

[2] "An Essay on Man," Epistle III, lines 303–304.

[3] "'Tis sweet and glorious to die for [one's] fatherland."

27TH.

No reciting this afternoon. A number of the Scholars are forming themselves into a military Company, and sent a Committee to the Governor, for some arms.

28TH.

I received a letter from Mr. W. Smith, informing me of my aunt Smith's Death.[1] She was here this Day week. Coll. Thatcher, the representative, for this Town, fell instantaneously dead, yesterday in Boston Streets. I went to Mr. Wigglesworth, to Mr. Sewall,[2] and to Mr. Pierson, in the afternoon. Almost all the Class met at Amory's chamber this morning.

[1] Letter not found; Mrs. Elizabeth Storer Smith, wife of Isaac Smith Sr. and sister of Deacon Ebenezer Storer, had died the previous day (Malcolm Storer, *Annals of the Storer Family, together with Notes on the Ayrault Family,* Boston, 1927, p. 48; Isaac Smith Jr. to AA, 8 July, Adams Papers).

[2] Stephen Sewall had been Hancock Professor of Hebrew and Oriental Languages from 1764 until 1785, when he was dismissed for intemperance. TBA lived at his house during his freshman year (Sibley-Shipton, *Harvard Graduates,* 15:107–114; JQA to JA, 30 Aug., Adams Papers).

29TH.

Went to Boston, and attended my aunt Smith's funeral. Sat about an hour with my old Companion Johonnot who shew me some more of his Poetry. We returned to Cambridge, in the midst of the Rain in the Evening.

30TH.

Mr. and Mrs. Cranch, Mr. W Smith, and Miss Betsey, came up here this afternoon and drank tea.
Fine Weather.

FINIS.

Nil tam difficile, quod non Solertia vincat.[1]

[1] This Latin proverb originally appeared at the beginning of JQA's first discourse before the A.B. Club (entry for 12 June, above).

Paris.   J. Q. Adams.   Aug: 20th
1783.

Ephemeris.

Vol II.[1]

From July 1st. 1786 to October 31st. 1787.

Tempora labuntur, tacitisque senescimus annis,
Et fugiunt, fraeno non remorante dies.

Ovid.[2]

1786

[1] Titlepage for D/JQA/11, covering the inclusive dates inscribed. The top line on this page is written in an earlier hand, presumably the date on which he purchased the blank Diary book. This same inscription appears on the top of titlepages of D/JQA/10 and 12, which are identical 380-page leather-bound books, all measuring $4\frac{1}{4}'' \times 6\frac{3}{4}''$.

[2] "Time slips away, and we grow old with silent lapse of years; there is no bridle that can curb the flying days," *Fasti,* Bk. VI, lines 771–772 (*Opera,* 5 vols., London, 1745, 1:[134], at MQA; *Publii Ovidii Nasonis Fastorum Libri Sex,* transl. Sir James George Frazer, 5 vols., London, 1929, 1:352–353). JQA purchased his own edition of Ovid, cited above, on 15 March 1785.

SATURDAY JULY 1ST. 1786.

The military company, having obtained a promise of 60 stand of arms, met immediately after Dinner, and chose their officers, and agreed to a Code of Laws. They were upon the business more than two hours. Vose, was chosen Captain, Fiske, and Packard lieutenants, and Chandler 1st. Ensign.[1]

[1] This was the college military company, founded in 1770, and named the Marti-Mercurian Band because of its motto, "tam marti quam mercurio." It was an association for exercise and recreation which marched and maneuvered with fife and drum, though it did not see service in the Revolution. The company was reformed in 1786, procured arms on loan from Gov. Bowdoin, and flourished for a year before it died away again. It was not reestablished thereafter until 1811. During the Shays' uprising the arms loaned to the band were returned and used by a regular infantry company against the insurgents (*Columbian Centinel*, 2 April 1828; Morison, *Three Centuries of Harvard*, p. 141).

2D.

I was unwell, and obtained leave of absence from meeting. The weather was so warm, I could not do much. I only wrote a Letter to my Sister.[1]

[1] Letter not found.

3D.

We had our private exhibition this morning. The Orations by Little and Beale, were both upon Education; that of Little was excellent, generally allow'd to be equal to that of Thomson, who has the greatest character as a composuist of the Senior Class. Beale's being in a dead language, was not so well understood but I thought it good; the Forensic, between Burge, and Abbot 1st. was on the Question, whether habit increases the criminality of an action. Burge appeared to have the best side of the Question. The Syllogistic on the Question, whether a promise extorted by force is binding, was read by the Sophimores, Abbot, Bancroft, Lincoln, and Prescott. The English Dialogue[1] was spoken by, Cabot, and Philips, the greek Oration by Sohier, and the Hebrew by Tappan.

We recited in the afternoon, but there were not more than a dozen of the Class, that attended.

[1] The dialogue between Apicius and Darteneuf, from George Lyttelton, *Dialogues of the Dead*, 4th edn., London, 1765, p. 212–227 (MH-Ar:Faculty Records, 5:226).

4TH.

Anniversary of American Independence; an Oration was delivered in the morning at Boston, by Mr. J. Loring Austin;[1] many scholars went to hear it, I was not of the number. It was said to be very good.

We have had fair weather several days, and the ground begins to be very dry. This morning Borland was restored, because, as the President, said his conduct had been circumspect, and he had shown a due sense of the Enormity of his Crime. This was indeed enormous.

¹ *An Oration, Delivered July 4, 1786,* Boston, [1786].

5TH.

Dull, and low spirited, somewhat, but it did not last long.

Mr. James, gave us a piece of Latin to make: the first the Class have had since I have been here. This is the last week that we attend the Latin Tutor, and last week we closed with Mr. Jennison. In the Senior year there are no languages, studied in College. It is very popular here to dislike the Study of greek and Latin, but it appears to me, that the recitations in these branches are much easier than in S'Gravesande's.

6TH.

ΦBK N:1. Whether civil discord is advantageous to Society.

There cannot be perhaps a Question, which at first view presents an aspect so unfavourable, as this does to the Person, who must support the affirmative. That discord, so frequently term'd a fiend of Hell, so heartily execrated by all mankind, though she possesses the breasts of so many of them; so generally allowed to be one of the greatest evils to which human Nature is subjected; that discord I say should be advantageous to Society, is what a superficial observer, must conclude to be impossible. It would be perhaps, to the honour of human Nature, if all the benefits which Society enjoys, were produced by good and virtuous Causes; but continual, nay, I may say perpetual experience, convinces us, that this is not the Case, and as it sometimes happens, that the best intentions are attended with very unhappy Circumstances, so, it is very common, that the most detestable principles are productive of the most beneficial effects.¹

Whatever is, is right. This maxim, I take it, holds good in the moral, as well as the physical world; there is no Passion, however base, that has been planted in the mind of man, which was not placed there to answer good Purposes; and when man was made, so prone to disagree with his fellow creatures, it was intended, that this Quality like all the rest should work for his general good: but men being seldom blessed with judgment, sufficient to Point out to them, how far they may suffer their Passions to lead them, without being detrimental to them, are in this Case, as in many others, sometimes hurried on to such a degree of discord, and hatred, as becomes highly prejudicial.

A Ship has frequently been used as the Emblem of an Empire, and the metaphor is very applicable here. When the Serenity of the ocean is ruffled by a moderate gale, the vessel pursues its course steadily, and is in perfect Security; but a total Calm, is almost always the forerunner of an outrageous tempest. In a State where the opposite Parties have any moderation; the heads of Government are never wholly in Peace, but the Empire is safe. But the Nation in which a perfect unanimity prevails is always threatened, with most violent commotions. Where there is no discord, there is no jealousy; and where there is no Jealousy, an ambitious intriguing man, and such there always are in all Nations, may pursue his schemes, without meeting any obstacle to prevent the execution of them. But where there are two parties, or more, continually watching each others Conduct, always endeavouring to pry into each others secrets, and the interest of each of which is to detect and bring to light, any evil design that may be form'd by the other, it will be very difficult to carry on an intrigue against the State, without being discovered. Which so ever of the Parties, is at the head of government, is sensible, that the other will take advantage of every error, every mistake, and even every ill success, that may attend the administration; and will consequently make more exertions to preserve, and increase the favour of the People in general, than if it was perfectly secure in Power. Besides this; emulation which in a well ordered government, is the primum mobile of all that is good and virtuous, will inspire the members of each party, with the desire of distinguishing themselves, by their Services to their Country; and every great action on one side lays an obligation on the other to equal it. Thus far Reason can teach us; if we consult facts, I believe they will coincide with these observations.

Let us single from ancient History, the Romans, whose fame has been extended further than that of any other Nation. From the expulsion of the Kings to the establishment of Augustus at the head of the Empire, we have one continued scene, of discord, and strife between the two great bodies which composed the republic, the Patricians, and Plebeians. In fact it was not civil discord, which brought such evils upon the republic, under the usurpations of Marius, of Sylla, and finally of Caesar; there were two Parties it is true; but each was violent against the other only because, it was too much attached to one individual. They acted as Puppets, as mere machines; set to work, by their leaders; and there was therefore no more discord between them, than there is between two sticks, which are struck one against the other. Any more Instances would be unnecessary; but I suppose the same Conclusion might be drawn from the history of every Nation antient and modern, and I think it may be inferred that as discord, sometimes proceeds so far as to be very injurious to Society, so when it is kept within proper bounds it is productive of the happiest Consequences.

There were only five of us present. Burge read a dissertation on the theme γνῶθι σέαυτον,[2] like most other People severe upon the Lawyers. While we were about it Mr. Packard came in. He affects to be very easy in his manners, but it is not natural ease. I made tea this Evening for the Club.

[1] After this point, paragraphing has been editorially supplied.
[2] Know thyself.

7TH.

The *Palladian band*,[1] have begun to exercise, and Captain Vose, feels quite important. I do not know, that I ever saw a man more gratified, with a distinction, of so little Importance. But ambition has almost always a trifle for its aim, and rattle for rattle, I do not see why this should not be as good as any other. I have not join'd this Company, because I fear there will be such disputes, and disorders, arising from it, as will make it disagreeable, if not wholly abolish it in a short Time: another Reason is, that it will employ more time, than I should wish to spend in mere amusement.

[1] That is, the Marti-Mercurian Band. Palladian, a reference to Pallas Athena, goddess of war and wisdom and guardian of cities, is probably JQA's own characterization of this college-based military company.

8TH.

At length we have some rain, the fruits of the Earth, have long been drooping for the want of it. There were two or three showers, in the morning after which it cleared up; but at about 5 in the afternoon, there arose some of the blackest Thunder clouds that I ever saw. Mr. Ware, who read a dissertation after prayers could scarcely distinguish, his own writing, it was so dark. There was no heavy thunder, but a very fine shower, which lasted about an hour; in the evening it cleared up again.

9TH.

The most comfortable Sunday, we have had, for many weeks past. Parson Hilliard preach'd in the forenoon from I Peter I, 3 and 4. "Blessed be the God and Father of our Lord, Jesus Christ, which according to his abundant mercy hath begotten us again unto a lively hope by the resurrection of Jesus Christ from the Dead. To an inheritance incorruptible and undefiled, and that fadeth not away, reserved in heaven for you." The text was enough for me; I heard nothing of the Sermon. It is the old Story, over and over again so repeatedly that I am perfectly weary of it. The afternoon text was from Proverbs IV. 23. "Keep thy heart with all diligence; for out of it are the issues of Life." Sin, and Salvation through Jesus Christ seem to be Mr. Hilliard's favourite topics, and he uses them so often, that they become words without any signification at all, like oaths in the mouth of a swearer. Walked two or three miles, over the bridge in the Evening.

10TH.

We recite this week to Mr. Hale; with whom we shall probably finish Locke: and next Quarter we begin in Reid on the mind.[1] It is said at present that Mr. Hale, does not intend to leave College: and he is determined to see what direction the Storm, that has lately been raised by Honestus,[2] will take, before he goes upon the practice of the Law. It is not very agreeable news here; though there will never be a Tutor I believe, who will be so easily satisfied at recitations, as he is. Mr. Williams brought some Letters for me, up, from Boston, dated as late as May 26th.[3]

We had a meeting of the A B. Gardiner Chandler, gave us an

Oration on Patriotism. Harris read an indifferent piece of Poetry, and the others read essays. There were only six of us Present.

[1] Thomas Reid, *An Inquiry into the Human Mind, On the Principles of Common Sense,* 4th edn., corrected, London, 1785. This is JQA's copy, now at MQA, which he may have owned at this time or used in his senior year.

[2] Under the pseudonym "Honestus," Benjamin Austin had published articles in the Boston *Independent Chronicle* between March and June which attacked the legal procedures in the Commonwealth and called for the abolition of lawyers, a profession which had become prosperous, it was alleged, during a period of economic hardship for others.

[3] Probably AA to JQA, 22 May; JA to JQA, 26 May; and possibly AA2 to JQA, 25–29 April (Adams Papers).

11TH.

We did not recite this day. As the quarter draws near to a close, the Students are falling off quite fast. A third of our Class are absent now. This day completes my 19th. year. I finished studying for this Quarter.

12TH.

The freshmen carry their enmity against the Sophimores, a great deal too far. They injure themselves both in the eyes, of the other Class, and in those of the government. This afternoon while Cabot, was declaiming, they kept up a continual groaning, and shuffling, and hissing as almost prevented him from going through. The freshmen, in the end will suffer for their folly, and before they get out of College, will repent it.

13TH.

We finished with Locke this morning, and were told to begin next Quarter, in Reid. In the afternoon we set off for Braintree, where we shall remain till commencement. All the Scholars, are put out of commons every year, the Friday before, so that the dinner may be prepared. We got home at about 6 o'clock. We found Mr. Weld, and Mr. Wibird here, and Miss Hannah Hiller, a friend of Miss Betsey's. About 15 I fancy, a beautiful countenance, and fine shape; but very unsociable owing either to too much diffidence, or to a phlegmatic constitution; which her countenance seems to express. The generality of our young Ladies are so apt to fall into the other extreme, that this now pleases me because it gives some variety, and furnishes matter for observations of a different kind.

14TH.

Gunning all the forenoon. Received this afternoon several Pamphlets,[1] from my Sister. Read the heiress;[2] a good play; much more regular, and more chaste, than those that are acted on the English stage generally are.

[1] Neither found nor identified except, presumably, *The Heiress,* mentioned in note 2 (below).

[2] London, 1786, a comedy in five acts by John Burgoyne, the defeated British general turned playwright. *The Heiress* met with enthusiastic popular success and went through ten editions in a year (James Lunt, *John Burgoyne of Saratoga,* N.Y., 1975, p. 324).

15TH.

Read part of the volume of anecdotes concerning Dr. Johnson.[1] He appears to have been a brute; a mere cynic, who thought himself the greatest Character of the age, and consequently, that he was entitled to do just as he pleased and to assume the lawgiver in Sentiments and opinions as well as in Literature, but neither his good opinion of himself, nor all his writings put together will ever place [him?] in the first rank of authors. He is represented as very charitable, and doing much good to People in Want, but the principle, seems to be no better motive than fear: and in one particular he was very remarkable; he could pity the poor and relieve them; but if a rich man, was upon any occasion peculiarly unfortunate, Johnson would sooner insult his distress than feel for it. He is represented as being in certain cases greatly biass'd by prejudices which would disgrace a school boy, and his Soul had not a spark of generous liberty in it. In short from what I have before heard of this man, and what I have now read of him, my opinion with respect to him, is a mixture of admiration and contempt.

We walk'd in the evening about a couple of miles with the young Ladies. Mr. Cranch returned this Evening from Boston.

[1] Hester Lynch Salusbury Piozzi, *Anecdotes of the Late Samuel Johnson, LL.D., during the Last Twenty Years of His Life,* London, 1786, which AA2 had sent to JQA. JQA's opinion of Dr. Johnson echoed that of other Americans and stemmed from the Englishman's prejudices against Americans and his antipathy for their revolution (AA to JQA, 21 July, Adams Papers; *Boswell's Life of Johnson,* ed. George Birkbeck Hill, 6 vols., Oxford, 1887, 2:312–313; 3:200–201; 4:283).

16TH.

Mr. Wibird preached all day upon the Same Subject. His text was in I Corinthians XV. 55, 56, 57. O! Death! where is thy sting? O grave where is thy victory. The sting of death is sin; and the strength of Sin, is the Law. But thanks be to God, which giveth us the victory through our Lord Jesus Christ. I did not hear much of it: and indeed I very seldom do. However it was said, that Mr. W. has not preach'd this Sermon so often, as he does some others.

17TH.

Mr. Cranch went to Boston. Miss P. Storer, N. Quincy and B. Apthorp, pass'd the afternoon, we play'd on the flute, on the harpsichord, and sung. There is always some fine music of one kind or another, going forward in this House. Betsey, and Miss Hiller finger the harpsichord Billy scrapes the Violin, Charles and myself blow the flute. Parson Wibird, was here all the evening.

18TH.

Rain'd a great part of the Day. Miss Hiller is only fourteen, her person comes very near to my ideas of a perfect beauty. A pair of large black eyes, with eyelids, an inch long, and eye brows forming beautiful arches, would be invincible if they had a greater degree of animated,[1] and if she was conscious enough of their power, to make use of it. She has not yet I believe been much into Company, and is therefore very silent: to an uncommon degree. I have not heard her speak three times in a day since I have been here. In short she does not appear to have sufficient sensibility

> her face is as white as the Snow
> And her bosom is doubtless as cold,

but she is not yet arrived to the age, where Sensibility is called forth, and when animation is necessary; the Time will come, when her eyes will be as sparkling, as they are pretty; and her countenance as expressive as it is beautifull.

[1] Thus in MS.

19TH.

At about 7 1/2 in the morning I set out for Cambridge, and arrived there just as the Clock struck ten. I found the Crowd large. At about half after eleven the procession arrived and took their Seats in the meeting house. The performances began, with a Salutatory Latin Oration by Champlin, which was followed by a Poem on Commerce by Fowle, which was very good. A Syllogistic on the Question whether the Soul thinks between Death and resurrection. Bradford respondent. A Forensic, "whether religious disputation promotes the interests of true Piety," supported by Crosby, and denied by Bigelow extremely well. A Poem, containing a sketch of the history of Poetry, by S. Gardiner, well written, and well delivered. A Syllogistic, "whether virtue consists in benevolence alone," Norton respondent. A greek dialogue, between Lincoln, and Warland. A Forensic between Lowell and Taylor. "Whether the happiness of a People depends upon the Constitution, or upon the administration of it." Lowell had as many antic tricks, and made as many grimaces, as any ape could have done. A Syllogistic, whether the mosaic account of the creation respects the solar System only. Simpkins respondent. A Conference upon History, Metaphysics, Poetry and natural Philosophy, between Parker, Dwight, Harris, and Hubbard, this Closed the morning performances, though it was past 3 o'clock.[1] I returned to the meeting house, at half past four, but the procession did not come till near 6. There were then. A Latin Oration by Andrews,[2] a Forensic "Whether the Powers of Congress ought to be enlarged" between Sullivan and Loring, who maintained the wrong side of the Question by far the best.[3] A Syllogistic Whether the heavenly bodies produce certain changes upon animal bodies. Wyeth respondent. Part of this was omitted which caused a pretty general clap, and finally an English Oration by Blake;[4] which did him credit.

The candidates for Master's degrees then came on, and an English Oration upon the present situation of affairs, was delivered by Mr. H. G. Otis, and after they had gone through the ceremony of receiving the degrees, a valedictory Latin Oration was spoken by Mr. Townsend.[5] The president then wound all up with a prayer. The house was as full as it could hold, and there was a little disturbance happened in the afternoon about some places. The Class are rather disappointed by the absence of their favorite Thomson who is so unwell, as prevented him from appearing this day.

I spent great part of the evening with Bridge. The new *Sirs,* got quite high, at Derby's chamber, and made considerable of a noise.

[1] The English oration by Thomas Thompson, which was to follow, was canceled because of his illness. Thompson's subject was "The obligation nations are under to keep their faith, fulfill their engagements and in all respects govern themselves by the strictest rules of justice; and the influence of such a conduct upon the public prosperity and happiness; with wishes that the United States of America may thus distinguish themselves" (MH-Ar:Faculty Records, 5:230–231).

[2] Upon "The importance of the Public's doing every thing in their power to promote the interests of the University; in which oration our political Fathers were particularly addressed, and their patronage warmly bespoken" (same, p. 231).

[3] The faculty records list Joseph Loring's name first, presumably taking the affirmative (same).

[4] Upon "The love of true glory, and its happy tendency, when united with public Spirit in virtuous men, to excite and engage them to accomplish themselves for great usefulness in the world—and the importance of fostering such a disposition" (same, p. 232).

[5] Horatio Townsend, of Medfield, who studied law with JQA in the Newburyport office of Theophilus Parsons and later practiced in Norfolk co. (*History of Norfolk County, Massachusetts, With Biographical Sketches of Many of Its Pioneers and Prominent Men,* comp. D. Hamilton Hurd, Phila., 1884, p. 15).

20TH.

A List of the Class that graduated yesterday.

John Andrews	Divinity.[1]
Samuel Andrews	Law
x John Bartlett died in 1786.	
Timothy Bigelow	Law
Joseph Blake	Do.
Samuel Borland	
Nathaniel Bowman	Physic.
Alden Bradford	Divinity
Christopher Grant Champlin	
Daniel Colt	
Amos Crosby +	
William Cutler	Physic.
John Derby	Commerce
William Dodge	Sea
Josiah Dwight	
Robert Fowle	Divinity.
Elias [Elisha] Gardner	
Samuel [Pickering] Gardner	Commerce

John Gibaut	Sailor
Robert Gray Settled at Dover	Divinity.
James Gray	
William Harris	Divinity.
Ebenezer Hill	
Nathaniel How[e]	
Dudley Hubbard	Law
Jonathan Leonard	
Henry Lincoln	Divinity
Joseph Loring	Physic
John Lowell	Law
Porter Lummus	
Jacob Norton + Settled at Weymouth	Divinity.
Isaac Parker	Law
David Pearce	Commerce.
Thaddeus Pomeroy	
Jonathan E[dwards] Porter	
Isaac Rand	
John Simpkins	Divinity
x James Sullivan + died in 1787.	
John Taylor	Law
Joseph Thomas	
Thomas Thompson	Law
John [Eugene] Tyler	
x John Warland died in 1788	
Joseph Warren	
Tapley Wyeth +	Physic

I set out from Cambridge between eight and nine. Stop'd and dined at General Warren's in Milton; and got home at about 4 o'clock. Mr. Shaw and my brother Tom, arrived soon after me.

[1] Death dates and occupations were probably added on at least two separate occasions. The reason for the crosses after the names of Crosby, Norton, Sullivan, and Wyeth is uncertain.

21ST.

Spent great part of the day in my fathers library, reading, and writing.

This day and to-morrow the Government of the College, are employ'd in examining, those that intend to enter the University this year. Tom waits till the end of the vacation.

22D.

Mr. Shaw went over to Weymouth. Mr. Cranch returned from Boston, and Mr. Standfast Smith came with him. My brothers and myself pass'd the night at the bottom of the hill.

23D.

Mr. Davies preach'd in the forenoon from Matthew V, 20. For I say unto you, that except your righteousness shall exceed the righteousness of the Scribes and Pharisees, ye shall in no case enter into the kingdom of heaven, and in the afternoon from I Corinthians I, 23, 24, 25. But we preach Christ crucified, unto the Jews a stumbling block, and unto the Greeks foolishness; But unto them which are called, both Jews and Greeks, Christ, the power of God, and the wisdom of God. Because the foolishness of God, is wiser than men; and the weakness of God, is stronger than men. This gentleman's composition appears to be very good, and his delivery, tho' not excellent, better than the common. He is the first preacher who has engaged my attention these many weeks. Coll. Waters and Mr. Foster came from Boston in the morning. The Coll. has a Son who entered College yesterday. There have been 35 admitted; two turn'd by for the vacation, and one for the year. We had a thunder shower came up, in the Evening, quite refreshing to the fields.

24TH.

The young gentlemen went down to Germantown: it was too hot for me. I spent almost the whole day in the library. Mr. Shaw and Miss Lucy went for Haverhill, in the morning; Mr. Smith, and Mr. Cranch for Boston after dinner.

25TH.

My Grandmamma spent the Day at Mr. Cranch's. General Palmer was up in the afternoon. I wrote part of a Letter to my Sister.[1]

[1] Not found.

26TH.

At about 6 this morning we set out I on horseback, Charles and Tom in a Sulkey; we got to Cambridge, at about 9. Went down to the President's to know what Chamber they had given me; he told me I could not have that which I have hitherto occupied because I was going to live with a Sophimore; so that I must put up with N: 6 which was held last year by Bigelow and Lowell, a senior Chamber, but a poor one in comparison, with that I am obliged to give up to Bridge, and Foster. I do not consider it as a mark of politeness in them to have petitioned for it; and I should have suspected almost any one in the Class rather than Bridge.

N. B. Bridge and Foster did not petition for the Chamber.[1]

Stay'd about an hour in Cambridge, after which we proceeded on our Journey, and at about half past two got to Wilmington, where we dined, at about 9 in the evening we arrived at Haverhill; with our horses almost tired out in coming 46 miles, a long day's Journey for this Country, and in this hot Season.

[1] Squeezed into the text and presumably added later.

27TH.

I perceive Charles has been guilty of a trick which I thought he would despise; that of prying into, and meddling with things which are nothing to him: and ungenerously looking into Papers, (which he knew I wished to keep private,) because I could not keep them under lock and key. If he looks here, he will feel how contemptible a spy is to himself, and to others.

I visited Mr. Thaxter and Mr. White's. Mrs. Allen, and Mrs. Welch, and Mr. Smith dined at Mr. Shaw's with us. There was a Company of Ladies drank tea here. Mr. Thaxter came in the Evening.

28TH.

Captain Wyer,[1] arrived a few days since from Ireland, and had caught a couple of Turtles in the course of his voyage; he presented one of them to the owners of his ship, Mr. White, and Captain Willis. They invited a large Company to dine upon it, in an island about two miles down the River. A little after one o'clock, we all went on board a flat bottom'd Boat, which had been prepared for the purpose, with a Tent over it, and we row'd to the Island where we landed at about 2. At about 30 Roods from the Banks of the River We found an elegant arbour about 50 feet long and 20 wide, with 14 arches form'd with boughs of trees, in such a manner that the leaves only could be seen. A number of flowers and grape vines were entwined with them, so that clusters of grapes were hanging over our heads. Beneath this romantic booth, four tables were spread with 20 plates at each. A number of stakes driven into the ground, with planks lain upon them served as seats. We sat down just before 4. Besides the Turtle, there were cold roast fowls and sallads. 74 Persons were seated at the Tables. One Toast only was drank after dinner, ("Captain Wyer, and all generous commanders at Sea"). By 5, all the company rose, rambled over the island, after which they returned to the Tables, and a number of songs were sung. Before 7 o'clock the whole Company returned to the Boat, several songs were sung on the way, and just after Sunset we landed at the Bottom of Christian Hill. There certainly never was a Party, composed of more than 70 Persons, conducted, with more decency and regularity; no one circumstance turn'd up, that could be disagreeable to the company, or any person in it, and I believe every individual return'd well pleased with the day.

I went to Mr. White's where I found Mr. Andrews who is going to Newbury to-morrow.

¹ Presumably Capt. William Wyer, shipmaster of Newburyport (*Life in a New England Town: 1787, 1788. Diary of John Quincy Adams, While a Student in the Office of Theophilus Parsons at Newburyport*, Boston, 1903, p. 46).

29TH.

Dined at Mr. White's, in Company, with Mrs. White of Boston, Mrs. Willard, Mrs. Parkman, and My Classmate Bil: Abbot, who belongs to Andover. Walk'd in the afternoon, and at Mr. Shaw's heard crazy Temple, talk an hour or two. He will not talk long to any body.

Fine weather.

30TH.

Mr. Shaw preach'd in the forenoon from Proverbs I. 5. A wise man will hear, and will increase learning, and a man of understanding shall attain unto wise counsels. A great deal was said about neglect in attending public worship on the Sunday. I rather doubt whether it be a matter of so much consequence as was supposed. It is however very proper for a minister to remind his People of their Duties from time to Time. The Sermon in the afternoon, was from Job I. 1. There was a man in the land of Uz, whose name was Job; and that man was perfect and upright, and one that feared God, and eschewed evil. As Job is here said to be perfect, Mr. Shaw proved, that no man ever was perfect, and shew that Job, himself, had grossly failed. He explained what was to be understood by the word perfection here; and that it was the Duty of every one to endeavour at attaining it.

31ST.

I paid a few visits in the morning. Dined with a pretty large Company at Mr. Duncan's. After Dinner I went with Mr. W. White, and Leonard, and paid a visit to Mrs. Stoughton. Miss N. Sheaffe,[1] was there, a celebrated Belle. Her appearance does not strike me; as extraordinary; she has a fine eye which gives her countenance a degree of animation. But her complexion is not clear, and she has no colour at all. She is supposed to be married to a Mr. Irving, but it is kept secret, because he depends upon an old uncle, who would not approve of the marriage at all. We drank tea at Mr. Harrods.

There appears a very considerable alteration in the behaviour of P. White within these 4 months. She is soon to be married to Mr. Bartlett, and has already adopted the course of behaviour which will be necessary: there is such a material difference in the manners of married and unmarried Ladies, that in a numerous company a person might I suppose easily distinguish them, though he should not be personally acquainted with any.

[1] Ann (Nancy) Sheaffe, of Boston, married John Erving Jr., mentioned later in the entry, on 30 Sept. (Boston Record Commissioners, *30th Report*, p. 413).

TUESDAY AUGUST 1ST. 1786.

There was a meeting of an association of ministers here this day; but there were only three present. Mr. Adams preach'd the Lecture, and was a whole hour in Sermon, endeavouring to prove, the Trinity, and the existence of hell. After all I believe he left all his hearers where he found them, and he was certainly much too long. After dinner I went with Mrs. White, Miss P. M'Kinstry, and Leonard to Hamstead [Hampstead, N.H.], a clever[1] ride although the road is bad for a Carriage.

[1] Nice, pleasing (*OED*).

2D.

We Lodged at Hamstead last night: it storm'd so all this morning, that, we could not think of returning. After dinner it was not quite so bad and we all return'd to Haverhill.

3D.

Spent part of the forenoon at Mr. Thaxter's Office. Mr. Dodge was there. I went with Mr. Thaxter and paid a visit at Judge Sargeant's. The young Ladies lately return'd from Rye, where they went last week to accompany their new married Sister Mrs. Porter. Mr. T. Leonard White and S. Walker dined at Mr. Shaw's. In the afternoon Mrs. Shaw and B: Smith, Mr. Thaxter and Miss Duncan, Leonard White and P. Stevenson, Miss Lucy and myself took a ride in four chaises, round the great Pond, Charles and Tom went on horseback. Miss Duncan and Miss Stevenson, pass'd the remainder of the afternoon at Mr. Shaws. We went down in the evening for an hour to Mr. White's. P. Stevenson, is not more than 16 I imagine, slender, not tall, a fine complexion, rather, too large a mouth, black eyes not quite enough animated, and a tout ensemble, which shows all the candour, and modest assurance of Innocence. But this is all outside. One trait only in her character I think I have seen more than once, which differs very much from her looks and indeed from her reputation, a contemptuous disposition, apt to ridicule small defects in the person or behaviour of other People. But this may be mere conjecture.

4TH.

Went in the forenoon, and pick'd blackberries with the young Ladies. Lucy Cranch tells me I have no Complaisance in me, and I suspected as much before. And for a person who has it not naturally, it is much too hard a task to undertake to be complaisant. Visited Dr. Saltonstall, and Mr. Bartlett in the afternoon. Drank tea at Mr. White's. Mr. N. Blodget was there; I knew him formerly but have not seen him before, these seven years.

5TH.

We were up at four in the morning; but were so long in preparing our things that we did not set out till the Clock had struck six, and before we started from the banks of the river on the Bradford side the clock had struck seven. Mr. C. Blodget was going to Boston on horseback, and we rode together as far as Mystic. He was in the army, almost all the late war, and told a number of anecdotes, which he was witness to in the course of it. I dined at Captain Brooks's in Mystic. Stopp'd about half an hour at Cambridge, and got to Mr. Cranch's at Braintree at about half after eight in the evening, as much fatigued as I ever was in my life.

6TH.

I felt so stiff all day that I did not go to meeting. I was unfit for almost every thing, and only read a few pages in the course of the day.

7TH.

I could not sleep last night. Lay restless till about 3 in the morning. Then got up, and read one of Bishop Berkeley's Dialogues against matter,[1] a curious System, and rather a new one to me. At day light I went again to bed, and slept till eleven o'clock. In the afternoon I went down to see my Grand-mamma, but she was not at home.

[1] Presumably George Berkeley, *Three Dialogues Between Hylas and Philonous . . .*, London, 1713.

8TH.

Read through the remainder of the Dialogues, which Reid says, "prove by unanswerable arguments, what no man in his Senses can believe."[1] There are however, great objections to the System which are not mentioned. This work appears to me, to confound the cause with its effect for ever. Thus if I burn my fingers, they say, the fire by which I burnt them is in my mind, because, the Sensation which it produced is there. Reasoning in the same manner might I not conclude, that there is a Bottle in this wine glass, because the wine that is in it was poured from a bottle? Every one readily agrees that the Sensations, which heat or cold, hardness or softness, solidity, extension, motion &c, raise in his mind, are not in the inanimate matter, which causes them but they are causes which produce those effects in our mind. But says Bishop Berkeley, no being, can communicate that which it hath not, which is as much as saying that a hone, cannot whet a razor, because, it is not sharp itself: in short if the ideal System be true, either every animal in creation has an immortal Soul, or else, man must have two; for I take it a horse, and a dog, have as clear ideas of heat and cold, and even of a tree or a river as man. The conclusion is evident, and for my Part, if ever I doubt of the existence of matter, I will likewise doubt of my own existence, and of that of every thing else, nor do I see, how one can be given up with out the other.

I went down in the afternoon, and drank tea at my uncle Quincy's. Charles Went to Cambridge yesterday to move our things, and returned this afternoon. Mrs. Apthorp and her Daughters spent the afternoon at Mr. Cranch's.

[1] Thomas Reid, *An Inquiry into the Human Mind,* p. 21–22.

9TH.

All the forenoon down in the Library; reading and writing. Pass'd the afternoon at my uncle Adams's. There was some conversation concerning Mr. T—r.[1] He has not many friends I believe in Braintree. I believe him at best a very imprudent man, or as Horace says of a character something like him

Nil fuit unquam, sic impar sibi.[2]

[1] Royall Tyler.
[2] "Never was a creature so inconsistent," Horace, *Satires,* Bk. I, Satire 3, lines 18–19 (*Satires, Epistles and Ars Poetica,* transl. Fairclough, p. 32–33).

10TH.

Spent the whole day in my father's library; wrote but little, I cannot indeed write half so much as I wish to, for if I leave off two minutes, I take up some book as if by instinct, and read an hour or two before I think what I am about. I intended to have written a great deal this vacation; it is now almost gone and I have not written twenty Pages.

11TH.

I went down with Charles and Billy to Mrs. Quincy's, in the afternoon. Mr. and Mrs. Gannett were there, Captain Freeman of Dorchester, and Mrs. Edwards, an antiquated Coquet, who was about half a century gone. Very much such a thing as Narcissa is at present; and if her face did not give the lye to her behaviour I should suppose her now to be 17 rather than 70.

> Her grisled locks assume a smirking grace,
> And art has levell'd her deep furrow'd face.
> Her strange demand no mortal can approve,
> We'll ask her blessing, but can't ask her love.[1]

[1] Edward Young, Satire V, "On Women," from "Love of Fame, The Universal Passion. In Seven Characteristical Satires" (*Poetical Works*, 2 vols., Boston, 1854, 2:120).

12TH.

Charles and myself went over to Weymouth, and dined at Doctor Tufts's. We were overtaken by a violent thunder shower. The lightening fell at a very small distance from an house where we took shelter while the Cloud pass'd over. When we return'd to Braintree we found Mr. Dingley at my uncle's.

13TH.

Mr. Weld preach'd all day from Micah VI. 8. He hath shewed thee O man, what is good, and what doth the Lord require of thee, but to do justly, and to love mercy, and to walk humbly with thy God. Mr. Weld proved, that to do justly, was to practice, all the Christian Virtues, and that a man who did not so, took things, for what they were not, and he likewise inculcated humility. The Sermon was as good as our President's from the same text the last fast day.[1]

[1] See entry for 6 April (above).

14TH.

Mr. Cranch went to Boston in the morning. My aunt and Miss Betsey, are both of them unwell. The weather being rainy and disagreeable Mr. Dingley determined to stay till to-morrow. Mrs. Apthorp, spent the afternoon here.

15TH.

Mr. Dingley return'd to Duxbury: he proposes returning here next Friday, to spend a fortnight. The weather was fine all day. We have had but very few disagreeable dog days.

16TH.

Charles came to Cambridge last Monday in order to move into our new Chamber. My Cousin and myself came from Braintree at about 9 o'clock, and arrived here just at Commons time. I found the Chamber all in Confusion, and it will be so probably all the rest of this Week, for Lowell and Bigelow, who lived in it last year were two of the greatest slovens in their Class. The studies must both be paper'd, which is a very disagreeable piece of Work. Leonard White came in the evening from Haverhill and brought me a couple of Letters.[1]

[1] Letters not found.

17TH.

The Scholars are coming in very fast, and are almost all of them busy, in putting their new chambers in order, and moving. Very busy all day in papering Charles's study, and part of mine, but before we finish'd the Paper fail'd us. Drank tea with Mead in his Chamber which is contiguous to mine. The Club are quite in a Dilemma, how to do since the boys are sent off. They are unwilling to send Freshmen, and think it beneath their dignity to go themselves for what they want. At about 10 o'clock this evening, Stratten, a crazy fellow came, and knock'd at my door; just as I was going to bed; I opened it, and he ask'd me for some water; I told him I had none, and shut the door upon him: "Damn you, says he, do you refuse a man a little water." After thumping two or three minutes at the door, he went away, knock'd at all the doors in the entry; ran up and down stairs, came again, to my door and stamp'd at it, and finally ran to the window in the entry, push'd it up, and leapt immediately out of it. I instantly got out of my bed, went to my window, and·saw him lying on the ground. After 3 or 4 minutes he began to groan "Oh! I've broke my leg." Charles had not gone to bed; I desired him to go and call up Dr. Jennison; who immediately came out. The fellow complain'd in the most doleful manner. However, after examining his leg, (for he was not at all hurt any where else) the Doctor said, there might be a bone crack'd but that none was displaced. It was with a great deal of difficulty that we were able to get Stratten, into one of the lower Rooms which is empty. He persisted for two hours in attempting to walk, for in addition

78

to his State of mind, he was then as drunk as a beast. At length however he was carried into the Room, and laid on a Straw bed. The Doctor, although the man was insulting him continually dress'd up his leg, and we left him just before 12 o'clock, at Night, upon which I immediately retired to bed again.

18TH.

They were obliged to carry off Stratten this forenoon, as he could not possibly walk. I finish'd papering my study this forenoon, and in the afternoon put the Chamber in order. I engaged Sullivan 2d.[1] for my freshman. Bridge made tea this afternoon for the Club, in Kendall's turn. Somehow or other we made out without employing a freshman finally.

[1] James Sullivan, the second of three brothers to graduate in that class, and son of Gen. John Sullivan. College customs enforced a system of freshman servitude under which any upperclassmen could demand personal services from first-year men. The well-advised freshman sought to attach himself to a senior "who protected him from the importunities of juniors and sophomores, and allowed him to study in his chamber, in order to be handy for personal errands" ([Thomas C. Amory], "Master [John] Sullivan of Berwick [Maine]—His Ancestors and Descendants," *NEHGR,* 19:304 [Oct. 1865]; Morison, *Three Centuries of Harvard,* p. 105–106).

19TH.

Leonard White Came from Boston, and Cranch return'd from Braintree this day. Almost all the College, have got here now, and the new monitors,[1] (who must always belong to the junior Class) took their Seats yesterday. They are Adams 2d.[2] and Underwood, who is about 35 years old. I have done little or nothing this day. The first week is almost always loitered away.

[1] Monitors were appointed by the college president to keep bills of absence and tardiness at devotional and other exercises (Benjamin Homer Hall, *A Collection of College Words and Customs,* Cambridge, 1856, p. 325–326).

[2] Solomon Adams, a sophomore, was regarded as "Adams 1" by the college until the end of July 1786 when he became "Adams 2." On the other hand, JQA, who entered late in his junior year, was first classified "Adams 3," but he became "Adams 1" by the beginning of his senior year (MH-Ar:Faculty Records, 5:228, 233, 237–238).

20TH.

Mr. Deane,[1] of Falmouth preach'd here this day, in the forenoon from Matthew. XI. 29. Take my yoke upon you, and learn of me; for I am meek and lowly in heart; and ye shall find rest unto your souls, and in the afternoon from Luke XVI. 31. And he said unto him, If they hear not Moses and the prophets, neither will they be persuaded though one rose from the dead. A whining sort of a Tone was employ'd by Mr. Deane, which would have injured the Sermons if they had been good.

> For what's a Sermon, good or bad
> If a man reads it like a lad,

but Mr. Deane's Sermons, were not hurt by his manner of speaking them.

[1] Samuel Deane was minister of the First Congregational Church, Falmouth (now Portland, Maine), from 1764 (Sibley-Shipton, *Harvard Graduates,* 14:591–598).

21ST.

We recite this week, and the next to Mr. Read; The juniors have now a leisure week; Mr. Hale having resign'd, and no other tutor being chosen in his stead. Every tutor when he resigns his office, has a right to nominate a person, for his successor; Mr. Hale nominated Mr. Paine the former Butler but they say he is too Popular among the scholars, to be chosen, there are four other gentlemen in nomination, three of whom (Mr. Abbot, Mr. Burr, and Mr. Webber) are his Class mates. The other Mr. Prescott, was in the Class before him.[1]

This afternoon after Prayers Charles read the Customs[2] to the Freshmen in the Chapel: they are read three mondays running in the beginning of every year, by the three first in the Sophimore Class, who are ordered to see them put in execution, immediately after prayers. The two Classes went out to have their wrestling match, a Custom which has for many years been established here. From 6 o'clock till twelve they were constantly at the work. They went on so close that the two Champions of each Class were fresh to take hold; but in less than five minutes Mitchell, the Sophimore, threw Babbitt and Fay, the Freshmen hero's. The Sophimores then set up a cry for three or four minutes, which resounded through the Colleges, for the Classes here make it a matter of great consequence.

[1] Jonathan Burr was eventually appointed to this position. Samuel Webber was chosen to replace another tutor, Nathan Read, in Aug. 1787, and two years later was made Hollis Professor of Mathematics and of Natural and Experimental Philosophy, succeeding Samuel Williams, who resigned in disgrace; he held that po-

sition until elected president of the college (in preference to Eliphalet Pearson) in 1806 (*NEHGR,* 35:289–290 [July 1881]; entry for 23 Aug. 1787, below; Morison, *Three Centuries of Harvard,* p. 190).

[2] See note for entry of 27 March (above).

22D.

Mr. Shaw came last evening with my brother Tom, who was examined this morning for the freshman Class, and admitted. He soon after set off for Braintree, where he is going to stay untill, a place is found for him to board at. I declaim'd this afternoon Collins's Ode on the Passions.[1] Coll: Waters and Mr. Cranch came up from Boston. I spent an hour in the evening with them at Waters's Chamber.

[1] *The Poetical Works of William Collins . . .,* London, 1786, p. 83–86 (MQA).

23D.

Went to Mr. Dana's in the forenoon. He proposes going to Maryland, to meet in a Federal convention.[1] We had the Club, at Mason's chamber this evening. Fay the Freshman was there, and sung a number of Songs extremely well. He also plays sweetly on the violin. He entertained us there charmingly for a couple of hours; and appears to be quite an agreeable companion.

[1] On 29 Aug. Dana and four others received commissions from Gov. James Bowdoin to represent Massachusetts at the Annapolis Convention, but neither Dana nor his colleagues arrived in time (MHi:Cushing-Orne Papers; Edmund C. Burnett, ed., *Letters of Members of the Continental Congress,* 8 vols., Washington, 1921–1936, 8:469).

24TH.

Went down to the President's, for an order to take a book from the Library, but he did not know whether he could give it me without leave from the Corporation.[1] Mr. Thaxter was here a few minutes; but was on his return to Haverhill. Mr. and Mrs. Cranch, Dr. Tufts, Mr. Isaac Smith, and his Sister Betsey were here at Tea.

Was at Bridge's chamber in the Evening.

[1] For Harvard's numerous and detailed laws regarding the borrowing of books, see Col. Soc. Mass., *Pubns.,* 31 [1935]:370–375.

25TH.

Mr. Read made a mistake, in calling over the Freshmen this morning, as it is customary to except them, the first week. Doctor Tufts was here this morning, and has engaged a boarding place for Tom, at Mr. Sewall's. I have not begun as yet to Study, with any Closeness, though it is full Time. Had Tea, and pass'd the evening at Williams's Chamber.

William Lovejoy Abbot,[1] was 21 January 18th. He belongs to Andover, and is the head of our Class. He purposes studying Physic. A very steady sober lad, he appears fond of being thought a dry, humourous fellow, and has acquired a great command of his Countenance. His wit would not please in the mouth of any other Person; but his manner of producing it seldom fails of raising the laugh. He is a very good speaker, especially such Pieces, as conceal the features of mirth under the mask of gravity.

[1] "Abbot 1st" later practiced medicine in Amesbury until 1794, when he moved to Haverhill (Russell Leigh Jackson, "Physicians of Essex County," Essex Inst., *Hist. Colls.,* 83:163 [April 1947]).

26TH.

Rainy weather all day. I had a number of the Class at my Chamber in the Afternoon. Immediately after Prayers we had a Class meeting for the Purpose of choosing a Valedictory Orator, and Collectors of Theses.[1] Eaton was moderator. A motion was carried that a majority of the votes of Class should be necessary for an Election. When the votes were collected it was found there was no choice. There were five votes, for Jackson, the last Person, that would have been suspected of obtaining any. A second attempt was made, equally fruitless. Jackson had ten Votes. It was then resolved, that the choice of an Orator should be deferred; and that the Class should proceed to that of the Collectors. The one for *Technology, Grammar,* and *Rhetoric* was first ballotted. Waldo, had 20 Votes; but as a majority of all the Votes was required there was no Choice. It was voted then, that the Person who should have for the future, the greatest number of Votes, should be duly elected. Waldo said, he was sensible of the honour done him by those gentlemen, that had voted for him; but that he wished to be excused. He was taken at his word, and *Abbot 2d.* was chosen. His modesty and diffidence were such that he earnestly requested to be excused; but with great difficulty was prevailed upon to accept. The second Collector for *Logic, Metaphysics, Ethics, Theology,* and *Politics,* was then Chosen. *Fiske* was the Person. The *Mathematical* Part fell to Adams, and the Physical to *Johnstone.* The choice of those was not so judicious as that of the others. *Cranch* and *Abbot* 1st would undoubtedly have been more proper Persons, but neither of them would probably have accepted, a second choice. The meeting at about 7 o'clock was adjourned till Monday evening, when we shall proceed to the Choice of an Orator. The Club then came, and drank tea at my Chamber. Fay was there, and entertained us with singing till 9 o'clock.

[1] Theses collectors prepared propositions, or arguments to be advanced and defended, in four branches of knowledge, basing them on subjects studied in the undergraduate curriculum. Hypothetically, if challenged, any senior was expected to defend these theses in Latin. The president, professors, and tutors chose from those submitted by the collectors a sufficient number suitable for publication on the theses sheet. For the 1787 sheet and JQA's mathematical theses, see the Descriptive List of Illustrations, Nos. 10 and 11 (Benjamin Homer Hall, *A Collection of College Words and Customs,* Cambridge, 1856, p. 458–459; entry for 8 May 1787, below).

27TH.

Mr. Hilliard preach'd in the morning from Philippians, IV. 11. Not that I speak in respect of want; for I have learned in whatsoever state I am, therewith to be content. And in the afternoon from Luke XIX. 8. And Zaccheus stood and said, unto the Lord; Behold, Lord, the half of my goods I give to the Poor; and if I have taken anything from any man by false accusation, I restore him four fold. They say Mr. H. has had his Corn stole from him lately, and that he preached this Sermon to perswade the thieves to return it.

I went after meeting to Williams Chamber, and remained there till almost prayer Time.

28TH.

We recite again to Mr. Read this week, but he did not attend in the afternoon because, we had a Lecture from Mr. Williams, at 3 o'clock. After Prayers the Class met by adjournment, and Fiske was chosen moderator. It was then resolved that if after the first ballot, there was not a majority for any one Person; the Class should the 2d. Time confine their Votes to the 3 Persons who

83

should have the most votes. I supposed that the greatest contest would lay between Bridge and Little, but to my great surprise, the second ballot Was between Freeman, Little, and Waldo. The third was between Freeman, and *Little,* who finally carried it by a considerable majority. The Class then all went to his Chamber, but did not stay there more than an hour.

After tea we had a meeting of the A. B. Beale and Cushman were admitted. Fiske, gave us a very good Oration, upon Ambition, closing with a number of very pretty Poetical Lines. We came to several New Regulations. There were two or three Pieces read. I had written the following, which I forgot to carry with me, and was excused from reading till the next meeting.

A.B.   N:3—Trifles light as air
Are to the jealous Confirmation strong
As proofs of holy writ.[1]

The Tragedy from which these lines are a Quotation, is such a complete History of the progress of Jealousy, that it would be the greatest presumption in me, to pretend saying anything new upon the subject. I shall therefore confine myself to a few remarks upon this play, which furnishes a more fruitful source than the trite and I may say worn out subject of Jealousy, which I suppose no person present is acquainted with, except merely by Speculation.

This Play is by many considered as the most perfect of all, that we owe to the immortal Shakespeare, and if we attend merely to the conduct of it, we may readily confess that few dramatic performances are better; but the very foundation upon which the whole fabric is erected appears injudicious, disgusting, and contrary to all probability.[2] Who can believe that the Senate of Venice, would give the government of an island belonging to the State, to a moor, when it is known how constantly the Venitian nobility have always enjoy'd every employment in the State? And how tenacious they have ever been of this Prerogative? And is it natural that a young Lady so virtuous and Chaste as Desdemona is represented would as Brabantio expresses it,

"Run from her guardage to the sooty Bosom
of such a thing as him, to fear, not to delight."[3]

In short I never could conceive what induced the Poet to take a negro for an example of Jealousy. But from this defect great

Beauties are derived. In particular the speech of Othello to justify himself before the Senate

                            "My Story being done
She gave me for my pains a world of sighs,
She swore in faith twas strange, twas passing strange
Twas pitiful, twas wondrous pitiful.
She wish'd she had not heard it; yet she wish'd
That heaven had made her such a man. She thank'd me
And bade me, if I had a friend that loved her,
I should but teach him how to tell my Story
And that would woo her. On this hint I spake,
She loved me for the dangers I had past
And I loved her that she did pity them."[4]

This is to perfection, the artless, and rough, but winning eloquence of a Soldier.

The manner in which Iago raises the jealousy of Othello, at
first by, obscure hints and insinuations, and afterwards by direct
accusations shows the nicest acquaintance with human nature. I
wish however to doubt, whether man be capable of the consummate villainy which is display'd in the character of Iago.

The Reasons which he gives for all his malice against Othello
and Cassio is, that he suspects they have both intrigued with his
wife, and moreover that Cassio was promoted before him. Jealousy, and disappointed Ambition, will easily prepare a man for
committing crimes; but Iago appears to care very little for his
Wife, and without love there cannot be much Jealousy. The
other Circumstance, I do not think sufficient to induce a man to
perpetrate such detestable deeds. For it may be considered as a
maxim that no man does evil for evil's sake, nor will any one injure his fellow creature unless it be to gratify Interest or Passion.
It is a fault too general with the writers of novels, Romances and
Plays, that their characters are either too good or too bad. Nature
deals not in extremes, and as the best man is he who has the least
faults, so the worst, is he who has the least virtues. An author
may indeed in drawing a good character, represent it more perfect, than is commonly found in real Life; because it may serve
as a model for others to imitate; but to represent men worse than
they really are, can be of no service, that I know, and, it is de-
grading human Nature.

It must however be confess'd that the character of Iago is absolutely necessary in order to work up the mind of Othello to such a pitch of Jealous fury as leads him to murder his wife, and herein consist the chief Beauties of the Play. But besides these, there are detached beauties of Sentiment and expression as in all the Plays of this inimitable author.

There is an energy and force in these Lines

> "The tyrant custom
> Hath made the flinty, and steel couch of war
> My thrice driven bed of down."[5]

There is a consummate hypocrisy in the following observation of Iago, which can escape the notice of no Sensible Reader

> "Who steals my purse, steals trash; 't'is something, nothing.
> T'was mine! t'is his, and has been slave to thousands.
> But he that filches from me, my good name,
> Robs me of that, which not enriches him
> And makes me, poor indeed."[6]

But to show all the excellencies of this Tragedy would almost be to transcribe it.

The Cloven foot was ascribed by the vulgar to the Devil, in Shakespeare's days as well as in our's, which appears from Othello's saying when he has full proof of his wife's innocence, and of the villainy of Iago.

> I look down tow'rds his feet; but that's a fable.[7]

The 13th. Scene of the second Act,[8] may I think be recommended to the serious attention of every young man. We may perceive how much the author detested a Vice, (which at this day is too common) by his representing it as attended with the most fatal consequences.

---

[1] *Othello*, Act III, scene iii, lines 324–326. Editorial citations to *Othello* are from *Shakespeare's Works*, ed. Quiller-Couch and others.

[2] Despite JQA's lifelong interest in the theater, so amply demonstrated in these early years, his critical, indeed damning, views of *Othello* became hardened at this young age and persisted throughout his life. They were publicly ridiculed in 1835 in Fanny Kemble's *Journal* and were published in several articles the following

year. For a detailed account, see CFA, *Diary*, 5:84–87.

[3] Act I, scene ii, lines 70–71.

[4] Act I, scene iii, lines 158–168.

[5] Act I, scene iii, lines 229–231.

[6] Act III, scene iii, lines 159–164.

[7] Act V, scene ii, line 288.

[8] From the context, JQA was most likely using the Warburton edition of Pope's *The Works of Shakespear in Eight Volumes . . .*, London, 1747, which divided Act II into 15 scenes. This was the edition

JQA had previously used for long quota-
tions in his Diary while in Holland (entry
for 9 June 1781, note 3, above); no copy of
this edition exists, however, in the Adams'
libraries. In the Quiller-Couch edition of
Shakespeare, this scene is scene iii, lines
254–328 of Act II. The "Vice" JQA is referring to is "the devil drunkenness," for
which Cassio berates himself.

29TH.

We had no recitation in the afternoon. After Prayers, we had a
meeting of the ΦBK at Freeman, and Little's Chamber; Mr.
Ware presided in the absence of Mr. Paine. Abbot 2d. was received. Freeman read a short Dissertation upon the love of our
neighbour; Little and Packard a Forensic on the Question,
whether the present scarcity of money in this Commonwealth be
advantageous to it. Harris and Andrews, were the extempore
disputants. Chandler 3d. and Cushman were admitted. Several
others were proposed, but an universal Vote, could not be obtained for them. The meeting was finally adjourned to Packard's
Chamber to-morrow morning, immediately after Commons in
Order to receive the two Persons, just admitted, and to make another attempt to admit others.

30TH.

The Society met, this morning at Packard's Chamber agreeable to their Resolution. Mr. Paine presided. Chandler and
Cushman were received. Beale and Harris were at length admitted; and it was resolved that they should be received, the morning of the anniversary, which will be next Tuesday. But all attempts to admit two others that were proposed were found
useless. It is a misfortune, that small and trifling prejudices,
should be the means of excluding worthy young men from a Society, which might be of Service to their Reputation. But of two
evils the smallest should always be preferred, and the Consequences would undoubtedly be more dangerous, if every member of the Society had not the privilege of excluding any other
Person.

We had no recitation this afternoon; Bridge was at my Chamber in the Evening. We had this afternoon from Mr. Williams,
one of the best Lectures, that I ever heard him deliver: it was
upon the importance of the mathematical Sciences. His Style
was nervous,[1] but too negligent. Such a Sentence as this, "There

is something in the *Nature* of Truth, which *naturally* is Pleasing to us," ought not to proceed from the Pen of a Professor at any University.

We had likewise a Lecture in the morning from Dr. Wigglesworth.

[1] Powerful, vigorous (*OED*).

31ST.

Charles went to Boston in the morning. I began upon Trigonometry in my mathematical manuscript. We had a Class meeting immediately after Prayers. The Committee of the Class that was appointed to inform the President of the choice, for an Orator &c. reported, that the President had not given his consent to have the Oration in English, because he thought it would show a neglect of classical Learning. I motioned that the Vote, for having it in English should be reconsider'd, but there was a considerable majority against it. It was then voted that the President should be inform'd that the Class had determined to have an English Oration, or none at all. The former Comittee all declined going again. Johnstone, Fiske, and Welch, were chosen, but declined. It was much like AEsop fable of the mice, who determined to have a bell tied round the Cat's neck: they were all desirous that it should be done; but no one was willing to undertake the Performance of it. The meeting was finally adjourned till monday next.

FRIDAY SEPTEMBER 1ST. 1786.

Studied Algebra all the forenoon. Took books from the Library, Brydone's Tour vol: 2d. Ossian's Poems, and Boswell's Corsica.[1] The weather begins to grow quite cold. This morning I shivered, almost all prayer Time. It is however to be hoped it will not set in, so soon.

[1] Patrick Brydone, *A Tour Through Sicily and Malta* . . ., 2 vols., London, 1774; *The Works of Ossian, The Son of Fingal, Transl. from the Gaelic by James MacPherson,* London, 1762, or 3d edn., London, 1765; James Boswell, *An Account of Corsica, The Journal of a Tour to that Island* . . ., London, 1768 (Harvard, *Catalogus Bibliothecae,* 1790, p. 73, 143, 55).

2D.

I have been too busily employ'd, to have much to say. Study, does not afford, a rich source for description. We had a moot

Court in the afternoon at Fiske's Chamber. Packard was condemned. Mr. and Mrs. Cranch were here.

3D.

Mr. Hilliard gave us a Sermon in the forenoon from Isaiah LV.
6. Seek ye the Lord while he may be found, call ye upon him
while he is near, and in the afternoon from John V. 22. For the
Father judgeth no man; but hath committed all judgment unto
the Son. I do not believe that Mr. H. has one new idea, in ten
Sermons upon an average. Some of his argumentation this afternoon appeared to militate with the Trinitarian System. He said
we ought to take it a peculiar favour, that we were to be judged
by Christ, because he had a practical knowledge of our natures,
and would make allowance for the frailty of humanity. Now this
appears to bring the Question to a Point. If Christ was God he
was omniscient and consequently wanted[1] no practical knowledge of mankind. But as he was not omniscient, the Consequence is plain, and may be easily deduced from Mr. H's own
Concessions. But all religious sects have their absurdities. It is
with them as with man. That which has the least faults is the
best.

[1] That is, "lacked."

4TH.

We were to have had a Class meeting, by Rights: but no one
thought to obtain Leave. As we have no metaphysical Tutor,[1]
here at present, we supposed, that, for the ensuing fortnight we
should have no reciting. But the government have determined
that we should continue to attend Mr. Reed in S'Gravesande's.
This is not an agreeable Circumstance; a Person who does not
belong to the University, and hears only the word reciting, naturally concludes, that the Scholars are an idle set of fellows, because they are always averse to recitations. Now the Fact is just
the Contrary. A Person fond of study, regards the Time spent in
reciting as absolutely lost. He has studied the Book before he re-
cites, and the Tutors here, are so averse to giving ideas different
from those of the author, whom they are supposed to explain,
that they always speak in his own words, and never pretend to
add any thing of their own: Reciting is indeed of some Service to

idle fellows; because it brings the matter immediately before them, and obliges them, at least for a short Time, to attend to something. But a hard Student will always dislike it, because it takes time from him, which he supposes might have been employ'd to greater advantage.

We had a mathematical Lecture from Mr. Williams, this afternoon, upon Dialling.[2] Probably the last we shall have this Quarter, as he Proposes setting out in the Course of this week upon a Journey. He expects to be gone about six weeks. I was at Little's Chamber in the Evening somewhat late. Freeman came from Sever's Chamber, and display'd such a brilliancy of wit, that I could scarcely come away. Beale and White endeavoured obtaining leave to go to Providence; to Commencement; but were refused.

[1] Tutor John Hale had resigned (entries for 6 May and 21 Aug., above).
[2] A method of surveying.

5TH.

Anniversary of the ΦBK, Society.[1] The members were, on that account excused from reciting. At 11. we met at The Butler's chamber. Harris and Beale were received, after which we proceeded on business. Mr. Paine, and the Orator, went first, and the others after them according to the order of admission. Mr. Andrews gave us a spirited, and well adapted Oration upon friendship. After it was finished, we returned to the Butler's Chamber. Packard then informed the Society, that there was in Town, a young Gentleman from Dartmouth College, by the name of Washburne; a Senior Sophister; who was very desirous of having the Society established there, and he was commissioned also, to express the same desire from several others of the same Class. It was questioned whether we had any right to grant a charter without consulting the Fraternities at New Haven, and Williamsburg. A number of arguments were used on both sides, and when it was put to vote there were 8 for consulting them, and 8 against it. It was again debated for some time, and, finally determined, by a considerable majority, that we should consult the brethren at New Haven, and Williamsburg; and at the same Time enquire whether it is their Opinion that each fraternity has a right to grant Charters out of their respective States.[2] These debates took up more than an hour; after this we proceeded to choose our Officers. Mr. Paine was elected President, Mr. Ware Vice President, Little Secretary, and Fiske Treasurer. At about half past Two, we went to Mrs. Nutting's, and had a very good Dinner. Wit and Wine, the Bottle and the Joke, kept nearly an equal Pace. When the Prayer Bell rung we broke up, and attended Prayers.

We dansed in the evening at Mason's chamber till 9 o'clock.

[1] Harvard's chapter was incorporated 5 Sept. 1781 (*Catalogue of the Harvard Chapter of Phi Beta Kappa . . .*, Cambridge, 1912, p. 100).

[2] A letter, dated 20 Nov., was sent to New Haven, asking for their opinion on the subject, but it was not received until the following May; in the meantime, the Yale chapter sent Harvard a similar letter (CtY:Phi Beta Kappa Records; *Catalogue of the Harvard Chapter,* p. 111; entry for 21 Feb. 1787, below).

6TH.

This day the annual Dudleian Lecture was preach'd by Mr. Symmes of Andover; the subject was the validity of Presbyterian Ordination. There are four subjects which are alternately treated the first Wednesday in September. They are Natural Religion, Revealed Religion, The errors of the Romish Church, and that above mentioned. The founder was Mr. Dudley:[1] who gave a Sum the annual interest of which is 12£ and is given to the Person who preaches the Lecture. The person is appointed by the President, the Professor of Divinity, the Senior Tutor, and the Minister of Roxbury, but they cannot choose a Person under 40 years old. Mr. Symmes's Lecture was a very good one, and the Sentiments he expressed were very liberal, though he was extremely severe in some places upon the Church of England.[2]

Mr. Cranch was here all the afternoon.

I was admitted into the Handel Sodality; and attended in the evening at Cranch's Chamber.

[1] Paul Dudley, a provincial Massachusetts judge, willed to Harvard £133 6s. 8d. for an endowment to be known as the Dudleian lectures (Sibley-Shipton, *Harvard Graduates,* 4:52–53).

[2] Unlike most other Dudleian lectures, Symmes' was never printed (same, 12:586).

7TH.

No reciting. Cranch went to Boston.

The Commonwealth is in a State of considerable fermentation. Last week at Northampton, in the County of Hampshire, a body of armed men to the number of three or four hundred, prevented the Court of common Pleas from sitting, and bruised the high-sheriff dangerously, as it is reported.[1] The same Court was likewise stopp'd the day before yesterday, at Worcester by 400 men. The Court went to a Tavern, and adjourned till yesterday. They were again prevented from proceeding yesterday, and adjourned without a day. The militia it seems could not be raised to quell them. The Governor issued a Proclamation,[2] calling upon the People at large to support the Constitution, attacked in such a flagrant manner, and directing the State's Attorney, to prosecute the abbettors of these Riots. The Militia in the Town of Boston, have already offered their Services, and declared their determination to support the government with their Lives and Fortunes. Where this will end Time alone, can disclose. I fear, it will not before some blood is shed. The People complain of grievances; the Court of Common Pleas, the Senate, the Salaries of Public Officers, the Taxes in general, are all grievances, because they are expensive: these may serve as pretences, but the male-contents, must look to themselves, to their Idleness, their dissipation and extravagance, for their grievances; these have led them to contract debts, and at the same time have, rendered them incapable of paying them. Such disturbances if properly managed may be productive of advantages to a Republican Government, but if they are suffered to gain ground, must infallibly lead to a civil war, with all its horrors. This will not I believe be the Case at present; but such struggles seldom end without the loss of some Lives. Such commotions, are like certain drugs, which of themselves are deadly Poison but if properly tempered may be made, highly medicinal.

[1] This event marked the first violence in what was to become Shays' Rebellion.
[2] Printed in *Massachusetts Centinel*, 6 Sept.

8TH.

I went in the evening to see Mrs. Dana; there was a large Company there, and I escaped as soon as I could. I intended to make a number of Sage Reflections, this evening, but I feel so ill-natured, that I will not attempt it.

9TH.

The inferior Court, is to sit according to Law, next Tuesday, at Concord; it is said, that the same People, who stopp'd it at

Worcester, are determined to join others, and proceed in the same manner at Concord. And they will probably carry their Point; for the People that are sensible, what evil Consequences must attend these disorders, yet are unwilling to use any exertions for putting a stop to them. We are now in a perfect State of Anarchy. No laws observed, and no power to Punish delinquents; if these treasonable practices, are not properly quelled, the Consequences must be fatal to the Constitution, and indeed to the Common-wealth.

The Parts for the next exhibition,[1] were given out this afternoon. *Freeman,* has the English Oration, *Bridge* the Latin, *Adams* and *Cranch,* a Forensic disputation, on the Question *Whether inequality among the citizens* be necessary, to the *preservation of the Liberty of the whole?*[2] *Beale, Burge, Fiske, Harris, Little,* and *Packard* have the mathematical Parts. The President told us to be ready, by a fortnight from next Tuesday, as the Corporation might possibly meet, then.

We had a beautiful Evening; I walk'd out with Cranch, round the Common, and on the Road till near 11.

[1] The exhibition was given on 26 Sept. At this time Harvard held exhibitions semiannually, and the various parts were assigned by the college government to members of the junior and senior classes. As the program outlined in JQA's entry here and that of 26 Sept. suggests, participants displayed their oratorical skills as well as their literary, classical, and mathematical learning. The exhibitions were open to all in the college and to interested outsiders and parents; about four hundred later attended the exhibition (Benjamin Homer Hall, *A Collection of College Words and Customs,* Cambridge, 1856; Mary Smith Cranch to AA, 28 Sept., Adams Papers).

[2] JQA spoke on the side affirming the necessity of inequality for liberty. Speakers were apparently given strips of paper each with the title of his part. See entry for 26 Sept., note 1 (below).

10TH.

Mr. Porter[1] the Minister of Roxbury, preach'd here; he is a pretty good Speaker. His discourse in the forenoon was from Revelations XI. 17th. We give thee thanks O, Lord God Almighty, which art, and wast, and art to come; because thou hast taken to thee thy great Power, and hast reigned. And in the afternoon from John I. 45, 46. Philip findeth Nathanael, and saith unto him, We have found him of whom Moses in the Law, and the Prophets, did write, Jesus of Nazareth, the Son of Joseph? And Nathanael said unto him, Can there any good thing come out of Nazareth? Philip saith unto him, Come and See. Mr. Porter's Language is Good, and his manner of preaching better than Common. But I suppose him not to be very deep, as a divine; he is indeed yet a young Man. Cranch and myself dined at the President's. Mrs. Willard is as different in her manners, from the President, as can be. They form quite a contrast. Mrs. W. is easy, and unaffected: and appears not to be made for Cerimony. He is stiff and formal; attached to every custom, and trifling form; as much as to what is of Consequence; however, he was quite sociable; much more so indeed than I should have expected.

¹ Eliphalet Porter was ordained at Roxbury in 1782 and remained there throughout his life (Walter Eliot Thwing, *History of the First Church in Roxbury, Massachusetts, 1630–1904*, Boston, 1908, p. 178, 184).

11TH.

We recite again to Mr. Read this week, and shall probably the whole of this Quarter. I finished the first part of my forensic. We had in the Evening, a meeting of the A. B. We had no Oration, Abbot 2d. being necessarily detained. Little and Cranch gave us a Forensic.¹ I read my N: 3. (p: 38.)² Several other Pieces were read, after which we determined to admit Abbot, Gordon, and Dodge, of the Junior Class; and finally adjourned to next Monday, evening.

¹ Punctuation in the preceding two sentences has been editorially supplied.
² See entry for 28 Aug. (above).

12TH.

Rain'd hard almost all day. We had a Class meeting, after Prayers for determining the matter, concerning a Valedictory Oration. By dint of obstinate impudence, Vociferation, and noise; the minority so wearied out those on the other side, that several of them went out, after which, a Vote was pass'd, ratifying the proceedings of the last meeting. Johnson, Sever, and Chandler 3d. were then chosen as a committee to inform the President of the proceedings in the Class, and the meeting was dissolved. We had a meeting of the ΦBK, at Burge's Chamber. Bridge, and Abbot, read a forensic, on the Question, "whether internal tranquillity, be a proof of Prosperity in a Republic." Freeman and ⟨*myself*⟩ Adams were the extemporaneous disputants. The Society then adjourned till this day fortnight, when they are to meet at Little's Chamber, immediately after Prayers.

94

13TH.

Finished my Trigonometry.

Immediately after Prayers in the Evening, the military Company, assembled, on the Common, and Captain Vose harangued them. He gave them a pretty Oration upon Patriotism. It contained several brilliant thoughts, and a well adapted Quotation from Cicero. After the Speech, the Company, went through the manual exercise, which was very well performed. After Commons the Sodality met, at Foster's Chamber; and play'd several Tunes. Broke up, as is customary at 9 o'clock.

14TH.

White went to Haverhill. I determined with Little upon two Pieces, to publish in the next Magazine for the A B. Concluded my Forensic, for the exhibition. Weather begins to be quite cold.

15TH.

I copied a part of Fiske's Oration, upon Patriotism, to be printed in the next Boston Magazine,[1] from the A B. Finished reading Jenyns's Disquisitions.[2] I think they show great judgment and deep penetration. I know not that I ever read, so small a volume that gave me greater Pleasure.

Abiel Abbot,[3] was 20. the 14th. of last December. He is one of the good scholars in our Class, and a pretty writer. His disposition is amiable, and his modesty so great, that it gives him a poor opinion of himself, which he by no means deserves. He proposes for the Pulpit, and has I believe every Qualification necessary to make him, a good Preacher: and his example, I have no doubt, as well as his Precepts, will recommend all the moral Duties.

[1] *The Boston Magazine* ceased publication with a combined November-December issue and without Fiske's article.

[2] Soame Jenyns, *Disquisitions on Several Subjects,* London, 1782.

[3] "Abbot 2d," after studying theology in Andover, returned to Harvard as tutor, 1794–1795. Following some years of preaching in Coventry, Conn., he became principal of Governor Dummer Academy, Byfield, Mass., in 1811 and later was minister at Peterborough, N.H. (Abiel Abbot and Ephraim Abbot, *A Genealogical Register of the Descendants of George Abbot . . .,* Boston, 1847, p. 7–8).

16TH.

Copied off my Forensic for the Exhibition, and prepared it, to carry for Approbation to the President. I received in the forenoon, a Letter from *Delia*.[1] White return'd this Evening from Haverhill.

[1] Letter not found. Delia was the name JQA gave to Nancy Hazen in his poem, "An Epistle to Delia," which he completed on 12 Dec. 1785 after resolving to put an end to his feelings toward her. The name may have been derived from the collection of 16th-century sonnets by Samuel Daniel about another Delia, the love of the poet's youth (M/JQA/28, Adams Papers, Microfilms, Reel No. 223).

17TH.

Mr. Hilliard preach'd in the forenoon from Isaiah V. 12. But they regard not the work of the Lord, neither consider the Operation of his hands. It might be a political Subject, and relate, to the Times, but I know not whether it really was. His Text in the Afternoon, was from Hebrews XII. 1. Wherefore seeing we also are compassed about with a great Cloud of Witnesses, let us lay aside every weight, and the Sin, which doth so easily beset us, and let us run with Patience the Race that is set before us. I seldom hear much of Mr. H's Sermons, except the Texts. Dined at Mrs. Dana's. She laugh'd at a certain Class mate of mine, who all at once, wears green silk before his Eyes, as if they were injured by hard Study. But certainly every one, who knows him, will exculpate Study from that fault.

After Prayers I went with Mead, and pass'd the evening at Professor Pearson's. Mr. and Mrs. Rogers[1] were there. The Professor, is a much more agreeable, and indeed a more polite Man, than I should have suspected, from what I have heard. I have not seen any Person belonging to the Government, so polite to Scholars, or show so few Airs. Mrs. Pearson is likewise very agreeable.

[1] Mrs. Daniel Denison Rogers was a sister of Henry Bromfield Jr., whom JQA met in Amsterdam. Their sister Sarah was the wife of Prof. Eliphalet Pearson (Daniel Denison Slade, "The Bromfield Family," *NEHGR,* 26:38–39, 142 [Jan., April 1872]).

18TH.

I have been so unwell all Day, that I have not been able to attend to any Studies at all. We had a Class meeting after Breakfast. The Committee that was Sent to inform the President of the proceedings of the Class, informed that he had said he feared he should be obliged to direct the Class to have the Oration in Latin; notwithstanding this it was voted by a majority of two, that the Class should still persist. I went in the forenoon to the President's to have my forensic approbated. I rode over the

Bridge through Boston, and returned by Roxbury, before dinner. The Sodality met in the Evening at Abbot's Chamber, to play over the Tunes for exhibition.

19TH.

Unwell again, so that I have not been able to Study. I have felt a kind of dizziness, which very much resembles Sea-sickness. I have been however much better than I was yesterday. Rain'd almost all day.

20TH.

This Evening, immediately after prayers, the President inform'd us that the Government, and Corporation, had chosen Mr. Jonathan Burr, for a Tutor, he had accepted the Office, and was to be attended accordingly. I went with Sever, to Mr. Tracy's and to Mr. Gerry's, but neither of them was at home. Attended the musical Society at Mayo's chamber, till 9 o'clock.

Jonathan Amory,[1] was 16. the 7th. of last July. His disposition is good and very easy. But he is too young to be possess'd of that steadiness and Reflection, which a Person just going into the world, ought to have. From the instances of Persons now in College, that came so very young, I think it may be concluded, that in general, it is a disadvantage to enter College before the age of fifteen; very few of those that come, before that age, make any considerable figure, in a Class.

[1] Amory became a Boston merchant. He was first in the countinghouse of his uncles Jonathan and John Amory, then engaged in business with James Cutler, and finally went into partnership with his eldest brother, Thomas Coffin Amory ("Memoir of the Family of Amory," *NEHGR*, 10:64 [Jan. 1856]).

21ST.

I really do not know what I have done this day. I am always sensible, that what with one trifle and another I lose too much of my Time, and yet I do not know how to employ more of it. I believe it is a disadvantage to have so many public exercises to attend. It is impossible to get seriously and steadily fixed down to any Thing. As soon as I get in a way of thinking or writing upon any Subject, the College Bell infallibly sounds in my Ears, and calls me, to a Lecture, or to recitation or to Prayers. This cannot certainly suffer any one, to engage in profound Study of any kind.

22D.

Mr. Read sent for me this morning, informed me, that the Exhibition was to come on next Tuesday; and offered to excuse me, from the recitations till then, in Case, I was not prepared, as the Time, that had been given for getting ready was so short. But as it happened I was not in want of more Time. I made tea for our Club.

23D.

I have done nothing all this Day. Every Day thus lost doubles the obligation of improving the next; but I fear if I was held to perform the Obligation, I should soon become a Bankrupt. Pass'd the Evening at Bridge's Chamber. We had considerable Conversation, as we frequently have, concerning our future Prospects. He is ambitious, and intends to engage in Politics. He expects more happiness from it, than he will ever realize I believe. But he is form'd for a political Life, and it is [he will?] probably show to advantage in that Line.

24TH.

Mr. Hilliard gave us an occasional Sermon, occasioned by the Death of Mr. Warland, a young Man, belonging to this Town. His Text was from Job. XIV. 1. 2. Man, that is born of a Woman, is of few days, and full of Trouble. He cometh forth like a flower, and is cut down; he fleeth also as a Shadow, and continueth not. It was one of the best Sermons I have heard from Mr. H: The idea that the diseases of the Body, are so many arrows taken from the Quiver of God Almighty, appears however, to be an instance of the Bathos.

In the afternoon, a Mr. Foster[1] preach'd from Isaiah LIII. 1. Who has believed our report? And to whom is the arm of the Lord revealed? I never heard a more extravagant fellow. His Discourse was a mere Declamation, without any connection, or train of Reasoning. He said that Religion, ought never to be communicated by raising the Passions, and mentioned it as a peculiar advantage of the Christian System, that it speaks to the understanding. Yet he made an Attempt, (a most awkward one I confess) to be Pathetic: talk'd, of a Grave, a winding sheet, and a Place of Skulls, all of which amounted to nothing at all, which was likewise the Sum total, of his whole Sermon. Yet this Man, is a Popular preacher, in the Place where he is settled. For the maxim of Boileau will hold good in all Countries, and in all Professions

Un Sot trouve toujours, un plus sot qui l'admire.[2]

[1] Probably Jacob Foster, minister at Nelson, N.H., 1781–1791. Foster was regarded as a moderate Calvinist (Sibley-Shipton, *Harvard Graduates,* 13:407–410).

[2] Nicholas Boileau-Despréaux, "L'art poétique" from *Oeuvres choisies,* 2 vols., Paris, 1777, 2:[11]. JQA quotes the last line of the first song.

25TH.

Almost all this Day was employ'd in preparing for the exhibition. The musical Parts take up some time. We had in the afternoon a Lecture from Mr. Pearson, upon Philosophical Grammar.

26TH.[1]

The exhibition began at about a quarter after 12, with, the Latin Oration by Bridge, it was a Panegyric upon the military institution which has lately been established. The forensic between Cranch, and me, came next. I read as follows. The second Part refers, to Cranch's reply.[2]

"Conscious of the insufficiency of my ability to perform the task allotted to me, I would fain implore the Indulgence, and Candour of this respectable Audience. But Apologies of this kind, are seldom of much avail, especially when they have any foundation: I shall therefore without any further Preamble, introduce the Question, Whether inequality among the Citizens, be necessary to the Preservation of the Liberty of the whole?

There are two views in which the word *Inequality,* as relating to the Citizens of a State, may be considered. Inequality, of Fortune, or of Rights, Privileges and Dignities. In the Case of Riches, the Inequality arises in the natural Course of Things; Nor is there an Instance of a State of any Consequence, subsisting without it. There were indeed several sharp Contests in the Roman Republic, with Respect to an equal distribution of Lands; but they were never of any Service, to the People, and were always attended, with the most unhappy Consequences. The Question appears therefore to be, in other Words, whether a pure democracy be the most favourable Government to the Liberties of a People.

It is a very general political maxim, that Men can never possess a great degree of Power without abusing it. Hence, so few Instances of despotic Monarchs, who have not been the scourges of their People. In an aristocratic government, the Power being in a number of hands, this tyrannical disposition becomes more dangerous, and extends wider its baneful Influence. But of all Tyrannies, the most dreadful, is that of an whole People; and in a Government, where all men are equal, the People will infallibly become Tyrants. What Protection can any Laws afford a Citizen in a State where every individual, thinks he has a right of altering and annulling them at his Pleasure, and where nothing is wanting, but the capricious whim of a vile Rabble, to overturn all Laws and Government? If a Prince is oppressive, at least he has been taught in some measure, the Art of governing an Empire, and has commonly been educated, for it. The same may be said of an Aristocracy, they will at least endeavour to support the Dignity of a State, and will take proper Measures for the safety of the majority, of the People, though they may be unjust to individuals. But when the Passions of a People, conscious of their Liberty and strength are raised, they hurry them into the greatest extremities: an enraged multitude, will consult nothing, but their fury; and their Ignorance serves only to increase their Obstinacy, and their Inconsistency.

The most simple forms of Government, are probably the most ancient: But Mankind soon perceived, the great inconveniences which naturally arise from a despotic Monarchy, an arbitrary Aristocracy, and an inconstant Democracy. They endeavoured therefore to form Constitutions, which might unite all the advantages, severally possessed by each of those Systems, without having their Defects. Such was the Constitution which raised a petty Village of Italy to the Empire of the World; and such in more modern Times was the Constitution which enabled Great Britain, to make such a splendid figure, in three Quarters of the Earth, and to prescribe terms of Peace to two combined Kingdoms, whose natural Advantages were so much superior to her own: happy would it have been for her, if Prosperity had not introduced Luxury and Corruption, which have undermined the

Pillars of her excellent Constitution, and exposed her to the Contempt and Derision of those very Nations by whom she was formerly view'd with Terror.

I am sensible, my Friend, that you have the popular Prejudice in your favour; and that in declaring against equality I am combating the Sentiments, of perhaps a large majority of the Inhabitants of this Common wealth. It is the Duty of every Person, and more especially of an unexperienced Youth, to show a proper Deference, and Respect for the Opinions of Mankind in general, and of his Countrymen in particular. But when his Reason tells him that these Opinions would lead him to a manifest absurdity, I think he has a Right to refuse his Assent to them, at least untill sufficient Arguments are brought to support them. Now, as Nature has in every other Particular, created a very great inequality among Men, I see not upon what grounds we can found the Supposition, that they ought all to share an equal degree of Power. And that too great a degree of equality among the Citizens, is prejudicial to the Liberty of the whole, the present alarming Situation of our own Country will I think afford us a sufficient Proof.

PART 2D.

It appears, my Friend, that you yourself are sensible of the weakness of your Cause, by your endeavouring to prove, what I never pretended to dispute, what I am as firmly persuaded of as you are, and indeed what I have already granted viz. That the People cannot be free in a despotic Monarchy, nor under an aristocracy; and that if the Proportion of wealth, possessed by Individuals, be unequal to a great degree, the Liberty of the Nation will be in Danger. I plead not for an excess of inequality, but I still maintain that a perfect equality is contrary to Nature and to Reason.

"In this Commonwealth" you say "The People apprehend some Persons have amassed too large a Proportion of Wealth, and acquired too large a share of Power, and thinking themselves injured have arisen, and demanded Satisfaction?"

But why do they think themselves injured? Is it because they have suffered Tyranny or Oppression? No! It is because other Persons have been more industrious, more prudent and more successful than they. When, regardless of every Principle which binds Man to Man, they laid violent hands on Justice herself, by stopping the proceedings of the Courts of Law, in diverse Places, was it because they had been injured by those Courts, and could not obtain Redress? No. It was because they were conscious they had injured others; and they wished therefore to put a stop to all means of obtaining redress. Now had the Notions of those People concerning equality been a little lower, and had there been really a greater degree of inequality among the Citizens, the Commonwealth would not have been thrown into a State of anarchy and Confusion, and instead of rebelling against the Laws and Government, those People would have sought in Oeconomy and Industry, that relief which they now endeavour to wrest by Violence.

If by Equality among the Citizens could be meant an equal right to Justice, and to the Protection of the Laws, certainly no Person, whose Soul is not debased by Slavery could object to it; but this construction cannot be put upon the word; it must be considered as relating to wealth or Dignity and in both Senses, I still must think inequality absolutely necessary for the Liberties of a People.

But here I would not be considered as an Advocate for hereditary Distinctions. Wealth may with Propriety be transmitted from Father to Son. But Honour and Dignities, should always be personal. The Man who to the greatest natural and acquired Abilities unites the greatest Virtues, should certainly not be view'd as on a Par with a vicious Fool, but the absurdity would I confess be equally great, if any one was obliged to enquire who were the Ancestors of a Citizen, to know whether he be respectable.

The History of Lacedemon certainly can produce no Argument in favour of equality. For 1st. it was an hereditary Monarchy. Two branches of a Family descended from Hercules were in Possession of the Throne for nine hundred years. 2dly. There was a Senate composed of 28 persons who formed an aristocratic Body with Power equal to that of the Kings; and 3dly. the Authority of the Ephori, who were chosen annually among the People was superior even to that of the Monarchs. So that in this Respect, the Spartan Constitution was similar to the Roman, and the British, which, I have already agreed were excellent. But Heaven forbid there should ever arise in our Country a Legislator to establish by Force, a Constitution which could form nothing but Warriors. The fine feelings of the Heart which render human Nature amiable, were entirely excluded from the System of Lycurgus. Many of his Laws, display a barbarous Cruelty, and beauteous Science, whose persuasive Voice, calms the impetuous Passions of Youth, sooths the cares, and asswages the infirmities of age, was discarded from within the walls of Sparta by this savage Legislator.

I doubt whether these arguments have convinced you, my Friend, of the necessity of inequality; but however we may differ in Opinion in this Respect, I am sure you will unite with me, in addressing to Heaven the most fervent Petition, that whatever the Constitution of our own Country may be, she may enjoy genuine Liberty and real Happiness forever."

After I read this Part Cranch concluded with a reply. The next Thing that came on, was the Syllogistic dispute, by the Juniors Grosvenor, Dodge, Clark, and Adams 3d. It was on the Question, *Whether there is a Sense of morality innate* in the human Mind. A Dialogue upon Eloquence from Fenelon[3] by Gordon and Lincoln succeeded, and after that the Greek Oration by Abbot 3d. the Hebrew by Gardiner, and finally the English by Freeman, which obtained an universal Clap, the first, known at an Exhibition. It was upon the political Situation of our affairs, and was delivered extremely well. The Oration would not read so well as Little's, but taken altogether would please almost any audience better.

We had Commons immediately after the exhibition. There were no Tutors Present, and there was a sad Noise in the Hall.

After Commons the Martimercurean band, escorted the President, with the Committee of the Overseers, over to the Steward's, where they performed the manual exercise. I pass'd part of the afternoon at Freeman's Chamber. Sullivan who took his degree this year was there.

I had Company to tea at my Chamber. Deacon Smith and his Son, Dr. Welch, and his Lady. Mrs. Otis. Mrs. Cutts, and Betsey Smith.

The Tea Club, who have formed a small Society for dancing, were here in the Evening till 9.

I had a very bad head ache, and retired to rest immediately after they went away.

[1] Between leaves of JQA's Diary at this point there is inserted a loose piece of paper, written in Joseph Willard's hand, which reads: "2. A forensic disputation

upon this question—'Whether inequality among the citizens be necessary to the preservation of the liberty of the whole'? By Adams and Cranch." Presumably this strip of paper was handed out by President Willard at the time parts were distributed on 9 Sept.

[2] Cranch's reply and rebuttal have not been found.

[3] Fénelon, François de Salignac de La Mothe, *Dialogues Concerning Eloquence in General; and Particularly, That Kind Which is Fit for the Pulpit . . .*, transl. William Stevenson, London, 1722 (Harvard, *Catalogus Bibliothecae,* 1790, p. 149). According to the faculty records, Gordon and Lincoln 1st were to give "an English dialogue between Demosthenes and Cicero, from [Fénelon, Archbishop of] Cambray's dialogues of the dead" [*Dialogues des morts anciens et modernes, avec quelques fables . . .*, 2 vols., Paris, 1752] (MH-Ar:Faculty Records, 5: 237).

27TH.

I feel quite indolent as I have finally got rid of the affair which has kept me employ'd this fort'night. Was part of the forenoon at Bridge's Chamber. The Sodality met in the Evening, at Putnam's. Rather Unwell.

28TH.

We had a meeting of the ΦBK, in the morning at Little's Chamber. Chandler read a Dissertation, Harris and Cushman a Forensic. Bridge and Cranch were the extempore disputants. Went with Freeman to Boston: paid a number of Visits; we dined at Mr. Sullivan's, in Company with Mr. Bartlett, Mr. Johonnot, and George Warren. Took a long walk with Johonnot in the afternoon. Return'd to Cambridge with Freeman, before 8. We had a very good supper at Mason's Chamber, after which we took a walk, and return'd there again; finally retired, between 11 and 12 o'clock.

29TH.

It is a most unhappy Circumstance, for a Man to be very ambitious, without those Qualities which are necessary to insure him Success in his Attempts. Such is my Situation,

> If it be a Sin to covet Honour
> I am the most offending Soul alive.[1]

But I have not the faculty of convincing the persons that compose the small Circle in which I move, that my deserts are equal to my pretentions and disappointment must naturally follow. I often wish I had just Ambition enough to serve as a Stimulus to my Emulation, and just Vanity enough to be gratified with small Distinctions. But I cannot help despising a fellow of such a Character. I esteem a Man who will grasp at all, even if he cannot keep his hold, but one who in the fifth or sixth Station can be content, whilst he has an equal Chance of obtaining the first must be despicable. May that Spirit, which inspires my Breast never be bent into an evil Course; and above all may Envy never find a corner of my Heart to lurk in!

These Lines have been suggested by an Event which happened this Day: If any one should read them except myself; I request he would not consider them as a proof, of my intolerable Vanity and self-conceit; but that he would think my heart is sometimes so full, that it spontaneously dictates to my hand Sentiments, which many would endeavour to conceal, with the utmost Care, and for which I must at Times condemn myself.

I went with Sever, passed the Evening, and supped, at Mr. Gerry's. Mrs. Gerry was not at home, Mrs.[2] and Miss Thompson were there, and a Coll: Glover,[3] a very curious sort of a Man. Miss Thompson, has a very Innocent Countenance, is pretty, and sensible of it, like all other fine Women.

[1] *King Henry V*, Act IV, scene iii, lines 28–29.

[2] Mrs. James Thompson, wife of a New York merchant and mother of Ann Thompson Gerry (entry for 9 Aug. 1785, note 3, above).

[3] John Glover, Marblehead merchant, brigadier general in the Continental Army, and political intimate of Elbridge Gerry (George Athan Billias, *General John Glover and His Marblehead Mariners*, N.Y., 1960, p. 35–37, 131).

30TH.

I see not why I should not relate what anecdotes I can collect concerning myself; and why I should not be at Liberty to record the Panegyrical speeches, that I hear made, by Chance. *Grosvenor* the Junior told my Class mate and neighbour, Abbot 1st., (without thinking I heard him,) that in his Opinion, Adams's forensic at the last Exhibition was the meanest that was ever delivered in the Chapel. It would not have been easy to express the Sentiment with more Energy, however I must bear it and only hope, that the generality of the Audience were more favourable.

Mr. and Mrs. Cranch were here in the Afternoon, the weather has been uncommonly warm ever since last Sunday. Learned was with me part of the Evening, and paid me several Compliments, which had they been true might have consoled me for the ill Opinion of Grosvenor.

SUNDAY OCTOBER IST. 1786.

Mr. Paine, preached here, in the forenoon from Acts IV. 12. Neither is there salvation in any other, and in the afternoon from I of Corinthians XVI. 14. Let all your things be done with Charity. The morning discourse was doctrinal, and therefore not so pleasing a Subject as the other; which was excellent. His arguments in favour of Charity, were such as naturally arise from the Subject, but well arranged, and in a very agreeable Stile. His delivery is good, but his length of Stature is such, as prevents his appearing so graceful as he otherwise might. Upon the whole he drew my attention more than any preacher I have heard for several months.

Bridge passed the evening in my Chamber.

2D.

We recite this week to Mr. Burr the new Tutor; but he was absent this Day. The A B Society met this Evening. The Juniors Bancroft and Lincoln were received; Abbot, and Dodge, were received the last meeting. The first Piece read, was the forensic between Fiske and myself upon the Question whether, a republican Government, be the most favourable for the advancement of Literature. I denied it, and read the following Arguments in the negative:

A. B. N 4. There is no Proposition however absurd, that will not be adopted and defended by some Man or other: and when an assertion is made contrary to all Sense or Reason, an ingenious Man can sometimes convince an Audience, that it is true, by representing only one side of the Question, and using only those arguments which incline towards that Side.

These Reflections naturally arise in my Mind, when I see you, Sir, endeavouring to show that a Republican Government, is the most favourable to Literature. You begin by laying down several of the most extraordinary premises that I ever heard: from these you draw natural Conclusions it is true, but which prove Nothing; for the Scriptures you know, tell us that an house built on the sand, must fall at the first blast. Your whole System seems to stand upon this maxim, that *the very Idea of a republican Government presupposes the Inhabitants in the highest State of Civilization.* I am willing my good friend, that you should presuppose whatever you please, if you will confess the fact to be far otherwise.

Without recurring to Athens or Sparta, Carthage or Rome, for Common Place arguments, as is too frequently done, let me ask whether at the present day the most civilized Nations are not subjected to Despotic monarchs: and whether Republics are not rather remarkable for being backward in the progress of civilization? And as to the scope, which a popular form of Government gives to Ambition, I should conceive that Circumstance more proper to form wise Politicians than men of deep learning. There cannot be in popular governments encouragements to literary genius equal to those which are given by Princes, who have themselves a Taste for the fine arts. They grant such rewards as kindle the latent sparks of genius, and enable it to shine with the brightest splendor. This is so consonant with experience, that the most distinguished aera's in the History of Literature are found in the Times and Countries of an Augustus, a Charles the 2d., and a Lewis the 14th. Indeed the prospect which every citizen in a free Government, has, of obtaining Offices of State, appears to me rather prejudicial than advantageous to Literature. A Man engaged in the Affairs of his Country can pay but little attention himself to the Art and Sciences; but when the desire of shining as a Statesman, or as a general is entirely restrained, and an ambitious man, has no other method to render his Name illustrious, than by his literary productions, all his attention will of Course be turned that way, and it must naturally follow, that his Exertions will be attended with Consequences more favourable to Literature than in a State where it is but a secondary Object, or (if I may so express it) an Instrument by which the Citizens raise themselves to public Employments.

PART 2D.

I have always supposed, my worthy Friend, that however certain a young Man might be of any Proposition, Decency and Modesty required he should not make it, with all that assurance, and confidence, which might be proper in a man of years and experience. I likewise suppose when I made the Question, which, I know not for what Reason, has not, I think been answered, that the Fact itself was so plain and Evident, as would oblige you yourself to answer in the affirmative. Had you done this your System must consequently have fallen; but rather than contradict a Proposition, which is next to self-evident, you have prudently avoided giving any answer at all, and have rested your Cause upon a Distinction, which would better suit a pleading at the Bar, than a candid Enquiry after Truth, viz. that a Question is no Argument. But since you can be convinced with nothing but positive assertions, I willingly indulge your inclination; and affirm, that the Idea of a republican government does not presuppose the highest degree of Civilization, and I trust I can prove it from your own Concessions. You grant that the most civilized Nations extant are governed by despotic Monarchs. It must follow that republics are not so much civilized; how then can you say, that republics have the greatest degree of civilization? It is just as reasonable, as if you should say, a yard is longer than a foot, but yet a foot, is longer than a yard.

To my other Question you reply, that had I confined my Attention to America, I must be sensible the answer would be in the negative: but Sir, suffer me to observe, that America, is not the only Republic now extant, and that the Question is not concerning the American but the republican form of government. You think my Distinction between a man of deep learning and a wise Politician is something new; I am happy to find that in the course of our Dispute, one new Idea has arisen, and I believe most of our hearers will agree that it is a just one. Politics and Literature are as different from one another as war and Literature; Nor is a very extensive acquaintance with the fine arts, more requisite for a Statesman, than for the general of an Army. You seem to think that Literature is like any particular Science, and that a small acquaintance with it is sufficient, if it can raise a Citizen to public Employments. I agree, it is sufficient for the Purpose of an ambitious citizen, but it is not sufficient for the promotion of Literature itself. Let us run a parallel between the progress of a man of genius in a republic and in a Monarchy. In both Cases, he will be employ'd while young in the pursuit of literature. In the republic, he will soon be called upon to serve the public, and from that time forth, he will be obliged to relinquish the Study of the Arts and Sciences, because the affairs of the Nation will employ all his Time. But in a Monarchy, his Talents will acquire him respect, reputation, and perhaps fortune, but they will not introduce him to a Situation which shall induce him to neglect the Sciences. On the contrary he will be continually improving his literary faculties, and his productions will do honour to himself and to his Country. This is my idea of the promotion of literature, and this is what a republic can seldom boast of. There is only one more argument of your's, that I shall endeavour to refute: (for I fear our friends that are present, will think I have taken too much time to prove a thing so evident.) You say we must not judge of the improvements of a nation by a few individuals, but by the People at large, and reasoning from this principle you conclude, that the progress of literature is greater in America than in any other country on earth. Let us examine your train of reasoning. "In America the common people can make out to read a chapter in the Bible by spelling about half the words. In Europe nine tenths of them cannot read at all. Here they can most of them write their names, there they are obliged to make a mark. Therefore, literature has made greater progress here than in Europe." If literature consisted in reading the Bible, or in writing a name, I should certainly concur in Opinion with you; but as the life of Man is barely sufficient to form a person deeply versed in literature, its progress must be the greatest, where there are Men, who can employ all their days, in cultivating the Arts and Sciences.

One or two Dissertations were read, and a character of Mr. James by Bridge, extremely well done. Abbot gave us an Oration upon Patriotism. We determined for the future to meet Sunday evenings, and then we all retired.

3D.

A number of the Students have been very ill in consequence of eating cheese from the Buttery. It operated very violently as an emetic.

We recited this morning to Mr. Burr in Reid on the Mind. The Tutor seems to be very unfavourable to the author, and treated him very cavalierly. He tells us we are to spend only this week upon the book, and that we shall go into Burlamaqui, upon natural Law[1] immediately.

There was a horse Race here in the afternoon, which prevented our reciting. The dancing Club met at Beale's in the Evening.

[1] Jean Jacques Burlamaqui, *The Principles of Natural and Political Law,* transl. Thomas Nugent, 2 vols., London, 1763 (Harvard, *Catalogus Bibliothecae,* 1790, p. 83).

4TH.

We had this morning a forensic given out, to be read next week, on the Question whether the diversities in national characters arise chiefly from Physical Causes. I am to support the affirmative, and think upon the whole it is the best side of the Question.

Our musical Society met in the evening at Vose's chamber.

5TH.

A very bad cold, has prevented my studying much, this day.

In the morning we finished reciting in Reid. We went over more than 300 Pages at this recitation. The next book we are to study, is Burlamaqui, which is said to be very good. I made tea for the Club. Bridge had a small dispute with me, upon the nature of Physical Causes. He thought the effects produced by sensual Appetites, could not be attributed to physical causes. I was of opinion that they must be. We appealed to Mr. Burr, and his Sentiments confirm'd mine.

6TH.

A stormy day. Very unwell, especially in the former part of the Day. I have had several Times little contests with Bridge, upon the Subject of our forensic. He is to support the negative side of the Question, and will write very ingeniously. He is the only person in the Class who is fond of discussing questions of this kind in Conversation: we frequently dispute, and it always, increases my acquaintance with the Subject. The objections he raises are commonly weighty, and they lead me to look further than I should otherwise do, into the point in debate; and our difference of opinion is attended with no bad Effects, as all acrimony, and ill humour is excluded from our Conversations.

7TH.

I have been studying almost all day what to write for a Forensic; the subject is so copious, that I find a great difficulty, in shortening my arguments, and making them concise. Charles went down to the Castle.[1]

[1] That is, Castle Island, situated off Dorchester in Boston Harbor, and formerly the site of the fortified post Castle William, burned down by the British in 1775.

8TH.

Mr. Hilliard preached in the morning from Ephesians V. 1. Be ye therefore followers of God, as dear children. A poor subject. His afternoon text was from Psalm XXX. 7. Thou didst hide thy face, and I was troubled. The Sermon appeared like an address to lunatic People; and to tell those who were so despondent, as to think they had committed the unpardonable Sin. There is not I believe much danger on that side; and that his Cautions were quite unnecessary.

Dined at Mr. Dana's. He got home from the Southward yesterday.

The A B, met in the Evening. We had several essays, and Orations from Beale and Harris, both upon, writing and Eloquence. We finally chose officers. Fiske president again. Little and Harris Secretaries. We adjourned before 9 o'clock to the first Sunday next quarter.

9TH.

No reciting. Mr. Burr is engaged to preach several Sundays at Hingham, and does not return early enough for the next morning recitation. We had a Lecture from Mr. Pearson, upon words and Letters: he enumerated all the different sounds of the 26 letters of the English alphabet. Mr. Williams who returned yesterday from his Journey, gave the Class a Lecture, upon Trigonometry. Pass'd the evening with Bridge.

10TH.

The ΦBK. met at Burge's chamber at 11 o'clock. Beale and Burge read dissertations. The extempore disputants were Packard and Chandler. We voted to admit White. Mr. Wigglesworth gave a Lecture in the afternoon. Several fellows in the two lower Classes were very indecent and noisy. The dancing Club met at Bridge's Chamber. After they broke up, I remained there; took a walk by the fine moon-light; and retired at about 11.

IITH.

The Class from 9 to near twelve were reading their forensic; I read in the affirmative as follows.

"Whether the diversities of national character, (taking the word, *character,* in its most extensive Sense) arise chiefly, from physical Causes?"

The many Arguments which naturally present themselves to defend each side of this Question, created in my mind, (and perhaps not in mine alone) a small difficulty. That many of the diversities of character, which distinguish so much one Nation from another, proceed from Religion, Government, or the intercourse between neighbouring States is what no Person can deny. That many others derive their origin from physical Causes, is what every man of sense and Candor must acknowledge: whether the moral or the physical are predominant, is an enquiry worthy the discussion of men of more experience and judgment, than are to be found among the students of this university: every one however must chuse one side of the question; and I have therefore adopted that which appears to me, to be the most probable. National character is the assemblage of those qualities which are predominant in the minds of the individuals who form a Nation; and by diversities are here meant (I imagine) those peculiar traits which distinguish so greatly the inhabitants of one Country from those of any other on Earth.

Should we consider the question, as relating to primary and original Causes, it would appear that there are none but physical; for a short reflection will convince us that moral Causes themselves are but the Effects of physical causes. A proof of this may be drawn from the national character of the Hollanders. Should the question be put to any one of our opponents, whence the three great characteristics of that Nation, (cleanliness, industry, and avarice) arose? probably he would answer, from moral Causes; and he would alledge the great power of education and habit. These I confess may at this day, serve to maintain, and may have served heretofore to increase those qualities; but they never can be said to have been the original Causes. The situation of the country, which is continually exposed to the encroachments of the surrounding Ocean, and the Climate which is so moist as causes, every thing that is not constantly kept clean, to moulder, absolutely require great neatness, industry and economy; and I am convinced in my own mind, that were the present inhabitants to migrate, and in their stead was a colony from any other nation to settle there, in the course of one century the new settlers would be distinguished by the same virtues and Vices, which now form the dutchman's character. But without taking all the advantages which the question seems to present, I will consider only the immediate causes of diversities in national characters, and even these, are, I believe, chiefly physical.

Let us single out from the european nations two, which notwithstanding their proximity to each other, and notwithstanding the constant intercourse between them, are so remarkable for their difference of character. The characteristics of the french nation are, contentment, vivacity, and a certain degree of levity; those of the English are thoughtfulness, melancholy, and a continual restless, uneasy disposition, whatever, their situation may be: In this case, we cannot imagine the difference to be owing to moral causes; for it would be natural to suppose, that a form of government which insures to every man his property, and personal safety, and a religion founded upon humanity and toleration, was calculated to make a nation happy, and contented; and on the other hand; that a Government in which the fortune, and even the Life of every individual depends upon the caprice of a despot, and a religion which enervates the mind, and corrupts the heart would render a nation miserable if it could be effected by moral causes. But when we consider the different physical causes which operate upon the minds of the French and English we can easily account for the facts as they stand.

Few Nations are favoured with a sky so serene, and a climate so temperate as the French. The air which they breathe is pure, and they are exempted from both the extremes of heat and cold. Their diet is generally light and salubrious; and from the Throne to the Cottage they are remarkably temperate. But the atmosphere of England is almost always loaded with vapours, there, the heart is seldom cheered, the spirits are seldom enlivened by the genial rays of the Sun; and the climate is so variable and unsteady; that frequently the resolution of the Seasons seems to be performed in the course of a day. The diet of the inhabitants is heavy and oppressive to the stomach; and they are too much addicted to the use of spiritous liquors: in both these instances it is evident, that the physical and moral causes counteract each other. But the contest is too unequal; the physical are so powerful that they destroy the influence of the moral, and yet appear to act, with as much force, as they could do, even if they met with no opposition. Arguments of a similar nature might be applied to other nations; but they could not be more conclusive, and would carry me beyond the limits prescribed to exercises of this kind. I shall therefore endeavour to refute some other objections which might be raised against the influence of physical causes.

It is evident that the characters of the same nations, have been very different at different periods. The modern Greeks and Romans, for instance are supposed to be as different from the ancient, as they possibly could be even if they did not live in the same countries. The alteration has been undoubtedly produced by a concurrence of physical and moral causes; and at first sight we should be led to think, the latter were chiefly influential: but it must be remembered that the physical causes have undergone a great change: the diet is extremely different, and the climates are most probably, far from being the same: if we were to judge of the Campania di Roma, from the enthusiastic accounts given of it by Pliny and Florus, we should suppose it to be a terrestrial Paradise; but this self same spot is now so unhealthy that it is intirely uninhabited, although the soil be as fruitful as any in Italy. This last Circumstance affords a presumption that the present situation of the country was the effect, not the cause of the alteration in the climate. If physical causes have operated so surprising a change upon one part of the country, we may reasonably conceive that the climate of the whole, has been in some measure effected by them. Why then should we expect to find in the Greeks and Romans of the present day, those characteristics, which distinguished the masters of the World?

I shall take notice but of one argument more, which might be used on the opposite side of the question. It respects the Jews. They have been for many Centuries, and still are dispersed all over the earth, yet they maintain to a great degree the same national character; but admitting that they have uniformly preserved the same peculiarities, whether the causes be moral or physical, they cannot be applied to any other Nation: it is by a particular dispensation of the Deity who for wise purposes has seen fit to keep them seperate and distinct from the rest of the world. But in fact the immediate causes may properly be called physical. They never mingle with other Nations, by intermarriages, which probably produce great effects, on the bodily frame, and they never make use of any animal food but what is prepared in their own peculiar manner.

But after all, it is in vain for Man, to attempt separating what the God of nature has united; the connection between the human mind and body is so intimate; that possibly whatever affects the one must necessarily have influence over the other; and perhaps after investigating the matter clearly and deeply, we should have reason to conclude, that physical and moral causes are really and essentially the same."

Johnson, whose great pride is in being singular, found fault with the question; and said he could not understand it. The only conclusion I can draw from his confession is that he is a very stupid fellow.

Mr. Shaw was here in the forenoon. Mr. Williams gave us a lecture upon the dimensions of the Earth.

The sodality met at Baxter's chamber in the evening. White brought me a couple of letters up from Boston. One from my mother, and the other from my Sister, signed A. Smith.[1] She was married it seems the 12th. of June.

[1] AA to JQA, 13 June; AA2 to JQA, 22–23 July (Adams Papers).

12TH.

Mr. Burr gave out this morning a subject for our next forensic. "Whether an extorted promise be obligatory." The affirmative is not so favourable, as in the last question. Though in many cases, it may be true.

The weather, extremely dull, which causes a very general depression of spirits.

13TH.

Had a great deal of fuss about some Tea spoons, which I lost some days since. I have found most of them however in an extraordinary manner. But it made me in manner lose all this day; as great part of it has been employ'd in making researches.

14TH.

Went to Boston, in order to get some books[1] which were sent by Callahan; but I could not get them: dined at Deacon Smith's.

Mr. Otis's family were there. Harry and his father had a dispute concerning the Roman *toga*. I came up with Beale; in the evening we held a Court of Law. Putnam, and myself were condemned to pay a bottle of wine each.

[1] JQA had earlier asked his father to send copies of "New Testaments in Greek and Latin" from JA's personal library, and Desaguliers' translation of van's Grave-sande's *Mathematical Elements* (JQA to JA, 2 April, Adams Papers). In addition to these volumes, JQA received others which he had not requested, "mostly upon philo-sophical subjects" (AA to JQA, 21 July, Adams Papers; entry for 16 Oct., below). Among these was François Soulès, *Histoire des troubles de l'Amérique ...*, London, 1785, now at MQA among JQA's books, which contains notes by JA in the second volume (JQA to AA, 30 Dec. 1786–11 Jan. 1787, Adams Papers).

15TH.

Was excused from attending meeting this day: being some-what unwell. Finished the first volume of Burlamaqui in the forenoon. Bridge was at my chamber after dinner.

16TH.

We recite two or three times more, in s'Gravesande's, but next quarter, we shall begin upon Ferguson's Astronomy.[1] Mr. Williams had a lecture, upon Trigonometry, very few of the Class attended. Charles went to Boston in the morning, and at length, brought the books, which are mostly upon philosophical subjects. Mead was at my Chamber in the evening. About half the Class are gone. I declaimed this Evening, a piece from Blair's Lectures[2] vol. 1. p: 14, 15, 16. on the cultivation of taste.

[1] James Ferguson, *Astronomy Explained Upon Sir Isaac Newton's Principles, And Made Easy to Those Who Have Not Studied Mathematics ...*, London, 1756. JQA requested of his father a copy of this work in his letter of 30 Aug. (Adams Papers), and his copy, 7th edn., London, 1785, is at MQA.

[2] Hugh Blair, *Lectures on Rhetoric and Belles Lettres,* 2 vols., London, 1783; Harvard had the 3-vol., 2d edn., London, 1785 (*Catalogus Bibliothecae,* 1790, p. 149).

17TH.

Charles and my Cousin, went away in the morning, immedi-ately after commons. Tom, went to Boston, and brought back Dr. Tufts's Chaise. Soon after dinner we set off, in the midst of the rain. We got to Braintree, just at five o'clock. We found Mr. and Mrs. Shaw here.

18TH.

Loitered away, a great part of my Time, as I most commonly do in vacation Time. I intend however to read considerable, before I return to College. Mr. Shaw and his Lady, this morning, left us to return homeward. Was down in my father's library part of the afternoon. The weather begins to be quite cold, and the leaves are all falling from the trees.

19TH.

Spent the day, in alternately reading, writing, walking, and playing. This is dull life, and convinces me, how grossly the whole herd of novel and romance writers, err, in trumping up, a Country life. Let them say what they will: the most proper situation for man, is that which calls forth the exertion of faculties, and gives play to his passions. A negative kind of happiness, like that of the brutes, may be enjoyed in the Country, but the absence of pain or anxiety is not sufficient for a man of sensibility. The passions of the mind, are what chiefly distinguish us from the brute creation, and as a country life tends to diminish their influence, it brings us nearer a par with them, and is therefore derogatory to the dignity of human nature.

20TH.

My two brothers were gone all the morning on a gunning party. My cousin and I went, in the afternoon, but we were unsuccessful. All kinds of game are scarce here, as there are several persons in the town that persecute the animals so much, that they have driven them all away.

21ST.

Mr. Thaxter stop'd about half an hour, this morning, on his return from Hingham, where he has been this week. In the afternoon I went with my cousin, and drank tea, at my uncle Quincy's. Just after we return'd, Leonard White and his Sister came in. Mr. and Mrs. Cranch arrived about an hour after. Leonard brought me a letter.[1]

[1] Letter not found.

22D.

Mr. Treadwell, preach'd in the forenoon from Matthew XI. 15 "he that hath ears to hear, let him hear;" and in the afternoon from Psalm IV. 4. commune with your own heart. Mr. T. appears to be a sensible man; but by no means a good speaker. In common conversation his voice, and manner of speaking is agreeable; but if he begins to pray or to preach, he immediately assumes a most disgusting cant. He spent the evening here; and talk'd of his Son, who is at college, in the junior class. He appears to have juster ideas of him, than parents commonly have of their children.

23D.

Mr. Cranch went this morning to Boston. His Son, went with him, and will proceed to Haverhill, for his Sister Lucy. Leonard and Peggy White, return'd to Boston. Thayer one of Charles's classmates, dined here, and after dinner they both set off to go to Scituate. Thus from a numerous company, we are all at once reduced to a very small party; I went down in the afternoon to the library. Miss Betsey Apthorp spent the evening here.

24TH.

Went down to my uncle Adams's in the afternoon, and spent a couple of hours. Finished reading Burlamaqui, upon natural and political Law. I am much pleased with the principles established by this author. The stile of the english translator is not agreeable.

25TH.

Thayer and Charles returned from Scituate this afternoon. Mr. and Mrs. Hilliard came to pass the night here. Mr. H appears much more to advantage in private conversation than he does in the pulpit. He appears to be a very sensible man.

26TH.

We have been left alone again this day. Mr. and Mrs. Hilliard went away this morning. I employ most of my time at present in reading the Abbé Millot's elements of history.[1] They are well written but very concise. He is quite philosophical: in some passages perhaps too much so. At least he calls in question many historical facts; without sufficient reason, I think. His reflections which seem to form the greatest part of his work, are for the most part just, and display, much humanity, which is an essential requisite in a historian.

[1] Claude François Xavier Millot, *Elemens d'histoire générale . . .*, 9 vols., Switzerland, 1778. JQA's copy, at MQA, was purchased in 1781.

27TH.

Mr. Read came here in the afternoon, to spend a day. Though he cannot entirely lay aside the Tutor, but retains a little of the collegiate stiffness, yet he endeavours to be affable, and is very sociable. These people when distant from their seat of Empire, and divested of that Power, which gives them such an advantageous idea, of their own superiority, are much more agreeable, than, they are, when their dignity puts them at such an awful distance from their pupils. Mr. Read conversed much upon several subjects and with a great deal of complaisance; but with most ease, and pleasure upon subjects which form part of the studies at the university.

28TH.

Mr. Read set out in the afternoon to return to Cambridge. In the Evening Mr. Cranch returned from Boston, and Lucy and her brother from Haverhill.

29TH.

Mr. Wibird preach'd all day from John I, 47. Jesus saw Nathanael coming to him, and saith of him, Behold an Israelite indeed in whom is no guile! Mr. W. is said to be so fond of his ease, that he seldom writes new Sermons, but preaches his old ones over and over, frequently. But this was new, and one of the best that I ever heard him deliver, full of judicious reflections, and wise instructions, which proves that if he is not of great service to the People, of this parish, as a moral teacher, it is not for want of sufficient abilities. The family here, are in affliction, on account of the Death of Mr. Perkins[1] in Virginia, a young gentleman, who resided in the house some months, and endeared himself to the whole family. A more particular attachment between him, and Eliza, renders his loss more distressing to her, than to the rest; and her great sensibility deepens the wound. Her grief is silent, but is painted expressively on her countenance.

[1] Thomas Perkins, of Bridgewater, had been a preceptor of the Adams boys and the Cranch children during 1781–1782, then left for Virginia to keep a private school. He returned the following year and studied law with Royall Tyler, but soon went south, to Kentucky, to return again once he had made his fortune. He died in Aug. 1786 (*Adams Family Correspondence*, 4:309; *Book of Abigail and John*, p. 367; Mary Cranch to AA, 22 May–3 June 1786; Elizabeth Smith Shaw to AA, 1–3 Nov. 1786, Adams Papers).

30TH.

Snow'd all the morning. Mr. Cranch went to Boston and Charles with him: he return to Cambridge. As the supreme judicial Court is to sit there this week, there will be two or three companies of militia, in order to prevent riots; for the insurrections of this kind, are not yet quelled, and indeed I know not when they will be. There is not sufficient energy in the government, and the strength of the party opposed to it is increasing. Unless some vigorous measures are taken the constitution of the commonwealth must infallibly fall.

31ST.

Miss B. Palmer, came from Germantown, this afternoon, to spend the night here. We prepared to return to Cambridge as our vacation closes this day.

WEDNESDAY NOVEMBER 1ST. 1786.

We returned through Boston, to Cambridge. The road from Charlestown was full of carriages coming here, to see the review of the militia of the County, under the command of General Brookes.[1] I found my chamber full of Ladies, who had a view of part of the troops from the windows: there were I believe about 2000 men, composed of the Cadet, and light infantry Company's, and the independent volunteers, which consist entirely of young gentlemen residing in Boston, the artillery companies of Charlestown and Roxbury, and about 60 companies of militia, from the different Towns in the County. The Governor, Lieutt. Governor, and Council, first went round them, after which, they all march'd by his excellency, who stood on the steps of the Court house door; after dinner they all march'd away except two companies which remained for the protection of the court. They have been here since monday, and stationed themselves in the college hall, and chapel. The Court sat in the afternoon. I went in but a short time before they adjourned, and heard Judge Dana deliver his opinion to the jury, upon a small case: he spoke extremely well.

¹ John Brooks, a veteran of the Revolution, led a militia division against Shays' forces (Charles Brooks, *History of the Town of Medford, Middlesex County, Massachusetts*, Boston, 1855, p. 129–134).

2D.

Attended the court in the forenoon, and afternoon, but there were no causes of any consequence tried. Pass'd the evening at Bridge's chamber, in company with Mr. Andrews, and Mr. Harris.

3D.

Reading, Reid on the Mind. This author in some places pleases me very much; but in others he is disagreeable especially when he attempts to be humorous. His Chapter upon seeing which fills three quarters of the book, contains, a long detail upon the construction of the eye, and a very curious dissertation upon squinting, but which seems, to have very little to do with the Mind. This and a laborous attempt to prove a proposition which no body can deny (viz, that there is no similarity between the cause of a sensation in the mind, and the sensation itself) takes up almost all this inquiry into the human mind.

4TH.

Charles and Cranch went to Boston. Wrote part of my forensic; and as I was obliged to support a side of the question, which I cannot believe; I found it very difficult to write any thing, and shall finally be very short.

5TH.

Mr. Hilliard preach'd in the morning from Matthew XXIV 13. But he that shall endure unto the end, the same shall be saved. I have no observations to make upon his Sermon, several of those I have made heretofore will apply. In the afternoon, Mr. Burr, the

Tutor preach'd from Titus II, 11, 12. For the grace of God that bringeth salvation hath appeared to all men. Teaching us, that denying ungodliness and worldly lust, we should live soberly, righteously, and godly in this present world. Mr. B. preaches well, but altho: it is but so short a Time since he begun, yet he has acquired a tone in speaking which approaches too near a cant. He paid the most attention to the last verse, which indeed is more proper to be expatiated upon.

6TH.

We recited this morning for the first time in Ferguson's astronomy. The part which I have read is pleasing, and the study in itself is as agreeable, as it is useful and important.[1] Mr. Williams began his course of astronomical Lectures this morning. The class attend in two divisions. He gave us the Theory of the earth's motion. We observed the Sun through a telescope; and saw several clusters of those spots which are mentioned in astronomical books. Mr. W told us, that he once saw one of them divide in two, while he was looking through the glass. He was to have given us a view of the moon this evening but could not because the weather was cloudy.

[1] JQA's interest in astronomy was to continue throughout his life. In 1816 he gave a set of celestial charts to Harvard and a few years later contributed money for building an observatory for the college. The need for a national observatory was included in his presidential inaugural address (Andrew Oliver, *Portraits of John Quincy Adams and His Wife,* Cambridge, 1970, p. 226–227 and references there).

7TH.

We had a lecture from Mr. Wigglesworth in the afternoon, and in the evening the weather being fair, we look'd through the telescope at the moon. The objects were not so much magnified as I expected, nor so plain, as they are represented in books. We held a court at Beale's chamber after tea.

8TH.

Mr. Williams gave a public astronomical lecture this afternoon, relating to the different theory's of the planetary System; he gave an account of the Ptolemean, the Tychonic,[1] and the Copernican. There was little more than what may be found in most astronomical books; but the lecture was entertaining and was very à propos, as it relates to the public course, and, to the book, which we have just begun to study.

Weather very comfortable.

[1] A *via media* between the Ptolemaic and Copernican systems, devised by the 16th-century Dutch astronomer Tycho Brahe, who believed that five planets rotated about the sun, which in turn circled around the immobile earth.

9TH.

Had the whole day to myself; as I did not attend the afternoon recitation. Spent my Time in reading Ferguson, and Saunderson.[1]

[1] Nicholas Saunderson, *The Elements of Algebra, In Ten Books . . .,* 2 vols., Cambridge, England, 1740 (Harvard, *Catalogus Bibliothecae,* 1790, p. 1). JQA may have used his personal copy of Saunderson, recorded among his books in 1784, which is no longer in his or the other Adams' libraries ([Christian Lotter], Inventory of JQA's books, 6 Nov. 1784, Adams Papers).

10TH.

We had a Lecture at 10 this forenoon from Mr. Williams, explaining the theory of the motion of the Earth and Moon. The astronomical lectures that we have already received, do not entirely answer my expectations; I have as yet got from them very little more than I knew before.

11TH.

We had another Lecture at 11 from Mr. Williams, to give us the theory of solar and lunar eclipses. In the evening after tea, we held a court at Foster's chamber, and tried a number of causes.

12TH.

Very unwell with a sore throat, so that I did not attend meeting. Dined with White at my chamber. We had in the evening a meeting of the A B. I read the following piece.

A B. N 5

> Without a sign, his sword the brave man draws
> And asks no omen, but his country's cause.[1]

Superstition is a quality, which in all ages of the world, has had peculiar sway, over the human mind: it seems to have been implanted there by the hand of Nature: when two uncommon events happen in the same place, and in a short space of Time, the ignorant vulgar will immediately conclude, the one to be the effect of the other: Imagination usurps the place of Reason, and forms very extravagant hypotheses, in which she herself places an implicit faith. Philosophy has always attempted to destroy this power of Fancy, and never fails convincing when she is heard; but she disdains courting the common herd of mankind, and the others are so few, that they are overpowered by the superior number of Fancy's votaries; and thus, many are obstinately fixed in error, till nothing can restore them.

I have often endeavoured to account for this proneness in the human mind, to whatever is marvelous, and I believe it can be attributed only to a strange combination of the powers of imagination and reason. It is a fundamental maxim, that nothing can exist without a cause: to gratify the curiosity of knowing those Causes, which is inherent in the human mind, is the business of natural, and moral philosophy: but their progress is always extremely slow; and as they can judge only from the concurrence of so many circumstances, as prove a fact to demonstration, they are upon every new and extraordinary occasion, forced at least to suspend their decision for a time; they are frequently obliged, to acknowledge, their ignorance, and the impossibility of obtaining a clear and distinct view of many things. But our Imagination is too impatient to be contented with a partial knowledge of any thing: if she cannot discover the real causes of things, she is ever ready, to invent fictitious; and she has almost always sufficient influence in the human mind, to induce it to adopt her own chimaera's. From these causes, arose probably, the ideas of ghosts, spirits, fairies, witches, and all those imaginary beings, of whose existence, the ignorant, (and consequently superstitious), of all ages, have never doubted. Hence likewise the fictions of astrology, and the confidence, placed in dreams, even by men, whose minds enlightened by Science, should soar, above those Clouds of the imagination, into the serene atmosphere of truth: hence the still more extravagant belief, that the flight of birds, or the entrails of an ox or a sheep, would discover, what should be the success attending any enterprize; and although mankind in general, at this day, are no longer imposed upon by these absurdities, yet it must be confessed, they are influenced by others equally contrary to reason, and common Sense. See a party at cards! If one of them be very unlucky, he will wish to change his seat, as if the chair he sit in, had any connection with the cards he is playing; ask the captain of a vessel, all ready to sail, and with an excellent wind, why he remains in the port? Because he is afraid to set sail, on a Friday; as if the success of the voyage, was to depend, upon the day of the departure. These, and many other notions of the same kind, of which we are daily made witnesses, sufficiently evince, that superstition is far from being entirely exploded, or even from being confined to the most ignorant and illiterate class of people; if we examine ourselves, with a severe, and impartial eye, few of us, I believe, will be able to say, that we are never influenced by this disorder of the imagination: but as it can never be serviceable, either to ourselves or to any of our fellow creatures, as it may be essentially injurious to society, and as it must infallibly tend to make us unhappy, it ought constantly to be our endeavour, to overcome every weakness of this kind, and to reduce, not only our conduct, but likewise our opinions and sentiments to the standard of unerring Reason.

[1] Homer, *Iliad,* ed. Pope, Bk. XII, lines 283–284. JQA's copy, 4 vols., London, 1759, with his bookplate and bearing the inscription "J.Q. Adams, 1781" is among JA's books at MB.

13TH.

The Class recite this week to Mr. Burr: but I was so unwell this morning that I did not attend. We had in the afternoon the last lecture upon Trigonometry. Mr. W. recommended to us to proceed upon the projection of the sphere and, upon conic sections. Mrs. Cranch and Miss Betsey were here in the afternoon. The parts for the next exhibition[1] were distributed. *Putnam* has the English oration, *Lloyd* the Latin, Chandler 3d. and White the forensic; and *Learned, Mayo, Prentiss, Vose, Welch,* and *Willard* the mathematical parts. The class are pleased with all except the first, which could not possibly, have been given more to the surprize, of almost every one. Mr. Williams in the evening pointed out to us, a number of the constellations in the Heavens.

[1] Given on 8 Dec. The parts and performers are discussed in more detail in JQA's entry for that day.

14TH.

We had a meeting of the ΦBK immediately after Commons in the morning, and received White. The meeting was then adjourned till twelve o'clock, as we were obliged to retire at 9. to read our forensic in the chapel. I made the following piece answer two purposes; but as I disliked the Question, I was quite short upon it.

Whether an extorted promise be obligatory?

The Question must be considered as relating only to such promises as are unjustly extorted; for if reason approves of the claim, of a man, who is reduced to the necessity of employing violence to obtain it, she will undoubtedly likewise justify that violence. The laws of nature, and the customs of all civilized nations justify it. It cannot therefore be made a question: under the head of promises justly extorted, must be taken, all contracts with an open and public enemy, whether made by a nation at large, or, by individuals. A doubt can be raised therefore, only when the person by whom the promise is extorted, acts contrary to the Laws of nature and of nations, and I am sensible that most moral writers agree, that in cases of this kind, all promises, are null of themselves and consequently cannot be obligatory. As it would argue the most unjustifiable arrogance in me, to maintain an opinion in opposition to that of many persons, whose productions have done honour to human nature, I shall only beg leave, to question, whether the consequences which must attend the breach of extorted promises, might not be very prejudicial to the interests of mankind in general? And whether the man who should not prefer enduring, the greatest evils, even Death itself, rather than make a promise with the design never to fulfill it, would not be blameable for loosening the bonds of Society.

We danced in the evening, at Tom Chandler's chamber; but I was unwell, and came away before nine. Cranch went to Lincoln, to day with his Mamma.

15TH.

Mr. Burr went to an Ordination, and consequently we had no reciting in the afternoon. Mr. Williams had a Lecture to demonstrate the truth of the copernican System, at 3, and in the evening: he shew us the planet Venus, which through a telescope, appears shaped like the moon, and was this evening horned. She is quite small view'd through our glasses, which magnify objects 90 Times.

16TH.

The weather begins to grow very cold: it has been remarkably fine all this fall. Mrs. Cranch return'd from Mystic, and will pass the night at Mrs. Hilliard's. Mr. Williams gave us in the evening a view at Jupiter, through the telescope. He appears like the moon when full, and attended with his four Satellites, at different distances. They are quite bright though invisible to the naked eye.

Bridge pass'd an hour with me after lecture.

17TH.

Took books from the library. Hammond's algebra; Burke, on the sublime and beautiful, and Smith's theory of moral sentiments.[1] Was employ'd a great part of the day, in calculating the Elements for a solar Eclipse. Snow.

[1] Nathaniel Hammond, *The Elements of Algebra in A New and Easy Method . . .*, 4th edn., London, 1772; Edmund Burke, *A Philosophical Enquiry into the Origin of Our Ideas of the Sublime and the Beautiful . . .*, London, 1761; Adam Smith, *The Theory of Moral Sentiments . . .*, 2d edn., London, 1761 (Harvard, *Catalogus Bibliothecae*, 1790, p. 1, 93, 95).

18TH.

Unwell, so that I could not do much all day. Finished my elements for an eclipse, and finally found it would be here before Sunrise, and consequently not visible.

19TH.

I was very sick with a sore throat, and head ache; so that I could not attend meeting. Dined in my chamber with Bridge, and Cranch. There was in the evening a meeting of the A B, but I could not attend. The weather quite cold.

20TH.

Snow'd almost all day. White set out early in the morning for Haverhill; his sister is to be married to-morrow.[1] The Class recite to Mr. Burr, this week. I did not attend this morning. Mr.

Pearson, gave a lecture, upon the analogy between philosophical grammar, and the human body. His divisions of Sentences, are those of Harris.[2] Sentences of assertion and volition. Mr. Williams gave a lecture upon the projection of the sphere but not one in the Class, had done any thing in it, as there are very few manuscripts upon the subject in college.

[1] Peggy White, Leonard's sister, married Bailey Bartlett (Haverhill, *Vital Records*).

[2] James Harris, *Hermes: Or, A Philo-* *sophical Inquiry Concerning Language and Universal Grammar . . .*, London, 1751, p. 17 (Harvard, *Catalogus Bibliothecae*, 1790, p. 135).

21ST.

The second division of the Class, read a forensic, upon the Question, whether the destroying of inferior animals, be a violation of the Laws of nature. Where so much may be said on one side, and so little on the other, there cannot I believe, be derived, much instruction from a debate. The pieces were almost all short, and I do not recollect, that any thing new was said. Mr. Wigglesworth, gave us in the afternoon, a lecture, and in the evening Mr. Williams, gave us a view at Saturn, through the telescope. The planet did not appear more than an inch in diameter, but the ring was quite plain. I could just perceive one of the Satellites, which appeared quite near the planet. We danced at Chandler 2d's chamber.

22D.

We had a lecture in the forenoon from Mr. Wigglesworth. Wrote off something upon conic Sections; for Mr. Williams's next Lecture. For the future it is left at the option of every individual in the class to attend him or not. The sodality met this evening, but I could not attend. Williams was part of the evening at my chamber.

23D.

Snow'd all the forenoon. We had tea at Cranch's chamber; Whitney arrived in the evening; he comes from Petersham, in Worcester county, and says the insurgents threaten coming to prevent the setting of the court of common pleas, in this Town, next week.

24TH.

This evening, just after tea, at Chandler 1st's chamber, we were all called out by the falling of a fellow, from the top to the bottom of the stairs. He was in liquor, and tumbled in such a manner, that his head was on the lower floor, and his feet two or three steps up. When we first went out, the blood was streaming from his head, his eyes appeared fixed, and he was wholly motionless. We all supposed him dead. He soon recovered however so as to speak, and was carried off, about an hour after he fell.

25TH.

Mr. Williams gave us a lecture this forenoon, to explain several astronomical instruments. Nothing new however. There are many flying reports concerning the coming of the insurgents next week. They have even been expected to arrive this evening, but none as yet have appeared.

26TH.

Attended meeting for the first time these three weeks. Dined at Judge Dana's. Captain Hobby, who was an officer in the late war, is there, and remains in town, by the desire of Genl. Lincoln,[1] who will take the command on Tuesday, to oppose the rioters, in case they should appear, and who wishes to place experienced officers, at the head of those companies of militia, that are not organized.

We had a meeting of the A B in the evening. Fiske had an Oration, one essay was read, and I spoke the following piece.

A. B. N: 6. "To a friendly, to an indulgent audience, instead of a formal discourse, of which I feel myself utterly incapable, I shall beg leave to offer only a few observations upon a subject, in which, as a member of Society, as a friend to the interests of mankind in general, and more particularly, as an inhabitant of this commonwealth, I feel myself deeply interested.

It is a trite observation, but no less true than solemn, that not only man himself, but the works of his hands, and the productions of his mind, while connected with his body, carry within themselves the principles of their destruction. All the arts and sciences, like our bodily frames, from an impotent and feeble infancy, generally rise gradually to that degree of perfection, by which, whatever pertains to humanity is bounded; after which, they imperceptibly decline, and finally return to nothing from whence they sprung.

We are however easily reconciled to these ideas, because we know, that such are the unalterable Laws, which have been established by the god of nature. But when by some unforeseen or unexpected accident, an individual is brought to an untimely end, we feel an involuntary pang, and lament the fate of one, who was not suffered to perform the course allotted to human nature. But if our hearts are thus taught by nature to sympathize for the misfortune of an individual, how painful, how distressing must our feelings be, when we behold a deadly blow aimed at the vitals of a constitution upon which our own happiness and that of millions depends; a constitution, purchased by the treasures, and sealed with the blood of our countrymen. These sentiments are dictated, gentlemen, by the present situation of public affairs in this commonwealth. At a time, when our property, our precious rights and privileges, and even our lives are threatened with destruction, it is undoubtedly, highly proper, for young men, about to enter upon the theatre of the world, to enquire, what were the causes of our present evils, what remedies, should at such a critical juncture be applied, and, what measures might be taken, in future to prevent the renewal of such dangers.

It must be universally agreed, that within these few years, there has been an astonishing decay of public virtue among us. Posterity will scarcely believe, that in the short compass of ten years, the same nation should have exhibited repeated examples of the most exalted heroism, and of the most abject pusilannimity—Young as we are, we all remember with what a noble ardor, and with what an undaunted fortitude, our countrymen resolved to support their liberty attacked by an arbitrary and powerful Tyrant: unacquainted, with the art of war, destitute of every kind of ammunition, without an army, and without a treasury to support one, the citizens of the united States resisted the forces of the most powerful nation on the face of the earth, assisted by an army of barbarous mercenaries, sold to the british monarch, by their more barbarous Princes—After suffering from the parent country, injuries, more than sufficient to weary the most enduring patience, the americans, perswaded, that as subjects, they could never obtain justice, finally declared themselves a free and independent nation: this action, was the result of cool reason, and mature deliberation. The declaration of independence drawn by the nervous and eloquent pen of a Jefferson, and the constancy, with which, for two years, they maintained a war, without the assistance of foreign powers, convinced the European Nations of the justice of their cause, and will convince posterity that their conduct was not dictated by the rage of party, or the temporary frenzy of enthusiasm.

The disadvantages under which, our countrymen laboured were such as precluded all possibility of raising immediately forces sufficient to oppose the veterans of Europe. The British armies were every where successful, and desolation, and rapine attended them, wherever they went. The invincible resolution display'd by the americans in the time of their greatest distress was never surpassed by the sublimest exertions of Roman magnanimity. At length, Fortune adopted the cause of Virtue, and after a struggle of seven years, the independence of America, was acknowledged by Britain herself. It is not necessary to mention, that during the whole course of the war, this State was particularly distinguished for her zeal, and spirited exertions in the common cause—But Oh! how altered is the scene! Instead of that noble spirit of freedom, which animated the breasts of our countrymen, we now hear of nothing but riots, and insurrections. Instead of an attachment to good order, and the Laws, we now behold nothing but violent attempts upon the administration of Justice, and so far have we degenerated, from that sacred regard to honour, which ought always to influence the conduct of individuals, and of nations, that thousands among us, publicly pretend to an abolition of all debts, whether public or private.

These evils are generally allowed to have proceeded from that luxury and dissipation, which have been introduced into our country since the Peace: and undoubtedly many of them originated from those Causes. But it is of little service to be acquainted with the disease, unless proper remedies are prescribed, and applied; what avails it, that public orators should lament our fondness for foreign frippery, our extravagance, and idleness unless, they recommend, by their precepts and example, the opposite virtues of industry and oeconomy? If but a few individuals of fortune and reputation, would agree, to confine themselves to the real necessaries and conveniencies of life, and to discard those superfluities, which have brought our Country on the verge of her ruin; their example would soon be followed by the generality of the People, and all complaints of imaginary grievances, with their lawless and destructive consequences would soon be at an end. What I propose, gentlemen, is not impossible: for the two or three first years of the late war, our intercourse with foreign nations was almost entirely interrupted, and the People lived upon the produce of their own Country, more happily than they could have done with all the imported fopperies of Europe. What has once been attempted with success can surely be performed again, and every one will allow that some measures of this kind, are as necessary at this time, as they ever were, in any period of our history. In short, unless some measures are soon adopted more effectual, than any that have yet been taken, we must soon submit to the most detestable of all tyrannies, that of a lawless, and unprincipled rabble. Our history will cast an indelible stain upon the annals of mankind. The name of american will be sufficient to brand any man with infamy, and our nation instead of holding, as they might have done, a distinguished rank, amongst the sovereigns of the Earth, will become, the scorn, the reproach, and the derision of mankind. Should this be the case,

> "Should men, for freedom born, renounce her cause,
> Refuse, her guidance, violate her Laws,
> Lose, first their Country's rights, and then their own,
> And bend before, a haughty despot's throne:
> Should liberty, desert this wretched land,
> And fly from fierce oppresion's iron hand;
> Secure, I follow where she leads the way,
> To shun a tyrant's arbitrary sway,
> Where'er the goddess chuses her abode,
> There too shall dwell, my tutelary god;
> Ignoble slavery, my soul disdains,
> My only country, is where freedom reigns."

[1] Benjamin Lincoln (1733–1810), of Hingham, had been appointed commander of the Massachusetts militia in April 1786. He raised $20,000 to finance the expedition against the insurgents which began in mid-Jan. 1787, when he marched westward to protect the Springfield arsenal (Sibley-Shipton, *Harvard Graduates*, 12: 416–438).

27TH.

Recite in Ferguson this week. Mr. Williams, this forenoon concluded his course of astronomical lectures, by explaining the orrery, and the cometarium.[1] I have not received from these lectures either the entertainment or the instruction, which I expected from them. Except having acquired a clearer notion of the figures of the different planets by viewing them through the telescope, I believe I have not attained one new idea, by the ten Lectures. However I do not know that more could be said than has been. In Sciences of this kind, little novelty is now to be expected. Few discoveries are probably left to be made, and those will be owing perhaps, rather to chance, than to any extraordinary effort of genius.

This evening, just before prayers about 40 horsemen, arrived here under the command of Judge Prescott[2] of Groton, in order to protect the court to-morrow, from the rioters. We hear of nothing, but Shays[3] and Shattuck[4]: two of the most despicable characters in the community, now make themselves of great consequence. There has been in the course of the day fifty different reports flying about, and not a true one among them.

[1] A mechanical device for illustrating the motion of comets in their elliptical orbits.

[2] General Oliver Prescott, the Groton physician, military officer, and justice of the peace who, upon hearing of Shattuck's intention of preventing the court from sitting, rode into Cambridge with a body of forty horsemen and secured the courthouse. Receiving word of the reception prepared for them, the rebels melted away (Sibley-Shipton, *Harvard Graduates,* 12: 569–573).

[3] Daniel Shays, Revolutionary officer, Pelham farmer, and local officeholder, prominent in the rebellion which bears his name. Shays, by this time the leader of the insurgents in western Massachusetts, had two months earlier established an agreement with the Hampshire co. militia to prevent the Supreme Judicial Court, meeting at Springfield, from hearing cases

involving indictments against the insurgents or concerning debts (*DAB*).

[4] Job Shattuck, Revolutionary officer, large Groton landowner, and prominent townsman, who had participated in the Groton riots of 1781, which involved the collection of taxes in specie. On 12 Sept., Shattuck assembled about one hundred men from Groton and nearby towns to prevent the sitting of the court of common pleas in Concord. Successful there, they decided to march to Cambridge, where the court was to meet on 28 Nov. The plan to join up with other rebel forces failed, and Shattuck was later captured, tried in Boston the following May, and sentenced to be hanged. After two temporary reprieves, he was unconditionally pardoned and retired to Groton (Samuel A. Green, "Groton during Shays's Rebellion," MHS, *Procs.,* 2d ser., 1 [1884–1885]:298–312).

28TH.

The weather very cold. No appearance of rioters as yet, tho' it is this evening reported that there are 1500, within four miles of Cambridge. We dansed this evening at Chandler 1sts. Last night the ΦBK met at Burge's chamber. Little and Cranch read dissertations. Freeman and Packard, a disputation upon the Question, whether good order is promoted more by the rewarding of virtue, than by the punishment of vice. Mr. Ware and Mr. Harris disputed extempore. Baron was admitted, after which the meeting was adjourned for a fort'night.

29TH.

No appearance yet of any body to prevent the sitting of the court; the reports have not yet ceased however. Had tea at my chamber this evening, and several of the club past the evening with me. Lovell, a classmate of mine, is half crazy, at hearing so much news. He wants to be doing something, and is determined by some means or other to fight the insurgents. He says he is no politician, he was made for an active life, but he cannot live in a place, where there is so much news.

30TH.

The reports of Shays, and Shattuck coming, at the head of thousands to stop the Court, grow more rare. It is now almost too late to spread any more stories of that kind. Shattuck instead of attacking, will have to defend himself, for, about 150 young volunteers, from Boston, under the command of Coll. Hitchborn[1] went through here this forenoon, on horseback, and are gone, with the design to seize two or three of the ring leaders of the mob, and bring them down to Boston. The Roxbury artillery company, under Major Spooner: went likewise from here in the evening. They would not say, which way they were going, but it is supposed they have the intention of seizing Wheeler[2] and Smith,[3] two of the leaders in the County of Worcester. There seems to be a small spark of patriotism, still extant; it is to be hoped, that it will be fanned, and kindled by danger, but not smothered by sedition. A republic must very frequently be called back to the principles of its government, and so long as it has sufficient virtue for that, its constitution will stand firm.

[1] Benjamin Hichborn was called on 29 Nov. to lead a corps of cavalry volunteers into northern Middlesex co. against the insurgents (Sibley-Shipton, *Harvard Graduates*, 17:36–44).

[2] Capt. Adam Wheeler, of Hubbardston, who with about one hundred men had kept the Worcester courts from meeting in September and again in November (Ellery B. Crane, "Shays' Rebellion,"

Worcester Society of Antiquity, *Procs....*
For the Year 1881, p. 72–73, 81–82).

³ JQA may be referring to Nathan Smith of Shirley, Middlesex co., who was

with Wheeler on 12 Sept. when the insurgents kept the Middlesex courts from opening at Concord (same, p. 74–76).

FRIDAY DECEMBER 1ST. 1786.

It was on Wednesday, that the troop of horsemen from Boston went up in search of Shattuck. They succeeded in their attempt, and this forenoon at about 11 o'clock, they return'd through this town, with two besides Shattuck; by the names of Parker, and Page.¹ These were taken by the horsemen, from Groton, before, the arrival of those from Boston. The circumstances of Shattuck's capture, are variously related, but the following are the most authenticated. The gentlemen pass'd the night on Wednesday at Concord; and yesterday morning, at about seven, they went to Shattuck's house. He was gone from thence but they could not discover which way. They then came about a mile on this road, and met a man, who by threats and promises was induced to tell them, that he had parted from Shattuck, but a short Time before, but he would not say where. They proceeded a little further, and saw in the snow the tracks of a man, going from the common road. They suspected them to be his, and followed them. Mr. Sampson Read, first saw him, on the opposite bank of a small river, and immediately cross'd it on the ice; Shattuck then came to a stand, and said to Read: "I know you not; but whoever you are you are a dead man." Read ascended the bank; a scuffle between them ensued. Read fell over the Bank, and the other, in making a violent push, at him, lost his sword, and fell upon him. He recovered his sword however, and was just about to pierce his antagonist with it, when Dr. Rand of Boston, arrived, and drew the sword from his hand, backwards by the hilt; at the same time Fortescue Vernon aimed at Shattucks arm, but the sword glanced, and wounded him dangerously in the knee, upon which he immediately surrendered himself; but said he should be rescued in half an hour: the gentlemen, were not molested however in bringing him off; but had every where every assistance given them, that they were in want of, and the apparent good will of every one, wherever they went.

¹ Oliver Parker of Groton, who led the insurgents in their march through Concord on their way to the Cambridge courthouse, and was later joined by Shattuck.

Benjamin Page was another Groton ringleader (Samuel A. Green, "Groton during Shays's Rebellion," MHS, *Procs.,* 2d ser., 1 [1884–1885]:303–304).

2D.

The party from Roxbury under the command of Major Spooner, which went from here, thursday evening, were not so successfull in their pursuit of Wheeler, and Smith, as those who went for Shattuck. They mistook the house where he was, and he got information of their being in quest of him, before they could find him, so that he made his escape. The Court adjourned from hence this afternoon, and Cambridge is not at present in danger of being the immediate scene of action. These rebels have for these three months, been the only topic of conversation all over the Commonwealth.

3D.

A number of the Class drank tea in the morning at Bridge's chamber. Attended meeting, all day; Mr. Hilliard preached in his ordinary stile in the morning, but after dinner he gave us, a sermon against swearing; the best I ever heard him deliver.

4TH.

We had after prayers a class-meeting, upon the subject of a private commencement. Freeman read the Petition, which he was desired by the class to draw up; it was voted that it should be carried up this week.[1] I went with Sever, and pass'd the evening at Mr. Gerry's. Just before we went it began to snow, but when we return'd, we had a violent storm, with the wind in our faces all the way. Sat with Sever about an hour after we got back.

[1] This petition and two others mentioned in later entries have not been found. The Corporation did not discuss the petition until 10 April 1787 and decided not to grant the request because "public exercises of commencement have an happy influence in exciting a laudable emulation among the students" and because displays of students' learning "are highly beneficial to the Commonwealth at large by stimulating parents to give their children an education which may qualify them to fill with reputation and honor the several offices in church and state" (MH-Ar:Corporation Records, 3:282–283). Joseph Willard added several more substantial reasons when he spoke to the class the following day. See below. The class made one final appeal on 1 May to the college overseers, but they eventually supported the corporation in denying a private commencement (MH-Ar:Overseers Records, 3:343–344).

In a letter to his sister, JQA explained what was at the heart of the matter. "The expenses of that day, to the class which graduates, are said to amount upon an average to £1000. In the present situation of the country," he continued, "this is a large sum, and the advantages derived from appearing in public [on a commencement program] are not adequate to it" (JQA to AA2, 14 Jan.–9 Feb. 1787, Adams Papers). To this argument the overseers made some concessions by ordering that the strictest economy be observed at commencement.

They omitted the usual entertainment and ordered that merely a cold dinner should be provided, for which the students would pay only $2.00. No entertainment was to be given by any candidate for a degree outside the walls of the college, except those whose parents lived in Cambridge. Students were advised to dress simply in inexpensive black worsted gowns, not to purchase new clothes, and not to entertain friends in their rooms in a lavish fashion (MH-Ar:Corporation Records, 3:282–283).

5TH.

The storm continued with unabated violence, a great part of the day. In the evening however it cleared up, and is now very cold. This day had been appointed for exhibition, but the weather was such as prevented it. Several of the Class had invited a number of the young ladies in town, to a dance, but were obliged to postpone it likewise for several days.

6TH.

The Weather fair, but the Snow, which drifted a great deal, is in some places so deep, that it is impossible to get through it. We danced in the club this evening at Foster's chamber.

7TH.

I have been rather idle, this week, and this day entirely so. This evening I went down with Mr. Andrews[1] to Judge Dana's, and spent a couple of hours there. Invited Miss Ellery[2] and Miss Nancy Mason, to the dance to'morrow.

[1] John Andrews, Harvard 1786, who was studying divinity at Harvard at this time.
[2] Almy, daughter of William Ellery (JQA to AA2, 14 Jan.–9 Feb. 1787, Adams Papers).

8TH.

It Snow'd in the morning till 10 o'clock, and it was feared the exhibition, must be again postponed. But it cleared before noon, and at about 3 o'clock, the president made his appearance in the chapel. *Lloyd* delivered an Oration, upon Commerce in Latin. He spoke so low that I could not hear him. *Abbot* 2d. and *Chandler,* then read a forensic, on the question, whether the natural reason of man be sufficient for the discovery of the existence of a God. The syllogistic, on the Question, Whether self love be the only spring of human actions, by *Bancroft,* respondent, *Baxter, Adams* 2d., and *Treadwell* opponents, followed; after this came the dia-

logue, between *Adams 3d.* and *Wier,* then the greek oration by
Prescott and finally the English Oration by *Putnam.* The forensic,
I was much pleased with: but of the last piece I could make neither head nor tail. *Agriculture* must find another panegyrist, before, it will be praised as it deserves. The mathematical parts
were then delivered up; and after an anthem had been sung, and
a few tunes play'd the company dispersed. A little after five, several of us went down, and supp'd at Bradish's: after which we
went for the Ladies; and danced till 2 in the morning. The
Ladies were Miss Ellery, Hill, Williams, Frazer, Wigglesworth,[1]
Jones[2] 2 Miss Kneeland, and 2 Miss Masons, Miss Cutts, and
Miss Badger. The Lads were Fiske, Little, Bridge, Freeman
Mason, Tom and Gardner Chandler, Beale, Amory, Lloyd, Foster, Williams, and myself, besides Mr. Andrews, who undertook
to be the manager. The dance was very agreeable, except, that
some partners were much better than others; and when we drew
the poorest, we were not so perfectly contented. After we had
sent the Ladies home, Mr. Andrews came to college and lodged
with me.

[1] Margaret (Peggy) Wigglesworth, daughter of Prof. Edward Wigglesworth, who
later married John Andrews (Paige, *Hist.
of Cambridge, Mass.,* p. 691).

[2] Catherine Jones, of Newburyport, a
distant relative of Prof. Wigglesworth
(Sibley-Shipton, *Harvard Graduates,* 5:410;
*Vital Records of Ipswich, Massachusetts, to
the End of the Year 1849,* 2 vols., Salem,
Mass., 1910).

9TH.

Very little fatigue, by the last night's party: but much fatigued
by the weather. For there came on this morning a second snowstorm which has raged all day with as much violence, as that
which came in the beginning of the week. All the former paths,
are filled up, and in some places the snow is more than 6 feet
deep, and what is worse than all; I am entirely destitute of wood,
and am obliged, to go about, and live upon my neighbours. The
storm is so violent, that it was with the greatest difficulty, we
could get to Williams's, where we drank tea this evening.

10TH.

The weather cleared up this morning; but the wind was so
high, and the snow so deep; that Mr. Hilliard could not get out to
meeting. The breakfast club were at my chamber, in the morn-

ing; and at noon we all went down and dined at Bradish's. We pass'd the afternoon, and supp'd there. Bridge, and I, made an attempt to go down to Professor Wigglesworth's in the evening, but the snow was so deep we could not succeed.

11TH.

We recite this week in Burlamaqui, to Mr. Burr, but he did not attend this day. I am reduced to the necessity of being idle; for I have no wood left, and must live where I can. Foster went off this morning to Boston, and I have for the present taken up my quarters with Bridge, who has a little wood left. Meeting of the ΦBK, this evening at Burge's chamber; the performers were absent: so there was nothing done except admitting Barron, and appointing performers for the next meeting, which is to be at Cranch's chamber this day fort'night.

12TH.

The government, this morning, determined that if more than half the students should be destitute of wood, the college should be dismiss'd. The president went to Boston, to consult the corporation, upon the subject, and he informed Little, who went this evening to request leave to go home, that the students would be permitted to disperse, to-morrow morning. Club danced at Little's chamber this evening.

13TH.

This morning, immediately after prayers, the president informed us that the vacation would begin at present, and be for 8 weeks, and hinted that the spring vacation, might on that account be omitted. As I thought I should be able to study much more conveniently here than any where else; I obtained leave to remain in town. Bridge proposes staying likewise, and we shall live together. In the afternoon we went down to Professor Wigglesworth's; found Miss Ellery just going home; I went with her, and pass'd half an hour at the judge's. Bridge engaged for us both to board at Mr. Wigglesworth's. Spent the evening at Mr. Pearson's.

By *Samuel Griffin, class of 1784.*

7. A WESTERLY VIEW OF HARVARD COLLEGE, CIRCA 1783–1784
See pages x–xi

14TH.

Thanksgiving day. Mr. Hilliard, preached a very long sermon, but none of the best. He appeared to have laboured much, and I thought quite without success. Indeed he thought perhaps there was no reason for giving thanks considering the Situation of the Country, and this makes him the more excusable. Bridge and I went down after meeting to Judge Dana's; dined, and passed the afternoon and evening there.

15TH.

Many families in town are distressed for want of wood; the snow, is so deep, that, the people in the Country cannot get into the woods, and there have been but two or three loads in town, since, the first storm. We begin to be shortened for it; and, are therefore prevented from studying, with any application, for the present.

16TH.

Tom, came from Boston this forenoon. Fifteen persons were buried there this afternoon, who perished, by different ship-wrecks in the late storms. The weather quite moderate; and so calm that we could hear the bells in Boston toll, as plain, as we can that in Town, from the chambers in Hollis.

17TH.

Chandler 1st. went off this morning; there are about 20 of the scholars, who have not yet been able to get home. They are how-ever going off, one by one. Attended meeting all day. Mr. Hil-liard preached in the morning, a sermon, which I have heard him deliver before. Thanksgiving sermon I suppose took up all his Time this week. Mr. Burr preach'd in the afternoon, and saved the Parson, the trouble, of reading another old piece. The young preachers are generally the most liberal minded; Mr. Burr was very particular, upon the insufficiency of faith without works, and strongly recommended morality.

18TH.

The young Ladies at Mr. Wigglesworth's, dined at Judge Danas, I went down there with Bridge; to tea, and pass'd the evening, very sociably. The conversation turn'd upon diverse topics, and among the rest upon love which is almost always the case when there are Ladies present. Peggy came away at about 10, but Miss Jones, concluded to stay there, to-night.

19TH.

Foster, and Lovell, and Cranch were here to day; all came for their cloaths &c. Several of the Class still remain, and untill they are gone, it will be impossible for us to study much. As they expect to go every day, they are rather dissipated, and more or less make us so. We got this day a load of wood. It is however still very dear.

20TH.

I have been rather more attentive this day, than for this week, past, and have written considerably. This evening a slay came from Petersham for Baron and Whitney. The person, who came with it informs us, that the insurgents have all disbanded, that numbers of them suffered extremely in the late storms, one or two perished, and several still remain, very ill at Worcester. They have had time to reflect on their conduct, and for their enthusiasm to cool down; I wish it may reform them.

21ST.

Miss Jones returned from Judge Dana's. I spent the evening with Bridge, and Freeman, at the Professor's. Miss Bromfield, Miss L. Kneeland, Miss Cutts, and Miss Ellery were there. [Of] all these ladies, the last are rather unsociable. We had however, upon the whole, a good time. Miss Cutts unluckily got a fall on the ice, as she was going out to the slay. Had her limbs, been rather more pliant, perhaps she might have saved herself. We came away before ten, and Freeman sat about an hour with us.

22D.

Miss Cutts's misfortune, last night, has been a subject of much diversion, to the Ladies; to Miss Jones especially, who is inclined to be satirical, and appears to take no pains to restrain that disposition; whence I conclude, she considers it as an accomplishment. This is a very common error, especially among the female sex. Satire they suppose, always includes wit, and many a severe reflection has been made, not from a principle of disapprobation, but with a view of appearing brilliant. Miss Jones, I fancy is not entirely faultless in that respect: she is but 18, rather giddy, and unexperienced. She has a very fair complexion, and good eyes, of which she is sensible; her face, is rather capricious than beautiful, and some of her features, are not handsome; of this she is not so well apprized; her shape is not inelegant, but, her limbs are rather large: she is susceptible of the tender Sentiments; but the passion, rather than the lover is the object of her affection; she is perhaps too sarcastic, but her real disposition which is good natured will excuse that; and a few more years may correct the foible.

23D.

Dined with Mr. Harris, Freeman, and Bridge at Mr. Pearson's. He has been very polite to me, and was quite complaisant, this day. Mrs. Pearson, did not appear; but Miss Bromfield, and Miss Cutts were there. Neither of them were peculiarly sociable, and the latter appears just proper to make a prude, in a few years.

The weather has been very moderate, it rain'd all the morning. This afternoon it grew colder, and began to snow. I hope we are not to have a third storm, like the two we have had already.

24TH.

Snow'd all night, and this forenoon. I attended meeting all day: Mr. Hilliard preached, but not in his best way. The meeting was very thin. It cleared up this afternoon, and the evening is very cold.

25TH.

Christmas day; and one of the coldest, we have had this Season. The snow which has fallen, will be very useful in the roads: it fell very even, and has filled up the bare spots; we spent the evening at the professor's with Mr. Ware, and Mr. Andrews. Had a good deal of chat with Peggy. Mr. Ware sung.

26TH.

Bridge went to Boston. Mason finally took his leave, and left us to ourselves; so that we shall henceforth, be able to study, with much less interruption than we have hitherto done.

27TH.

Bridge went to Boston again: in the evening we went down, with Mr. Ware, and Freeman, to Judge Dana's. We convers'd and play'd whist, and sung till 10, o'clock. The ladies seem to have settled that we are to be in love: but ideas of this kind, are very common with the ladies, who think it impossible to live without Love.

28TH.

Studying Saunderson; Mayo was here in the afternoon. Mr. Ware likewise paid us a visit and sat about half an hour. The weather has been very good for several days, but the weather-wise foretell a snow storm.

29TH.

Continuation of the same course. We got us some wood, this afternoon. Bridge, pass'd the evening with the Ladies, at Mr. Mason's;[1] but for particular reasons I preferr'd staying at home. Lloyd was here in the forenoon. Bridge, and Freeman return'd late from Mr. Mason's. Freeman pass'd an hour with us, after he came back.

[1] Thaddeus Mason, holder of various provincial offices, including clerk of the Middlesex court of common pleas from 1735 to 1789 (Paige, *Hist. of Cambridge, Mass.*, p. 606–607).

30TH.

The week has closed as it began, and I shall be content if for the six remaining weeks of the vacation I can make, an equal progress, in my present course of studies. Williams spent the evening with us. The weather is quite moderate; and has the appearance of rain.

31ST.

Sacrament day. Mr. Hilliard preach'd an occasional sermon in the forenoon; and in the afternoon from Acts IV. 28. We pass'd the evening at the professors, in company with Mr. Andrews.

This day completes two years, since, I attempted to commit to paper, the transactions, which daily occurr'd, in which I was concerned. It is a question, whether amidst the quantity of trivial events, to which I have given place, and the heap of trash which I have here inserted, there is sufficient matter worthy of remembrance, to compensate for the time I have spent in writing. For these 15 months, the Scenes before me have been so much alike, that these pages have not even the small merit of variety: but to myself I have always spoken, for myself I have always written, and to myself only, I am accountable for the nonsense, and folly in this and the preceding Volume.

MONDAY JANUARY IST. 1787.

I received, two letters,[1] and a couple of Packets of newspapers, from Europe, they were the more acceptable, as it is almost three months, since I have had any direct news from thence, before. After playing a few tunes to the young Ladies, In the evening, I went with Bridge, and paid a visit to Mr. Hilliard; a sensible man although his Sermons are rather cold.

[1] AA2 to JQA, 1 Sept.–12 Oct. 1786; AA to JQA, 27 Sept.–14 Oct. 1786 (JQA to AA2, 14 Jan.–9 Feb. 1787, all Adams Papers).

2D.

I pass'd the evening with Mr. Andrews, at Professor Pearson's. He is fond of music, to enthusiasm. We play'd several tunes together, but I was not a proper person to accompany him. He is quite an adept in the art; and like all connoisseurs in music, extravagantly fond of Handel.

3D.

Dined at Mr. Hilliard's, in company with Mr. Stedman,[1] Mr. Ware, Mr. Andrews, Freeman, and Bridge. Stedman is a student in Law; said to be a man of Sense. However that may be, he does not strike me, at first sight as a very exalted genius. We pass'd the evening, at the Professor's. Miss Jones display'd some of her satirical wit.

There was a total eclipse of the moon, between 6, and 9 in the evening; but the weather being cloudy, rendered it invisible, the greatest part of the Time.

[1] William Stedman was completing his legal studies in Newburyport with Theophilus Parsons, with whom JQA would begin studying law in September ("Descendants of Gov. Bradstreet," *NEHGR*, 8:317, 318, 320 [Oct. 1854]).

4TH.

For want of sufficient exercise, I have been unwell, for several days: there is no walking at this Season, and we are consequently obliged, to keep too recluse for health. Mr. Andrews, and Freeman, pass'd the evening with us, at the professor's. Miss Jones as usual was severe. Her disposition would be much more amiable, if she was not so sensible of her satirical talents, and so fond of them as to gratify her passion upon all occasions.

5TH.

We passed the evening at Freeman's chamber. He proposes setting off for Newbury, to morrow morning. The weather for several days, has been uncommonly moderate, but this afternoon it grew somewhat cold, and began to snow.

6TH.

Very cold this morning, Freeman went for Ipswich. Mr. Andrews called upon us in the afternoon.

I got through Montesquieu's spirit Laws;[1] and I much admire the author's penetration, in discovering the origin, and causes of diverse Laws in diverse Countries, and in the same Country, at different periods. His ideas of the principles, upon which the different forms of government are founded, appear very just; though I think he says not all he would have said, had he lived in a Country where a man might with impunity publish his sentiments.

[1] *The Spirit of Laws,* transl. Thomas Nugent, 3d edn., 2 vols., London, 1758 (Harvard, *Catalogus Bibliothecae,* 1790, p. 84). JQA may have owned at this time an edition of Montesquieu (3 vols., Amsterdam, 1749), containing his bookplate, now at MQA.

7TH.

Mr. Hilliard preach'd all day; pretty much in the common stile.

Dined at Judge Dana's; and conversed with Miss Ellery upon the subject, of two young Ladies. I find, that her opinion, as well as that of Mr. and Mrs. Dana, coincides with mine in that respect. Benevolence, candor, and innocence, are more amiable, and more estimable ingredients for a character, than wit without judgment.

Weather very cold. Mr. Andrews was at tea, with us.

8TH.

We went down this evening with the young ladies, to Mr. Dana's. I passed several hours agreeably. I had an essay upon philosophic Love given me to read; a little allegorical tale, in the composition of which, fancy, rather than reason predominated. For, as Terence says

> ――― incerta haec si tu postules
> Ratione certa facere, nihilo plus agas,
> Quam si des operam, ut cum ratione insanias.[1]

[1] For complete quotation and translation, see entry for 5 March, note 1 (below).

9TH.

Snow'd part of the day. Reading Watson's chemical essays.[1] They are written in a very plain intelligible manner, and are quite entertaining. The subject I have never before paid any great attention to. We pass'd the evening at the professor's. Small conversation, with women, can be interesting, only at the time it is going forward.

[1] Richard Watson, *Chemical Essays,* 3d edn., 3 vols., London, 1784 (Harvard, *Catalogus Bibliothecae,* 1790, p. 37). There is a four-volume set of this 3d edn., London, 1784–1786, among JA's books (MB).

10TH.

Mr. Paine was ordained, minister of Charlestown, but as it snow'd all the fore part of the day, I did not attend. Cabot, the junior was here: I am still pursuing the study of algebra; which is as entertaining as it is useful. I could wish I had time for proceeding in all the mathematical branches of Science: but the time will soon come, when I shall be called to studies of a very different nature.

11TH.

The weather is yet unsettled, but it has not storm'd this day. Saunders, and Barron of the junior Class were here.

Our time flies away extremely fast; one half of the vacation has already eloped, and I shall soon, with a mixture of pleasure and pain, see my fellow students again assembled, and be called again to attend to the public exercises. They will it is true diminish; as our Class are henceforth to attend recitations only once a day, and that only for nine weeks, after which we shall in a manner be left to ourselves.

12TH.

The weather cleared up in the morning, and the cold since noon has increased very fast. We pass'd an hour in the evening at Mr. Gannett's; he was not at home: Mrs. G. is quite historical; that is she gives a very minute history of whatever occurs to herself or her family.

Up late reading parliamentary debates.[1] Packard came to see us, this afternoon.

[1] JQA may have been preparing for his declamation, given on 27 Feb. (below), on "part of one of Mr. Fox's speeches."

13TH.

The weather very cold all day with a strong wind. We had a Quantity of company, in the forenoon Hill, who graduated last commencement, Learned and Williams; in the afternoon Angier, Cushman and Tufts:[1] Bridge set out after dinner for Lexington, where he intends to pass two or three days.

[1] Either Cotton Tufts, Harvard 1789, or Abijah Tufts, Harvard 1790 (Sibley-Shipton, *Harvard Graduates,* 11:480; *Harvard Quinquennial Cat.*).

14TH.

Mr. Hilliard preach'd all day. It is a long time since he has given us any variety: but on the other hand he writes short Sermons, which is very much in his favour, in cold weather. Dined at Mr. Dana's. Forbes came up from Boston this afternoon, and lodg'd here. I pass'd the evening at Mr. Wigglesworth's. Miss Jones, has recovered from the sour fit which she has been in for several days, and is quite complaisant. *Quere*. is caprice, a necessary quality to form a fine woman?

15TH.

The weather very moderate. The snow went off quite fast. Drank tea at Mr. Hilliard's. His daughter look'd prettier, than she ever did before. Mr. Paine was there, and appeared quite happy, in his new situation. The People of Charlestown, who never could be united in their opinions, for a minister, are universally very much attached to him, and his talents and virtues are such as will probably preserve him that esteem, which he has every where acquired. Mr. H. appears to be very fond of him, and proud of him as a brother.

16TH.

Dined at Mr. Dana's, and pass'd part of the evening with the Judge and his Lady at Mr. Gerry's. Miss Thompson, is very handsome; but whether she possesses all the other qualities which are requisite to render a Lady amiable, I shall not take upon me to decide.

Bridge returned this evening from Lexington.

17TH.

My Chum went to Boston, but return'd early in the afternoon. After tea we went down to Mr. Dana's. Miss Ellery was there, and Miss Jones with her; Bridge accompanied this Lady home, and after they were gone, I had a deal of chat, with Miss Ellery, who has a larger share of Sense, than commonly falls to an individual of her sex. We conversed upon diverse subjects, but I can never give any thing but general accounts of conversations, for I cannot always keep this book under lock and key; and some people have a vast deal of curiosity.

18TH.

Fine weather, till the evening, which was very blustry. The men have been selected who are to go from this Town, against the insurgents. They have taken almost all the servants in Town; the troops are to march to-morrow, for Worcester, under the command of General Lincoln. We passed the evening at Professor Williams's. Jenny look'd handsomer, than she has for several months past; and was very agreeable.

19TH.

The troops from this Town, went this afternoon to Waltham, from whence, they are to proceed to-morrow towards Worcester. After tea, I went with Bridge, Williams and Learned to Mystic, and had a very good dance. There were several very fine girls; but being entirely unacquainted with them all, I could not be very sociable with them. A Miss Dixey struck me, as being uncommonly beautiful; but from the few observations I could make, I thought she had the qualities which are commonly the companions of beauty: at about one in the morning we broke up, and, we reach'd home, at about two.

20TH.

Snow'd all day. We were rather tired after our expedition. I have been idle; and do not by any means feel disposed to write at present.

21ST.

Mr. Hilliard again entertained us all day, with his own composition. Bridge, and I dined at Mr. Dana's. Miss Almy informed us of all the circumstances which attended our party the other day; and among many other anecdotes, told us that Bridge was deeply smitten with a Miss Hall, who had I thought much of a sleepy appearance and I forsooth, am the humble admirer of Miss Dixey. If personal beauty was my only object of admiration, I should certainly be in this predicament, but I must look a little further, before I surrender my liberty entirely.

> For all the gifts which nature can impart,
> Are vain without the virtues of the heart.[1]

Mr. Andrews, who returned from Hingham yesterday, drank tea with us this evening.

[1] JQA here quotes from his own poem, "An Epistle to Delia," lines 27–28, written in 1785 (M/JQA/28, Adams Papers, Microfilms, Reel No. 223).

22D.

Employ'd all day, in translating some german observations for Mr. Dana: finished them: and in the evening I went down there to carry them. Miss Ellery and Miss Jones, keep up a correspondence in writing. Almy has a larger share of Sense, than commonly falls to the lot of her sex, and, that sense is cultivated and improved, a circumstance, still more uncommon.[1]

[1] In spite of JQA's favorable disposition toward Almy Ellery and his critical and repeated comments about the "sour fits" or "unsociable" attitude of Catherine Jones, he was able to compose an acrostic about the latter on this day, which he wrote into his Diary on 16 April 1788 (below). The original is in M/JQA/28, Adams Papers, Microfilms, Reel No. 223.

23D.

Miss Ellery pass'd the day at the professor's, and was very agreeable; I am more and more pleased with this Lady, every time, I am in company with her. Miss Jones who is treated both by Bridge and myself with a distant reserve, appeared this day for the first Time to be mortified by it: she could not help forming a contrast between our behaviour to her, and to the two other Ladies, and her Vanity was piqued. But she has drawn it upon herself. Thomson pass'd part of the evening with us: her spirits were revived while he was present, but droop'd again, when he went away.

24TH.

Miss Ellery, went home this morning, after breakfast. Miss Jones, rather unsociable; her spirits low. Charles and Tom, arrived here, this afternoon from Haverhill: left all our friends well. I went down to Mr. Dana's with Charles, had a long conversation with Miss Almy, upon a subject, interesting at the present moment. Williams came home with Mrs. Dana, and we return'd together, at about 10. Charles remained.

25TH.

The weather has been all along quite unsettled. Yesterday was very cold, but to day, it thaws fast again. Mr. Andrews past the evening with us at the professor's. Miss Jones, rather more agreeable, than I have sometimes seen her, but not perfectly sociable. Mr. Andrews and she appear to go on as easily, and with as little rubbing as any person: less indeed than I should expect from the dissimilarity of their dispositions.

26TH.

General Lincoln, it seems, finds more difficulties in the affair he has undertaken, than were expected. He has sent for a reinforcement of troops: there are about 2000 men assembled to oppose him. They have the start of him, and it is supposed they intend first to attack, Genl. Shepard,[1] who is at Springfield, with about 1200 men. Part of the militia are going from this town. I pass'd the evening at Mr. Dana's, and lodg'd there. Saw Mr. Winthrop.

[1] William Shepard, major general of the Hampshire co. militia, repulsed the attack on the Springfield arsenal by Daniel Shays' forces on 25 Jan., before Lincoln arrived (*DAB*).

27TH.

Fay was here this morning, and Freeman return'd this day from his Tour to visit his friends. Part of the company of militia in this town, march'd this morning towards Worcester. Dispatches were expected this evening from Genl. Lincoln, but none appeared.

28TH.

Mr. Fiske[1] supplied Mr. Hilliard this day: and gave satisfaction in general. His sentiments are very liberal, more than those of any preacher I have heard of late. It is perhaps to be feared lest some of our future divines may go too far in that respect, and assert that Christianity consists in morality alone. If this were the case, in what point would its excellence be shown, above the Systems of many heathen philosophers? For even the sublime maxim, "do good to those that hate you" was inculcated and even practised by some of them. The harsh, discouraging doctrines held up, by many of our old preachers, are absurd, and impious; but the other extreme may be more dangerous to Christianity; and our young divines would do well, to remember

Dum vitant stulti vitia, in contraria currunt.[2]

Dined at Mr. Dana's, with Mr. Winthrop. He had a letter from his brother, but not of a very late date. There have been no accounts from Genl. Lincoln this day.

[1] Thaddeus Fiske, of the Second Church of Cambridge at Menotomy (now Arlington), 1788–1828 (Paige, *Hist. of Cambridge, Mass.*, p. 546).

[2] "In avoiding a vice, fools run into its opposite," Horace, *Satires,* Bk. I, Satire 2, line 24 (Horace, *Satires, Epistles and Ars Poetica,* transl. Fairclough, p. 20–21).

29TH.

Bridge went to Salem, upon some business this day, and returned.

Miss Ellery and Miss Williams, her brother, Mr. Andrews and Freeman, drank tea at the professor's; I was sociable with Miss Jane, for the first Time. She is not destitute of personal charms, and has I believe a very good disposition. Mr. Andrews was quite elated with the news from Springfield, which arrived this evening. A party of 700 insurgents commanded by Luke Day,[1] were put to flight, without a gun fired, and about 30 of them taken. Genl. Shepherd, had however been obliged to fire at a party headed by Shays. 3 men were killed, and 3 mortally wounded. Upon the whole, affairs in that quarter appear to take quite a favourable turn.

[1] Day, of West Springfield, had his orders intercepted, and failed to lend support to Shays at the battle of the Springfield arsenal. After Lincoln's arrival in Springfield, both he and Shepard scattered Day's men in West Springfield; then Lincoln pursued Shays. Unable to secure a general pardon, Shays withdrew to Petersham, where, after a forced march in a snowstorm, Lincoln surprised and routed the insurgents. Most surrendered, although Shays and a few others escaped into New Hampshire. Within a month most insurgent opposition had ended (Ellery B. Crane, "Shays' Rebellion," Worcester Society of Antiquity, *Procs. ... For the Year 1881,* p. 92–99; Robert J. Taylor, *Western Massachusetts in the Revolution,* Providence, 1954, p. 160–163).

30TH.

Mrs. Cranch, Miss Betsey, and her brother, came from Braintree this morning, dined at Mr. Gannett's and returned after dinner. Bridge, and I were quite alone at tea this evening: the

Ladies were at Mrs. Forbes's, and the professor was gone to Judge Dana's. The Ladies returned however immediately after tea, and Miss Ellery came, and pass'd the evening there:

> In fairest forms can evil passions dwell?
> The virgin breast, can envy's venom swell?
> Can malice dart her rage from beauty's eye?
> And give the snow white cheek, a crimson dye?
> Where then are all the tender virtues flown?
> And why was strength dispensed to man alone?
> The lamb, to vye with Lions neer pretends,
> The timid dove, with eagles ne'er contends,
> Attempt not then, ye fair, to rule by fear,
> The surest female weapon is a tear.[1]

[1] These verses were later included in JQA's "A Vision," lines 163–172, a poem generally thought to have been written at Newburyport while he was a law student. These verses, however, clearly show that its origins were somewhat earlier. Compare JQA's "An Epistle to Delia," lines 41–52, a poem dated 12 Dec. 1785, with "A Vision," lines 91–102 (both in M/JQA/28). To the verses in this entry JQA later added six additional lines at the beginning (157–162): "*Almira* next in dubious form is seen,/Her face is female, masculine her mien,/With equal skill no mortal can pretend,/The varied faults of either sex to blend./To woman's weakness add the pride of man,/And wield alike the dagger and the fan" (same).

"A Vision," a satirical sketch about several girls JQA knew in Newburyport, was patterned after, though more sophisticated in style than, the "Receipt for a Wife," which JQA had read and portions of which he had copied while staying in New York in the summer of 1785 (entry for 3 Aug. 1785, above; JQA to AA2, 1–8 Aug. 1785, Adams Papers). Later evidence confirms that Almira is Catherine Jones, whom he first met at Dr. Wigglesworth's house in Cambridge, and whom he later saw occasionally in Newburyport, though, like the Delia piece mentioned above, the sketch here may have been written about one subject and applied to another when the poem was completed later. For a discussion of the subsequent development of "A Vision," see note for entry of 28 March 1788 (below).

31ST.

Mr. Harris arrived this afternoon from Springfield, but did not bring any further accounts of consequence from that quarter. He saw on the road several of the insurgents who had returned home, sick of their expedition. Bridge and I drank tea at Mrs. Forbes's, and spent the evening. Mr. and Mrs. Hilliard, Mrs. Willard, and Mrs. Miller were there. After tea, Cards being proposed Mr. Hilliard went his way. We had a rubber of whist, with Mrs. Hilliard and Mrs. Willard; in the midst of which the president made his appearance. He soon went off however. After Cards, we had a dish[1] of music. We play'd on the flute, and Mrs.

Hilliard sang a few songs. She has a very good voice, and is by no means ignorant of it. Between nine and ten we escorted Mrs. Willard and Mrs. Miller home, after which, we retired to our Chamber.

[1] Figuratively, an indefinite quantity (*OED*).

THURSDAY FEBRUARY IST. 1787.

It snow'd, the greatest part of the day; but gently, and without wind. Miss Jones, this forenoon, quite suddenly, resolved to go to Boston and went in the midst of the Snow. She proposes passing a fortnight there, and as our vacation is to close, next Wednesday, I shall probably not have an opportunity of seeing her frequently again. I went to tea to Mr. Pearson's, and in the evening accompanied his viol with my flute. Mr. Fayerweather[1] and his family were there. An extraordinary character. The greatest range of his ideas, is between the counter of a shop, and the potatoe-hill behind his House; these furnish him with an universal topic of conversation, which he commonly enjoys alone, for he gives no other person time to express either approbation or dislike of his sentiments.

[1] Thomas Fayerweather, ardent Cambridge Whig before the Revolution, whose house was converted into a hospital for soldiers in 1775 (Paige, *Hist. of Cambridge, Mass.,* p. 418).

2D.

Drank tea again at Mr. Pearson's. Miss Ellery, Miss Williams, Miss Mason, Miss Wigglesworth, Miss Foster and Miss Fayerweather were there. Mr. Andrews, Freeman, Bridge, Williams, Forbes, and Clarke. After a pretty long consultation, we had a little dance, and broke up a little before ten. I drew Miss Williams, and found her very sociable and agreeable. Miss Ellery, was obliged to go away early, because her brother[1] arrived this afternoon.

[1] Presumably either William Ellery or Edmund Trowbridge Ellery, brothers-in-law of Francis Dana (Harrison Ellery, "Ancestors of Hon. William Ellery, Signer of the Declaration of Independence," *Newport Historical Magazine,* 4:182 [Jan. 1884]).

3D.

A Snow storm came on, in the afternoon, and continued in the night. We saw Mr. Ellery this evening at the professor's. Something further than the common sentiments of friendship, subsists between this gentleman and Miss Peggy. If his disposition be, but one half so amiable as her's, their union must be lasting, and productive of much happiness.[1]

Freeman and Forbes pass'd the evening at our chamber.

[1] Peggy Wigglesworth married John Andrews in 1789.

4TH.

The wind was very high all the forenoon; and although the sky was clear, the drifting of the snow, has made it very disagreeable walking. We dined at the President's: he was more sociable than I have seen him before. Mrs. Willard and Mrs. Miller, are both very agreeable. The weather in the evening being fine, we walk'd down to Mr. Dana's, and pass'd two or three hours with them; Mrs. Dana, removed from our minds an impression unfavourable to Miss Foster.

> Curst be the wretch, whose soul, to nature deaf,
> Views with indifference another's grief
> Without a sigh, afflictions voice can hear
> And even mock misfortune with a sneer!
> The human lot is misery and woe
> And evils, from unnumber'd sources flow.
> When dire misfortune with her baleful train,
> Oerwhelm a mortal with excessive pain,
> The kind emotions of a tender heart
> Command the sympathetic tear to start.

5TH.

The occurrences of the day, were not remarkable. I did not study much. I have been reading Sheridans lectures upon elocution,[1] and am pleased with them. They contain many usefull instructions, and ought to be perused by every person who wishes to appear as a speaker. His praises of the Greeks and Romans, may be warmed with the heat of enthusiasm, and his censure of modern Oratory is perhaps too severe: but every candid reader must acknowledge, that the contrast, which he shews, is but too well grounded.

We passed the evening with Forbes at his chamber.

[1] Thomas Sheridan, *A Course of Lectures on Elocution* ..., London, 1762 (Harvard, *Catalogus Bibliothecae,* 1790, p. 149).

6TH.

This being the last day before the close of the vacation, I was part of the day employ'd in getting my chamber in order. Williams was with us all the forenoon. We spent the evening at his Father's. Miss Jenny appears more amiable to me, than she did formerly, and her behaviour has eradicated a small prejudice, which *misrepresentation,* had raised in my mind against her. It has been observed, that since she has lost much of that beauty, which was formerly celebrated; the young ladies of Cambridge allow, that her disposition is good. This may be easily accounted for without charging the other Ladies with envy: beauty of person, is frequently, if not always injurious to the mind, and the loss of it may convince a lady, that something more than a pretty face is requisite to make her amiable.

7TH.

This morning I returned to my old quarters N: 6. My Brothers and Cousin got here just before dinner. There were commons at noon, but it is most generally somewhat confused in the hall, the first day in the Quarter: I preferred not attending: Miss Ellery dined at the professor's: After dinner I took my leave of the folks of the house: in the evening White arrived from Haverhill. Very few of our class mates however, got here this day.

8TH.

White lent me his horse this morning, to go to Boston. Dr. Tufts, had sent by my brothers, desiring me to see him; I had not been in Boston before, these three months. Called at my uncle Smith's, at Dr. Welch's, and at Mr. Storer's. I likewise went to see Miss Jones, who appeared rather surprized to see me. Dined at Mr. Foster's, with Mr. Cranch and Dr. Tufts: they are now attending the general Court; who conduct themselves finally with great spirit, and a proper sense of their own dignity. A *rebellion* was (on Saturday, the first day of the Session) declared to exist in the Counties of Worcester, Berkshire, and Hampshire, and the legislature are determined to use every exertion, in order to suppress it.

Returned to Cambridge, in a violent snow storm, which had indeed begun in the morning, and been all day increasing.

9TH.

Return'd to the library the books I had taken out, and took the second volume of the Idler.[1] After prayers this evening Charles and I went down to Mr. Dana's. Mr. Ellery was there, and appeared to greater advantage than I have seen him before.

[1] [Samuel Johnson and others], *The Idler,* 2 vols., London, 1761 (Harvard, *Catalogus Bibliothecae,* 1790, p. 115).

10TH.

Very few of the students have arrived. Not more than 15 of our Class have yet appeared. The tea Club were at my chamber: only 6 of them however were assembled. We had a supper and spent the evening at Freeman's chamber.

11TH.

Mr. Hilliard entertained us all day, with a couple of Sermons, upon the whole armour of god. The shield, and the helmet, the sword and the arrow, afforded subject for description, and application. The improvements which might result from these two discourses, are wholly concealed to me; that it is the duty of man, to avoid Sin, is a self evident maxim, which needs not the assistance of a preacher for proof; yet it was all Mr. H. aimed to show: how barren must the imagination of a man be, who is reduced to give descriptions of warlike instruments, to fill up a discourse of 20 minutes!

Charles dined with me at Judge Dana's.

The weather was somewhat dull, all day, and in the evening it rained very hard:

Miss Ellery told me I was vapourish.

12TH.

We recite this week to Mr. Burr, but this disagreeable exercice returns at present only once a day, and that only for this quarter. Mr. Pearson gave us a lecture this afternoon, upon the division, of languages into the different parts of speech. Bridge and I pass'd part of the evening at Mr. Wigglesworth's.

13TH.

At nine o'clock this morning, the Class read a forensic disputation: I had written in the course of the vacation as follows.

Whether the infliction of capital punishments, except in cases of murder be consistent with equity?[1]

Had the question admitted other exceptions, or had it admitted none, I should have felt a greater degree of diffidence, in maintaining the affirmative. It has frequently been doubted by men who reason chiefly from speculation, whether it were equitable to punish any crime, with death, Sovereigns have attempted to abolish capital punishments entirely, but this scheme, like many others, which appear to great advantage in theory has been found impracticable, because it has been attended with consequences very injurious to society; but if it be acknowledged, that death is the only equitable atonement which can be made for the commission of murder, I cannot see, why other crimes, equally, and perhaps still more, heinous, should not deserve a punishment equally severe. The question naturally occurs here; what is the end of punishment? Certainly, to give satisfaction, to the injured, and to insure the safety of individuals and of Society: but as the man who falls by the hand of an assassin, cannot receive satisfaction; the punishment in that case, must be inflicted only for the benefit of Society in general. No one, I presume will deny, that Treason is a crime, more dangerous to a community, than murder; as it threatens the destruction of each individual, as well as of the whole commonwealth: to inflict a milder punishment therefore upon this crime, would be destroying that proportion, in which alone, justice and equity consist. The celebrated Montesquieu observes, that the punishment should always derive from the nature of the crime, and consist in the privation of those advantages of which the criminal should have attempted to deprive others. He confesses however, that in many cases, this would not be effected: most frequently the man who robs the property of another, possesses, none himself, and therefore a corporal punishment, must supply the place of confiscation. Those who plead in favour of a lenient system of punishments, may engage the passions of their hearers, by expatiating upon the virtues of benevolence, humanity and mercy: far be it from me to derogate from the excellency of those exalted virtues; but if mildness in punishments instead of deterring men from the commission of crimes, encourages them to it, the innocent, and virtuous part of the community, who have surely the greatest claim to the benevolence of a legislator, would be the greatest sufferers.

It is customary with persons who disapprove of capital punishments, to say that confinement during life to hard labour, would be a punishment, much more severe, than immediate death, and that a criminal thereby, might be rendered useful to Society, whereas a dead man is entirely lost to the community. A zealous student in surgery might deny the latter part of this proposition; but I shall only reply, that admitting confinement and hard labour for life, to be a more rigorous atonement for a crime, than death it will not follow, that it is equally terrifying, and this ought to be the principal object of a legislator. The addition of confinement will be but a small restraint to the greatest part of mankind who know, that whether innocent or guilty, they must depend upon hard labour for their subsistence. But Death is more or less terrible to all men; I have frequently heard persons who supposed themselves in perfect security, express the most intrepid contempt of death, but I conceive their philosophy would be somewhat deranged if the prospect of a sudden, and violent dissolution were placed before them. In such a situation all mankind would reason like the criminal represented by the inimitable Shakespear, as being condemned to die.

> Ay, but to die, and go we know not where,
> To lie in cold obstruction, and to rot;
> This sensible, warm motion, to become
> A kneaded clod, and the delighted spirit,
> To bathe in fiery floods, or to reside
> In thrilling regions of thick ribbed ice,
> To be imprison'd in the viewless winds
> And blown with restless violence round about
> The pendent world;—'tis too horrible!
> The weariest, and most loathed worldly life,
> That age, ache, penury, imprisonment
> Can lay on nature, is a paradise
> To what we fear of Death.[2]

Mr. Wigglesworth gave a public lecture this afternoon. We danced in the evening at White's chamber.

¹ JQA's draft of the disputation, dated 11 Jan., contains no major changes (M/JQA/46, Adams Papers, Microfilms, Reel No. 241).
² *Measure for Measure,* Act III, scene i, lines 117–125, 127–131.

14TH.

Mr. Wigglesworth gave us this morning a private lecture, and Mr. Williams had a public one, in the afternoon. Bridge and Freeman went over after dinner to attend an exhibition of Cushman's school in Mystic.¹ I could not go. Mr. Thaxter and Mr. Duncan, were here a few minutes; they came from Haverhill this morning. I made tea for the club this evening, and I believe it will be for the last Time. It is too troublesome to return so frequently as once a week, and there are only 9 or 10 now left. Was part of the evening at Mason's chamber and supp'd with him there.

¹ JQA's classmate Joshua Cushman taught school in Medford during the winter of 1786–1787 (Charles H. Morss, "The Development of the Public School of Medford," *Medford Historical Register,* 3:24 [Jan. 1900]).

15TH.

I went down in the morning to Mr. Pearson's, with an intention of inviting Miss Bromfield to dance with us this evening but she was out of town. There are several young ladies in this place, who have not attractions to charm the gentlemen, but in the case of a dance, there is no choice, we must either take up with those ladies or have none. We drew lots therefore, to determine, who should go to one house; and who to another. It fell to my lot to go no-where, but Foster who was to have invited Miss Bromfield, not being acquainted with her, requested me to go in his stead. We assembled at about 7 o'clock, and danced till 2 in the morning after which we broke up. The Ladies were, Miss Ellery, Wigglesworth, Jones, Foster, two Miss Mason's, Miss Williams, Hill, Eustis, and two Miss Kneelands. Mr. Ellery, Mr. Harris, and Mr. Andrews, with my Class mates Amory, Bridge, Chandler 3d., Cranch, Forbes, Foster, Freeman, Lloyd, White, and Williams compleated the company. Of the Ladies, some had beauty without wit, and some wit without beauty; one was blest with both, and others could boast of neither. But little was said, and sentiment did not thrive, when the feet are so much engaged, the head in general is vacant. After we return'd several of us pass'd

161

a couple of hours at Cranch's Chamber, and at about 4 o'clock I retired to bed.

16TH.

I rose just before the commons bell rung for dinner, quite refreshed, and not more fatigued, than I commonly am. The other lads were all up, in the morning, and had been to my chamber though I knew nothing of it. After dinner we were an hour at White's chamber. Several of the gentlemen were nodding, and most of them appeared quite worn out. I went with White to Mr. Mason's and to Mr. Wigglesworth's: the Ladies were all well, but somewhat fatigued. There was a lecture, in the afternoon; but few of us attended: I pass'd the evening, with Cranch, at Judge Dana's. Miss Ellery had a head ache, and was much fatigued. Miss Hastings was there, but she has neither youth nor beauty, and if she has wit it is somewhat beneath the surface. We retired at about 10.

17TH.

Was at Kendall's chamber after dinner; and likewise drank tea there. At home all the evening reading and writing; a number of junior's had quite a frolic in Clarkes chamber.

Samuel Angier[1] from Medford, was 20 the 8th. of last November. Although his chamber is directly opposite to mine, I have but little intercourse with him. His character is far from amiable. Envy and vanity appear to me to be the most remarkable traits which distinguish him. He always appears discontented with himself and with all the world beside. There is but one person, of whom he speaks uniformly, and invariably well; and perhaps this is because, no one will ever take the task from him. Such is his admiration for this gentleman, that being incapable of displaying the same talents he is contented with aping his foibles which are sufficiently numerous and conspicuous. He proposes studying physic, and in that profession I hope, he will be useful; for any other he would not be suited, for I believe he would be a surly lawyer, and, an illiberal bigoted divine.

[1] Angier, who had transferred from Dartmouth, was later licensed to practice medicine (*The Massachusetts Medical Society: A Catalogue of Its Officers, Fellows, and Licentiates, 1781–1893*, Boston, 1894, p. 199).

18TH.

Mr. Hilliard preached to us in the forenoon, and the president in the afternoon, when we were improved by a very laborious encomium upon Moses. Whatever the president's literary talents may, be, he is certainly not an elegant composuist, nor a graceful orator. His reasoning may be sound, but the charms of his stile, if any there be, are hidden from a vulgar audience. Dined at Mr. Dana's. Pass'd the evening at Bridge's chamber, and made it rather late before, I went to bed.

19TH.

We recite this week to Mr. Read. So few of the Class have yet arrived, that we have all something to say at one recitation, and Mr. Read always goes completely through a lesson. Mr. Pearson gave a very long lecture in the afternoon, upon *the article,* in the greek, Latin, French and English Languages. He was rather tedious, and before he got through, the Sophimores and Freshmen, shew their impatience, by shuffling. White, Cranch, and myself were the only persons in the Class, who attended Mr. Williams's mathematical lecture at 3. Seeing so few, he hinted he should not attend any more. I shew him my manuscript upon algebra. In the evening a number of us danced at Mason's chamber till 9 o'clock, having transferred to this time the Tuesday club. We were to have had this evening a meeting of the ΦBK, but Mr. Ware being unavoidably called away, it was postponed.

20TH.

Was part of the afternoon at Bridge's chamber. Had tea at Little's. Charles and Cranch, pass'd the evening at Mr. Hilliard's. I was with Mr. Andrews at White's chamber.

William Amherst Barron[1] of Petersham was 18. the 10th. of January. By the death of his father, which happened since he entered the university, he has been involved in some difficulties, and has been able to spend but a small portion of his Time here. Notwithstanding these disadvantages he is said to be a good scholar, and his disposition is amiable. Since I came, he has been present only one quarter, so that my personal acquaintance with him is not intimate. He intends studying Law.

[1] Barron returned to Harvard from 1793 to 1800 as mathematics tutor; thereafter, he entered the U.S. Army, where he was acting professor of mathematics at West Point, 1802–1807, and then served in the department of the quartermaster general until 1821 (Sidney Willard, *Memories of* *Youth and Manhood*, 2 vols., Cambridge, 1855, 1:275–276; George W. Cullum, *Biographical Register of the Officers and Graduates of the U.S. Military Academy, at West Point, N.Y., From Its Establishment, March 16, 1802, to the Army Re-Organization of 1866–67*, 2 vols., N.Y., 1868, 1:78).

21ST.

Mr. Williams gave us a public lecture this afternoon, containing, an account of the different constellations in the Heavens. We had at Little's chamber a meeting of the ΦBK. Mr. Andrews read a dissertation, containing a panegyric, upon the Ladies. A Letter from the branch of the Society at New-Haven was read,[1] containing some queries respecting the granting a charter to Dartmouth, and an account of their transactions, upon a certain affair. After the letter was read a committee of 3,[2] was appointed to answer it. The meeting was then adjourned to Monday March 5th. I pass'd a couple of hours with Freeman.

[1] Not found, but dated 2 Jan. and referred to in Harvard's reply of 8 March.
[2] Henry Ware, JQA, and James Bridge.

22D.

Very cold weather. We drank tea at Williams's. Bridge, and I went and pass'd the evening at Judge Dana's; he himself is attending the court at Boston. We found Mr. Read and Mr. Burr there, and endeavoured as much as possible to behave like gentlemen. After we returned to college, I got engaged in conversation with Bridge, so deeply, at his chamber, that it was near 1 in the morning, before I left him.

23D.

About one half the Class are here at present: they have been coming in, quite slowly; and they will be chiefly here, I suppose, before the end of the Quarter. Yesterday afternoon, I met with Mr. Ware, and Bridge, upon the subject of the letter to New Haven; we thought it would be best for each of us to write, and to select from the three. Accordingly I wrote this evening.[1] I made tea this evening, and at the same time quitted the club, for a number of substantial reasons.

¹ JQA's draft letter has not been found. The letter sent to New Haven was dated 8 March and is printed in the *Catalogue of the Harvard Chapter of Phi Beta Kappa* ..., Cambridge, 1912, p. 111–113. The RC at Yale indicates that it went out in Ware's hand and over his signature, as senior officer of the Harvard chapter. Yet, as JQA reports in the next entry, it was he, not Ware, who decided which of three letters was sent to Yale; thus he undoubtedly shaped the reply.

The committee's letter presented the case for granting the charter to Dartmouth. Because the William and Mary chapter was so distant and "by this unavoidable delay a number of worthy characters now at Dartmouth College would be deprived of the benefit resulting from the institution," the Harvard chapter deemed it advisable to draw up a charter, provided such a move received Yale's approbation. Yale agreed, and the charter was signed on 21 June at Cambridge. Two months later it received Yale's ratification (*Catalogue of the Harvard Chapter*, p. 114–115).

24TH.

Committee met again at Mr. Ware's chamber; after reading all the letters, I was requested to select from them. White went to Boston, and spoke to Mr. Dingley, who sent back my volumes of Gibbon's roman history.¹ Drank tea and passed the evening in Mead's chamber, and retired very early. The weather has grown quite moderate.

¹ The only extant copy of Edward Gibbon's *The History of the Decline and Fall of the Roman Empire* in the Adams' libraries is a broken six-volume set of at least two editions, London, 1727–1788, containing the autograph of JA and bookplates of JQA (*Catalogue of JA's Library*).

25TH.

I was absent from meeting all this day. Bridge dined with me, at my chamber. I begun, and read 100 pages in Gibbon's history; with the stile of which I am extremely pleased. The author is not only an historian but a philosopher. The only fault with which I think he may be charged, is, an endeavour sometimes at the point of an epigram, when a serious reflection, would be more proper.

26TH.

We recite again in Ferguson. Mr. Pearson gave a lecture this afternoon; it was still upon the *article,* very dry, and abstract, by no means the most entertaining that I ever attended. From six this morning when I arose till near twelve which was the time when I retired to bed, I have been as busily employ'd as I have any day these two years.

27TH.

Almost all our Class have arrived. This morning I was not waked by the ringing of the prayer bell and therefore did not attend the recitation. I declaimed this afternoon, part of one of Mr. Fox's speeches, from the Parliamentary debates, in December 1783.[1] N. B. Did not speak loud enough, and changed feet too often. We danced in the evening at Putnams chamber till 9 o'clock. Read after I came home, a chapter or two in Gibbon.

[1] Charles James Fox was foreign secretary in the coalition ministry of the Duke of Portland. The speech was undoubtedly Fox's highly "republican" one of 17 Dec., filled with sound Whig principles and made because the King used his personal influence to defeat Fox's India bill. Fox passionately defended the rights of the Commons and liberties of England: "The deliberation of this night must decide whether we are to be freemen or slaves; whether the House of Commons is to be the palladium of liberty or the organ of despotism." Fox and the rest of the ministers were dismissed the following day, and Pitt formed a government (*The Parliamentary Register; Or a History of the Proceedings and Debates of the House of Commons ...*, 112 vols., London, 1775–1813, 12:428–429).

28TH.

Mr. Williams gave us an astronomical lecture this afternoon. The sodality met, in the evening at Putnam's chamber, and play'd till nine. Spent an hour with Mead after I return'd.

Benjamin Beale[1] was 18. the 6th. of June last. His father was from Braintree, but he was born at Liverpool in England. He entered the Class just before they commenced sophimores. His disposition is amiable, and he is a good scholar; but the government of the university have so repeatedly taken notice of him at exhibitions, that it has given offence to many of the young gentlemen in the Class, and they affect to despise his abilities; and to deny his scholarship. His talents have perhaps been rather overrated by the government, but I fear they are still more underrated in the Class; and he is not the only person whose popularity with his fellow students, has been greatly diminished by the favours of the government: notwithstanding all the reports circulated by malice and envy, I believe him very deserving: he displays no vanity, either of his person, which is elegant, or of his genius, which has been flattered by distinction, and this I think, is a sure mark of good Sense. Commerce, will probably be his profession, and from his general character, I think he has a good prospect of success. May he obtain it!

¹ Beale, son of the merchant Benjamin Beale and his English wife, who became the Adamses' nearest neighbors in Quincy after 1792. Young Beale studied law and was admitted to the Suffolk bar in 1792, but decided to turn to foreign trade a few years later (*Hist. of Suffolk County, Mass.*, 1:286; JA to AA2, 29 Oct. 1792, in AA2, *Jour. and Corr.*, 2:124; JA to James Monroe, 6 March 1795, DLC:Monroe Papers).

THURSDAY MARCH 1ST. 1787.

Charles went to Boston this morning: in the afternoon, I was at Foster's chamber; he introduced me to his father and to Mr. Bissi, a young french gentleman, who lives with the french Consul. He had been three years at a school at Passi, which I left in 1780, so that we had a fund of conversation, ready to our hands. We accompanied the gentlemen, into the library, the museum, and the philosophy chamber. Mr. Bissi, was most entertained with the elegant paintings of Mr. Copley, with which the philosophy chamber is adorn'd: and for a cursory view, more entertainment may be derived from one good portrait, than from an hundred thousand volumes, however elegantly bound, if the outsides only can be seen. I was up very late this evening reading Gibbon.

2D.

Mr. Andrews was at my chamber in the forenoon. I went with him, and Cranch and my class mate Harris, to take tea, at Mr. Pearson's. Miss Ellery, Miss Hastings, two Miss Mason's and Miss Foster were there. I got seated between Miss Ellery and Miss Hastings, but could not perfectly enjoy the pleasures of conversation, because, the music, was introduced. Music is a great enemy to sociability, and however agreeable it may be sometimes, there are occasions, when, I should wish it might be dispensed with.

James Bridge,¹ of Pownalborough in the Province of Maine, was 21 the 23d. of last September. As a scholar and as a gentleman, he is inferior to no one in the Class, and with no one, have I contracted since I entered the university, so great a degree of intimacy. His natural abilities are very good, and they have been greatly improved by Study. His passions are strong, but in general he keeps them well under command. His genius is metaphysical, rather than rhetorical; in reasoning with him we are rather convinced by the force of his argument, than seduced by the brilliancy of his imagination. He is possessed of much benevolence, and ambition occupies a large share of his mind; he does not endeavour to conceal this, but freely owns his expectations; which are so sangwine, that I somewhat fear, he will not entirely realize them all. His advantages however will be peculiar, and it is I think very probable that he will one day be eminent in the political Line. Law will be his Study; and I have long hoped that we should be together in one office, but many difficulties attend the scheme, and I fear much that it will not take place. My friendship for this gentleman, and three or four more of my classmates, saddens very much the anticipation of commencement, when we must part, perhaps forever.

[1] After a year of virtual self-study, Bridge entered Theophilus Parsons' law office in Newburyport, and he became JQA's roommate. He practiced law in Augusta, Maine, made a fortune as agent and attorney for the proprietors of the Kennebec purchase, then gradually retired from the profession and became president of a bank in Augusta in 1814. Although JQA thought him "form'd for a political Life" and believed he would "probably show to advantage in that Line," Bridge never so distinguished himself, serving only a single term in the legislature and the governor's council and as a member of the Maine constitutional convention of 1819 (Bridge to JQA, 28 Sept., Adams Papers; entry for 23 Sept. 1786, above; Willis, *Hist. of the Law, Courts, and Lawyers of Maine*, p. 154–159; James W. North, *History of Augusta, From the Earliest Settlement to the Present Time* ..., Augusta, Maine, 1870, p. 507–509).

3D.

Dined with, Bridge, Cranch, Freeman, Little and White, at our classmate Foster's in Boston. Just before dinner I went with Mr. Foster, and paid a visit to the french Consul. The family, at Mr. Foster's are all very agreeable; Miss Foster amused us, with a few tunes upon the harpsichord. It began to snow early in the afternoon, so that we were obliged to return sooner than we had intended. We were not half an hour coming from Boston, and got here just before prayers. Pass'd the evening at Lovell's chamber. The storm was violent till midnight, after which it abated. Charles came back from a little tour to Lincoln.

4TH.

Was absent from meeting all day. Read a Sermon, from Blair, in the forenoon, upon the duties of the young.[1] Dined with White, Foster and Lovell, at my chamber. Weather cleared up in the afternoon.

Josiah Burge,[2] of Hollis, in New Hampshire, County of Hillsborough, was 20 the 19th. of last April; he is possessed of one of those calm, easy minds, which enjoy happiness, under almost all circumstances. His serenity is seldom ruffled by passion, or oppressed by melancholy. His circumstances are not fortunate, and he is obliged to be absent frequently from college. Careless of futurity, he views all objects in a fair light, and always hopes for the best. It were natural to suppose, a character of this cast, would be indolent in study; yet he is acknowledged to be a very good scholar, and his mental capacity, is far from deficient. With such a disposition, he cannot be disliked, and accordingly he is much esteemed. He intends to preach, and should he be settled among men, of liberal sentiments, I have no doubt, but he will be successful. Died. 1790.[3]

[1] Hugh Blair, *Sermons*, 2 vols. [1:13th edn., 2:10th edn.], London, 1785, 1:306–340 (Harvard, *Catalogus Bibliothecae*, 1790, p. 156).

[2] Burge had been prepared for Harvard at Philips Academy by Eliphalet Pearson, who was preceptor there until 1786. Burge was one of a handful of students unable to pay his bills and thus ineligible to graduate in July. When Pearson found out about it only days before graduation, he offered to advance the money and sought out a group of seniors, including JQA, to help locate their classmate and bring him back for commencement. During the remainder of his short life, Burge taught school and studied for the ministry. He preached at Rindge, N.H., for about nine months before he died of consumption following an attack of measles (MH-Ar:Quinquennial File; Samuel T. Worcester, *History of the Town of Hollis, New Hampshire, From Its First Settlement to the Year 1879 ...*, Boston, 1879, p. 290–291; entry for 16 July, below).

[3] An interlineation written at a later date.

5TH.

Snow'd moderately, a large part of the day. We recite to Mr. Burr. Professor Pearson, gave a lecture with which he concluded his observations upon the article. I did not hear many of them.

At 7 this evening we had a meeting of the ΦBK at Cranch's chamber. Mr. Ware, was excused from reading a dissertation. I had written with White in opposite composition, and read the following piece.

Whether Love, or fortune ought to be the chief inducement, to marriage?[1]

Was I not perswaded of the benevolent candor, and kind indulgence of this audience, I should not venture to express my sentiments upon a subject, which, most men, will affirm, admits not of a question: there are certain prejudices among men, which it is dangerous to oppose: and was I in a Company of

Ladies, to avow, the following opinions, they would be universally combated, by the flash of indignation and the sneer of contempt, which too frequently supply the place of argument: but liberality of sentiment, is a chief characteristic of this Society: and if my reasoning is judged erroneous, I shall at least be sure of being forgiven.

No proposition perhaps, affords a fairer scope for the ridicule of commonplace reasoners, than that which I endeavour to maintain. Was mankind, in that primitive state of innocence, of which, the only traces that remain are to be found in the descriptions of poetry, I confess it would be unnatural and absurd to consider wealth as a requisite, for the union of two persons of different sexes: but in this iron age, when fortune is so important an article, to the happiness of men, it appears not to me repugnant to the principles of reason and virtue.

It is a very old observation that words have more influence than things in forming the opinions of men: and to this perhaps may be ascribed the universal applause bestow'd on love matches, and the detestation of interested marriages. The word *Love,* raises very agreeable ideas in the mind, and *avarice,* has always been branded with infamy. Should we, however investigate the nature of the two passions, the most strenuous advocates for the former would perhaps acknowledge, that the comparison would not be greatly in its favour. That pure, refined, and elevated passion, which we term Love, is an heterogeneous compound of *Lust,* and *Vanity,* most frequently attended with *Jealousy,* a passion formed by the furies for the misery of mankind. It is captious, imprudent, whimsical, and utterly inconsistent with reason. If you think this definition too severe, attend to the words of a celebrated ancient author.

> In AMORE, haec omnia insunt vitia, injuriae
> Suspiciones, inimicitiae, induciae,
> Bellum, pax rursum: incerta haec si tu postules
> Ratione, certa facere, nihilo plus agas
> Quam si des operam, ut cum ratione insanias.[2]

Such is the passion which most men consider, as the indispensable foundation, of an union for life between the sexes. But very soon after marriage, Lust is satiated by enjoyment, and vanity remains the only ingredient, this, instead of being gratified, will be subject to frequent mortifications, because it will not be supported by fortune; discord introduces herself into the family, and the astonished couple, find themselves chain'd to eternal strife.

Now suppose a man should make wealth the chief, though not the only object in his matrimonial pursuit. The connection may be formed by the mild warmth of mutual esteem, but without one spark of that blazing flame, which is dignified, with the name of Love. The Husband by the acquisition of a fortune, will be put in possession of the conveniences of Life, and out of the reach of want; and his wealth, will give him consideration, and importance. A Sentiment of gratitude will induce him to treat his wife with complaisance and affection; and she in her turn, perceiving him, sensible of the advantages, she had bestowed upon him, from a principle of generosity, would never remind him of her favours. They would have reason to be pleased with themselves, and it would naturally, follow, that they would please each other: no disappointed passion would divide them; no troublesome wants would make them burdens to each other; the sentiments of friendship with which the connection had been formed at first, will be greatly increased; and the happy pair would never have reason to regret the absence of that extravagant passion, which like the Sirens of ancient fable, charms but to destroy. They will labour under no difficulties, with respect to the education of their children; and their hopes for their prosperity will with reason overbalance their fears of misfortune.

Perhaps I may be charged with delivering the general opinion, with the mere alteration of words; and it may be said that the ideas which I express by the appellation of mutual esteem, are in fact the same, which the rest of the world understand, by Love: but were this the case, love might subsist between Man and man, which is contrary to the received System; I have heard a brother of this Society, whose judgment, was I to name him, would not be called in question, say, in speaking of a certain Lady, that she was too perfect to be the object of Love: the observation was very just; and I dare say many of our brothers now present, have experienced the truth of it. In short, the only difference between mutual esteem and Love is, that the one is founded only upon Reason, to which the other is diametrically opposite.

Such are the sentiments, which with diffidence, I venture to acknowledge as mine: I am not however obstinately attached to them; and should any arguments be produced sufficient to convince me, that they are erroneous, I shall retract them without hesitation.

A revision of the Laws was voted; and Freeman and Little were appointed as a committee to make alterations in the ceremony of admission.

[1] JQA's draft, dated 4 March, contains only minor variations (M/JQA/46, Adams Papers, Microfilms, Reel No. 241).

[2] Terence, *Eunuchus,* Act I, scene i, lines 14–18: "Love has all these Inconveniences in it, Injurys, Jealousys, Resentments, Truces, War, then Peace again: to endeavor to make these Incertaintys certain, by Reason, is just the same as if you should strive to be mad with Reason" (*Comoediae Sex,* London, Brindley edn., 1744, p. 47; *Terence's Comedies* ..., transl. T. Cooke, 2d edn., 2 vols., London, 1755, 2:26, 27; both are among JQA's books at MQA).

6TH.

Engaged an horse, to go to Haverhill to-morrow; White went to Boston for the same purpose. Mr. Burr gave out for our next forensic, the following question. "Whether Christianity has been promotive of the temporal interests of mankind." It is to be read the week before the close of the vacation, and will be the last exercice of this kind, for our Class.

John Chandler[1] of Petersham, County of Worcester, was 19. the 21st. of last July. Without great genius, or an uncommon share of knowledge, he has sufficient of both to render him, an useful and respectable member of Society. His disposition is very obliging, and with an handsome fortune, he unites, a laudable frugality to a proper spirit of generosity; he proposes following commerce, and as a merchant, will I doubt not, promote his own interest, without injuring any other individual.

[1] "Chandler 1st" later became a partner with his brothers in and then headed a mercantile house which traded at Petersham and Coleraine, Mass. (George Chandler, *The Chandler Family, The Descendants of William and Annis Chandler, Who Settled in Roxbury, Mass. 1637,* Boston, 1872, p. 508, 854–855).

7TH.

At about 11, in the morning I set off, with Foster and White, for Haverhill. At half past one, we got to Dick's tavern in Wilmington; we dined there, at three we started again, and at a quarter after five arrived in Haverhill: we rode in the snow the greater part of the Time. The slaying is very good; but we could not trust to its continuing so, three days at this Season of the year: I stay'd but a few minutes at Mr. White's and then went up to Mr. Shaw's. I was extremely fatigued; and retired early to bed.

8TH.

In the forenoon, I went and paid a number of visits, to my old acquaintance in this place; Mr. Thaxter; I pass'd a couple of hours with. Was at Mr. Osgood's, Mr. Duncan's, and Mr. Bartlett, who has sacrificed to Hymen,[1] since I saw him last. "Cupid by Hymen was crown'd," but at 37 it is to be supposed a man of sense, would be able to repel the attacks of the young tyrant, whose empire is generally composed of more youthful subjects. The flame, by which the torch was lighted, was not I imagine very ardent, but it will probably be lasting. It was not like the impetuous, crackling blaze of the faggot, but like the mild, and constant heat of the walnut.

I finished my visits, at Miss Hazen's; she has lately been a journey with her brother, to a remote part of the State, and return'd last week. She appears not quite so handsome, as she used to be, fourteen months since; though she is yet too young to begin to fade. We conversed about half an hour, but rather in a distant ceremonious manner.

Dined at Mr. White's. At about 4 afternoon, I went with Mr. and Mrs. Bartlett, two Miss Codman's, Miss Hazen, and her brother, Foster and White, in two double sleighs down upon the river, to Russell's tavern. Just before we went upon the ice, in going down a steep descent, one sleigh overset, men and women, all pell mell one on the other: no person however was hurt: not two minutes after; one of our horses went through the ice, just off the banks of the river: we thought the sleigh would follow; the ladies screamed, and leapt out; but we soon extricated ourselves from that difficulty likewise: we then cross'd the river, stop'd an hour at the tavern; then rode, up on the river 4 or 5 miles, and return'd just before dark: drank tea, and pass'd part of the evening at Mr. White's, and at 8, went up the hill.

[1] See entry for 10 Sept. 1785, note 2 (above).

9TH.

Walk'd about the town, with Mr. Hazen, White and Foster. Went to see Miss Hazen, the Miss McKinstry's, Mr. Thaxter, and Judge Sargeant, who was very much fatigued by riding from Boston yesterday. He proposes going into Berkshire next week, and is already imagining all the difficulties of travelling that way, with terror. His journey thither will probably be more fatiguing than his jaunt from Boston. We drank tea, with Miss McKinstry, went to Mr. Duncan's to show Foster the beauty;[1] and spent the evening at Mr. Bartlett's, in singing, playing cards &c.

Snow'd and rained the greatest part of the day.

[1] Elizabeth Duncan.

IOTH.

We had not obtained leave to be absent from College, and were therefore obliged to be at meeting, in Cambridge, to-morrow, or to submit to the fine. This morning therefore, between 9 and ten, we left Haverhill, with beautiful weather, but sloppy riding, as a great deal of snow, was melted by the rain last night: we got to the half way tavern by twelve, we stop'd and dined there, after which we again proceeded; and arrived at College while the prayer bell was tolling, just before Sun Set. Foster quitted us in Mystic, and went to Boston. Soon after prayers I heard with equal grief and surprize, that Judge Dana was seized with an apoplectic, and paraletic fit, on thursday in the forenoon: that his life was for sometime despaired of, and that he is still in a very dangerous situation. To me, he has been a second father, and his instructions, though too much neglected at the Time when he gave them, have since been more attended to; and have at least check'd some of my failings, and were calculated to reform them entirely. I have therefore reason to revere him in a peculiar manner: but a man of his Talents and virtues, filling one of the most important offices in the State, is precious to the whole Commonwealth; and should his disease prove fatal, his loss will not be easily repaired.

IITH.

Attended meeting all day. Mr. Hilliard preach'd; but not very much to the purpose: what with the fatigue of my yesterday's ride, the little sleep I had last night, and some soporific qualities in the discourses which were read, I was much refreshed by a couple of naps which I took; one beforenoon and the other after. In the evening I went down to Judge Dana's, but did not see him: the president was there: stiff as ever. Mr. Dana, had a second attack last night; but not so violent as the first: they have some hopes, and many fears with respect to his recovery.

12TH.

This morning the parts for the ensuing exhibition were distributed. *Foster* has the English Oration, Waldo the Latin: *Freeman, Little,* and *Adams,* a conference in English, upon the comparative utility of *Law, Physic,* and *Divinity,*[1] *Eaton* and *Harris,* a forensic dispute, upon the Question, whether the destruction of inferior animals by Man, be agreeable to the Laws of nature. *Bridge, Cranch, White* and *Adams;* the mathematical parts. Waldo, who proposes obtaining leave in about a month, to go to Europe, requested to be excused from performing.[2]

Mr. Pearson gave us a lecture this afternoon, upon the noun: rather abstruse. Judge Dana, had another fit of his disorder. I fear exceedingly, that he will not recover. Drank tea at Williams's Chamber.

[1] The parts were actually assigned as follows: Little on physic, Adams on law, and Freeman on divinity.

[2] Waldo was granted this request, and the part was reassigned to William Amherst Barron (MH-Ar:Corporation Records, 3:280–281).

13TH.

Somewhat idle, the greater part of the day: rather dull, and low spirited: the Sophimores this evening got more than half seas over, in Wilson's chamber, directly under mine, and made, a most outrageous noise till almost 9 o'clock. Weather moderate.

14TH.

Was employ'd almost all day, in thinking upon the subject of my conference; wrote a few Lines, with much difficulty. Did not like the subject. Wished the conference to the devil: the junior Class being displeased with the distribution of parts for exhibition; so far as respected their Class; assembled this evening at Prescott's chamber, and made a great deal of noise. The Sodality met at my chamber this evening.

Thomas Chandler[1] of Worcester, was 19 the 11th. of last January. His father was formerly one of the most opulent individuals in N. England; but in consequence of his siding with the british, in the late war, a large part of it was confiscated; he had 15 or 16 children, so that Tom has not the prospect of a very great estate. His disposition is good; he is extremely irascible, but

he carries anger, as the flint bears fire.[2]

A trifle will throw him off his guard, but a moment's recollection, reforms him. In the space of five minutes I have seen him calm, raging violent and repenting: excepting at such times his temper is easy, and contented: his happiness however proceeds chiefly from want of thought, and reflection: in short, he appears to be influenced so entirely by his Passions, that I should think him rather an instrument of action, than a moral agent.

[1] "Chandler 2d," son of John, was afterward a merchant at Chester, Vt., and Worcester, Mass. (George Chandler, *The Chandler Family*, Boston, 1872, p. 140, 526–527, 255–259).

[2] O Cassius! you are yoked with a lamb/that carries anger as the flint bears fire (*Julius Caesar*, Act IV, scene iii, lines 109–110).

15TH.

All day, engaged again, in writing my part of the conference; I do not know that I ever found so much difficulty, to write upon any subject: Little, and Freeman, are not much better pleased: in the night however, between 12 and 2 o'clock, I began to have something like a flow of ideas; I wrote more, than I had done, in two whole days. I Dined, with Freeman and Little, Cranch, and Lloyd at Mrs. Forbes's. Charles brought me a letter this evening from Boston; it was from my Sister, but dated so long agone, as last July.[1]

[1] Probably either AA2 to JQA, 22–23 July, or 27 July–22 Aug. 1786 (Adams Papers).

16TH.

Attended the library.

After prayers we had a Class meeting. It seems reports have been spread about, that many of the Class are in reality desirous to have a public Commencement, and were induced merely out of complaisance, to sign the petition, which was presented; as we conceived this might be injurious to our Cause, we voted that an additional petition should be presented to the corporation, in order, to prevent any suspicions of our sincerity. Freeman was chosen to draw it up but declined: I wished not to be alone, and finally, Fiske Little, and Adams, were chosen, to draw up the petition and present it to the Class, for approbation;[1] after which the meeting was dissolved.

Gardner Leonard Chandler[2] of Worcester was, 18, the 29th. of November. Notwithstanding his youth, his fortune, (which is supposed to be greater than that of any other student in College,) and the unbounded indulgence which his mother has always shown him, he is neither vain, extravagant nor idle; without being considered as in the first rank, either for natural or acquired abilities, he is however respectable for both: his disposition is amiable, and his moral character is without a blemish: he may be a great man; but will certainly be a good one. He intends to follow the profession of the Law.

[1] Not found. See note for entry of 4 Dec. 1786 (above).

[2] "Chandler 3d" studied law in the office of Levi Lincoln Sr., of Worcester, but soon abandoned his practice to become a Boston merchant (George Chandler, *The Chandler Family*, Boston, 1872, p. 259, 263, 530).

17TH.

I at length finished my part of the conference, this forenoon, and was employ'd all the afternoon in transcribing it; Although I have not been able, even to please myself; yet I now feel, as if an heavy burden had been taken from my shoulders. I have still however a great deal of business, upon my hands. Late up this evening. The Government met this forenoon to make enquiries concerning the noise at Prescott's and at Wier's chamber: *Cabot* it seems receive'd from them a private admonition; and something further is expected for the others.

Caleb Child[1] of Brookline was 26 the 13th. of last May; his name, and his years for a student at College, do not by any means agree. He has been absent a great part of the Time since I entered so that I have but very little acquaintance with him. Those who know him, say, that were it not for a considerable degree of envy his disposition would not be bad. As a scholar he is not remarkable; and although he has endeavoured more than once to display his genius by declaiming his own composition, yet the most common opinion is that he has not succeeded. Divinity will be his profession, and he has already acquired a ministerial cant, which is such an essential quality to a preacher.

[1] After graduation, Child taught school in Boston and preached in Roxbury; he later moved to New York, where he was a preacher, physician, and apothecary in Poughkeepsie and Troy (Alfred B. Page, "Some Graduates of Harvard College," *Dedham Historical Register*, 4:48 [Jan. 1893]).

18TH.

Mr. Hilliard preached for us the whole day: his text in the afternoon was in these words, "righteousness exalteth a nation."[1] A political Sermon; upon the present situation of affairs; the first Mr. H. has delivered since I became one of his hearers.

We had this evening a meeting of the A B. for the first time this quarter. We chose officers, to continue, untill our Class shall cease to meet at the Society. A couple of essays were read; and it was voted that, Adams 3d. Barron, Gardner, Grosvenor, and Phillips, of the junior Class, should be admitted: after which the meeting should be adjourned till next Sunday evening, at half after seven.

[1] Proverbs 14:34.

19TH.

This morning the junior's Prescott, and Wier, were publicly admonished for having had riotous noises at their chambers, last week. The sentence is considered all over college, as uncommonly severe, and by many as wholly unmerited, at least on the part of Prescott.

We had in the evening a meeting of the ΦBK. at Fiske's chamber. A dissertation was read by Freeman, but the other exercices were omitted: it was voted that a number of books should be bought to add to the library belonging to the Society. Andrews and Fiske, were chosen as a committee to purchase them.

William Cranch of Braintree, was 17 the 17th. of last July. The ties of blood, strengthened by those of the sincerest friendship, unite me to him, in the nearest manner. Our sentiments upon most subjects are so perfectly similar, that I could not praise his, without being conscious of expressing a tacit applause of my own. His manners I can however pronounce amiable; his spirit, nobly independent: his judgment sound, and his imagination lively. His thirst for useful knowledge, and his fondness for study is not surpassed by that of any individual in the Class:

happy were it for me; if with a perfect coincidence with his opinions in general, I could unite, the same talents, and the same accomplishments.

20TH.

Lines, upon the late proceedings of the College Government.
By a Student.[1]
The government of College met,
And Willard rul'd the stern debate.
The witty Jennison declared
That he had been completely scared.
"Last Night, (says he) when I came home,
I heard a noise in Prescott's room:
I went and listen'd at the door,
As I have often done before;
I found the junior's in a high rant.
They call'd the President a Tyrant.
They said as how, I was a fool,
A long ear'd ass, a sottish Mule,
Without the smallest grain of spunk;
So I concluded they were drunk.
From Xenophon, whole pages torn
As trophies, in their hats were worn
Thus all their learning, they had spread
Upon the outside of the head,
For I can swear without a sin,
There's not a line of greek within.
At length I knock'd, and Prescott came;
I told him t'was a burning shame,
That he should give his Class mates wine,
And he should pay an heavy fine.
Meanwhile; the rest grew so outrageous,
That though I boast of being courageous,
I could not help being in a fright,
For one of them, put out the light.
And t'was as you may well suppose
So dark, I could not see my nose.
I thought it best to run away
And wait for vengeance till to day:
For he's a fool at any rate,

Who'll fight when he can rusticate.
When they found out, that I was gone
They ran through college, up and down,
And I could hear them very plain
Take the Lord's holy name in vain!
To Wier's chamber they repair'd
And there the wine they freely shared,
They drank and sung till they were tired,
And then they peacefully retired."
When this Homeric speech was said,
With drawling tongue, and hanging head,
The learned Doctor, took his seat,
Thinking he'd done a noble feat.
Quoth Joe "the crime is great I own
Send for the junior's one by one;
By this almighty wig I swear,
Which with such majesty I wear,
And in its orbit vast contains
My dignity, my power and brains,
That Wier and Prescott both shall see
That College boys must not be free."
He spoke and gave the awful nod
Like Homer's Dodonean god.
The College to it's center shook,
And every pipe, and wine glass broke.
Williams, with countenance humane,
Which scarce from laughing could refrain
Thought that such youthful scenes of mirth
To punishments should not give birth.
Nor could he easily divine
What was the harm of drinking wine.
But Pearson with an awful frown
Full of his article and noun:
Spoke thus. "By all the parts of speech,
Which with such elegance I teach,
By all the blood which fills my veins,
By all the power of Handel's strains
With mercy I will never stain
The character which I maintain:
Pray tell me why the laws were made
If they are not to be obey'd,

Besides, that Wier I can't endure
He is a wicked rake I'm sure.
But whether I be right or not
I'll not recede, a single jot."
James saw twould be in vain t'oppose,
And therefore to be silent chose.
Read, with his two enormous eyes
Enlarg'd to thrice their common size,
And brow contracted, staring wild,
Said, government was much too mild.
"Were I, (said he) to have my will
I soon would teach them to be still:
Their wicked rioting to quell,
I'd rusticate, degrade, expel;
And rather than give up my plan,
I'd clear the college, to a man."
Burr, who has little wit or pride,
Preferr'd to take the strongest side;
And Willard soon receiv'd commission
To give a public admonition.
With pedant strut, to prayers he came,
Call'd out the criminals by name:
Obedient to his dire command;
Before him Wier and Prescott stand.
"The rulers, merciful and kind,
With equal grief and wonder find
That you should laugh, and drink and sing,
And make with noise the college ring:
I therefore warn you to beware
Of drinking more than you can bear:
Wine, an incentive is to riot
Destructive of the public quiet:
Full well your Tutors know this Truth,
For sad experience taught their youth:
Take then this friendly exhortation,
The next offence is rustication."

This afternoon Dr. Welch, and Deacon Smith came up from Boston, and were here about half an hour: This evening we danced for the last Time, at Lovell's chamber. After which I was some time at Mead's.

¹ Since its publication in Benjamin Homer Hall's *A Collection of College Words and Customs,* Cambridge, 1856, the first known printed version, this poem has been attributed to JQA, partly because JQA's Diary entry is still the only known contemporary MS version. Hall claimed that he published the poem "from a MS. in the author's [JQA's] handwriting, and in the possession of the editor of this work" (p. 233–235). Hall, Harvard 1851, a lawyer of Troy, N.Y., had no known contact with the Adams family, although he may have been acquainted with JQA2, who graduated in 1853. He provides no documentation for JQA's authorship, and the MS he used has not been found. Many of the poem's sentiments about college officials, tutors, and the incident itself mirror JQA's own, but the severe judgments on Harvard officials and the benign condonation of the students' behavior seem out of character. Moreover, the style of "The Late Proceedings" is untypical of JQA's productions. Until new evidence is forthcoming, JQA's authorship should be accepted with some reservation.

A partial answer for these doubts may come from another copy of the poem, transcribed in the late 19th century and among the Charles Grenfill Washburn papers at the American Antiquarian Society. (See also *Harvard Graduates' Magazine,* 26:343–344 [Dec. 1917].) Unlike Hall's version, which was a looser rendition containing freer punctuation and many small word changes, the Washburn copy is a truer, though far from an exact, reproduction of JQA's, or JQA's version as published in the late 19th century by HA ("Harvard College. 1786–1787," in *Historical Essays,* N.Y., 1891, p. 118–121). In an endnote to the Washburn transcription the poem is assigned to "J. Q. Adams and J. M. Forbes, March 1787." Such a collaborative effort was not impossible. JQA described Forbes as having "an uncommon share of wit" and a classmate who "always found his fellow students ready to laugh at his satirical wit"; he had been a close friend since JQA entered college (entry for 28 March, below). Moreover, the two remained friends well past their college days, both studying law and practicing their profession in Boston, and eventually leaving their country for foreign service. So, while the Washburn copy sheds no new authoritative light on the authorship of "The Late Proceedings," it provides a clue, albeit unsubstantiated, which may better explain JQA's role in the poem's development.

21ST.

This usually an holiday to the junior Class who now cease reciting at eleven in the forenoon. The greatest part of the Class generally join and go to some tavern at a distance from Cambridge, where they spend the evening, in mirth, and festivity: but several circumstances have induced the present juniors to omit this custom; and the President a few mornings since read in the chapel, a vote of the corporation, expressing their approbation of the conduct of the young gentlemen in that respect, and recommending to the ensuing Classes to imitate their example: several of the Class however, determined to adhere to the good old cause; in consequence of which a number of the windows in the Philosophy chamber were broken.

22D.

Fast day. Attended Mr. Hilliard the whole day; but to no great purpose: in consequence of the late severity of the College Governors, there has been yesterday and this day, a subscription paper handed about among all the Classes, to procure a meeting of the whole college to-morrow evening in the chapel, every person having a pipe, a glass and a bottle of wine, and there to convince the government that the Students are possess'd of "a noble spirit, a spirit which shall nip the bud of tyrannical oppression," they will get as drunk as beasts, and probably break every tutors window in College: this absurd, and ridiculous plan has found so many votaries, that a large majority of every Class except ours have already subscribed; but I am happy that in our Class; there are but few who have joined the association, and as it is to take place only upon condition that there be a majority of every Class, the plan will most probably fail.

I went down this evening to Mr. Dana's: I saw him for the first Time since his illness. They say he is much better, and recovering fast; but I was shock'd at seeing him; pale, emaciated and feeble, he scarcely looks like the same man he was three weeks agone.

Beautiful weather, and the warmest we have yet had, this Season.

23D.

Charles went down to Mr. Dana's this evening; the judge is mending but quite slowly:

I had thoughts of carrying up some algebraic calculations, for the mathematical performance at exhibition, but, Cranch takes the next transit of Venus. Bridge and White, who do not choose, to take much trouble, have both taken lunar eclipses; and as there was no solar eclipse presented at the last exhibition I determined to project one, for the next. I went to Mr. Read to find out, when there will be a large one, and finally calculated the elements for that which will happen, May 15th. 1836.

Joshua Cushman[1] of Bridgewater will be 23 the 11th. of next month. Poverty appears to be his greatest enemy; she opposes his progress, and he has a very great struggle with her, to go through College. For genius he is neither at the Zenith nor at the Nadir; but somewhere about half way between. For improvements, he has made as many perhaps, as his circumstances would allow him. In composition, an admiration of beautiful periods, and elegant expression, have taken from the natural taste for that simplicity in which alone true beauty and elegance consist. His conversation sometimes degenerates into bombast; to express that he wants a glass of water he will say, that within the concave excavation of his body, there are certain cylindric tubes which require to be replenished from, the limpid fountain or the meandering rivulet. In the public exercices of composition his greatest fault is prolixity. He will write two sheets of paper full, for a forensic, while scarcely any other of the Class will scarcely fill half one. He is however esteemed by the Class in general, as an amiable character, if not as an uncommon genius.

[1] Cushman studied theology and was ordained at Winslow, Mass. (now Maine), where he was minister from 1795 until 1814. His contract was not renewed, possibly because of his liberal religious views. While still a minister, he sat for two terms in the Massachusetts legislature. He later served in the U.S. House of Representatives, 1819–1825. Afterward he served in the Maine legislature (*DAB*).

24TH.

We had last evening a Class meeting; a petition drawn up by Little, as additional to that already presented, was read to the Class, and approved by them: the Committee, were ordered to carry it down to the President. I was employ'd the greatest part of this day in projecting my Eclipse for exhibition. The elements are as follows.

Elements.

for a solar Eclipse. May 15th. 1836.	D.	H.	M.	S.
1. True time of New Moon at Cambridge, in May 1836.	15:	9:	29:	13
		°	′	″
2. Semidiameter of the Earth's Disc............		0:	55:	0
3. Sun's Distance from the nearest solstice		35:	17:	42
4. Sun's Declination, North		18:	58:	0
5. Moon's latitude, north ascending		0:	26:	26
6. Moon's horary motion from the Sun........		0:	28:	14
7. Angle of the Moon's visible path with the ecliptic		5:	35:	0
8. Sun's Semidiameter		0:	15:	55
9. Moon's Semidiameter.............................		0:	15:	0
10. Semidiameter of the Penumbra..............		0:	30:	55.

Charles watch'd at Mr. Dana's this night.

Peter Eaton[1] of Haverhill was 22 the 15th. of this month. I have not the pleasure of an intimate acquaintance with him; but all those who have, speak well of him. As a speaker he is distinguished, and as a scholar respectable; his public exercices have been in general equal if not superior to any in the Class since I belonged to it: but he is very modest and diffident, so that he has not brought himself so much into notice, as several others in the Class, who without his abilities have a much greater share of confidence.

[1] Eaton was ordained at West Boxford in Oct. 1789 and remained there as minister throughout his life (Sidney Perley, "The Dwellings of Boxford," Essex Inst., *Hist. Colls.*, 29:85–86 [April–June 1892]).

25TH.

We heard Mr. Evans preach, all day: he attempted to be quite pathetic in the afternoon; but when art is seen through it must be disgusting; and when a person appears deeply affected upon a subject, which cannot be very interesting, we must conclude, that he grieves for the pleasure of grieving.

This night I watch'd at Mr. Dana's. I read a couple of novels in the course of the night; both of them perfectly insipid.

26TH.

Breakfasted at the judge's, and then returned to College. Finished the projection of my eclipse, for exhibition. Mr. Read gave out this morning to the Class, the calculation of a solar Eclipse for 1791 as the last exercice, on that score. This afternoon I calculated the elements for it.

Oliver Fiske[1] of Brookfield, will be 25. the 2d. of Septr. next. Solidity of judgment; independence of spirit, and candour of disposition, are the chief characteristics of this gentleman; as a scholar, he stands on the first line in the Class; and his honour is unblemished: his circumstances are not fortunate, and he has been often absent from College. He was with General Lincoln in Berkshire the greater part of the last winter: and wishes to follow a military life, after leaving the University: he would make I believe a very good officer, and whatever his profession may be, he will be certainly an excellent man.

[1] Fiske was a volunteer in the Revolution, and at Harvard he was instrumental in reorganizing the Marti-Mercurian Band. He studied medicine and practiced throughout his life in Worcester (William Lincoln, *History of Worcester, Massachusetts, From Its Earliest Settlement to September, 1836* …, Worcester, 1837, p. 259–260).

27TH.

It was late before I retired last night, and this morning I arose between 10 and 11. Little called me up to go to the President with our petition. We called Fiske and went all together. Mr. Willard conversed with us upon the subject of a private Commencement; but from what we could collect we rather suppose the Corporation will deny the favour which we requested. He said however, there would be next week a meeting of the Corporation, when they would probably give their final decision.

28TH.

Employ'd, part of the day in projecting the Eclipse for April 1791. We had a meeting of the musical society this evening at Foster's chamber. It was after 8 before we could make the instruments accord; and at 9 we were obliged to break up; this indeed is most frequently the case. It would not be easy to collect a set of worse instruments than we have, among eight or ten violins and as many flutes there are not more than two or three that will accord together, without scraping and blowing an hour or more, so that we can seldom play more than three or four tunes at a meeting. Wrote a little after I came from Foster's, and retired a little after ten.

John Forbes[1] of Cambridge was 15. the 13th. of last August. He is the youngest person in the Class, and his entering the university at so early a period, has been an essential injury to him; by being left so much to his own direction at twelve years of age, he acquired habits of indolence, and idleness, which are not easily shaken off. He has an uncommon share of wit, and an extraordinary memory: but he has not sufficiently learnt to respect himself; as he has always found his fellow students ready to laugh at his satirical wit, he has acquired a great degree of impudence, and rather then miss a joke fills his conversation frequently with the most low lived scurrility: as he seldom loses much of his time in thinking he is not sensible, that the very persons who applaud his satire despise the speaker, or that the reason why no notice is taken of his insults, because he is supposed to have no meaning in what he says, his mind like the sand will receive any impression; and the impression will last about as long. All these foibles however may be attributed to his youth, and it is to be hoped a few years of experience, will correct them; he is always

8. JOHN QUINCY ADAMS'
HANDWRITTEN MUSICAL SCORE FOR FLUTE, 1787
See pages xi–xii

good-natured, and has a great deal of sensibility; with an excellent genius which wants nothing but cultivation to make it flourish among the first. I have been intimate with him, since I entered College, and have always endeavoured to retain the same Sentiments concerning him though his friendship for me, appears to ebb and flow as frequently as the tide: if he should throw off those childish follies which now disgrace his character, and apply with diligence to study, he would be an honour to his friends and an ornament to Society.

[1] Forbes studied law following graduation and practiced in Boston until about 1796, when he went to Europe. Five years later he was appointed consul, living at Hamburg and Copenhagen until 1819; the following year he went to Buenos Aires as commercial agent and eventually rose to chargé d'affaires (*DAB*).

29TH.

I went this evening with Bridge, and pass'd half an hour at Mr. Wigglesworth's. Ned is very ill of a pleurisy fever, and Peggy looks low spirited. The Professor has been all along, and still is much opposed to a private Commencement, and when he has once adopted an opinion, I believe it would require supernatural powers to convince him that it is erroneous.

Dr. Jennison had one or two square of glass in his windows broken this evening, and has lately received several other insults of the same kind: it was owing to a complaint made by him that Prescott and Wier were admonished, and this Circumstance has made him very unpopular.

Bossenger Foster[1] of Boston was 19. the 9th. of last December. Of him I can say but little: he is a very good speaker, and has a good natural genius, but has not been very assiduous in improving the talents entrusted to him by nature: his conversation and manners are often puerile, and very seldom show him to great advantage: his chief excellency lies in declaiming an elegant piece of composition, and in playing on the violin: in these particulars there is not, perhaps his superior in College. He is remarked by some, as being of a narrow disposition, but this stigma is cast by certain characters upon every person who keeps within the bounds of common frugality. And if this were Foster's only fault I should set him down, as an excellent character.

[1] Foster later studied law in Theophilus Parsons' office with JQA (entry for 20 Sept. 1788, below).

30TH.

Charles went to Boston this forenoon.

I have been somewhat idle for several days: and expect to continue so till the exhibition is over; for so long as that is before me I can pay very little attention to any thing else. I found this to be the case last fall, and do now, still more so but, thank fortune I have only one more trial at the worst, of this kind to go through; which will be at commencement unless we should obtain a private one. Distinctions of this kind are not, I think, very desirable; for besides the trouble and anxiety which they unavoidably create they seldom fail of raising the envy of the other students. I have oftentimes witnessed this with respect to others and I am much deceived if I have not lately perceived it, with respect to myself.

31ST.

The Class recited in Doddridge this morning, but I did not attend, being rather unwell. The weather has been very pleasant for several days: and indeed the whole month has been much more agreeable than March generally is.

SUNDAY APRIL 1ST. 1787.

Attended meeting the whole day, to hear Mr. Hilliard; and had moreover the supreme felicity of waiting on the amiable Miss Williams to her home. After meeting, at night, I wrote part of my forensic, for next Tuesday. Attended the meeting of the A B. in the evening: not many of the members present. Two or three pieces however were read, and a forensic dispute between Abbot 3d. and Dodge, upon the curious question, whether wine be beneficial to mankind. A little after nine, we dispersed.

2D.

Recite this week in Burlamaqui: This is the day on which the election of a governor is made throughout the Commonwealth: in this Town, there were only 37 votes for Mr. Bowdoin, and 154 for Mr. Hancock: this gentleman has likewise a majority of 50 votes in Boston; indeed it is supposed he will have a considerable majority throughout the State. Mr. Cushing has the majority of votes, as lieutenant Governor, both here, and at Boston.

The Martimercurian band assembled this afternoon to choose their officers for the ensuing year. Gardner was chosen Captain, Gordon lieutenant, and Barron ensign.

We had this evening a meeting of the ΦBK, at Cushman's chamber; he read a Dissertation, but the dispute was omitted. Little business was done; and after appointing writers for the next meeting, we all retired. I pass'd the remainder of the evening at White's chamber.

Up late.

Nathaniel Freeman[1] of Sandwich, County of Barnstable, was 21. the 1st. of last month. Few persons are so liberally gifted by nature as this gentleman. He is of a middle size, but extremely well proportioned, his countenance is very handsome, and full of dignity: as an animated speaker he shines unrivaled in our Class, and for brilliancy of imagination he is inferior to none of his fellow students. He appears to be well acquainted with his peculiar excellence, and has therefore chiefly attended to composition; perhaps he has gone too far in this respect, so as to neglect other studies equally useful. In the languages, in the mathematical, and philosophical pursuits, and in metaphysics; though superior to the generality of the students, he is however surpassed by many individuals. He was formed for an orator,[2] and as such he will be distinguished whether he plead at the bar, or administer at the altar. With great sensibility he unites great ambition; but notwithstanding his numerous advantages he is as free from vanity as any person of my acquaintance. He is warm in his friendship, and perhaps rather too keen in his resentments. His passions are strong, but their violence is counteracted by the generosity of his heart. He has many imperfections, which are the concomitants of humanity; but upon the whole it would be difficult to find at this university a more promising character.

[1] Freeman later studied law and practiced in Sandwich, served as brigade major in the militia, and was a representative in the congress 1795–1799 (Freeman, *Hist. of Cape Cod*, 1:561–562; 2:137).

[2] Freeman, the "preferred rival" to JQA in oratory at commencement, was described as "superior in style, elegance and oratory" to JQA by the *Massachusetts Centinel*, 21 July. "Freeman was not deficient in elegance of diction; in mellifluousness he was unqualled. He has happily imitated the plain and just model of eloquence which has been attended with the most flattering success in this country" (JQA, *Memoirs*, 6:77).

3D.

At nine this morning the Class in two divisions read their forensics one part upon the Question "Which is the best form of government;" and the other upon that *"Whether the introduction of Christianity has been serviceable to the temporal interests of mankind:"* on this question, I read the following piece in favour of the affirmative:[1]

It is a subject of astonishment to me, that, at an University, where a liberal system of religion is generally professed, a question should be proposed which implies a denial, either of the goodness, or of the wisdom of omnipotence. In a Country where the forcible arguments of an infallible inquisition, reduce the opinions of all men to one standard, this question might with some decency be debated; because, those who deny the temporal advantages, which Christianity affords, might shelter themselves, under the protection of a future world; and this would be entirely consistent with the practice of putting a man to Death, in order to insure his eternal salvation. But here, thank Heaven!, religion does not stifle every sentiment which can counterbalance the vices and follies of humanity: here, without the dread of momentary, or of eternal flames, a man can affirm as his opinion, that all those who fear god and love their neighbours as themselves, will enjoy an equal share of felicity in a future State, whatever their mode of worship, may be. I am happy to say I have heard this sentiment inculcated from the sacred desk; and sorry I am to hear it now, publicly called in question. For if it be doubted whether Christianity be of service to mankind in this world, it must either be supposed necessary for salvation in the world to come, or acknowledged entirely useless and even injurious to the welfare of men.

I am sensible, however, that those persons who maintain the negative of this question, will have a rich plunder of argument from the history of the civilized part of the earth, ever since the introduction of Christianity: From the days of Nero to those of Constantine, the bloody banner of Persecution was almost continually display'd, against the peaceful standard of Christ: a short lucid interval ensued, after which the divine institution was again attacked by the absurd imposture of Mahomet and his followers: The enthusiastic spirit of crusading, which was calculated to maintain and support the faith, increased the importance of religion, by the murder of millions; and when the Christian world grew weary of contending with foreign enemies, they soon discovered, that they had sufficient to do, to defend the glory of Christ against one another: Every trifling deviation of sentiment was supposed sufficient to corrupt the whole System, as the imperceptible sting of an asp is sufficient to taint the whole mass of the blood. The different sects of Christians persecuted one another with such envenomed fury, and such unbounded malice, that an impartial observer would suppose, the principles by which they were actuated had been delivered by a fiend of hell, rather than by the Son of God.

All this I say, may be urged by our opponents with a very specious appearance of truth. But even admitting all these facts to be incontestible, I cannot for my part, see, what they prove against Christianity. I would ask, have there been more wars, and have those wars been more cruelly conducted since the introduction of this religion, than before that aera? Certainly not: and therefore we must attribute the discord of men, to an infernal spirit which cannot be rooted from their hearts, and not to a religion whose main object is to oppose that spirit. Christianity, it is true, has been the immediate object of many contests: but when mankind have an inclination to quarrel with one another, a motive is easily found; the causes of dispute are innumerable, and had Christianity never appeared; the power of Discord would probably have been much greater than it has been. Every candid reader of history will acknowledge that the Christian institution, has gradually inspired into the hearts of men, sentiments of compassion, benevolence and humanity even towards their enemies, which were entirely unknown to the savage barbarians of antiquity. Nero and those who imitated his persecutions, would still have been tyrants, had the religion never appeared; and the innocent victims of their execrable despotism, would have been equally numerous, without acquiring the glory of martyrdom: the Saracens would equally, have borne desolation through the Earth: and conquest would have been a sufficient motive for crusading, if devotion had failed but mercy would have been unknown among the conquerors, and perpetual slavery would have been the mildest lot of a vanquished army. If from these considerations we conclude, that Christianity has been beneficial to mankind collectively, how much more reason have we to think it has promoted their happiness individually: it has strengthened the influence of every sentiment of humanity and benevolence: it has taught us, our real duties towards one another, and towards ourselves. It has vindicated the rights of nature, which before its introduction had been violated, even by the principles of civil Society: it has restrained within proper bounds, even the sacred rights of parental authority, and shewn the cruelty, and the absurdity of abandoning an infant to destruction for any deformity in its bodily frame: it has enlarged our views, and taught us, not to confine our goodwill and friendship, to the small circle from whom we have received, or to whom we have granted favours, but to embrace in the arms of our affection the whole human race: it has inculcated the sublime maxim of loving our enemies, and of praying for those who persecute, and in short, if it does not enable us to reach the summit of perfection, it is because we wilfully depart from its guidance and direction.

At 11 o'clock Mr. Williams, began his course of experimental philosophy, by a lecture on the properties of matter.

[1] JQA's draft, dated 2 April, contains only minor variations (M/JQA/46, Adams Papers, Microfilms, Reel No. 241).

4TH.

Employ'd great part of the day in collecting the theses. I have now as many as I shall want excepting five or six in fluxions[1] which I cannot easily find, as I do not understand the doctrine enough for my own satisfaction: in the evening the sodality met at Mayo's chamber, and play'd till 9.

I was very much fatigued and retired to bed quite early.

Timothy Fuller[2] of Needham, Suffolk County, will be 22. the 26th. of next July. I have very little acquaintance with this person, and his character is such as will not induce me to cultivate an intimacy with him. His countenance is perfectly stupid, and has no other expression than that of gin or brandy, his chief talent lies in drinking largely of these liquors without apparent intoxication, and in smoking tobacco; and this talent he improves by incessant application; as a classmate I insert his name, and my plan obliges me to give the traits which distinguish his character. I would fain mention his virtues; but if he possesses any they are too deep to be perceived by common observation.

¹ That is, differential calculus (*OED*).
² Fuller became a physician in Needham (Francis H. Fuller, "Descendants of Ensign Thomas Fuller, of Dedham," *Dedham Historical Register,* 5:128 [July 1894]).

5TH.

At eleven this forenoon, Mr. Williams gave us, the second, philosophical lecture: it was upon the incidental properties of matter, and excepting very few deviations, was expressed in the same terms with that we had last year upon the same subject: indeed, whether the professor's time is taken up by other studies, or whether he is too indolent to make any improvements in his lectures, it is said he gives every year the same course, without adding or erasing a line.

However interesting the subject may be, there are many students who find no entertainment in the repetition of what they have already heard and frequently read; and I must myself confess that these lectures which were highly entertaining last year, afford me little amusement or instruction at present: if the experiments and the observations upon them were somewhat varied, I should now attend the lectures with as much satisfaction as I received from them last year.

Drank tea at Foster's chamber. Mr. Bissi was there. In the evening I went with Cranch, and Mead to Mr. Pearson's; I invited the ladies to my chamber exhibition day: the professor himself was not at home. We also went and passed about an hour at Mr. Hilliard's.

6TH.

We this day returned our books to the library.

I went immediately after prayers to Mr. Wigglesworth's; where I found only Mr. Ellery and Miss Peggy: I waited there a short time and went from thence to Mr. Williams's, but did not find a soul at home. I spent a couple of hours in the evening with Sever at Mr. Gerry's. Mrs. Gerry was quite unwell, so that we neither saw her nor her Sister.

*Thomas Hammond*¹ of Rochester, Plymouth C: was 20 the 17th. of last August. He has a mixture of good and bad qualities, so equally poised, that it is difficult to determine, whether his character may be called good or bad. He has it is said an independent spirit; but I believe few students at this place distinguish properly between independence and impudence: it is certain that Hammond, by this same independent spirit has indisposed every governor of the university against him; and whether this circumstance is much to his credit, an impartial world may determine: he is studious, and has a good knowledge of the Latin Language in particular. As a metaphysician some think him acute, but I have more frequently known him to dispute about words, and dabble with trifles, than to reason with superior judgment or genius. His moral conduct is not wild or extravagant, but at times his profanity, will make the most abandoned, stare. In short if he has any principles they are certainly not such as I should wish a friend of mine to adopt.

¹ Hammond became a lawyer and settled in New Bedford (*Fleet's Pocket Almanack and Massachusetts Register,* 1794).

7TH.

Mr. Williams gave us this forenoon a lecture upon motion: the same which we heard a twelve month past; upon that subject. Fine weather.

I have been this day chiefly employ'd in making preparations for exhibition. White brought me some things from Boston. Spent great part of the afternoon at Cranch's chamber.

8TH.

Mr. Burr preach'd to us this afternoon, a pretty good Sermon. In the evening I attended the meeting of the A B. and read an essay. Several other pieces of the same kind were presented but the Oration and forensic were omitted. Freeman requested a dismission from the Society, and it was granted: Cranch was chosen in his stead to deliver the anniversary Oration on the 12th. of next month. It was 10 o'clock before we had perform'd all our business.

A B. N. 7.

> Oh! sovereign of the willing soul,
> Parent of sweet, and solemn-breathing airs,
> Enchanting shell! the sullen cares
> And frantic Passions, hear thy soft controul.
>
> *Gray.*¹

The influence of music and Poetry, upon the human mind, have so frequently been expatiated upon, that it would be needless to attempt producing any new ideas on the subject: but we may derive entertainment and instruction, from the repetition of what has already been said, and this exercice of the mind preserves its health, and enables it to execute greater projects.

There is something unaccountable in the human mind, by which it is obliged (if I may so express myself) to receive pleasure from harmony. It is certainly involuntary, nor can it be subjected to the laws of reason. It appears to be peculiar to the mind of man, for notwithstanding all the splendid tales told of Orpheus and Amphion, it is plain that none of the beast creation are sensible to the charms of music: if any of the domestic animals, received pleasure, from a concert of instruments, many of them have a faculty of manifesting their sensibility which certainly, would not lay dormant upon such Occasions. Sound it is well known, has a great effect upon many animals, but seldom otherwise than to strike them with terror. The generous horse, is startled at the rumbling of the drum, and roused at the clang of the trumpet: but he does not appear at all affected by instruments which convey gentler sounds, and it is plain, that martial music, instead of affording him pleasure, always terrifies him. It is not the harmony, which actuates him, but the noise.

There are indeed birds, which by the mere strength of nature, will warble strains, scarcely to be surpassed by the most admired compositions of art. But it must be supposed that these powers are only mechanical, for those birds, that utter only harsh, disagreeable notes, are as fond of hearing themselves, as the nightengale. It is not necessary to produce many arguments in favour of a proposition, which perhaps no one would deny. Enough therefore has been said, to this Point.

This fondness for harmony is then one of the characteristics which distinguish man from the brute creation: and it is one of the richest sources of enjoyment, that an indulgent providence has granted him. Harmony, under various forms can rouse, soften or restrain all the passions in the human breast. There is scarce a sensation in the heart, but there may be found a musical note in unison with it. I appeal to the experience of every person, whether all their passions have not been influenced by the power of harmony?

"If in the breast tumultuous joys arise,
  Music her soft assuasive voice applies.

> And when the soul is prest with cares
> Awakes it with enlivening airs.
> Warriors she fires, with animating sounds,
> Pours balm into the bleeding lovers wounds."²

It is remarkable that this charm is rather falsified, and corrupted, among civilized nations, than perfected: its efficacy appears to be diminished in proportion to the advancement of civilization. If we carry our researches so far back as the fabulous ages of antiquity, we shall hear of its influence not only over lions, and tygers, not only over rocks and Forests, but even over the stern, unrelenting tyrant of the infernal regions. We know how far these accounts are to be credited; but at the same Time, it must convince us, to what a degree of enthusiasm the fondness for harmony was carried in those days. As soon as the light of history begins to dawn, we find the effects of music to be much diminished. Still however we hear of a Tyrtaeus, who by a song, rallies the retreating forces of Sparta, and turns the scale of victory: still we hear of an Homer deified for his verse, and that verse, consulted as an oracle upon all occasions; still we are told of a Timotheus, who "bids alternate passions, fall and rise

> While at each change, the son of Libyan Jove,
> Now burns with glory, and then melts with Love,
> Now his fierce eyes, with sparkling fury glow,
> Now sighs steal out, and tears begin to flow
> Persians and greeks, like turns of nature found,
> And the worlds victor stood subdued by sound!"³

Yet if we examine the subject, with attention, I believe we shall have reason to conclude, that the power of music has been gradually declining to our own times. There is but one modern story which is any thing like those of antiquity concerning the influence of harmony: it is told by Dryden, in his ode to St. Cecilia.

> When to her organ, vocal sounds were given
> An Angel heard, and strait appear'd
> Mistaking Earth for Heaven.⁴

If such always have been, and such always must be the effects of music, what can be said of the man, who is not affected by it? Let us conclude with the great master of human nature.

"The Man that hath no music in himself
Nor, is not moved with concord of sweet sounds,
Is fit for treasons, stratagems and spoils,
The motions of his spirit are dull as night,
And his affections dark as Erebus."[5]

[1] Thomas Gray, "The Progress of Poesy," lines 13–16 (*Poetical Works of Mr. Gray,* new edn., London, 1785, p. 25, at MQA). This poem was copied by JQA as early as Sept. 1782, while he was living in St. Petersburg (M/JQA/26, Adams Papers, Microfilms, Reel No. 221).

[2] "Ode for Music on St. Cecilia's Day," lines 24–29. JQA copied Pope's poem into another of his commonplace books in Aug. 1782 (M/JQA/24, Adams Papers, Microfilms, Reel No. 219). The poet's lines 26–27 read: "Or, when the soul is press'd with cares,/Exalts her in enlivening airs."

[3] "An Essay on Criticism," lines 376–381.

[4] "A Song for St. Cecilia's Day," (1687), lines 52–54—also copied by JQA in Aug. 1782 (M/JQA/24, Adams Papers, Microfilms, Reel No. 219). In the first line JQA substituted "sounds" for "breath."

[5] *The Merchant of Venice,* Act V, scene i, lines 84–88.

9TH.

This is the last week in which our Class attend recitations; and, this morning Mr. Burr gave us the last 30 pages of Burlamaqui for to-morrow morning.

Preparing for exhibition; wrote a little.

In the evening the two musical Societies met together in Putnam's chamber, and perform'd the anthem. Not in the best manner possible.

Thaddeus Mason Harris[1] of Malden, Middlesex, will be 19 the 7th. of next July. As a scholar he is respectable, and his natural abilities are far from contemptible; he has a taste for poetry and painting which wants cultivation, and a benevolent heart, which wants judgment to direct it. He has a great share of sensibility, which has led him into an excessive fondness for pathetic composition; so that all his exercises appear to be attempts to rouse the passions; though frequently the subject itself will not admit of passion. His speaking is injured by the same fault; for in endeavouring to call up the affections of his hearers, he runs into a canting manner, which disgusts instead of pleasing: this failing is however amiable, because it proceeds from the warmth of his heart. His disposition I believe to be very good; and if the picture is a little shaded by Vanity, a foible so universal ought to meet always with our indulgence, his constitution is feeble, and his Circumstances are penurious, but his spirit is independent, and his mind is cheerful.

[1] Harris afterward studied divinity, but served as Harvard Librarian from 1791 to 1793 before holding the pulpit at the First Church, Dorchester, from 1793 to 1838 (Nathaniel L. Frothingham, "Memoir of Rev. Thaddeus Mason Harris, D.D.," MHS, *Colls.*, 4th ser., 2 [1854]:130–155).

10TH.

The weather in the morning was disagreeable, but cleared up, at about ten. Had company at my chamber. Major Cabot and his Lady, Miss Bromfield, Miss Thomson, and Miss Fayerweather, Miss Williams, and Miss Wigglesworth; Mr. Ellery, Mr. Ware, and Miss Andrews, with several of my Classmates. It was almost twelve before the president made his appearance, immediately after which the performances began. The Latin Oration was omitted: B Barron, has been prevented by indisposition from writing it: the forensic dispute between *Eaton,* and *Harris,* came on, first. It was upon the question, "Whether Man, has a natural right to destroy inferior animals" very well supported on both sides: Though Harris in one or two passages, could not help indulging, his fondness for the pathetic: the next thing was the syllogistic dispute, by *Treadwell* respondent, *Hill, Underwood,* and *West,* opponents. The two first only performed, and *Hill,* blundered a little. The Question was, "whether the origin of all our ideas may be referred to the senses." The Dialogue between Tamerlane and Bajazet[1] was next spoken by the juniors *Barron* and *Abbot.* The greek oration, by *Phillips,* followed; after which I mounted the stage with *Freeman* and *Little.* I read the following piece. *Little* spoke immediately after me, upon Physic, and *Freeman,* closed, with a panegyric upon Divinity, which he performed so well that we were honoured with a clap.

A Conference

Upon the comparative utility of *Law, Physic,* and *Divinity.*

Law[2]

At a time when the profession of the Law, labours under the heavy weight of popular indignation; when it is upbraided as the original cause of all the evils with which the Commonwealth is distressed; when the legislature have been publicly exhorted by a popular writer[3] to abolish it entirely, and when the mere title of Lawyer, is sufficient to deprive a man of the public confidence, it should seem, this profession would afford but a poor subject for panegyric: but its real utility is not to be determined by the short lived frenzy of an inconsiderate multitude, nor by the artful misrepresentations of an insidious writer: with this consideration, I shall rely upon the candor of the audience, without being terrified by the prevailing prejudice of the day.

It is a melancholy reflection, that the utility of all the learned professions, depends entirely upon the errors, the infirmities, and the vices of mankind: Were the conduct of men towards one another directed by the invariable and eternal rules of reason, and equity, there would be no occasion for the laws of Man: if the human frame were not subject to disorders and convulsion, the skill of the physician would not be required; and if our passions were never to lead us astray from the duties which we owe to the creator, and to our fellow mortals, an order of divines would be wholly unnecessary. Unfortunately these very institutions, which were calculated to correct the frailties, and to supply the deficiencies of humanity, afford striking examples of its weakness. The lawyer depends for his subsistence, upon the breach of those Laws, whose dignity his profession obliges him to maintain; the interest of the Physician, is benefited, by the loss of that health which he is employ'd to restore; and were those vices and follies to cease, which the preacher condemns with abhorrence, and laments with pathetic eloquence, *his* welfare would not be promoted so much as that of religion: I am sensible, gentlemen, that the profession of the law, has been charged with this defect in almost all nations, and under all governments, whilst the physician, and the divine, have more frequently escaped the imputation. The law, labours under peculiar disadvantages in this respect. Whenever two individuals appeal to the Laws of their country to decide a dispute between them, one of them, must necessarily be in the wrong; yet such is the influence of the passions, that very frequently each of the parties is confident in the justice of his cause; and consequently, whatever the judgment may be, one of the parties, at least will consider himself injured: instead of imputing his misfortune to his own imprudence or folly, his passion will immediately suggest that it was owing to the ignorance or negligence of his lawyer, or to the sophistical refinements of the pleader for his adversary: to circumstances of this nature, more than to any peculiar depravity of the lawyers, is owing the general odium which the profession has incurr'd: The physician has the same temptation to lengthen out a disease, that the lawyer has to protract the final issue of a cause; but if it should overcome his virtue, he is not in an equal danger of being detected; because he can easily convince his patient that the obstinacy of the disease is invincible: and should the patient die, such is the discretion and politeness of the dead, (as a dramatic author has observed) that they are never heard to complain.[4] The opposite interests of religion, and of the preacher are still less exposed to public view: the Divine may continue year after year in the same round of exhortation: he may point out to his people the evil tendency and pernicious consequences of sin: with the most ardent zeal, he may recommend to them to practice humility, moderation, sobriety, and every other Christian virtue: so long as he addresses his discourses to men, he will never be in want of fruitfull topics for declamation; and so long as he performs all that is enjoined him by his profession, his people can never censure *him,* because they do not reform their manners.

But, gentlemen, general reflections against any particular order of men, are as false as they are illiberal; and while I freely acknowledge the abuse which may be made of the learned professions, with the most heartfelt satisfaction, I can affirm that in this country they are generally filled with men incapable of using base and ignoble arts; men, whose virtues place them beyond the reach of malice, and whose talents must always command respect.

I shall not attempt to prove the superior utility of this profession over the others; they are all absolutely necessary for the happiness, nay for the very existence of a civilized Society; and therefore I conceive their utility to be equal: their objects are to secure the possession of the three greatest blessings which contribute to the felicity of mankind, *health, liberty,* and *innocence.* Deprived of either of these, a man must necessarily be wretched; but so long as he possesses them all, he will never be overwhelmed by the torrent of other misfortunes. I shall leave it to you, gentlemen, to expatiate with superior elegance upon the utility of Physic and divinity, and shall only beg leave to mention some of the particular advantages, which are derived to Society from the profession of the law.

Before the establishment of Society, the only law by which the conduct of men towards one another could be directed, was that of benevolence, which nature has implanted in the human heart, and the influence of this amiable virtue, was frequently overpowered, by the irresistible violence of unrestrained passions.

When men first began to unite in small communities, it was necessary, that the rights and obligations of every individual, should be ascertained, by some permanent regulations: the Societies being neither extensive nor numerous, the laws at first were simple and few in number: but in proportion as the wealth the prosperity and the numbers of the Society increased, the duties and the rights of every citizen increased with them: as soon as an intercourse was opened between different States, an additional System of Laws was requisite, to regulate the communications between different nations; and finally by a continual and unavoidable multiplication of the laws, the system became so complicated, that a perfect knowledge of it, could not be obtained, without assiduous attention and laborious application: the greatest part of the community engaged in other pursuits, could not attend sufficiently to this study: it was however necessary that the laws should be executed: judges were therefore necessary who should know exactly what proportion had been established by the laws, between the punishment and the crime: it was necessary that the man to whom nature and fortune might have dispensed their gifts with liberality, should in a court of Law, have no advantage, over him, whose mind should be neither enlightened by science, nor dignified by genius: it was necessary that wealth and talents should not be taken as proofs of innocence, nor poverty and ignorance of guilt: hence arose the necessity of this profession, and whatever may be the insinuations of Envy, or the aspersions of Malice, it has certainly been the means of placing men upon a more equal footing in the courts, than they would be if every man, were obliged to plead his own cause. What employment can in fact, be more truly respectable and useful, than to defend the cause of innocence, and to vindicate the rights of injured justice: to protect the feeble, and defenceless son of poverty, from the cruel[5] fangs of Oppression, and to detect the villain who either publicly or in secret violates the laws of Society, or endangers the safety of individuals.

The intimate connection between the science of the laws, and that of government must be obvious to everyone. The liberty of a State consists in the unlimited obedience of its citizens to the laws alone: every breach of a law, is therefore a breach of the liberties of the Community: and consequently, the man, whose profession obliges him to enforce the execution of the laws, must naturally be jealous, and tenacious of the liberty of his Country.

In free governments, lawyers have been more frequently admired by posterity, than rewarded by their contemporaries, for their ardent patriotism, and their generous spirit of freedom. The name alone of a Demosthenes or a Cicero conveys the idea of the father of his Country; yet, it is well known, that one of these exalted patriots, to avoid being given up by his ungrateful countrymen to the tyrant of Macedon,[6] was obliged to put a period to his own existence: the other was banished from the very city, which by his vigorous exertions, and indefatigable vigilance, had been saved from impending destruction; and was finally murdered by the unhallowed hands of an execrable miscreant[7] whose life had been preserved by his eloquence.

In absolute monarchies, where the physician has not the most distant connection with public affairs, and where the clergy, are frequently used as the blind but powerful instruments of despotic sway, the lawyers, are the only set of men, who oppose any barrier to the arbitrary proceeding of tyranny. "The parliaments of Paris" says Dr. Moore "can remonstrate to the throne; and have done it, with such strength of reasoning, and energy of expression, that if eloquence were able to prevail over unlimited power, every grievance would have been redressed. Some of these remonstrances, not only display examples of the most sublime and pathetic eloquence, but also breathe a spirit of freedom which would do honour to a british house of commons—indeed the lawyers in France, have display'd more just and manly sentiments of government, and have made, a nobler struggle against despotic power than any set of men in the kingdom."[8] Such was the testimony of a writer who *was not* a lawyer and who was an Englishman. Yet he adds with equal truth that they are both in private society, and upon the stage, the objects of continual ridicule. The only inference that I can draw from this is, that the man who undertakes to promote the welfare of his fellow creatures, must be actuated by some nobler motive, than the desire of obtaining their gratitude and applause.

But, gentlemen, I must repeat, that notwithstanding my partiality in favour of this profession, I have the highest veneration for those, in praise of which you are about to speak: a bigoted attachment to one course of life, joined to a contempt or hatred, of any other, is the sure characteristic of a trifling genius, and a contracted mind: and you will acknowledge with me, that the man, who unites the talents of the mind to the virtues of the heart, will always render whatever profession he embraces, respectable, and useful.

After the conference, *Prescott* delivered the Hebrew Oration; but had not got it by heart. *Foster* then spoke the english oration, which was applauded by a clap. It was upon the political situation of affairs: but in the old stile of invective against luxury, and foreign gewgaws.

After the performances closed, the company escorted the Corporation and overseers to the stewards. It was after 3, before they finished their exercices. Charles and I dined at Mr. Williams's, in company with Mr. Ward, a young gentleman who graduated at this university, a few years agone; a Miss Miranda Woodward, and my classmate Phelps: the professor himself was not at home: but came in before we went away: He was uncommonly merry and witty: he had several spats with Dr. Waterhouse who called there after dinner.

I pass'd the evening at Judge Dana's: he recovers but slowly.

[1] Nicholas Rowe's play *Tamerlane, A Tragedy,* first produced in 1702, in which the Mongol Tamerlane defeated Bajazet, leader of the Turks, was very popular throughout the 18th century as a result of its political allegory, "an unsubtle presentation of the struggle between William III and Louis XIV abroad and the Whigs and Tories at home" (*Tamerlane, a Tragedy,* ed. Landon C. Burns, Phila., 1966, p. 5, 6). Harvard had two copies of Rowe's *Tamerlane,* which appears in the second volume of his *Miscellaneous and Dramatick Works,* 3 vols., London, 1733 (Harvard, *Catalogus Bibliothecae,* 1790, p. 131).

[2] Two other copies of JQA's piece, with minor variations, exist among the Adams Papers: one, enclosed with JQA's letter to JA, 30 June; the other, a draft copy, in M/JQA/46 (Adams Papers, Microfilms, Reel No. 241).

[3] Honestus, or Benjamin Austin. See entry for 10 July 1786, note 2 (above).

[4] The draft version reads: "the descretion, and the prudence of the dead, (as a ⟨witty french⟩ dramatic writer has ⟨said⟩ observed,) ⟨is surprising: for⟩ is so great that they are never heard to complain of

the physician, by whom they were destroy'd." This comes from Molière, *Le Médecin malgré lui* (1666), Act III, scene i. JQA purchased Molière's works in St. Petersburg in Sept. 1782 (*Oeuvres,* vols. 1–4, 6–7, Paris, 1760, vol. 8, 1753, at 4:167; *Catalogue of JQA's Books*).

[5] Unclear in Diary, but rendered as "cruel" from both copies of JQA's speech.

[6] Philip II (382–336 B.C.), King of Macedon and father of Alexander the Great.

[7] JQA is apparently referring to Octavianus, or Augustus (63 B.C.–A.D. 14), who did not oppose Antony's nomination of Cicero as victim of proscriptions under the new triumvirate of 43 B.C., composed of Antony, Lepidus, and Augustus. Cicero was murdered by soldiers shortly thereafter (*Harper's Dictionary of Classical Literature and Antiquities,* ed. Harry Thurston Peck, N.Y., 1898).

[8] John Moore, *A View of Society and Manners in France, Switzerland, and Germany: With Anecdotes Relating to Some Eminent Characters,* 6th edn., 2 vols., London, 1786, 1:102 (Harvard, *Catalogus Bibliothecae,* 1790, p. 75).

11TH.

I went down this morning to the president to know the determination of the Corporation with respect to a private Commencement; and was told that the petition of the Class was rejected: because they supposed that if public Commencements were lain aside, there would be no stimulus to study among the scholars: and they are afraid, that by granting our petition, they might establish a precedent which the following Classes, would take advantage of, and claim as a right, what we only request as a favour. Another reason which Mr. Willard said, had weight, although the gentlemen did not choose to avow it publicly, was their fear of offending the future governor by depriving him of that opportunity to show himself in splendor and magnificence.[1]

I walked down to Boston with Forbes. The weather was very fine. Dined at Dr. Welch's, and soon after dinner set off, for Braintree: drank tea at My Uncle Adams's, and got home, at about 7 in the evening.

[1] Relations between the College and John Hancock were uneasy because of the unsettled problem of Harvard's finances arising from Hancock's tenure as treasurer. Hancock, who had been appointed in 1774, neglected to receive or pay the College accounts. Finally, in 1777, he was eased out of office, which he considered an insult, and Ebenezer Storer was appointed in his place. Hancock was slow to clear up the overdue accounts, and in 1780 Harvard renewed its request for a settlement to no avail. Four years later Hancock took fresh offense over the seating plan of the Lafayette dinner, but nevertheless paid up some of the debt shortly thereafter. The whole matter, however, was not settled until 1795, two years after Hancock's death. His heirs even then paid only simple, not compound, interest on the arrears (Morison, *Three Centuries of Harvard,* p. 153–156).

12TH.

By using so little exercice, as I have done for these 18 months; and leading a sedentary life; I have got into a very indifferent state of health: and have determined to attend to nothing further this vacation, than to get into a better way: for this purpose I have begun to take much exercice, from 9 to 1, and from 3 to 6, I was rambling about with my gun. Mr. Gannett and his Lady, got here just before dinner, on their road to Sandwich; and the weather being rather disagreeable they will tarry here this night.

13TH.

Mr. and Mrs. Gannett went away at about 11. this forenoon, and left their daughter here. I pass'd the greater part of the day again in strolling: I wrote however a little. I am much afflicted with the heart burn, and have always been in the vacations at Braintree, much more than at any other time.

14TH.

Spent the day very much like the two former. We have destroy'd almost all the birds within five miles about: I am reduced to neglect the improvement of the mind for the sake of the body. This is as dull and insignificant a manner of doing away a man's life, as any that could possibly be invented.

15TH.

Went to meeting in the forenoon, and heard Mr. Wibird preach. That most pleasing part of his performances is his reading the psalms: I never heard any person read Poetry with so much propriety, and energy. He appears inspired at those times, though never in his own discourses. I did not go in the afternoon.

Mr. and Mrs. Gannett pass'd by in the afternoon, on their return to Cambridge. When they got to Hingham, Mrs. Gannett found herself so ill, that she could not proceed any further, and therefore determined to come back.

We went in to Mrs. Apthorp's with the young Ladies this evening. Miss Charlotte, who but a twelve month agone, was as stiff as buckram, and speechless as a Statue, has been for a few months at school in Boston, and is become quite a prateapace, full of airs and laughter: a few years more however may give her judgment, and they say she is not destitute of sense.

16TH.

A very fine day. At about 10 this morning, the president and his Lady, Mr. and Mrs. Hilliard, Mr. Tucker and Mr. Ware, arrived here on their way to Sandwich. They breakfasted here, and proceeded forward, at about eleven. I was just mounting with my Classmate Vose when Foster and Lloyd came up, in company with Dr. Howard and Mr. Foster. They stopt to refresh their horses; we waited for them, half an hour, and finally set off without them at half past eleven. A little after one, we arrived at Hingham and all dined there. After dinner I went with Vose and Lloyd as far as Plymouth.

We stopped a few minutes at Kingston where we found Fiske and Sever. Mr. Tucker and Mr. Ware came on with us. Dr. Howard and Mr. Foster came no further than Pembroke, 11 Miles back. The president and Mr. Hilliard stopped at Kingston, so that we were sufficiently divided, not to be inconvenient to one another. The roads in general were pretty good: but very dusty, the weather being very dry: the soil is not very good, especially on this side of Pembroke. The last 8 miles shew us a large proportion of pine trees and barren sands.

17TH.

The whole company arrived here early this morning: we went up into the burying ground and saw the ruins of the first fort built by our ancestors in this part of the world.[1] We found several ancient grave stones but none dated prior to the commencement of the present Century. Between 9 and 10 this morning the Cavalry set off; Mr. Ware, Mr. Tucker, Mr. Gannett, Mr. Whitman, Mr. Haven, Vose, Lloyd, and myself. The President had been very careful to desire almost every individual, that proceeded forward, to bespeak a dish of clams for him at Ellis's a tavern about 9 miles from Sandwich, famous for the excellency of the shell fish which abound there; but alas! how uncertain are the hopes of men, how liable to disappointment: when we got to the tavern the tide was high and no clams could be got: we left the President to comfort himself with his own reflections, and before two o'clock we arrived at Mrs. Fessenden's tavern at Sandwich: we found Freeman and Little, just mounting their horses to go and meet the Company. We drank tea and supp'd at Mr. Freeman's, and returned to the tavern to lodge. Parson Whitman, of Welfleet, a man that professes to be a wit, Mr. Damon, a young clergyman, and a Mr. Green, supped with us, and endeavoured as much as possible to make us merry.

[1] The fort at Plymouth, built in 1622 in response to the news of the Indian massacre of settlers in Virginia that year, was repeatedly repaired and extended (James Thacher, *History of the Town of Plymouth . . .*, Boston, 1835, p. 48, 72, 77).

18TH.

At about 11, this morning, we went from Mr. Freeman's to the meeting house: it was much crowded: a number of anthems were sung by the People of the town, and the buxom beauties of the Cape, had collected together in one gallery. By twelve the young candidate made his appearance preceded by the gentlemen who were to consecrate him to the service of God: Mr. Hilliard began the ceremony with prayer: Doctor Howard then delivered an excellent Sermon, to the general satisfaction; full of candor, benevolence, and piety, with the most liberal sentiments. Mr. Shaw[1] of Barnstable then gave the charge, and spoke very curiously; his language and ideas, however, were good; a Mr. Stone gave the right hand of fellowship, in such a manner that he appeared to me to be a man destitute of all feeling. Mr. Reed of Bridgwater made the last prayer, and the whole ceremony was concluded by another anthem; it was past 2 before they finished: all the students returned then to Mr. Freeman's, where we dined. In the afternoon we went to Mrs. Williams's,[2] who is the widow of the late minister of this place, and at whose house Mr. Burr entertained his Company. The house was full; but we crept in with the crowd. After tea, we went with a number of Ladies to a certain house where we were to have had a dance, but we were so much crowded there was no room left to move in, not till after 11. Here was an odd scene: at about two we conducted the ladies to their homes, and then retired to our own lodgings. A young lady by the name of Caroline Williams is the celebrated beauty of Sandwich; she is fair extremely delicate, and her features are regular and well proportioned: but I cannot think her so uncommonly beautiful, as many persons suppose, and as she appears convinced herself: her Sister Patty is more agreeable.

[1] Oakes Shaw, minister of the West Parish Church and elder brother of John Shaw, JQA's uncle (Nahum Mitchell, *History of the Early Settlement of Bridgewater, in Plymouth County, Massachusetts, Including an Extensive Family Register*, Boston, 1840, p. 291).

[2] Anne Buckminster Williams, wife of Abraham Williams, who had been minister at Sandwich from 1749 until his death in Aug. 1784 (Sibley-Shipton, *Harvard Graduates*, 11:498–501).

19TH.

Between 10 and 11 this morning I set off with Vose and Lloyd, and Clark, and arrived at Plymouth, before 2 in the afternoon. We found Sever and Henry Warren as soon as we arrived, and dined with them at a Mr. Russells; I paid a visit to Mrs. Thomas, and pass'd the afternoon at Warren's chamber. We drank tea at Mr. Russell's: he has two fine Sisters; one of them remarkably handsome. After tea we adjourned to Bartlett's tavern, where we amused ourselves with cards till 11 at night and then went to supper. The company consisted of Captain Thomas, Mr. Russell, H. Warren, Sever, Vose Lloyd, and me. After supper the glass circulated so briskly, that one of the Company, became immensely foolish. Cards were again proposed; at three in the morning the travellers retired, and left the other four at whist, where they continued, till an hour after Sun rise.

20TH.

At nine this morning we left Plymouth, and proceeded with Sever, and Warren, to Kingston. They had been up the whole night, and we were upon the run, the greatest part of the two last nights; we were consequently very much worn out and fatigued. Just as we arrived at Mr. Sever's in Kingston, we found the President and his Lady, going from there. We rambled about before and after dinner: and finally kept ourselves awake, with backgammon and whist till 9 o'clock, after which we retired to bed.

21ST.

Snow'd quite fast this morning, and the weather was very cold. Between 10 and 11 however we departed from Kingston, and arrived a little before two at Cushing's tavern in Hingham, where we dined, after which we proceeded forward; I stopp'd at Dr. Tufts's, where I found, my brothers and Cousin. At about Sunset I started again, and got home, just after dark. I then heard of a terrible fire, which happened in Boston last night,[1] and consumed an hundred buildings among which three or four belonging to Mrs. Amory, the mother of an amiable classmate of mine, whose misfortune I peculiarly lament.

[1] The fire was centered along Orange (now Washington) Street near Beach Street in what was then the southern part of Boston. The fire's destructiveness was eclipsed up to that time only by the great fires of 1711 and 1760 (*Independent Chronicle*, 26 April).

22D.

Somewhat fatigued in consequence of my journey: for which reason, I did not go to meeting to hear Mr. Taft[1] comment upon the scriptures. Was at the office, writing the greatest part of the day.

[1] Moses Taft, minister of the south precinct of Braintree (now Randolph) (Sibley-Shipton, *Harvard Graduates*, 13:135–136).

23D.

Rambling about with my gun all the forenoon; but with little success: went and dined at my uncle Quincy's and pass'd the afternoon there: when I return'd I found Mrs. Warren, had been at Mr. Cranch's; with her Son.

Weather very dry.

24TH.

Very warm this forenoon. After dinner, I had just set out with my aunt to go down to Mr. Beale's in Dorchester, when we met Mrs. Williams, and her daughter in a Chaise; we returned, and about ten minutes after Mrs. Beale, and Miss Mayhew, with Ben and Miss Street, came in. Mrs. and Miss Williams propose passing the night here.

25TH.

The other young gentlemen, went off at about 8 o'clock: I waited about an hour longer, in order to accompany Mrs. Williams. Stopp'd about a quarter of an hour at Genl. Warren's, and arrived at College before 12: found very few of the students arrived; pass'd the evening at Mr. Dana's: he is still upon the recovery, but not very fast.

Walter Hunnewell,[1] will be 18 the 10th. of next August. His misfortune is to have been born in low life, and to have been kept in it to this day. The company which his education necessarily led him into has been such as students are not used to keep; and his Classmates, consequently treat him with the most perfect neglect: as a scholar he is remarkable on neither side; and his genius appears suited to the condition in which he was born; he is a mere cypher in the Class, and was it not for the public exercices which he is obliged to attend; I should never have known there was such a person in College.

[1] Hunnewell later became a physician and practiced in Watertown (James Frothingham Hunnewell, *Hunnewell: Chiefly Six Generations in Massachusetts*, [Cambridge], 1900, p. 30–31).

26TH.

The students return, slowly. Cranch went back to Braintree last night. Clark arrived from Plymouth, where he left Sever and Fiske. Rain'd almost all the forenoon, and cleared up at about dinner time.

Joseph Jackson[1] of Brookline was 19 the 27th. of last October. His countenance is of a brown inexpressive cast, and his face is as perfect a blank, as his mind. His eyes are black, and always in an unmeaning stare. He is extremely dull of apprehension, and possesses no other talent, than that of pouring forth with profusion the language of Billingsgate. If I was called to point out the smallest genius in the Class, I should show him: if the most indolent and negligent student, he would be the man: but at the same time I must do him the justice to say he is not vicious; and when all the faults which a man has, may be attributed to nature, perhaps we ought not to find fault with him. Died. August. 1790.[2]

[1] Jackson later studied medicine with his uncle, Dr. Clement Jackson, and with Ammi Cutter in Portsmouth, N.H. (John Pierce, *Reminiscences of Forty Years . . . in Brookline,* Boston, 1837, p. 33; Russell Leigh Jackson, "John Jackson and Some of His Descendants," *NEHGR,* 97:9 [Jan. 1943]).

[2] Added at a later date.

27TH.

Went into the library, and took out one Volume of Wolff's mathematics.[1] Charles went to Boston: this evening Cranch return'd from Braintree: we had a class meeting this evening, and voted to present a petition for a private Commencement to the overseers, who are to meet next Tuesday. I was desired, with Barron and Packard to draw up the petition. The meeting was adjourned to monday night.

[1] Christian Wolff, *Elementa Matheseos Universae,* 5 vols., Geneva, 1743–1754 (Harvard, *Catalogus Bibliothecae,* 1790, p. 92).

28TH.

The Boston Scholars come up this evening, after entering their names at the buttery on Wednesday.

I drew up the petition, this day, but it was little more than a repetition, of what has been said in those which were presented to the Corporation.

Asa Johnson[1] of Bolton, Worcester County, was 28 the 6th. of this month. He is the oldest person in the Class, and without possessing a superior genius, he is literally mad with ambition:

What shall I do to be forever known?[2]

appears to be the question he has frequently asked himself: but unfortunately he has hit upon a method which will not succeed: he has determined never to be of the same opinion with any other person; and to set the world at defiance: the first point which he establishes is, that the existence of a God is an absurd chimaera, which little minds only can conceive: and such a violent antipathy, has Johnson to the idea of a supreme being that no one can even hint an idea which has the most distant connection with religion, without being flatly contradicted by him: if you pretend to reason with him, he will not argue, but by cavilling upon words, and pouring forth round assertions, he keeps to his point, and never acknowledges himself in an error: Upon all other subjects he has likewise peculiar ideas; and if any one expresses an opinion, similar to that of the generality of the world; he must submit to contradiction from Johnson, as he would from a parrot, without noticing it: but the gentleman is not content with opposing the opinions of men, he must likewise follow different customs: this is a late improvement upon his System: and as his Circumstances are rather penurious, he must go upon an economical plan: last winter he cut off the tops of his boots, and they served as the upper leather for a pair of shoes: his coat was longer than necessary and folds in the skirts were entirely useless; he therefore cut them off, and had a waistcoat made with them. His hair he has cut short, but in the winter, he suffers it to grow; so that it may keep him warm. But it takes whatever direction chance may give, and

Each particular hair does stand on end,
Like quills upon the fretful porcupine.[3]

He even carries his singularity so far, that in eating a piece of bread and butter he holds the butter downwards, so that it may come upon the tongue. In short he is determined to be distinguished from the rest of the world, and he has succeeded: but he will always find I believe, that the world, will not respect the notions of a man, who pays no respect at all to theirs.

[1] Johnson was later a Worcester co. lawyer and, for a short time, postmaster of Leominster, Mass. (*Hist. of Suffolk County, Mass.,* 1:523; Fitchburg Historical Society, *Procs.,* 1 [1892–1894]:91).

[2] "What shall I do to be for ever

known, / And make the age to come my own?" (Abraham Cowley, "The Motto," lines 1–2, *Works,* 11th edn., 3 vols., London, 1710–1711, 1:1, at MQA).

[3] *Hamlet,* Act I, scene v, lines 19–20.

29TH.

Attended meeting all day. Mr. Hilliard preach'd in the forenoon, and Mr. Willard,[1] brother to my Classmate, after dinner. Quite a young man; and his sermon was a proof of it. It was upon justice, temperance fortitude, godliness brotherly kindness, and charity: and not contemptible: his pronunciation however was not perfectly accurate, and there were some little improprieties in his language. Mr. Hilliard and he, very devoutly pray'd for one another.

William Samuel Judd[2] of Hartford, in Connecticut, was 21, the 10th. of January last. He was almost three years at New-Haven College, and entered this University, since last Commencement, he has boarded out of college till this quarter, and I have consequently had but little opportunity to be acquainted with him. As a scholar he is not very conspicuous, if we judge from his public exercices. He appears rather to have a disposition towards low-life, and trades, with hair dresses and tailors, in fiddles and old cloaths. This however I only have from common report; as I have never seen any thing in him, of that kind: but there is not one of the scholars from any other College, in our Class, that leads us to suppose their method of education better than that which is pursued here.

[1] Both brothers of Samuel Willard were ministers; but this one presumably was Joseph, minister at Wilbraham, Mass. (Joseph Willard and Charles Wilkes Walker, *Willard Genealogy: Sequel to Willard Memoir,* ed. Charles Henry Pope, Boston, 1915, p. 91, 176).

[2] After graduation, Judd returned to Connecticut, where he entered trade in New Britain (Sylvester Judd, *Thomas Judd and his Descendants,* Northampton, Mass., 1856, p. 19–20, 28).

30TH.

Cranch and my Chum went to Boston this morning to see a pompous funeral of one Mr. Webb, who was grand master of the lodge of free-masons at Boston.

We had a philosophical Lecture this forenoon, upon the central forces, with an explanation of some of the conic sections.

After prayers this evening we had a class meeting. The petition to the overseers was read, and signed by those of the Class that were present. We had a thunder shower in the afternoon. It cleared up in the evening and was very pleasant. After ten o'clock I walk'd with Cranch and Foster across the common.

TUESDAY MAY 1ST. 1787.

It thundered this morning from seven to nine, with some rain. I went with Barron to Mr. Hilliard's, and gave him the petition, which we desired him to deliver to the board of overseers. He told us we should not be so likely to succeed as we might if the Senate were to attend; they are detained by Boston by public affairs, as this is the last day on which the general Court propose to sit.[1] However, the matter was not determined this day; but the gentlemen adjourned till Friday, at Boston when some of the Senators may attend.

Samuel Kellogg[2] of Hebron, in Connecticut will be 26 the 7th. of this month. After having spent some time both at New Haven, and at Dartmouth Colleges, he entered here just before last Commencement: he proposes preaching, and is very superstitious and bigoted: he agreed after last Commencement to chum with Child; but before they had lived together three months, Child gave him six dollars to renounce his right to part of their chamber. Sever was the first person who noticed him, when he came to College, and he rewarded him by telling some lies concerning Sever, to a young lady, and in consequence of this he had a violent dispute with him. He introduced himself to several of the best families in town, and desired Mr. Read to introduce him to the worthy lads in our Class, because, said he, "I wish to be intimate with those only that bear good characters." A character thus compounded of Superstition, impudence, hiprocrisy, and Avarice, will not probably be popular any where: here he is universally despised or hated.

[1] Under a provision of the Massachusetts Constitution, the governor, deputy governor, governor's council, and the senate of the Commonwealth, together with the ministers of Cambridge, Watertown, Charlestown, Boston, Roxbury, and Dorchester, were all members of the Harvard Board of Overseers (Ch. V, Sect. I, Art. III).

[2] Kellogg returned to Hebron to study divinity and later lived in Westfield, Mass., and Wethersfield and Hartford, Conn. (Timothy Hopkins, *The Kelloggs in the Old World and the New*, 2 vols., San Francisco, 1903, 1:171, 364).

2D.

This morning I went out with Forbes and Mason, on a gunning party. The game was very scarce, but among us all, we kill'd a large variety of birds. We dined at one Richardson's, living beyond the fresh pond, and did not return till almost six o'clock; pass'd the evening with Cranch, and was much fatigued.

3D.

Cranch went to Braintree this morning. I pass'd the greater part of the day in writing. I do not expect to get properly at the study which for one fortnight I wish to pursue till next week; and then I must attend to it with great diligence.

Weather fine.

Ephraim Kendall[1] of Ipswich, Essex C. was 20 the 28th. of last Novr. There is something peculiar in this character. He is said to be one of the hardest students and one of the poorest scholars in the Class: his natural abilities are so small, that they can scarcely be improved even by cultivation. He appears to be totally destitute of literary judgment at least; for I have heard him declaim a piece in very plain english, which I was convinced he did not understand. At recitations he was never distinguished for taking the meaning of an author, and in short all his public exercices have been inferior to the common run. Yet he is possess'd of extreme sensibility, and his temper is very irascible. His person is handsome, but there is an unmeaning stare in his eye, which is too expressive of the vacancy in his mind. It would require a very metaphysical genius to prove this to be a good or a bad character; but it is not certainly one, which any person would wish to possess.

[1] Kendall became an Ipswich merchant and, presumably, owner of several ships (*Columbian Centinel,* 12 Sept. 1798; Essex Inst., *Hist. Colls.,* 40:232, 333 [July, Oct. 1904]; 41:376 [Oct. 1905]; 70:86 [Jan. 1934]).

4TH.

Mr. Williams at 11 o'clock gave us a philosophical lecture in which he blended two of those he gave last year; upon the centripetal force; and upon the lever.

Wrote a great deal this day. Mrs. Cranch, and Miss Lucy, were here this afternoon.

5TH.

A sultry, disagreeable day. Mr. Williams gave a philosophical lecture this morning; but I had forgotten his announcing it, and when the bell rung, supposed it was for some other exercice; this is the first lecture of any kind which I have not attended, since I entered the university; after dinner several of the Class went a fishing: I set out with them; but turn'd back as there was too much wind, for sport. Cranch returned from Braintree this evening.

Nathaniel Laurance[1] of Woburn, Middlesex C. was 21 the 21st. of last July. I have not much acquaintance with him; but those who know him are not enthusiastic in their praises. He professes a vast deal of independence, and assurance; his heart he says never palpitated at the presence of man: and the heart which never palpitated with fear, cannot surely beat for joy. As a scholar, and as a speaker he is not conspicuous; though in his declamations he has frequently display'd that matchless impudence, of which he is so fond of boasting. His moral character is good I believe, and it is said, he has assisted his chum (Jackson) very much in the article of composition.

[1] Lawrence became a minister at Tyngsborough, Mass., 1790–1839 (*History of Middlesex County, Massachusetts, with Biographical Sketches of Many of Its Pioneers and Prominent Men,* comp. D. Hamilton Hurd, 3 vols., Phila., 1890, 2:372).

6TH.

Attended Mr. Hilliard all day. He preach'd rather better than usual, I think.

Dined with my brothers at Judge Dana's. He looks much better, than I have seen him at any time since he has been sick. The weather in the course of the day was disagreeably warm; more so than it has been at any time this Season, but in the evening it grew cooler, and, rained very plentifully. Pass'd the greatest part of the evening at Mason's chamber.

7TH.

This morning I went up, with Cranch, Learned, Lloyd, Mason, Phelps and Putnam, to the fresh pond, on fishing; and did not return till after four in the afternoon: we caught only a few small fish; and had the pleasure of rowing a clumsy boat all over the pond.

I miss'd two lectures by this party: one from Mr. Williams at 11. and the other from Mr. Pearson at 2.

Pass'd the evening in Angier's chamber.

Ebenezer Learned[1] of Medford, Middlesex C: will be 25 the 30th. of next Octr. Without possessing a superior genius; by mere dint of application he has become a respectable scholar: his mind is perhaps more attentive to matters of small moment, than is necessary: he has candour enough to confess himself envious, but says he cannot help it: he appears to be sensible that his abilities, are not of the first rate, yet he acknowledges, that his soul is tortured with ambition. I would not give a fig for life said he, one day to me, if I could but plant immortality upon Ebenezer Learned: There is not at present any prospect that his name, will obtain immortality. But he intends to be a preacher, when he may comfort himself with the idea, that his soul, must be immortal. He was as he says himself too old when he entered the University. From 14 to 18 I should suppose the best age for entering. The studies which are pursued here, are just calculated for the tender minds of youth; but the degree of liberty that is enjoyed, renders it dangerous to young persons, before they have acquired a certain degree of judgment.

[1] Learned studied medicine with Edward Augustus Holyoke in Salem and briefly practiced in Leominster, Mass., before moving in 1793 to Hopkinton, N.H., where he resided for the rest of his life (C. C. Lord, *Life and Times in Hopkinton, N.H....*, Concord, N.H., 1890, p. 248, 426, 427).

8.

Began to pay some attention to my theses. Studied fluxions, a little in the forenoon: and the afternoon, translated a few. Was at Putnam's chamber before dinner. Leonard White returned from Haverhill, this day, and brought me a letter:[1] at prayers Mr. Ware read a latin theological dissertation. We had a meeting of the ΦBK at Freeman's chamber. The usual performances were exhibited, and it was voted to admit the juniors Abbot, Bancroft, and Lincoln.

[1] Letter not found.

9TH.

Mr. Wigglesworth gave a private lecture this morning, and we had likewise a philosophical lecture from Mr. Williams; the subject was fire; and there were a number of curious observations, which, I do not recollect having heard last year: Charles pass'd part of the evening with me, at my chamber.

Moses Little[1] of Newbury, will be 21 the 4th. of next July. Great application, joined to very good natural abilities, place him in the first line, in the class as a scholar: he has been attentive to all those parts of Science which are pursued here, and in all, he has made considerable proficiency: as a speaker, he is inferior to several, but his composition, is perhaps rather too flowery: to a large share of ambition he unites great modesty, and he has the peculiar talent of being favour'd by the government of the College, without losing his popularity with his Classmates. His disposition must of course be amiable, he seldom contradicts the opinions of any one, yet when he is obliged to declare his own sentiments, he can shew, that he thinks for himself. But notwithstanding all of his good qualities; he is sometimes censured, and such is the instability, of all populaces, that a small trifle might induce two thirds of the Class to deny the improvements and the abilities even of this person.

[1] Little after graduation studied medicine with John Barnard Swett in Newburyport, at the same time JQA was pursuing his legal studies there; afterward he practiced in Salem (Russell Leigh Jackson, "Physicians of Essex County," Essex Inst., *Hist. Colls.*, 84:89 [Jan. 1948]).

10TH.

A violent north east storm continued the whole day, with copious rain: there has fallen more this day, than in any other two for a twelve-month past: and it will be very serviceable to the ground: Mr. Thaxter and Mr. Greenleaf were here this afternoon from Haverhill; but notwithstanding the storm, they proceeded to Boston.

Pass'd the evening with Cranch.

11TH.

Storm'd again the whole day: we had a lecture from Mr. Williams, upon heat, in which he introduced his own system, which he first made public last year. Charles declaimed this evening in public, for the first time. Pass'd the evening with Mead.

James Lloyd[1] of Boston, was 17   . He is said to be a good scholar, and a hard student; but his disposition is far from amiable. He is an only son, of a physician of eminence, and fortune in Boston; and has been too much indulged in every childish caprice, to make him studious to please others: his ideas appear to be, that the beings which surround him were created to administer to his pleasures, but that he was born wholly independent of them: whatever he sees, different from his own taste, he honours with a sneer, but when any person has boldness enough to return the sneer

Then his fierce eyes, with sparkling fury glow.[2]

He has not the least command of his passions, and any person of coolness might play upon his mind, and direct his rage, just as he should please.

But he can never be an agreeable companion; I was with him continually, for one week; and I should never wish to be with him again. His chum (Amory) is the only person that could live with him without quarreling, and he preserves peace only by giving way in every particular: a greater contrast of characters could not be found. Amory has every virtue which conspires to win the hearts of men, and Lloyd would be discontented, if he was placed at the right hand of omnipotence.

[1] Lloyd became a Boston merchant, and, after JQA's resignation, served in the U.S. Senate from 1808 to 1813 and from 1822 to 1826 (*Boston Directory*, 1796; *Biog. Dir. Cong.*).
[2] "An Essay on Criticism," line 378.

12TH.

The storm continued the whole day with unabated violence. Mr. Williams gave a philosophical Lecture upon hydrostatics, something different from that which we had on the same subject last year. Indeed several of the late lectures have been much diversified; and are the more agreeable on that account.

We had in the evening a meeting of the A B. Cranch gave us the anniversary Oration, which was well written and delivered. After this a subject of importance was discussed; and then, the officers for the next quarter, were chosen from the junior Class: Abbot was elected president, Barron secretary, and Gardner deputy secretary. The members from our Class, then took their leave; and for the future are to attend only as spectators, and at their option.

13TH.

The storm continued violent through the whole day. The rain pour'd down, with as much force, as if there had not fallen a drop before. I felt dizzy in the head, and therefore did not attend meeting: in the evening at half past eight we met by adjournment from last night, at Fiske's chamber; we finally concluded, the business which we met upon by the expulsion of the person, who had betray'd the Society; after which we returned all to our Chambers.

James Lovell[1] of Weymouth, Suffolk C. was 19. the 1st. of January last. It would be almost impossible to trace, the sources of this person's principles of action: it might perhaps be said with truth that he has none: his natural abilities appear to be good, but they have never been improved by much cultivation: his education before he came to this university was not brilliant, and he now exhibits the mingled qualities of a buck and a clown. His passions rule him, with unrestrained sway; yet his mind is so pliant that it is easily directed by any kind of reasoning: such a disposition cannot be perfectly amiable: and accordingly he has lived with five different Chums, since his admission to College: and, if he had to remain here any longer, he would certainly change again at Commencement. He might make a good military officer; but I believe he will never shine very conspicuous, in any other capacity.

[1] Lovell later practiced medicine in Weymouth (*History of Weymouth, Massachusetts*, 4 vols., Weymouth, 1923, 3:399–400, 402–403).

14TH.

We had a philosophical lecture at 11. A Class meeting was called this evening, to determine, whether the Class should take any further measures, upon the ill success of our petition for the overseers: it was proposed that the whole Class should refuse to perform the different parts that may be allotted to them for Commencement. A Committee of three was appointed, (Barron, Freeman and Packard,) to draw up a solemn declaration to be signed by all the Class. After an adjournment of one hour, we returned to the chappel: the declaration was read, and signed by 29 members of the Class: some requested time to reflect upon the subject, and some peremptorily refused to sign: it was finally voted to adjourn the meeting till to-morrow morning, that those who wish for time to think on the matter, may then insert their names. I, opposed the measure, because, I perceived that more than half of those who signed, were influenced merely by the fear of being thought desirous of honourable parts: and I am morally certain an engagement of that kind, when contracted with so much reluctance, would never be regarded, if the person who contracted it should find it for his interest to violate the agreement.

15TH.

Mr. Williams gave us a lecture upon pneumatics: The parts for Commencement were not given out this morning as was expected: but the Class met by adjournment and tore up the agreement, as they found there was not sufficient unanimity, to carry the measure into execution.

William Mason,[1] of Salem, Essex C. will be 19 the 12th. of next September. His natural abilities are very good, and he has a peculiar taste for the Science of natural philosophy: this he has cultivated much by reading, and observation: but in all the other branches of learning, he has been rather remiss, and to all the college exercices, he has been very inattentive; his moral principles are not very severe, and in general since he has been a member of this university, he has been as indolent, and dissipated as any in the Class: his disposition is naturally good, and he is possessed of an innate generosity of soul, which even when it is carried to an excess, is at least an amiable failing: but he has not that command over his passions, which is requisite to a man, who wishes to be popular in the world; and he has always borne the character of a buck: his faults however may all be attributed to youthful imprudence; and a few years may probably render him a very useful member of Society.[2]

[1] Mason later became preceptor at "Smith's Academy" in Charleston, S.C. (Bentley, *Diary*, 1:178, 182, 322; 3:147).
[2] Found at this point in the Diary on a loose sheet of paper are ten lines of poetry in JQA's hand about JA which were copied from Joel Barlow's *The Vision of Columbus; A Poem in Nine Books,* Hartford, 1787, p. 165.

16TH.

The parts for Commencement have been expected for a day or two, with some degree of impatience by the Class: they have not yet, however been delivered. I pass'd last evening with Freeman at the Butler's chamber: he said he had seen the different parts at the president's; and that there were several of a different kind, from what have been usual in former years. Mr. Williams gave us another lecture this forenoon, upon pneumatics; he proceeds faster this year than he did last, and may close sooner, although it was a week later, when he began.

Daniel Mayo[1] of Roxbury, Suffolk C. will be 25 the 30th. of next September. Little can be said of this person, except that his disposition, is very amiable: as a scholar, and as a speaker he is neither contemptible nor excellent: his chief attention has been turn'd to the study of geometry, Surveying, trigonometry, and those parts of the mathematics which are usually studied here. In these he has made some proficiency: but his virtues are more the objects of our esteem, than his abilities of our admiration: he will certainly be a good man: and that reputation is much more meritorious than the fame of extraordinary talents; because the qualities of the head are given to us, by nature; but those of the heart depend chiefly upon ourselves.

[1] Mayo went west in 1788 with Col. Ebenezer Battelle, Harvard 1775, to Belpre, Ohio, where he taught school for a few years. Eventually he settled in Newport, Ky. (Clara Paine Ohler, "Frontier Life in the Old Northwest," *Journal of American History*, 2:305 [1908]).

17TH.

This morning the different parts for Commencement were distributed by the president, in the following order.

1. A Latin Salutatory Oration, by *Little*.

2. An English Poem by *Harris*.

3. A Syllogistic disputation upon the question—"Whether thought be the essence of the soul"? by *Hammond*, respondent. *Whitney*,[1] *Phelps, Mason*, and *Lovell* opponents.

4. A Forensic disputation, upon the question,—"Whether it be possible for civil liberty long to subsist in a Community, without three orders in the government, vested with such powers as to make them mutualy checks upon, and balances to each other? by *Bridge*, and *Cranch*.[2]

5. A Latin conference, upon the happy effects of industry and Economy in a Community. By *Abbot 1st.* and *Abbot 2d.*

6. A Forensic disputation, upon the question—"Whether the world has been and is, continually increasing in useful knowledge and morality. By *Chandler 3d.* and *Fiske.*

7. A Syllogistic disputation, upon the question—"Whether any man be so depraved as to have left all sense of virtue"? by *Johnson,* respondent. *Judd, Jackson, Hunnewell* and *Fuller,* opponents.

8. An English Oration, upon the importance and necessity of public faith, to the well-being of a Community, By *Adams.*[3]

9. A conference in greek, upon the excellencies of some of the greek writers. By *Eaton* and *Vose.*

10. An English conference, upon this question,—"Whether, to attain the end of civil government, it be as necessary to reward the virtuous as to punish the vicious? By *Foster* and *Putnam.*

11. A Latin Oration, upon agriculture, by *Beale.*

12. An English conference, upon this query—"Whether mankind in general are most influenced in their conduct, by a desire of wealth, power, or fame. By *Amory, Lloyd* and *White.*[4]

13. A Latin conference upon this topic—Whether learning, really promotes the happiness of those who possess it? By *Chandler 1st.* and *Mead.*

14. A Forensic disputation, on the question—"Whether self-love be the ultimate spring of all human actions. By *Burge* and *Packard.*

15. An Hebrew Oration. By *Learned.*

16. A greek Conference upon the advantages of Peace, for cultivating the arts and Sciences. By *Morton* and *Welch.*

17. Astronomical calculations, and projections, algebraic deductions, geometrical demonstrations, solutions of problems in conic Sections, and in Trigonometry—Surveying &c. By *Angier, Barron, Chandler 2d., Child, Cushman, Forbes, Kellogg, Kendal, Laurance, Mayo, Prentiss, Rand, Sever, Willard,* and *Williams.*[5]

18. An English Oration. By *Freeman.*

The distribution of the parts, is generally approved: some indeed who are disappointed in receiving such as they suppose, less respectable than what they expected, complain, and Eaton I think is with reason displeased. On the other hand Amory, who was so certain himself of having an opponent's part, that he had engaged Hammond to write his syllogisms, for him; was agreeably disappointed, with an english conference. All the Class agree that he deserves it not, as a student, but all are pleased with his allotment because his disposition is so uncommonly amiable.

I pass'd the evening at Mr. Dana's; in company with Mr. Reed and the librarian. The Class this evening confirmed their reputation for propriety of behaviour, by avoiding all those excesses, which have frequently disgraced the characters of the students. There were no disorders of any kind.

[1] Whitney did not perform in the commencement ceremonies, apparently because his unpaid college bills kept him from graduating with the others (MH-Ar:Faculty Records, 5:259; entry for 18 July, below).

[2] Bridge was excused from the commencement, and Cranch read an oration on the same subject (MH-Ar:Faculty Records, 5:259–260).

[3] A slip of paper assigning JQA's part, written by Willard and limiting him to ten minutes, is inserted between pages 290 and 291 of the Diary.

[4] In the Diary nos. 1, 2, and 3 are placed above "wealth, power, or fame," respectively. Above "Amory, Lloyd and White" are nos. 2, 3, and 1, in that order.

[5] Barron and Cushman did not perform, presumably because they had not yet paid their bills; Williams was officially excused from the ceremonies (MH-Ar:Faculty Records, 5:261; entry for 18 July, below).

18TH.

Concluded my theses, and carried them to him[1] for examination. Began my part for commencement, and wrote about one page. The good parts as they are called, are so much more numerous this year, than they ever have been before, that the president was obliged to limit the time, to be taken up by the different performances. Mine is restrained to ten minutes; so that I shall not be able to write much.

Samuel Mead[2] of Harvard, Worcester C. will be 25 the 30th. of this month. His oratorical and scholastic talents, are not remarkable on either side; he has a command of his countenance, which gives him a great advantage in declaiming humorous pieces. He is an exceeding kind neighbour, and I have lived, in the chamber adjoining his, upon very friendly terms, this year: but his politeness, I fear goes too far, for it appears to me, he is always of the same opinion with his Company however opposite that may be at different times. He has even been accused of hypocrisy; this charge however I hope is entirely without foundation, and I have no reason, to doubt of his honour or of his sincerity. The greatest defect which I have observed in him, has been, a jealousy, and suspicion, of what others have said of him: this circumstance has set him at variance with several of his class-mates; and has probably been the cause of those reports which have been spread, injurious to his honour.[3]

[1] President Joseph Willard.

[2] Mead was ordained minister at Alstead, N.H., in 1791, but his congregation grew dissatisfied with his Unitarianism and dismissed him in Aug. 1797. He then went to Walpole, N.H., where he occasionally preached, but he was never again settled in a pulpit (George Aldrich, *Walpole ... Containing the Complete Civil History of the Town From 1749 to 1879 ...*, Claremont, N.H., 1880, p. 327–328).

[3] Found between pages 244 and 245 in the Diary is a loose scrap of paper with the following words: "Ἐ'χθρος γάρ μοι κεῖνος, ὁμῶς ἀΐδαο πυλῃσιν, /'ός χ' ετερον μὲν κεύθει 'ενὶ φρεσὶν, αλλοδὲ Βάζει. Iliad: 9. v: 312. Who dares think one thing, and another tell, /My heart detests him as the gates of Hell. Pope."

Evidently JQA was comparing with Pope's the original version (lines 312–313), rendered as "for hateful in my eyes, even as the gates of Hades, is that man that hideth one thing in his mind and sayeth another" (Homer, *The Iliad With An English Translation,* transl., Augustus T. Murray, 2 vols., London, 1924, 1:404, 405; *Iliad,* transl. Pope, Bk. IX, lines 412–413).

19TH.

Mr. Thaxter was here, about half an hour, on his return to Haverhill. Mr. Williams, gave us yesterday a lecture; still upon the subject of air: in the afternoon, I carried down my theses to the president, for approbation: I went with Mrs. and Miss Williams, and Miss Betsey Cranch into the Museum, where the professor diverted them, with a number of experiments. He was very sociable, and full of wit upon the effect of the pulse-glasses.[1] We returned just before prayers, and drank tea, at Mr. Williams's: he conversed much, upon the distribution of the parts, and upon the opinions of the students, with respect to the transactions of the government of the University. White pass'd the evening with me.

[1] Pulse-glasses: Glass tubes filled with rarified air and enclosed at each end with a bulb "which when grasped by the hand exhibits a momentary ebullition, which is repeated at each beat of the pulse" (*OED*).

20TH.

Attended meeting all day. Dined at Mr. Dana's, with the butler.[1] The weather was warm, the fore part of the day, but in the afternoon, got round to the east.

Ephraim Morton[2] of Boston was,   . He has been absent from college, on account of sickness, ever since Commencement, till this quarter; so that I have had less opportunity to form any acquaintance with him, than with any other person belonging to the Class. His character however is not very conspicuous in any line; he is said to be a very good scholar in the Latin and greek languages; but even when he is here, he is little noticed by the Class in general, and I have seldom been in Company with him: his disposition is good, and he has at least the merit, of not being the author of any mischief.

[1] William Harris served as butler from July 1786 (MH-Ar:Corporation Records, 3:260).

[2] Morton afterward studied medicine and became a surgeon in the East India Company's service (*Massachusetts Centinel,* 16 Dec. 1789).

21ST.

Mr. Williams this forenoon closed the subject of Pneumatics, with an account of the different kinds of air. Was employ'd, the chief part of the day in writing my part for Commencement, and have not yet finished it. As I am conscious, of having no talent at rhetorical composition; this allotment has given me a vast deal of anxiety. As my part is of the same kind with that of Freeman, whose chief talent, among many others, lies in this kind of Compositions; I dread the comparisons which may be made; and although my friendship for him is such, that I shall rejoice to see him perform his part with universal approbation, and unbounded applause, yet I cannot help fearing that contrasts may be drawn, which will reflect disgrace upon me.[1]

[1] Even after four decades, the signs of competitiveness with Freeman over the commencement orations were still evident. JQA wrote: "The incidents attending it were of a nature to make and leave a deep impression upon my mind. The appointment to deliver it was itself a high distinction. Yet it was but the second honour of the Class; and he who took the first, the preferred rival [Freeman], sunk at the age of 35, to be forgotten" (JQA, Diary, 7 Oct. 1822, *Memoirs,* 6:77).

22D.

Our lecture this day, was upon magnetism; but I think it was nearly or exactly the same with that which was delivered last year upon that subject: I concluded my piece this afternoon, and propose to lay it by for some time; and to make such alterations from time to time, as shall appear proper. This afternoon Mr. Wigglesworth gave us a lecture; but was scandalously interrupted.

Hezekiah Packard,[1] of Newtown, Middlesex C. was 24, the 6th. of last December. He has a good share of original wit; but his genius is not uncommon: his improvements are greater than those of the students in general, but not such as to place him in the first rank of scholars. As a speaker he is too much addicted to a monotony, whatever his declamations are. His disposition is good, and his moral character is unimpeachable.

[1] Packard became mathematics tutor at Harvard, 1789–1793, and later served as minister in Chelmsford, Mass., in Wiscasett, Maine, and in Middlesex Village (Lowell), Mass. (Samuel P. Hadley, "Boyhood Reminiscences of Middlesex Village," *Contributions of the Lowell Historical Society,* 1:216 [July 1911]).

23D.

This day, we had a lecture upon electricity: we received a shock, which was much more violent than that given us last year. I felt it only by a very disagreeable twitch in the joint at both elbows; but it was a kind of pain different from any thing else I ever felt. It is so instantaneous, that the sensation is known only by recollection: it was over before I was sensible of the stroke: it had however a powerful effect upon my nerves, as indeed I recollect, the small shock which we received last year, had likewise: Mr. Williams informed us, that for the future his lectures would depend upon the weather; as the optical experiments could not be exhibited, unless the sky were clear. Cranch went to Braintree with his Sister to-day: she intended to have spent a week more here; but was taken ill on Sunday, and is still so unwell, that she wishes to be at home.

24TH.

Weather was so cloudy all day, that we had no philosophical lecture. Tuesday evening we had a meeting of the ΦBK. Admitted Abbot, Bancroft, and Lincoln, and yesterday morning, we met again at Packard's chamber, and voted to admit *Barron, Gardner* and *Grosvenor.* Our Class having no college exercices to attend to, and many of them having now finished their parts for Commencement, are generally very indolent. Riding, and playing, and eating and drinking employ, the chief part of their time.

John Phelps[1] of Westfield, Hampshire C, will be 19 the 16th. of next month. He entered this University, with Judd, since last Commencement and has not made a conspicuous figure in the Class. This College indeed cannot boast much of the acquisitions it has made from New-Haven and Dartmouth. Angier, Kellogg,

Judd, Phelps and Willard are all either harmless and inoffensive, or malicious, and hypocritical characters. Phelps however would come under the first description; for no body ever complains of being injured by him. He is I believe one of those indifferent characters, which are neither virtuous nor vicious.

[1] Phelps studied law and practiced in Granville, Mass., where he also became a town officer, state representative, and sheriff of Hampden co., 1813–1831 (Oliver Seymour Phelps, *The Phelps Family of* *America and Their English Ancestors . . .,* 2 vols., Pittsfield, Mass., 1899, 1:184; Albion B. Wilson, *History of Granville, Massachusetts,* [Hartford, Conn.], 1954, p. 126–129).

25TH.

Rain'd all day; but cleared up in the evening. We had last night a class meeting, to determine, concerning the printing of our theses; and notwithstanding the vociferous clamour of certain characters, who always glory in creating confusion, it was finally determined, that Mr. Freeman should print 2000, and a Committee was chosen, to make the agreement with him: it was then voted, that the sum which has been subtracted from the usual expence for a Corporation dinner at Commencement, be applied to the relief of the indigent scholars in the Class: a Committee was chosen to collect the money on or before the 18th. of next June, after which the meeting was dissolved. I pass'd this evening at Freeman's chamber.

26TH.

The weather was fair this forenoon, and Mr. Williams gave us a lecture, upon the nature, reflection, and refrangibility of light. Took a long walk this evening after prayers. Sever spent the evening at my chamber.

Nathaniel Shepard Prentiss[1] of Charlestown, will be 21, the 7th. of next August. He is a pretty good speaker, but as a scholar he is not conspicuous; notwithstanding his age, his countenance and his manners have a puerility, which indicates a boy, rather than a man: his disposition however is good: he has none of those distinguished traits of character, which bespeak a man extraordinary, whether in a good, or in an evil sense. His abilities are such as may carry him through the world with decency, if fortune should not be unfriendly; but he never will be a Cromwell nor an Hampden.

[1] Prentiss, sometimes spelled Prentice, practiced medicine in Marlborough, Mass., and from 1801 in Roxbury, Mass., where he combined the role of doctor with that of principal of the grammar school. He also served as town clerk and town representative in the General Court (Harrington, *Hist. Harvard Medical School,* 1:193–194).

27TH.

Attended Mr. Hilliard, the whole day: he preach'd in the afternoon a Charity Sermon, and a contribution was made, for the benefit of the unfortunate sufferers, at the late fire in Boston. There was a scandalous stamping, by some of the students, at the time of singing. Such conduct must always bring disgrace upon the University itself.

Samuel Putnam,[1] of Danvers, Essex C, was 20, the 13th. of this month. To the stature, he unites the manners and the behaviour of a boy: he is a pretty good speaker, but as a scholar he is extremely superficial: his vanity, which was puff'd up in the winter, by the allotment of an english Oration at an exhibition, has of late received considerable mortification. The circumstance, at the time surprized every one in the Class himself excepted, but the late allotment to him was a subject of astonishment to no one but himself. He sometimes proposes to pursue the study of the Law, and sometimes, to turn his attention to physic: and in this indecision as in all the rest of his conduct, he exhibits the weakness and instability of his mind. Unless years bring wisdom to him, he can never make a respectable figure in life.

[1] Putnam eventually decided to study law, but went to Judge Theophilus Bradbury's office in Newburyport, for Parsons' was full. There JQA noted that "he is not exempt from that puerility which I mentioned as constituting his character," a reference to this earlier character sketch, but was "more pleased with him than I was while we were classmates." Putnam opened his law office in Salem, married into the Pickering family, served as state senator from Essex co., and judge of the state supreme court from 1814 to 1842 (Elizabeth Cabot Putnam and Harriet Silvester Tapley, "Hon. Samuel Putnam, LL.D, A.A.S. ....," Danvers Historical Society, *Historical Collections,* 10 [1922]: 1–5, 13–15; entry for 5 April 1788, below).

28TH.

I wrote off my piece for Commencement this forenoon, and carried it to Mr. Reed for his examination: and henceforth I believe I shall be very idle till Commencement. Having got through the business of my theses, and being prepared for the important day, I shall now be at leisure, and shall attend in some measure to my health which has been in a declining state for this twelve-month; a sedentary life, and the little exercice which I have used, have been attended with their usual consequences, and now my principal business, will be to recruit.[1] Mr. Pearson gave us a lecture this afternoon, in which he attempted to prove the non-existence of complex ideas.

[1] To recover one's health and vigor (*OED*).

29TH.

The junior's, this forenoon read a forensic in the chapel, upon the question, whether the soul be material: I pass'd the whole day, in indolence, and amusement. Pass'd the evening with Fiske at Mr. Hilliard's. Mr. Reed and Mr. Ware were there.

Isaac Rand, of Cambridge, was 18 the 8th. of this month. He has been if common fame may be believed very idle and dissipated. As he lives not in College, I have had no opportunity to become much acquainted with him. His disposition I believe is very good, and his natural abilities are not despicable: his youth may be an excuse for his levity; and every one has not even that.

30TH.

Election day. About two thirds of the Students went to Boston. Those of us who remain'd pass'd the day, in amusement; I was at Cranch's chamber the whole day. The Sophimore Class with their civil Officers at the head march'd in procession to the Hall, and as soon as they came in a pistol was fir'd by their governor. The same ceremony was repeated after commons were over. In the evening they were at Thomas's chamber, much intoxicated and very noisy. Dr. Jennison paid them a visit at nine o'clock, and sent them all to their chambers.

31ST.

The Sophimores are very fearful that their yesterday's conduct has brought them into difficulties. Mr. Reed, who found his door broken through, when he return'd from Boston, is very much incensed and will probably, take measures to discover the persons who offered the insult. Mr. Williams gave us a lecture upon a number of optical instruments. I trifled away this day.

John Sever[1] of Kingston, Plymouth C, was 21 the 7th. of this month: His genius is very good; but he is destitute of all moral principles; and he has ever been remarkable for dissipation and disregard to the laws of the University: he is however ambitious of ruling and had when he first came to college so great influence, that he led the Class as he pleased: his imprudence has since that made him as unpopular as any individual in the Class.

[1] Sever after graduation returned to Kingston, where he became a merchant (*Columbian Centinel,* 19 Nov. 1803).

FRIDAY JUNE 1ST. 1787.

At 11, we had another lecture upon the optical instruments; the solar microscope,[1] the telescope, the cylindric mirror,[2] and the magic lantern came under consideration; we should have seen likewise the camera obscura, but the Clouds overshadowed the Sun so much, that the effect could not take place. I carried down my part to the president, for approbation: was not quite so indolent the whole day, as I have been two days past.

[1] The solar microscope was mounted on a window shutter and used in a darkened room; a mirror reflecting sunlight through the instrument projected the image of the specimen on the wall (David P. Wheatland and I. Bernard Cohen, *A Catalogue of Some Early Scientific Instruments at Harvard University Placed on Exhibition in the Edward Mallinckrodt Chemical Laboratory, February 12, 1949,* Cambridge, 1949, p. 31).

[2] Probably an anamorphoscope, or semicircular mirror. When purposefully distorted drawings were viewed through the mirror, they appeared regular and properly proportioned. The instrument was used for demonstration rather than practical purposes (David P. Wheatland, *The Apparatus of Science at Harvard, 1765–1800,* Cambridge, 1968, p. 124–125).

2D.

This day the government met, upon the subject of the disorders of which the Sophimores were guilty, last Wednesday. I was examined, but could give no information, upon the subject. Wilson is in sad terrors, and will I think probably come under censure: I past an hour or two with Mr. Ware, this evening after prayers.[1]

Solomon Vose[2] of Milton, Suffolk C, was 20 the 22d. of February; a vain, envious, malicious, noisy, stupid fellow, as ever disgraced God's Creation; without a virtue to compensate for his Vices, and without a spark of genius to justify his arrogance; possessing all the scurrility of a cynic with all the baseness of a coward

A Dog in forehead, but in heart a deer.

A soul callous to every sentiment of benevolence, and incapable of receiving pleasure, but from the pain of another. This severity of description is not dictated merely by personal resentment: he has done all in his power to injure me it is true, but his attempts have been made with the concealed, poisoned arrows of dastardly envy, not with the open arms of a generous enemy: independent however of every selfish sentiment I cannot help despising him, and his injuring me, has only added a sentiment of aversion, which I never will disguise.[3]

[1] Written later in JQA's more mature hand, enclosed in parentheses, and placed just before the sketch of Vose is "carried too far."

[2] Vose studied law and set up his practice at Northfield, Mass.; in 1805 he moved to Augusta, Maine (Albert K. Teele, *The History of Milton, Mass., 1640 to 1887*, Boston, 1887, p. 511).

[3] Written at the end of the entry in a different hand and encircled: "rather warm John." This was possibly written by CA, who not only roomed with JQA but also had a history "of prying into, and meddling with things which are nothing to him" (entries for 27 July 1786, and 17 Jan. 1787, above).

3D.

Attended meeting in the forenoon. Sacrament day: I went to dine at Judge Dana's: soon after I got there, he was taken ill, and thought it was with his old disorder. He sent immediately to Boston, for Doctor Lloyd,[1] and Dr. Danforth;[2] and for Dr. Jennison at College. We rubb'd him with a flesh brush, and with blankets, for two hours without intermission: he recover'd and the Physicians supposed this attack was only the consequence of a cold which he has caught. It rain'd hard all the afternoon, and evening. I remain'd at Mr. Dana's and lodg'd there.

[1] Dr. James Lloyd, a popular and successful Boston physician trained in London, who maintained strong loyalist sympathies and ties during the war as well as warm friends among Boston whigs; his son James was one of JQA's classmates (Sibley-Shipton, *Harvard Graduates,* 12:184–193).

[2] Dr. Samuel Danforth, another popular Boston physician, who also had maintained tory views, albeit less outspoken, and served as president of the Massachusetts Medical Society, 1795–1798 (same, 14:250–254).

4TH.

The judge was much better this morning. At 11 o'clock I came up to College. Mr. Williams closed his course, with a lecture upon astronomy. He finished with an affectionate farewell to the Class, advising them to carry into life the spirit of Philosophy, which was the spirit of business: a spirit which could not fail to make useful members of Society. I return'd and dined at Mr. Dana's. Pass'd part of the afternoon there, and just before college[1] came up to college again.

John Jones Waldo,[2] of Boston will be 19 the 15th. of September. He has had his education till within these two or three years in England, and seems to pride himself upon his european acquisitions. He has seldom associated much with any of the Class, which some have attributed to haughty arrogance, and some to an independent disposition. His talents, natural and acquired, are very good but he has not always improved his time to the best purpose. He is not popular throughout the Class, but has one enthusiastic admirer, whose name is among the first in the Class. Waldo, at the latter end of the last quarter obtain'd leave to be absent from that time till Commencement, as he wished to embark soon, for Europe; and he has not appeared, this quarter.

[1] Thus in MS.
[2] Waldo was later a merchant in Bordeaux (John J. Waldo to JQA, 10 April 1797, Adams Papers).

5TH.

This morning after Commons we had a meeting of the ΦBK, at Cranch's chamber: We began by admitting the junior's Grosvenor, Gardner and Barron, after which the performances for the day came on; I read the following Essay.

> A Maid unask'd, may own, a well-plac'd flame,
> Not loving first, but loving wrong is shame.

This proposition, though it be strictly true, will not obtain the assent of mankind in general. Very few persons, can so far overcome the prejudices of Education, as to think that a young lady of strict virtue and chastity, can, with propriety make the first advances in what is term'd courtship: but if we submit the Question to the judgment of Reason, it will perhaps be found that the opinion of the generality of mankind is erroneous and unjust.

Let us take a view of the situation of the female sex, with respect to man, which is nearly the same, in all the civilized nations on Earth: they are taught that it is their duty, to submit implicitly to the will of their lord: this is but reasonable; he is bound to protect and defend them: and his mental and bodily

233

strength is so much superior, that he may with propriety claim the right of commanding: But this is only one point among many, in which they are made sensible of their inferiority: they are always told that their studies should be confined to domestic life, that their science should be to take care of their families, that they should never aspire to any distinctions, military, civil, or even literary, that they should deny themselves frequently, the pleasures of society, and in short that they were made scarcely for any thing else, but nursing children, and keeping an house in order. This too if it were not carried to an extreme would be reasonable: but this is not all. From their childhood, they have the idea inculcated in their minds, that honour, virtue, reputation, and in short every thing good and great with respect to them is comprized in chastity: they are led to suppose that a woman if she has only such a command over her passions, as to resist all the temptations that assail her chastity, she is then perfect, though her disposition be ever so bad: and that, however numerous the good qualities of a female may be, they can be accounted for nothing, if she has not chastity. Now if the real virtue was inculcated, if the chastity of the mind could be taught them, the System might be justified: but this, is scarcely attended to. The purity of the Body is considered as all, and if a woman preserves that, she claims esteem and respect, though her mind, should be corruption itself. From this System has arisen the maxim, that no woman should first disclose an affection for a man. Now if we reflect, that the female sex, is form'd with a deeper sensibility, and with warmer passions than the other; that the power of those passions is not weakened by the pursuits of an active life, that the retirement from the hurry and bustle of business increases them, and suffers them to prey with more violence upon the heart, and that nature, as well as the laws of society obliges them to be collected and fixed on one object, is it not most absurd, unnatural and cruel to condemn them to silence and to deprive, a young woman even of the small satisfaction of expressing those feelings which are so deeply imprinted on the heart? The sexes were created the one for the other. Nature has made an union between them equally necessary to both: but a number of circumstances arising from society, concur in making the necessity greater on the female side.

A Man is always able to support himself: he can go through life honourably by means of his own industry, nor does he (comparatively speaking) require the assistance of others: but a woman, whatever her station in life, may be, is still a dependent being. She must trust either in a parent, or an husband, for protection and support. The latter must be preferred because she is enabled to return the obligations she is laid under and acquit herself of the debt: but a father's care, she cannot repay; and the dependence must consequently be greater and more burdensome: add to this that an old maid is despised and neglected by all the world: she no longer possesses those charms, which formerly had engaged the affections of men; nor can she command respect for being of service to the world. A married woman, who has a family lays society under obligations to her by bearing and educating her Children: she fulfills the design of the great author of nature: but an unmarried woman, is a mere dead weight upon the community; she must be maintained; and yet she cannot be useful to Society. Most women are sensible of this, and the male part of mankind, are all united in the opinion: but a man is not the less respected for being unmarried. He can serve his friends, or his country equally well, and perhaps better; he has many other inducements to continue single, and few that engage him to marriage. Is it not therefore consistent with reason and justice, that the fair sex should have a right to express the tender passions, of which they are so susceptible? And if so, the customs of most Nations in this respect are erroneous, and it would be the duty of a wise legislator, to establish a more equitable System.

Cranch and Fiske read a disputation, on the Question, "Whether Agriculture or Commerce, should be most cultivated in this Country." Mr. Abbot, and Mr. Ware, disputed ex tempore on the same subject. After this we proceeded, to choose, according to Law, two anniversary orators. Thomson was chosen for the first, and Freeman for the other. We then chose Barron for secretary, and Abbot for treasurer from the junior Class; to serve till the 5th. of September. A committee was appointed to examine the books of the treasurer and secretary. Adams 3d., Clarke, and Phillips, were ballotted, for admission, and the votes in their favour were finally unanimous. After being assembled more than two hours, the meeting, was adjourn'd for a fortnight, and I went with Mr. Andrews to Judge Dana's. Return'd and dined at College, and pass'd the afternoon in Clarke's chamber.

6TH.

Past the day at Judge Dana's. It rain'd almost all day. Miss Peggy Wigglesworth was there; amiable as usual. Mrs. Dana read some pages in the sorrows of Werter.[1] Women are better judges of sentiment than men: the ladies were pleased with parts of these letters, which to me appeared very trifling. The arguments in favour of suicide, are sophistical; and subtile, but when well examined, they must appear false: as all arguments that can be brought in favour of this unnatural crime ever must.

Francis Welch[2] of Plastow in New Hampshire was 21 the 31st of last month. His talents are not striking, and his mind is contracted. His disposition is very unamiable, and his heart is not good. Envy of the worst kind has established her dominion in his breast, and her snakes appear to play around his head. His eye, is the eye of the basilisk, and his every feature expresses the base passions which reign in his soul. His disposition renders him miserable, and cannot fail to make unhappy all those who are connected with him.

[1] Johann Wolfgang von Goethe, *The Sorrows of Werther,* transl. Daniel Malthus, 2 vols., London, 1779, and subsequent English translations; first published in German in 1774.

[2] Welch became minister of the West Parish, Amesbury (later Merrimac), Mass. (William Prescott, "Philip Welch of Ipswich, Ms., and His Descendants," *NEHGR,* 23:421 [Oct. 1869]).

7TH.

North-east winds, still chill the blood, and with a dull cold principle affect our spirits. This evening, immediately after prayers, the Marti-mercurean band paraded; the members belonging to our Class appeared for the last Time. They performed the manual exercices, and the different evolutions, very well. Supp'd at Bradish's with Bridge and Foster: the former has obtained leave to be absent at Commencement, and expects to go, in a few days: more than twenty of our class are already gone.

Otis, Upham and Wilson were admonished yesterday morning.

8TH.

Took books from the library for the last time. I took Mason's Poems and Abbadie, upon the truth of the Christian religion.[1] This afternoon the president returned me, my part for Commencement! I feel quite low-spirited, at seeing my Class-mates falling off, one by one: we shall never meet again, all together; and these youthful scenes which now are so delightful, will soon be remembered, with sensations of mingled pain and pleasure. Here void of every care, enjoying, every advantage, for which my heart could wish, I have past my time, without the perplexities with which life is surrounded, here without the avocations of business or the hurry of affairs, I have pursued those studies, to which my inclination led me. Soon, too soon I shall be obliged to enter anew upon the stage of general Society on which I have already met with disgust, and which with satisfaction I quitted. These disagreeable reflections haunt me continually and imbitter the last days, of my college life.

Leonard White of Haverhill was 20 the 3d. of last month. As I lived at Haverhill some time, and as he Chums with my cousin, I was acquainted with him before I came to the University, and have been very intimate with him since: his natural abilities without being very great, are such as will enable him to go through life with honour, and his disposition is amiable. His virtues are numerous, but among them all modesty is the most conspicuous. I never knew any other person so intimately as I am acquainted with him, without having perceived in him some sparks of Vanity: but I believe he never experienced the feeling. A remarkable neatness of person is likewise one of his characteristics, and is the more extraordinary because he has so few imitators here. He has so much candor[2] that I never heard him speak ill of any one of his Class-mates, and very seldom of any one: his defects are only trivial foibles, and he will certainly be an useful member of Society.

[1] Jacques Abbadie, *A Vindication of the Truth of Christian Religion, Against the Objections of All Modern Opposers . . .*, transl. H[enry] L[ussan], 2d edn., 2 vols., London, 1694 (Harvard, *Catalogus Bibliothecae*, 1790, p. 151).
[2] Freedom from malice (*OED*).

9TH.

This morning the president returned my theses to transcribe a fair copy for the press. I past the day at Judge Dana's. Mr. W. Ellery is there: his first address is certainly not in his favour. He talks too much about Newport; and our State, and his State; First impressions if they are not favourable, should not be attended to; but unless I am much mistaken this gentleman, is very far from being either a Statesman, or an hero. The wind has finally quitted its corner in the east, and this day has been fair, with two or three showers.

10TH.

Attended meeting all day. Mr. Burr, preach'd two very good sermons. Dined at Mr. Dana's, in Company with Mr. Parsons of Newbury-Port: a man of great wit, as well as of sound judgment and deep learning.[1]

I was at Mr. Wigglesworth's in the evening with Beale; but Peggy was not at home.

The weather has been very warm this day. The thermometer was at 83.

[1] After graduation, JQA studied law with Parsons in Newburyport.

11TH.

A very warm day. I loitered away my time, as I have, every day for these three weeks.

Classmates dropping off. Very few will be left by the 21st. This evening the sodality went serenading and at 3 in the morning they play'd in our entry.

Richard Whitney[1] of Petersham, Worcester C, was 20, the 23d. of last February. His circumstances are low and he will find it very difficult to get through College; this situation distresses him, and affects his spirits: notwithstanding which his native humour, and his originality of genius, frequently break out; and appear conspicuous. I am fond of his character because there is some thing new in it: he has manners and ideas of his own, and does not keep forever in the old and beaten track; the generosity of his soul is admired, although it is cramped by poverty. His heart is benevolent and his disposition is amiable. As a scholar, the disadvantages under which he has laboured have prevented him from appearing to so great advantage, as he would if he could have spent all the time here, since his admission. As a speaker I know but little what improvements he has made; for he has been so much absent that I never heard him declaim but once.

[1] Whitney, the son of Dr. Ephraim Whitney, whose strong tory sympathies apparently led to the confiscation of his property. Young Whitney became a lawyer in Brattleboro, Vt., and served as clerk of the Vermont House of Representatives, 1793–1797, and secretary to the governor and council (Frederick Clifton Pierce, *De-*

scendants of John Whitney, Chicago, 1895, p.
81; Zadock Thompson, *History of Vermont,
Natural, Civil, and Statistical . . .*, Burling-
ton, 1842, pt. 2, p. 118; *Records of the Governor and Council of the State of Vermont*, 8
vols., Montpelier, 1873–1880, 5:92).

12TH.

Went to Boston this morning with Bridge, Cranch, White and
Whitney in the stage. I attended the debates in the house of representatives; they were debating upon the subject of the instructions to the different members. I dined at Mr. Jackson's, with
Mr. Lowell,[1] and Mr. Brimmer. They conversed much upon gar-
dening.

At half past 6 in the evening we return'd to Cambridge, and
past the evening at Cranch's chamber.

[1] John Lowell, former member of the congress and a judge on its Court of Appeals in
Cases of Capture, 1783–1789. Later he was United States district court judge for Massachusetts (Sibley-Shipton, *Harvard Graduates*, 14:650–661).

13TH.

Mr. Wigglesworth gave a lecture this forenoon, but I did not
attend; engaged the chief of the time in writing off my theses:
read Mason's Caractacus, and was much pleased with it. I think
he has made it more interesting than his Elfrida. The Catastrophe it is true is not more tragical; but the speech of the Chorus
which closes the Poem of Elfrida, is cold and inanimate, and that
of Caractacus is noble and pathetic.[1]

Weather very fine and warm, all day.

[1] William Mason, "Caratacus. A Dramatic Poem: Written on the Model of the Ancient
Greek Tragedy" and "Elfrida. A Dramatic Poem: Written on the Model of the Ancient
Greek Tragedy" (*Poems*, London, 1764, p. [169]–289, [75]–168; Harvard, *Catalogus Bib-
liothecae*, 1790, p. 142).

14TH.

Return'd a copy of my theses to the president, who informed
me, that they would all be ready to send to Boston in a day or
two. Cranch and Amory, and Beale, went over to Mystic with
Learned, who took his final leave of College.

The weather was very warm all day; but in the evening, a
beautiful thunder shower refreshed the air very greatly. Pass'd
the evening at Foster's chamber.

15TH.

A warm day, but the air has been much more pure, than for several days past. Yesterday Mr. Dana set off for Newport where he proposes tarrying till after Commencement. Drank tea with Bradbury, and my Chum, at Mr. Williams's. After tea, we walk'd with the young ladies. Jenny has been handsome, but at the age of nineteen she has lost all her beauty, and must henceforth charm only by the sweetness of her disposition: after returning from our walk, we past a couple of hours there, chatting, and singing songs, after which we retired.

16TH.

Charles went to Boston this morning, and return'd at night. After prayers I went with Cranch to Mr. Williams's. We walk'd with the young Ladies. Miss Frazier from Boston[1] was of the party: she appears sensible and agreeable. We went and viewed Mr. Brattle's gardens, and ponds and other conveniences,[2] which his ingenuity has invented for the gratification of his sensuality. This man, who enjoys an handsome estate has pass'd his whole life in studying how to live; not in a moral but in a physical sense. The ladies were disappointed when they found he had very few flowers in his garden, but it was observ'd that he was so much engaged in the service of his palate, that he could have no leisure to give his attention to any one sense in particular.

After we return'd to College I pass'd the remainder of the evening at Cranch's chamber.

Samuel Willard[3] of Stafford in Connecticut, will be 21 the 26th. of next December. He was about two years and an half at Dartmouth college, and entered at this University, about a fortnight after me. He has never been much used to what is called genteel company, and is somewhat awkward in his address, which sometimes makes him an object of merriment among his satirical class-mates. His genius is not of the first rate, and his acquirements are not very extensive; he is said how ever to be a very good mathematical scholar: and in the languages he is not deficient. If he is not in wit, a man, he may at least be said to be, in "simplicity a child." Mediocrity is his sphere and will ever remain so.

[1] Perhaps Rebecca, the only unmarried daughter of Boston merchant Nathan Frazier (Thwing Catalogue, MHi).

[2] The estate of loyalist William Brattle, JA's newspaper antagonist in the early 1770s, was willed to his son, Maj. Thomas Brattle. The house still stands on Brattle St., just up from the square. The father's death in 1776 improved the title, but Thomas, then a refugee in England, was formally proscribed and the estate was confiscated in 1778. After six years' effort he regained title. His interest in horticulture aroused during his stay in England, Brattle planted his spacious grounds, which extended to the Charles River, with flowers and fruit trees and had a small pond, shaded by willows, stocked with fish. For the benefit of Harvard students he laid out a long walk bordered with trees and built a bathing house on the river, where students might learn to swim (Paige, *Hist. of Cambridge, Mass.,* p. 170, 203; Sibley-Shipton, *Harvard Graduates,* 14:568–572; "Old Cambridge and New," *NEHGR,* 25:233 [July 1871]).

[3] Willard, the nephew of President Willard, afterward studied medicine and practiced in Stafford (Joseph Willard and Charles Wilkes Walker, *Willard Genealogy: Sequel to Willard Memoir,* ed. Charles Henry Pope, Boston, 1915, p. 46, 176–177).

17TH.

Attended meeting all day. Mr. Hilliard preach'd us two good occasional sermons from Proverbs II. 3. 4. 5. If thou criest after knowledge, and liftest up thy voice for understanding. If thou seekest her as silver, and searchest for her as for hid treasures: Then shalt thou understand the fear of the Lord; and find the knowledge of God. The Sciences were his topic, and the importance of learning, his theme in the afternoon, he said he should omit the address which he usually makes to the young gentlemen about to leave the University, because so many of the present senior Class were already gone; he paid us however an handsome compliment upon the uniform propriety of conduct which had ever distinguished the Class, and concluded by exhorting the following Classes to imitate so laudable an example.

I wrote a letter this evening to Freeman;[1] in answer to one which I receiv'd from him yesterday.

[1] JQA to Nathaniel Freeman Jr., 16–[17] June (owned in 1963 by H. Bartholomew Cox, of Maryland); Freeman's letter has not been found.

18TH.

Took a long walk with Cranch this afternoon.

Foster took charge of the theses and of my letter, and promised to deliver them to Mr. Freeman in Boston.

I went with Amory, Cranch, Mason, and White and supped at Bradish's. They pass'd the remainder of the evening with me.

19TH.

This forenoon Mr. Cranch pass'd through here on his way to Boston. We are to return to Braintree in the chaise. Billy went with his father to Boston, and brought back the Chaise this evening. The idea of leaving College threw me into a train of gloomy and disagreeable reflections; which however in the evening were dissipated by conversation.

Samuel Williams of Cambridge, son to our professor of Mathematics, and natural Philosophy, will be 17 the 6th. of next Octr. His being introduced so young into the world has been essentially injurious to him. An immoderate share of Vanity appears to be one of the characteristics of this family, and Sam, appears more particularly influenced by this passion. His vanity is so extensive that it not only inspires him with a great admiration for his useful abilities whether natural or acquired, (and of these he has no great reason to be vain) but he likewise descends to self approbation upon every trivial, and even useless accomplishment. He is so fond of hearing himself talk that he seldom suffers any one with whom he is [in] conversation to say much; and yet I do not recollect ever hearing him discourse, unless he himself was his theme,

"And *I* the little hero of each tale."

Of his genius he does not talk often, and only by modest hints: of his knowledge, he gives information by telling what he has done; his spirit he discovers by relating, how many times he has insulted the president and the tutors, particularly Mr. Read, and by declaring how he would have treated such a fellow, if he had received such an insult from him, as another fellow did, without resenting it. He values himself much upon drinking hard, and never getting drunk, but at shooting, wrestling, playing ball, and boxing he supposes himself perfectly irresistible. He damns Mr. Read, for being partial towards those, who have always treated him with respect, and against those, who have always made it a practice to insult him: and he knows the president has a personal pique against him: his opinions change like the wind, and he adopts affections and aversions, equally without knowing why or wherefore. I have at different times heard him express the most exalted ideas, of *Bridge, Little, Barron, Freeman, Lloyd* and *Cranch;* and at other times I have heard him speak with perfect contempt of the same persons, the last excepted. In short he has not yet any fix'd principles; and untill he has, he never will be a respectable character.

20TH.

The weather was extremely warm: I had a long contest with Johnson, in the barber's shop. We finally agreed to drop the subject: for we were perswaded that we should each retain his own sentiments let the dispute be ever so long. Williams, Mason, and Cranch were at my chamber till commons' time: in the afternoon I pack'd up some of my things. As Mr. Read had desired, that those of the Class who should still be here, might stop in the chapel after prayers this evening, we determined to wait and hear his address. He had committed it to memory: it was friendly, and contained some very good advice. Soon after we came out; Cranch and I set off for Braintree, where we arrived at about 10 o'clock.

It is not without many melancholy reflections that I bid a last adieu to the walls of Harvard! The scenes through which I have past since my entrance at the university have been for the most part agreeable, I have formed an intimacy, with a number of amiable and respectable characters of my own age, and with dispositions corresponding to my own. I have never once regretted, but have frequently rejoyced that I left Europe, to come and pass a twelve-month here. It has been productive of very good effects; particularly, in reducing my opinion of myself, of my acquirements, and of my future prospects, nearer to the level of truth and reality. I hope, that in two or three years more, I shall have taken down, without any violence, all the elegant castles which my imagination had built in the air, over my head, and which for want of a foundation, were liable, to be overset, and crush the builder, if any accident had happened. And I believe that even now, (making allowance, for a little vanity, which has frequently been flattered,) I do not exaggerate my prospects, more than other young people of my age, and circumstances, do.

21ST.

This is the day, when our Class should by rights, have quitted college; but they have been dropping off by degrees, these three weeks, so that there were not left more than three or four to go away, to-day. For my own part I have been dull and low spirited; the whole day. We took a walk this evening with the two young ladies.

22D.

My Cousins went in the morning down to Mrs. Quincy's, and in the afternoon to Milton. I remain'd at home all day. The young folks did not return till after ten this evening. I idle away my time here, pretty much as I did the last three weeks at College: nothing to do; eating drinking and sleeping are the chief of my employments.

23D.

Mr. Cranch and Dr. Tufts came from Boston this afternoon. The Dr. informs me, that Mr. Parsons, has agreed to receive me; and consequently I expect to go in August or September, to Newbury Port. The papers mention the death of young Sullivan who graduated last year: this is another victim added to the millions that have been destroy'd by debauchery. He was not yet 19, and had been blest by nature with a very good genius; but the fashionable vices, (not of this age in particular, but of all ages) have cut him down, in the early dawn of life, and have laid in the dust, the head which wisdom might have inspired, the heart which patriotism, might have animated, and the tongue upon which Eloquence might have dwelt.

24TH.

Attended meeting all day. Mr. Shuttlesworth preach'd; I was much better pleased with him, than I had expected to be. His language is not perfectly correct, nor his stile remarkably accurate; but his delivery is agreeable, and his composition cannot be called bad. I was much pleased with his manner of praying. I walk'd with Mr. Cranch and his son, this evening, and ascended the highest hill within several miles. We had a view of the harbour, the sea, and the cluster of islands, which are spread about thick in the bay; the prospect is beautiful: but a prospect pleases only for a few moments, and affords no satisfaction to a man, when it has once lost its novelty: near the top of this hill, we found a living spring, which it is said, in the driest Seasons, is always supplied with water. Mr. Cranch started doubts concerning the common theory, by which this phenomenon of springs is accounted for: it does not perfectly satisfy him: and indeed I think his objections very just.

25TH.

My Cousin and his mamma, went to Milton this afternoon. I went to see my Grandmamma. Miss N. Quincy, was here when I return'd: she proposes passing the week here. Two thousand pound, and an amiable disposition have not yet married her. It is strange how some girls, without either fortune, beauty, or any amiable qualities, have a talent at engaging a man's affections, so as to escape, the name of an old maid, which next to death is most dreaded by a female: and yet others with every qualification of the heart, which could promise happiness to an husband, with sense, and fortune, are forced to enter the ridiculous sisterhood; but there is no accounting for the opinions and caprices of mankind; they must be taken as they are; for better, for worse.[1]

I read the beggar's Opera,[2] this evening, for the first time. ... did not admire it.

[1] In 1790 Nancy married Rev. Asa Packard, minister at Marlborough, Mass. (Joseph Allen, *The Worcester Association and Its Antecedents: A History of Four Ministerial Associations: The Marlborough, The Worcester (Old), the Lancaster, and the Worcester (New) Associations ...,* Boston, 1868, p. 114–116). After Nancy's marriage, which, according to JQA, "blasted even before the bud" AA's *darling* project for the advancement" of her eldest son, JQA refined his ideas on the role of fortune in a prospective bride. Your son "never will be indebted," he wrote to his mother, "to his wife for his property. I once seriously thought that I should easily be enabled to make matrimony an instrument of my Avarice or my Ambition. But really it is not so, and I am fully persuaded like Sancho, that if it should rain *mitres* in this way, there would be never an one to fit my head" (JQA to AA, 14 Aug. 1790, Adams Papers).

[2] John Gay, *The Beggar's Opera,* London, 1728.

26TH.

Mr. and Mrs. Boyes [Boies] with Miss Lucy, came over and dined here. After dinner we went to Squantum, to Mr. Beale's:[1] there was a large company. Mr. and Mrs. Woodward, Mr. A. Alleyne, and his mother, Mrs. Quincy, Mr. Woodbridge and his Sister from Salem, with Miss Robertson and Miss Peale. Miss Woodbridge is called very handsome, but her features are too regular: She has a very fine set of teeth, which every body must know who has ever seen her. She appears sociable, and of an open, frank disposition. Miss Robertson, would not generally be called so handsome, nor has she so amiable a countenance; but her complexion is still fairer, and there is an expression in her features which the other wants. She wears a small patch of court-plaister on her cheek, which has a pretty effect. But, when I see a patch of this kind, on a Lady's cheek, I consider it as I do a brand on a man's forehead; the one convinces me that the man is a rogue; the other that the woman is a coquet; and I endeavour equally to avoid them. After tea we walk'd down to the chapel, form'd by the cavities between the summits of several sharp rocks. These rocks are broken off, so that the sea, bathes their foundation, and the perpendicular descent is not less I suppose than 50 feet. The perpendicular surface is not smooth, as at the cliffs of Dover, but craggy, and rather concave. The tops of the rocks are sharp and verge to a point. From this place, it is said, one of the female leaders of the indians, in former days, plunged into the sea, after the loss of a battle; preferring this death to captivity, like the bard of Snowdon.[2] But what foundation there may be for this tradition, I have never heard. After a pretty long ramble, we set out and return'd home, in the evening. Miss B. Apthorp, stopp'd for a few minutes at my uncles.

[1] Benjamin Beale, a merchant with trading interests in Liverpool, where he married and had a family. He was the father of JQA's classmate and later was JA's neighbor (Pattee, *Old Braintree and Quincy,* p. 241; AA2, *Jour. and Corr.,* 2:124).
[2] Probably a reference to Thomas Gray's Pindaric ode, *The Bard,* about the Welsh bard who jumped to his death rather than face execution at the hands of the conquering English (Thomas Gray, *Poetical Works of Mr. Gray,* new edn., London, 1785, p. 33–39, at MQA).

27TH.

Two Miss Greenleaf's[1] came here this forenoon, and still remain. Mr. Cranch went to Boston this morning. Mr. Weld and his lady, and Parson Wibird drank tea here, and we had a quantity of music in the evening.

[1] Probably Rebecca, who later married Noah Webster, the lexicographer, and Anna (Nancy), who married William Cranch, JQA's cousin, in 1795; they were daughters of William Greenleaf, the Boston merchant (James Edward Greenleaf, *Genealogy of the Greenleaf Family,* Boston, 1896, p. 218, 222).

28TH.

Took a long walk in the morning with my Cousin and the Ladies. When we return'd we found, my brother Charles, with

Mrs. Hillard and her daughter; who dined here, and return'd to Cambridge in the afternoon.

We all drank tea, at Mr. Apthorp's, and pass'd the evening there: this man is certainly a little crack-brain'd; his conversation, is ingenious, but he flies from one topic to another, with the utmost rapidity, and some of his speeches are extravagant. The least that can be said of him is that he is very singular, and between singularity and positive madness the distinction is but small.

29TH.

I intended to have gone to Cambridge this afternoon, but could not get an horse. My Cousin went and will return to-morrow night. Wrote a letter to my father.[1]

I do not relish this life of idleness and expectation. I am very desirous that Commencement should be over, and shall certainly, not feel easy, till then. And indeed after that, till I get settled at some business, I shall not be contented.

[1] JQA to JA, 30 June, which enclosed a copy of JQA's speech on law, given 10 April at Harvard (Adams Papers).

30TH.

Mr. Cranch and his son, return'd from Boston, this afternoon. Dr. Tufts stopp'd here on his way home. Mrs. Quincy drank tea here, and soon after went away with Nancy, who has pass'd the week here. Her mamma, has been so extremely careful to prevent her being a coquet, that she has in fact made a prude of her. If she should live to be an old maid, she will be terrible to all young ones. It is a pity, that it should be so difficult to avoid one extreme, without falling into its opposite.

Wrote a letter to my friend Bridge,[1] and read a little in Lord Bolingbroke's philosophical works.[2]

[1] Letter not found.
[2] *The Philosophical Works of the Late Right Honorable Henry St. John, Lord Viscount Bolingbroke*, 5 vols., London, 1754 (*Catalogue of JQA's Books*).

SUNDAY JULY 1ST. 1787.

Attended Mr. Wibird all day: in the afternoon, four children were baptised. We remain'd after meeting to hear the singing.

Read some of Bolingbroke's metaphysical speculation in the evening. Dull times.

2D.

Miss Betsey and her brother pass'd the afternoon at Mrs. Quincy's. I was quite indolent and idle almost all day.

I was walking alone in the church-yard, rambling through the grass which waves unmolested over the alternate hillock, and reading or endeavouring to read the inscriptions, which love and friendship have written on the simple monuments, which the indefatigable hand of Time, had nearly worn out, and as if envious even of their humble pretence to fame, had scatter'd over with moss. I was startled by a rustling noise, look'd round and saw a large snake, winding himself along between the bending blades. I pursued him, but he soon found his hole, into which he slip'd and escaped my pursuit. Was it the genius of the place? Or was it the guardian spirit of any one whose bones are here deposited? Yet methinks, if it were *a gentle spirit,* some more amiable shape than that of a serpent might have been assumed; some shape, which might engage the affections, and call forth the soft and pleasing passions.

3D.

At about 8 this morning I went set off with my Cousin, for Cambridge, where we arrived, just after 10. At 11 the exhibition began, with the Latin Oration by *Prescott.* It was upon the military art, and the composition appeared to be very good, but it was not very well deliver'd: this person indeed was never form'd for an Orator. This part was followed by a forensic disputation, upon the question, whether the conduct of mankind in general is much influenced by a prospect of future reputation? between *Grosvenor* and *Baxter.* The former appeared to much better advantage than his opponent. Both introduced perhaps more scripture than was necessary. The syllogistic dispute came on next by *Weld* respondent. *Bradbury, Churchill* and *Payne* opponents. The question was, whether the approbation of conscience makes any action virtuous. This was followed by the dialogue between *Haven* and *Thayer* both of which spoke very well. *Cutts* delivered the greek Oration and *Kirkland* the Hebrew, and both were approved; the literary performances closed with the English Oration, by *Gordon,* the subject was patriotism. It was well written, and well spoken; though he took rather too high a pitch of voice, and imitated Mr. Otis rather too much. An anthem was sung, and several pieces of music perform'd extremely well.

I dined with Mr. Andrews in company with a number of other gentlemen; among the rest several of his class mates. Cranch went over to Mystic, and pass'd the evening there, but as I had some business to transact I remain'd at Cambridge.

4TH.

Breakfasted with Forbes, and at ten o'clock set off for Boston in company with Clark: as soon as I got into town I went to the chapel, where Mr. Dawes was delivering the anniversary Oration;[1] but he had almost finished, when I got there. He closed very prettily: after which his ode to independence, set to music by Mr. Selby[2] was perform'd: from thence I went immediately to the old brick meeting house, where another Oration[3] was deliver'd by Genl. Brooks, for the Society of the Cincinnati. It was cautious and well guarded: but although the claws of the eagle may be concealed or withdrawn, they are always ready as a weapon to attack or to defend, whenever an opportunity shall present itself. After he had done, I went up to the common, in order to see the military parade. It is surprizing what a martial spirit has been raised in this capital within these twelve months; on the last anniversary of independence; a few undisciplined militia, with as many colours of dress as there were men, would scarcely have been collected; whereas this day, there appeared, no less than six independent companies besides a regiment of militia, all in their respective uniforms. They paraded and exercised on the common till four o'clock. It was three, before I went off, to dinner with Mr. E. Freeman. I was with him the greater part of the afternoon; saw the Companies again, who at about 5 o'clock, march'd down State street, and up again, with which they closed their exercices. I drank tea at Mr. Foster's and at seven o'clock, we mounted our horses, and return'd to Braintree: we got home just after nine.

[1] Thomas Dawes, *An Oration Delivered July 4, 1787, at the Request of the Inhabitants of the Town of Boston ...*, Boston, 1787. Dawes was a Boston lawyer (*Hist. of Suffolk County, Mass.*, 1:246).

[2] William Selby, British-born composer and organist at King's Chapel (David McKay, "William Selby, Musical Émigré in Colonial Boston," *Musical Quarterly*, 57:609–627 [Oct. 1971]).

[3] John Brooks, *An Oration, Delivered to the Society of the Cincinnati ...*, Boston, 1787.

5TH.

Mrs. Cranch and Miss Betsey, went to Boston this morning, and propose not to return till Saturday. I read partly through, Wraxall's tour into the northern parts of Europe[1] which is much inferior to Moore and Brydone.[2] These letters are full of incidents which however interesting they may have been to the author, are not so in the least, to the public. His observations appear very superficial, and such as any youth might naturally make at the age of 19. We were going to walk in the evening, but were called back by the arrival of Mr. Tufts, and Miss Lucy Jones.[3] They stay'd however but about a quarter of an hour, and proceeded to Weymouth.

[1] Nathaniel William Wraxall, *Cursory Remarks Made in a Tour through Some of the Northern Parts of Europe . . .*, London, 1775.

[2] Patrick Brydone, *A Tour through Sicily and Malta . . .*, 2 vols., London, 1774 (Harvard, *Catalogus Bibliothecae*, 1790, p. 73).

[3] A niece of Cotton Tufts, who later married Joshua Cushman, one of JQA's classmates (Henry Wyles Cushman, *A Historical and Biographical Genealogy of the Cushmans . . .*, Boston, 1855, p. 185).

6TH.

Finished Wraxall's tour, and am confirm'd in the opinion I had formed of it: the poor young man, is really to be pitied, when the tenderness of his heart, is always ready to overflow at the sight of a female. His great ardor in the pursuit of knowledge is very laudable, and would be equally meritorious if he had not said so much of it.

The weather was extremely warm.

Miss Charlotte Apthorp came in the evening and pass'd a couple of hours here.

7TH.

Mrs. Cranch and Miss Betsey return'd from Boston this evening.

A ballad, founded on fact.[1]

Now ponder well, ye students sad,
   The words which I shall write,
The people of the town are mad,
   And ready for the fight.

250

T'was once upon a sabbath day
  A day, which you shall rue
That parson H——d² could not pray
  And laid the fault to you,

And when with melody of heart,
  The people rose to sing
A noise was heard from every part,
  Which made the Church to ring.

And, what can scarcely be believ'd
  Though I the truth attest
E'en Foxcroft's³ voice was scarce perceiv'd
  Discordant with the rest.

No wonder then his pious rage
  Burst forth into a flame,
He vow'd an holy war to wage,
  And Winthrop⁴ did the same.

Thus by the hand of mighty power
  Which good from evil draws,
Men who were ne'er devout before
  Espouse religion's cause.

"A seperation must ensue,
  Cries Winthrop all on fire,
Or I will surely quit my pew,
  And from the church retire

"What satisfaction can I reap
  From either pray'r or sermon
If I am thus bereft of sleep,
  By this audacious vermin."

"My voice, no longer will I raise"
  The worthy Foxcroft said
"The lord, no longer will I praise,
  If such a noise be made

"No more the accents of my tongue,
  Shall you, with rapture hear
No more the harmony of song
  Shall please the ravish'd ear."

"Oh spare, (cried Winthrop,) spare that threat
  For should it once, be known,
They soon would make a noise as great
  Or greater than your own.

"Refer the matter to the laws
  And I can surely find,
A Witness in the pious cause
  Just suited to my mind

"On any two that we shall name,
  The punishment must fall,
To save religion's injur'd fame
  Let them atone for all."

Yet after all, our pious friends,
  The people of the town,
Found they could not obtain their ends
  And laid the matter down.

A mountain once, as I am told,
  The pangs of child-birth felt,
Her moanings frighten'd young and old
  Who near the borders dwelt.

Full long the mountain had remain'd
  In this distressful plight,
And when her pains were at an end,
  A mouse was brought to light.

[1] Presumably this was written by JQA and is the piece to which he refers in his entry for 24 Jan. 1788 (below).
[2] Rev. Timothy Hilliard, minister of the First Church in Cambridge.
[3] John Foxcroft, a justice of the peace and county registrar of deeds, whose suspected sympathy for the British lost him his positions. Foxcroft continued to live in Cambridge a life of "luxurious idleness," and students remembered his loud voice while singing hymns and psalms in services at Hilliard's church (Sibley-Shipton, *Harvard Graduates,* 14:268–270).
[4] James Winthrop, the college librarian. On student antipathy toward Winthrop, see his sketch in the Descriptive List of Illustrations, No. 3.

8TH.

I did not attend meeting this day.

We had a thunder shower in the afternoon. Tired to death of living thus doing nothing. On many accounts I wish Commencement was over.

9TH.

Mr. and Mrs. Cranch went to Boston this morning, and re-turn'd in the evening.

Arose at 8 o'clock, breakfasted at 9; after which I loiter'd and rambled about till 1. Dined; after dinner, smoked a pipe; slept till 6. Drank tea: play'd upon the flute, and sung all the evening. Supped at 10. Went to bed.

This is my history at present: is it not an edifying manner of passing one's time.

10TH.

All the forenoon out, shooting birds. Much fatigued. At about three this afternoon, we had the smartest thundershower, that I have seen within these two years. Clear'd up again in the evening.

11TH.

This day completes my twentieth year: and yet I am good for nothing, and cannot even carry myself forward in the world: three long years I have yet to study in order to qualify myself for business: and then—oh! and then; how many more years, to plod along, mechanically, if I should live; before I shall really get into the world? Grant me patience ye powers! for I sicken, at the very idea: thus is one third of a long life employ'd in preparing to act a part during another third; and the last is to be past in rest and quiet waiting for the last stroke, which places us just where we were 70 years before. Vanity! Vanity! all is vanity and vexation of spirit.

12TH.

Mr. Cranch and his Son went to Boston this morning: my Cousin proposes to go this night to Cambridge, and return home to-morrow. For my own part I have spent my time this day as usual. I have even discarded thought, and live more like any of the domestic animals, than like a man.

13TH.

I found something to do, this forenoon, and have pass'd it with less tediousness, than any for several weeks.

Went over to Weymouth and dined with Doctor Tufts. Conversed with him upon a variety of subjects. Came away just after Sunset: I found the two Miss Apthorp's at my uncle's and my Cousin return'd, when I got home.

There was a bright northern light this evening.

14TH.

Went with my cousin in the forenoon to the meeting house, in order to exercice ourselves in speaking our pieces.

This evening, our classmate Willard came here from Cambridge, and proposes passing Sunday with us.

15TH.

I attended meeting the whole day, and heard Mr. Everett of Dorchester. He prays well and preaches good sermons, but is destitute of the smallest spark of animation. Willard after meeting went this evening to the upper parish, whence, he intends to return to Cambridge to-morrow morning.

16TH.

This morning at about 10 o'clock, in the midst of the rain, I mounted on horse-back and went to Cambridge: here I arrived at about half after twelve. Found several of my Class-mates already arrived: dined at Braddish's: after dinner I went to Freeman's chamber and found him and Little, both there. We went down to get the key of the meeting house; in order to speak our parts: we could not find a key: as we were returning to College, we met Mr. Pearson, near the meeting-house. He said he was just going to college to find some one of our Class upon a subject of some consequence, and desired us to go with him to his house. When we were there he told us, he had just heard that our classmate; Burge, was here last week, and inform'd the President he should not be able to pay his bills, nor should he come to Commencement. Mr. Pearson, said he felt particularly interested in the case of Burge, whose circumstances were peculiarly unfortunate, and who had formerly been one of his pupils; after premissing these, and several observations he finally told us, that if we would engage, to send for burge, and have him here before commencement, he would advance the money for the payment of his bills.

In the midst of a violent thunder shower we immediately went up to college, and endeavoured to discover, which direction Burge had taken when he went from here; but of this no-body could inform us: upon this Freeman gave up all further hopes and left us: but as soon as the shower was over I went with Little and endeavoured to find a person, who would undertake to go immediately to Hollis; where we think it probable that Burge is at present. Blake 1st. the Sophimore, finally agreed to go, and we immediately set about getting an horse: after some difficulty, we found one; and notwithstanding several other delays, Blake finally set off for Hollis at just 9 this evening: he has to go 45 miles, and then there is a chance, that he will not find Burge, who must be here within 36 hours, and have all his bills paid, in order to get his degree. The probability is not much in our favour: but any thing ought to be done, when there is a prospect of saving a classmate.

I was employ'd this evening in preparing for Commencement.

17TH.

Breakfasted and dined with Mr. Andrews, in company with Mr. Thomson, who is studying law, with Mr. Parsons.

Mr. and Mrs. Shaw were at our chamber this afternoon, and lodge in town to-night. Very busy all the afternoon and evening, till Mid-night, in preparing for Commencement. At about 7 o'clock Blake arrived here with Burge, after riding 90 miles in 22 hours: this success affords me inexpressible pleasure; the satisfaction I feel, in having been instrumental to save a worthy and unfortunate class-mate from losing a degree, would be sufficient to compensate for thrice the trouble and expence I have been at, in this case: happy should I be, if I were in a situation to relieve several other class-mates who are so much indebted that they have not the least prospect of paying their bills: four or five, I fear will fail.

WEDNESDAY JULY 18TH. COMMENCEMENT DAY.

At about 11 o'clock the procession began from the door of Harvard. The succeeding Classes went before us; and we preceded the President and fellows of the University, who, were follow'd

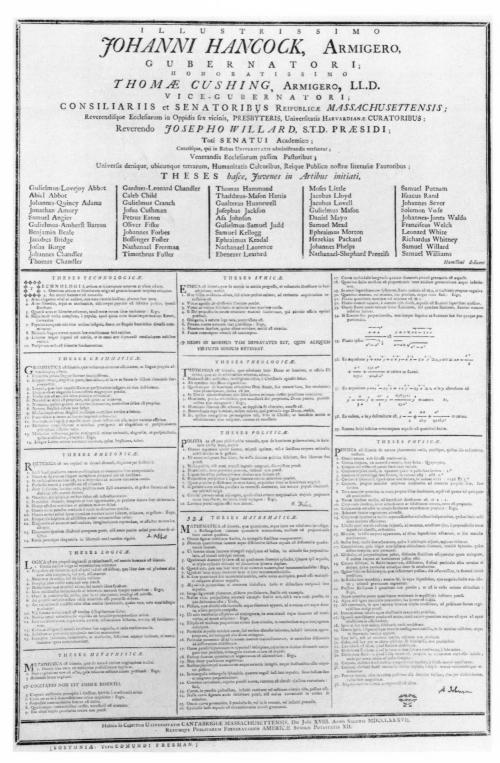

9. HARVARD THESES, 1787: THE THESES SHEET
See page xii

324 THESES MATHEMATICÆ.

M ATHEMATICA est scientia, quæ quantitates, atque inter eas relationes investigat.

1. Rectangulum duorum quorumvis numerorum, medium est proportionale inter eorum quadrata.

2. Omnes figuræ rectilineæ similes, de triangulis similibus componuntur.

3. Duarum quantitatum summæ atque differentiæ factum æquale est differentiæ quadratorum suorum.

4. Ut summa trium laterum trianguli cujusquam ad basim, ita altitudo sua perpendicularis, ad circuli inscripti radium.

5. Quadratum diametri sphæræ est ad quadratum diametri cylindri, sphæræ ipsi æqualis, ut tripla cylindri altitudo ad diametrum sphæræ duplam.

6. Quantitates, quæ non sunt inter se ut numerus numero, sunt incommensurabiles : Ergo,

7. Quadrati latus atque diameter inter se sunt incommensurabilia.

8. Si duæ quantitates sint incommensurabiles, nulla unius multiplex, potest esse multiplici cuiquam alterius æqualis.

9. Æqualium pyramidum et conorum isoscelium bases et altitudines reciproce sunt æquales.

10. Imago figurarum planarum, picturæ parallelarum, similis erit exemplo.

11. Nullus visus perspectivus accurate exemplo similis erit, nisi à vero visûs puncto, ex quo delineatus esset : Unde,

12. Pictura, quæ directo visa invenusta atque abnormis apparet, ad normam erit atque decora, a loco proprio conspecta.

13. Ut axis transversus ellipseos ad conjugatum, ita area circuli cujus diameter est transversus, ad aream ellipseos : Ergo,

14. Ellipsis est medium proportiona e inter duos circulos, in transversum atque conjugatum descriptos.

15. Parabolæ æquales eundem axem, sed vertices diversos habentes, infinite invicem appropinquant, sed nunquam alia aliam attingunt.

16. Parabolæ parameter est ad summam duarum semiordinatarum, ut earundem differentia ad differentiam abscissarum.

17. Omne parallelogrammum in hyperbola inscriptum, cujus latera duabus diametris conjugatis sunt parallela, rectangulo duorum axium est æquale.

18. Factum duarum quantitatum negativarum est affirmativum : Ergo,

19. Non datur quadratum negativum.

20. Radices plerumque numerorum neque numeris integris, neque fractionibus ullis exprimi possunt.

21. In triangulis rectangulis sphæricis, quorum anguli basi sunt æquales, sinus basium sunt ut tangentes perpendicularis.

22. Centrum curvationis, cujusve puncti curvæ, centrum est circuli ejusdem curvationis : Sed,

23. Curvæ, in punctis quibusdam, infinite curviores vel rectiores circulo ullo, possunt esse.

24. Nulla curva figuram arcûs describere potest, nisi radius curvationis in vertice fit infinitus.

25. Omnis curva geometrica, si producta fit, vel in se revertit, vel infinite procedit.

26. Cycloidis basis æqualis est curcumferentiæ circuli generantis.

27. Curvæ cycloidalis longitudo quatuor diametris circuli generantis est æqualis.

28. Quantitas finita medium est proportionale inter nihilum geometricum atque infinitatem.

29. In omni logarithmorum systemate, fluxio unitatis est $= 0$, et fractionis propriæ negativa.

30. Quantitas maxima, vel minima, nec prorsum, neque retro fluit : Ergo,

31. Fluxio quantitatis maximæ vel minimæ est $= 0$.

32. Fluxio numeri cujusive, à numero ipso divisa, æqualis est fluxioni logarithmi ejusdem.

33. Omnis fluens unam tantum habet fluxionem, sed quædam fluxiones, fluentes numero infinitas habent.

34. Si fluentes sint proportionales, non semper sequitur ut fluxiones suæ sint quoque proportionales.

35. Fluxio ipsius $\dfrac{x+a}{\overline{x^2-a^2}\,\big|^{\frac{1}{2}}}$ est $\dfrac{x+a\times\overline{\dot{x}+a\dot{x}}-2a\dot{x} \quad -\dot{x}^2}{x-a\times\sqrt{x^2-a^2}}$

36. Ex æquatione $y^3 + a\,\dot{x}\,x\,\dot{y} + a\,\dot{x}\,y - \dot{x}\,x - 2a\,\overset{\cdot\cdot\cdot}{x} = 0$, y crit $= ax - \dfrac{x^2}{8}$

$\quad + \dfrac{x^3}{192a} + \dfrac{131\,x^4}{2048\,a^2} +$ et cætera fluenti.

37. Ex æquatione $2axy - a\,y\,\overset{\cdot\cdot}{x} + 2\,x\,\overset{\cdot\cdot}{y} - 2\,y\,\overset{\cdot\cdot}{x} = 0$, x in y ascendente est

$\quad y^2 - \dfrac{9}{5a}\,y^4 + \dfrac{27}{5}\,y^6 - \dfrac{8985521}{45\,a^3}\,y^8$ et cætera. At,

38. Ex eadem, x in y descendente est, $y - \dfrac{a}{2} + \dfrac{aa}{16y} + \dfrac{a^3}{9216\,y^2} +$ et cætera.

39. Summa seriei infinitæ nonnunquam æqualis est quantitati finitæ.

2. Omnia corpora, ex materia concreta, sunt finita : Quapropter,

10. HARVARD THESES, 1787: DETAIL FROM JOHN QUINCY ADAMS' MATHEMATICAL THESES

See page xii

by the governor and council of the Commonwealth: the company of light horse, headed by Coll. Swan, were drawn up before the meeting house. As soon as we all got placed, the president opened the Ceremony by prayer: the performances then were delivered, in the order, in which they are mentioned, (page 242)[1] except that Cranch spoke an Oration instead of a forensic. When it came to my turn to speak I delivered the following piece.

An Oration.
Upon the importance and necessity of public faith,
to the well-being of a Community.

The solemnity of the present occasion, the numerous concourse of this brilliant audience, and the consciousness of my own insufficiency, all conspire, to fill my breast, with terrors hitherto unknown, and although my heart would fondly cherish the hope, that the candor, and indulgence, which have ever been the distinguished characteristics of this assembly, will at this time be exerted, yet, this involuntary palpitation expresses fears which cannot be subdued.

Suffer me however, while the united powers of genius and of science are here display'd by others for your entertainment, to call your attention for a few moments to a subject of the utmost importance to our country, and to every individual as a citizen.

To every reflecting mind the situation of this Commonwealth, for some months past, must have appeared truly allarming. On whatever side we turn our anxious eyes, the prospect of public affairs is dark and gloomy: the distressing scarcity of a circulating medium has been continually increasing: the violent gust of rebellion is scarcely dissipated, and threatning clouds of sullen discontent are still lowering round the horizon; luxury and dissipation, like baneful weeds have obstructed the growth of all our useful virtues; and although the hand of patriotism, has of late been stretch'd forth to crop the noxious plant, yet the fatal root, still lies lurking beneath the surface:[2] the bonds of union which connected us with our sister States, have been shamefully relaxed by a selfish and contracted principle, and the sails of commerce furled within our ports, witness the lamentable declension of our trade.

At this critical period, when the whole nation is groaning under the intolerable burden of these accumulated evils, and while the most tremendous calamities are suspended, by a slender thread over our heads, it is natural to enquire, what were the causes which tended to reduce the commonwealth, from a state of happiness and prosperity to the deplorable situation in which we now behold it placed, and what measures might still be adopted, to realize those happy days of national wealth and honour, which the glorious conclusion of a just and successful war, seemed to promise.

In this enquiry, the first question which will naturally occur must be, what is the situation of our national credit? and what are the dispositions of our fellow citizens, with respect to the fulfillment of those engagements, which in times of difficulty, and danger, in times "when the souls of men were tried" they were under a necessity of contracting? And let me ask, can any man whose generous soul disdains every base sentiment of fraud or injustice, answer these questions without dropping a tear of shame, or uttering an expression of indignation? Will he not be constrained to acknowledge, that the divine enthusiasm, and the undaunted patriotism, which animated the bosoms of his countrymen, in their struggle for liberty, has abandoned many so soon as they had attained the darling object of their wishes? But what is liberty, and what is life, when preserved by the loss of honour? Would not the most abject state of slavery to which tyranny and oppression could have reduced a people, have been preferable to standing as an independent nation exposed to the scorn, the reproach, and the derision of mankind. Forbid it Heaven, that this should be our fate! From the well known honour and integrity of the distinguished patriot, who by the suffrages of a free people, has repeatedly been called to fill the seat of government, and from the present dispositions of the majority, of my countrymen, I would still hope, that they will adhere inviolably to every maxim of justice and equity;[3] yet, an indolent carelessness, a supine inattention to the solemn engagements of the public are but too conspicuous among us: numbers indeed, without even assuming the mask of dissimulation, openly avow their desire to evade the performance of those engagements, which they once esteemed supremely sacred.[4]

It is frequently suggested, that nations are not subjected to those laws which regulate the conduct of individuals; that national policy commands them to consult their own interests; though at the expence of foreigners, or of individual citizens; that it is the duty of every government to alleviate the distresses of the people over whom it is placed, and in short that a violation of the public faith could not subject any individual to censure: but an idea, so palpably absurd can be formed upon no other principle, than the probability of escaping the punishment due to the most flagrant enormities: one of the basest principles which can blacken the human heart: the principle, which impels the hand of the lawless ruffian, and directs the dagger of the midnight assassin. Can it be pretended, that there be more than one kind of justice and equity? Or that honour and probity be qualities, of such an accommodating nature, that, like the venal sycophants of a court, they will suit themselves at all times to the interest, of the prevailing party? Does not the very idea of a right whether possest by an individual or by a Society, imply that of a correspondent obligation? And can a nation therefore, have a right to form treaties or enter into contracts of any kind, without being held by every bond of justice to the performance?

The contracted bosom, which was never expanded, by the warm and generous feelings of benevolence and philanthropy, may slight all public engagements for the sake of a paltry profit, but to a mind not bereft of every virtuous sentiment, it must appear that if any obligations can be more peculiarly solemn than others, they must be those for the performance of which, the honour, not of one individual, but of millions has been pledged: and to a person whose views extend beyond the narrow compass of a day, every breach of public faith must appear equally repugnant to every principle of equity and of policy. Survey the faithful page of history, peruse the annals of the civilized world, and you will always find, that the paths of rectitude and justice, have ever been to a nation the paths of wealth and greatness, as well as of glory and honour: that public credit has ever been the foundation, upon which the fabric of national grandeur has been erected.

So long as the grecian states adhered inviolably to the bonds by which they were connected, the innumerable armies of the persian despot, only served as trophies to adorn their victories: when a disregard to their public faith, with its inseperable companion, Discord, crept in among them, they soon fell, an easy prey to the ambition of a less powerful tyrant.

Rome, the imperial mistress of the world, exhibits to our view the most illustrious example of the grandeur to which a nation may arrive, by a sacred regard to public faith: it was not by the splendor of her victories, it was not by the pageantry of her triumphs that she extended her dominion over the submissive world: but it was by her insuperable attachment to the laws of justice and equity; and her punctilious observance of all the contracts in which she engaged. On the other hand, the disastrous fate of Alba,[5] and of Carthage, the faithless rival of the roman power displays the melancholy consequences of an unjust system of policy in a Nation.

In modern times, Britain attacked at once, by the united power of four mighty nations, and born down by the load of an enormous debt, exhibits an example, of national honour, for the admiration of the world, and for the imitation of the american States. The punctual observance of every agreement, and the scrupulous fulfillment of every contract are the only props which have supported, the sinking reputation of that ill fated kingdom.[6] This alone has arrested the progress of threatening conquest, and suspended the uplifted arm of ghastly Ruin.[7]

In this country, I am persuaded there yet exists a spark of patriotism, which may still rekindle a vivid flame. On you, ye lovely daughters of Columbia, your country calls to revive the drooping public spirit: Without recurring to the examples of distant ages, let me only recommend to you, to imitate yourselves: you have already given ample proofs that the patriotic virtues, are not confined to man: Nature it is true, has not formed you, to tread the rugged paths of active life: but your's is the nobler influence of the mind: tis your's to encourage with the smiles of applause every virtuous undertaking, and when the warrior returns from the field of battle with the laurel in his hand, 'tis your's to twine it round his head. Oh! may you every instill into the tender mind the principles of liberty and of patriotism; and remember that the man who can violate his country's faith, must ever be regardless of his own.

Suffer me, my friends and class-mates to address you upon this interesting subject. Warm'd by that friendship, which will ever be the pride, and comfort of my life, I can attest the sentiments of honour and integrity which I have ever heard you express. To recommend to you a spirit of patriotism, and of public zeal would be needless; I can therefore only exhort you, when you shall be advanced upon the theatre of the world; when your Country shall call upon you, to assist in her Councils, or to defend her, with your fortunes and your lives against the sword of

Invasion, or against the dagger of Oppression, to retain those severe republican virtues, which the pamper'd minion of a tyrant
may deride, which the debilitated slave of luxury may dread,
but which alone can effectually support the glorious cause of
Freedom and of Virtue. Above all, may your ruling passion ever
be to preserve pure and immaculate the reputation of your
Country. May an insuperable attachment to this, ever shine
forth in your actions, ever be the favourite theme of your discourse: for it may safely be asserted, that all the distresses in
which the commonwealth is involved, are immediately connected, with the loss of our national credit, and that of an invincible resolution to abide, by all the agreements to which we have
consented, were display'd in the conduct of our citizens in general, we should soon rise superior to every temporary evil: gentle
Peace, and smiling plenty would again appear and scatter their
invaluable blessings round the happy land: the hands of Commerce would recover strength and spread the swelling sail: arts
and manufactures would flourish here, and soon would vie with
those of Europe, and, Science here would enrich the world, with
noble and useful discoveries.[8] The radiant Sun of our union
would soon emerge from those thick clouds, which obscure his
glory, shine with the most resplendent lustre, and diffuse
throughout the astonished world, the brilliant light of Science,
and the genial warmth of freedom. Our eagle, would soon extend
the wings of protection to the wretched object of tyranny and
persecution in every quarter of the globe.

The Muses, disgusted, with the depravity of taste and morals
which prevails in Europe, would soon take up their abode in
these blissful seats of liberty and peace: here would they form
historians who should relate, and poets who should sing the
glories of our country.

And shall we from a sordid motive of self-interest forego all
these advantages? Shall we draw upon our country the execra-
tions of injured foreigners? Shall we deprive the man, who nobly
fought and bled to establish our freedom, of that subsistence
which he no longer can procure? Or shall we reduce his mourning widow and his orphan child to beggary, as a reward for his
services? Forbid it ye powers, who are the protectors of innocence and virtue! May a detestation of so base a principle, be en-
graved upon the heart of every american! May it be expressed in
the first accents of the lisping infant, and in the last words pro-

nounced by the faltering voice of age! And may national honour and integrity distinguish the american commonwealths, till the last trump shall announce the dissolution of the world, and the whole frame of nature shall be consumed in one universal conflagration![9]

The performance, as well as several others, was honour'd with a mark of approbation from the audience: after the conference, between Amory, Lloyd and White, the four following parts were omitted: the mathematical performers then delivered up their parts to the governor, and the morning exhibitions were closed with the english Oration by Freeman, who perform'd extremely well, and with general applause. We then return'd in procession to the hall, where the dinner had been provided, and where according to custom, we attended them: after dinner a psalm was sung, and Bil: Abbot served as deacon: after the ceremony was over I return'd to my chamber, where I found some of my company at dinner. It was near three when we left the meeting house before dinner: and at about five, we return'd thither in procession again, but with the candidates for masters degrees. The president spoke a farewell address to our class in latin which was clap'd: this was followed by Mr. Stedman's english oration, which was as good as I expected from him. We then proceeded to the ceremony of taking our degrees. That of batchelor of arts was conferr'd on the following persons.

William Lovejoy Abbot.	Bossenger Foster
Abiel Abbot	Nathanael Freeman
John Quincy Adams	Timothy Fuller
Jonathan Amory	Thomas Hammond
Samuel Angier	Thaddeus Mason Harris
Benjamin Beale	Walter Hunnewell
James Bridge	Joseph Jackson
Josiah Burge	Asa Johnson
John Chandler	William Samuel Judd
Thomas Chandler	Samuel Kellogg
Gardner Leonard Chandler	Ephraim Kendal
Caleb Child	Nathanael Laurence
William Cranch	Ebenezer Learned
Peter Eaton	Moses Little
Oliver Fiske	James Lloyd
John Forbes	James Lovell

William Mason	Isaac Rand
Daniel Mayo	John Sever.
Samuel Mead	Solomon Vose
Ephraim Morton	John Jones Waldo
Hezekiah Packard	Francis Welch
John Phelps	Leonard White
Nathanael Shephard Prentiss	Samuel Willard
Samuel Putnam	Samuel Williams.

Barron, Cushman and *Whitney,* will be obliged to wait till they can get money to discharge their bills. *Bridge, John Chandler, Lovell, Waldo,* and *Williams,* were declared to be necessarily absent so that in fact there were only 43 of us who really went through the ceremony. When we had return'd to our seats, the candidates for the master's degree went through in the same manner; after which the latin valedictory Oration was pronounced by Mr. Timothy Williams. The whole was closed by a prayer from the President. We then conducted the government of the State and of the University, to the President's house, where we left them; and return'd to college. I found our chambers as full of company as they could hold and was complimented and flattered on every side.

One such day every year, would ruin me. However; I still think that all the advantages of a public Commencement proceed from a gratification of vanity: and if this passion is foster'd in two or three persons it must be mortified in many others; and may therefore very probably do more harm than good.

All our company was gone at about 9 this evening; and at about 10, I retired to bed.

[1] See entry and notes for 17 May (above).

[2] In JQA's draft, the lines "luxury and dissipation ... beneath the surface" read as follows: "and altho' the spirit of extravagance and luxury, which ⟨had disgraced⟩ was advancing with such rapid strides in this Commonwealth, has been checked, by the infallible hand of Necessity, yet it ⟨is far from being progress⟩'s baneful influence is rather *impeded* ["obstructed" is written above *"impeded"*] than effectually ⟨stopped⟩ suppressed" (M/JQA/46, Adams Papers, Microfilms, Reel No. 241).

[3] Followed in JQA's draft by these words: "which serve to promote not only

the honour, but the real prosperity of nations as well as of individuals" (same).

[4] The draft version reads: "without affecting the dissimulation of hypocrisy" and "promises" for "engagements" (same).

[5] Alba Longa, an ancient city near Rome which lost its primacy in Latium when it was destroyed by the Romans in the 7th century B.C.

[6] Followed in the draft with "⟨and this alone, has as yet prevented their final and total ruin⟩" (same).

[7] The following two paragraphs and part of the third are not in the draft, which reads: "But without going any further than our own Country, it may safely

be asserted, that all the distresses in which this commonwealth is involved ..." (same).

[8] The remainder of this paragraph and the next are not in the draft (same).

[9] Besides the copy printed here and the draft already mentioned, the Adams Papers contain two other copies of this oration: one, separately filed under the date of 18 July, endorsed by JA in advanced age, which was possibly enclosed in JQA's letter to AA, 1 Aug. (Adams Papers); and another undated copy (M/JQA/46) with MS changes and additions which indicate that it was the copy JQA enclosed with his letter of 30 July to Jeremy Belknap (MHi:Belknap Papers) in reply to Belknap's proposal to print the oration in the *Columbian Magazine*. Only the original draft has substantive differences from the others, as indicated in the notes above.

Almost immediately after hearing JQA's commencement oration, Belknap asked to have the oration published in the Philadelphia periodical. "Highly honoured" by Belknap's solicitation, JQA sent him a copy and seemed willing, albeit cautiously, to have it published, provided that the commencement poem of his classmate Thaddeus Mason Harris also be included, since "it might with reason perhaps be considered a mark of presumption in me to assume a distinction, which others, much more meritorious, had declined through modesty." He also requested that Belknap have it printed anonymously. Unable to secure a copy of Mason's poem, Belknap asked JQA to soften his restrictions. "Can your Modesty suffer by yielding to a proper solicitation, especially if the publication be prefaced with a hint of the difficulty with which a Copy was obtained for the Press?" Belknap also urged him to reconsider suppressing his name, arguing that Harvard would be denied its honor, that "the friends of Liberty and Virtue will have the farther Satisfaction to see the features of the Parent in the Son," and that the "Country will have a pledge of a succession of abilities in the same Family still to aid her Cause and espouse her Interest" (3 Aug., Adams Papers). After several days of reflection JQA wrote to Belknap reaffirming his desire not to be singled out from among his classmates, but in the end left the whole matter up to Belknap. Again he raised the objection of using his name and of the difficulty in obtaining a copy, but then, as before, expressed confidence in the minister's judgment (6 Aug., MHi:Belknap Papers). In his Diary that day, he fatalistically observed that he had "ventured upon a step, which perhaps some persons may censure," but one which he felt he could, with justification, take. The piece was published in the September issue and appears at 1:625–628, with only minor changes in spelling and grammar from the Diary copy.

Belknap's gentle cajolery contrasted sharply with the adverse comments JQA received at the hands of two Boston newspapers. The *Massachusetts Centinel* of 21 July described JQA's oration "upon a well chosen subject" as performed "in a manly sensible and nervous style of eloquence," but found that "the publick expectations from this gentleman being the son of an Ambassador, the favourite of the officers of the College, and having enjoyed the advantages of European instruction, were greatly inflated." "The performance justified the preconceived partiality," it noted; "He is warmly attached to the republican system of his father and descanted upon the subject of public justice with great energy." Still the *Centinel* found Freeman "superior in style, elegance and oratory." Indirectly more damning, however, was a remark in the *Boston Gazette* of 23 July. While finding JQA's adherence to the republicanism of his father not unusual and defending the young orator from the "bombastic, inflated and ridiculously partial account" of the *Centinel*, Aristides, the *Gazette*'s writer, concluded his article with apparent reference to JA's recently published *A Defence of the Constitutions of the United States of America* by stating that "it is truely singular to see certain people whose whole importance has been created by the partiality of their countrymen, affect to decry the merits of a democracy because forsooth they cannot be noblemen." JQA's oration could not escape the criticism reflected in the worsening social, economic, and political conditions of what he himself described as the "critical period."

In spite of the political crossfire, JQA long maintained that the delivery of his commencement oration was "one of the most memorable events of my life." When George M. Dallas, son of the former editor of the *Columbian Magazine,* returned the Belknap copy to JQA in 1822, the author "reperused" it, "now with humiliation; to think how proud of it I was then, and how much I must blush for it now" (JQA, Diary, 7 Oct. 1822, *Memoirs,* 6:77).

19TH.

Rose early this morning.

The booths and tents before the colleges continue standing as yet, but the chief of the genteel company is gone. From the contrast between the appearance of objects yesterday and this day, every thing looks at present dull: and the idea of bidding a long and last adieu to all my classmates and fellow students, and of quitting these scenes so pleasing to the heart; presses upon me with double force at this time: I endeavoured however to shake off these unpleasing Sensations, by frequently changing the scene and the company. Breakfasted and dined with Mr. Andrews, and pass'd a sociable evening at Mr. Wigglesworth's.

20TH.

Very few of the Class remain yet in town. At about 11 I went with Willard, and took a cold breakfast with Forbes: between 12 and 1. I set out for Boston. Mr. Pickman was at my chamber for about an hour before I came away; he has a brother who passes examination this day for admission.

Dined at Mr. Foster's in Boston; and after paying several visits, set off for Braintree, at about 5 o'clock, and arrived there between 7 and 8. Found Parson Wibird and Mr. Tufts at Mr. Cranch's.

And thus the great business of Commencement is compleated; and as happily as I could have expected personally; though I feel for my three classmates who were obliged for the present to forfeit their degrees. Charles and Tom, are to return to-morrow.

21ST.

Pretty much fatigued, after all the business of the week.

Charles and Tom came from Cambridge this afternoon: my

Cousin, went to Boston in the morning, and return'd with his father at night.

22D.

Staid at home from meeting the whole day, and was busily employ'd in writing; and yet have not been able to get letters ready to sail by Captain Folgier, who proposes sailing very soon for London.

23D.

Beale paid us a visit this forenoon, and dined with us all at Mr. Apthorp's: where we likewise past the afternoon. There is a degree of singularity, running through all this family: I never feel myself under so much restraint any where as in that house: Mr. Apthorp, is disgusting by his eternal admiration of every thing that is english. His lady is agreeable; but perhaps too pointedly civil and polite, to make company perfectly easy: Betsey is sensible and amiable; but extremely diffident and remarkably silent. I know not why, but I believe I never could be sociable with her: Charlotte is more talkative, and at first view more pleasing: but she is affected and fantastical, and in her manners amazingly stiff, and unpliant. In short they are different from the rest of the world and as such I must always view them.

George Blake was over here this afternoon.

24TH.

Went out in the morning with young Quincy,[1] and My brother Tom, on a shooting party: we went down on the marshes and had very good sport.

Lost the afternoon in idleness: Charles went over to Weymouth.

[1] Probably Josiah Quincy III, a classmate of TBA's, later a congressman, mayor of Boston, and president of Harvard (Robert A. McCaughey, *Josiah Quincy, 1772–1864: The Last Federalist,* Cambridge, 1974).

25TH.

Was all the forenoon again on the marshes, with my cousin and my brother Tom: Charles set out this morning for Haverhill. I wrote but little this day, and lost all the afternoon.

Rainy and foggy weather.

26TH.

Employ'd myself the whole day in writing. Dr. Tufts was here in the forenoon. I am now waiting here, and preparing for a tour of three or four weeks, before I take up my final abode at Newbury.

27TH.

Wrote all the forenoon. In the afternoon I read a novel, which arrived from England by the last vessel. The title is *Louisa*, or the cottage on the moor.[1] It is light and airy like most novels. The stile is rather unequal; in some places pretty, and in others very defective: it appears to be a lady's stile. There are no marked characters in it; and very little acquaintance of human life. In short this novel cannot give instruction but it will, entertainment: the story is interesting, and affecting. The incident of Danvers' carrying off Louisa, from Dover is theatrical, and related with more circumstances of probability than are usual in Scenes of that kind, but it must be confest that probability is but little consulted in the general course of the story. I imagine it is the production of a lady, and that is sufficient to screen it from the severity of criticism.

[1] By Elizabeth Helme, 2 vols., London, 1787.

28TH.

Writing all the forenoon. In the afternoon I went out, with my brother Tom, upon a shooting party: indifferent sport. Somewhat fatigued in the evening. I sit down every day to write journal, but here events in general are so trifling, that a relation of them is not worth committing to paper: and as to sentiment, there is nothing here to raise it in the mind; if I had a brain as fertile as that of some of my friends I could write without a subject, and fill up page after page, upon nothing: but gifts of this kind are very partially distributed; and I was never yet able to write without knowing upon what. I frequently think hour after hour, and with a great deal of pains endeavour to call up some wise reflection or observation, but so sure as I attempt this I always find, that some wild association of ideas, will carry me off in a tangent, and after half an hour's reverie, I awake, and am almost ready to ask myself where I am. At present I am a mere cypher in creation; without any employment and without any character: when I get to Newbury I expect the study of the Law, will furnish me with something to say.

29TH.

Attended parson Wibird the whole day. He recommended very highly humility, or spiritual poverty; his sermons were I thought, better than usual. Miss Sarah Taylor, a young lady between 60 and 70 years old dined here this day. I have seen, when I was a child in books of fairy tales, figures very much like this lady, astride upon a broomstick riding Jehu-like through the air. This is a sufficient description of her person, and as to her mind, it will be enough to say that she has been a genuine old maid, these forty years.

30TH.

Writing all day. Dr. Tufts was over here in the afternoon. Weather very cold; a fire in dog-days seems quite unnatural; but is very comfortable at present.

31ST.

A cold north-east storm.

Reading and writing all day. Wrote a letter to my mother, and one to my Sister.[1] Read some pages in Bolingbroke's philosophical works: the stile and matter both inferior to his political writings.

[1] JQA to AA, 1 Aug. (Adams Papers); his letter to AA2 has not been found.

WEDNESDAY AUGUST 1ST. 1787.

Tom set out this morning for Haverhill. I expected to be there before now; but one thing and another has prevented me from going, and I suppose I shall be kept here as much as a week longer. I wrote a short essay this forenoon,[1] but was not pleased with it, when I had done. Ben. Beale, was here in the afternoon, and drank tea with us; I proposed to him to go with me to Haverhill next week, but he said he could not make any positive promise.

We pass'd the evening as usual in playing on the flute and singing.

¹ Not found.

2D.

One of the Miss Greenleaf's and a married sister of her's dined here, and withal Miss Taylor, the amiable lass that I mentioned, two or three days ago. She is an original character, with a good deal of natural sense, but a brain, which has been some how out of order, and does not at present appear to be wholly right: she is an incessant talker and like most other persons who bear that character, she says a great many foolish things, and makes now and then a very good observation. She is the daughter of a lieutenant governor of this Colony, but the family is greatly reduced. The revolutions in private families are similar to those of States and Empires. There is scarce one family in Boston possest of great wealth, or having much political importance that can trace a genteel ancestry, or even such as lived comfortably and creditably, for three generations past. But nothing is more common than to see the descendants from honorable, and opulent families now in the greatest obscurity and poverty. It seems as if fortune herself was resolved to put the republican system into practice here. I could name many families now in high repute for wealth, or political trust, that appear to me to be upon the decline, and the younger branches of which are I think in a fair way to be at the lowest ebb within thirty years; and there is a great chance, that I myself shall at some future period serve as an additional example of this truth.

Mr. Tufts came over this afternoon in company, with Miss Brookes¹ and Miss Jones, and drank tea here: they return'd to Weymouth just after Sun-set.

¹ Presumably Mercy Brooks (1763–1849), of Medford, who later married Cotton Tufts Jr., JQA's cousin.

3D.

I went over to Milton this forenoon, and dined at General Warren's. I found my Class-mate Sever there, and his mamma. They left Milton at about 4 in the afternoon, and proceeded to Boston. Soon after they were gone Mrs. Scott, and Miss H. Otis, (a sister to Mrs. Warren,) Mrs. Parsons and Miss Nancy Russell of Plymouth, came in, and drank tea. I had never before seen either of these ladies, except the last, who has one of the most amiable countenances that ever I beheld

> Fair as the blooming flowers that cheer the vale,
> And lend their fragrance to the gentle gale,
> Her cheek with lilies and with roses vies,
> And innocence adds lustre to her eyes.

It is impossible that such an heavenly form, should contain any other than a good mind. How was I disgusted, how much was I griev'd in the spring to see what this young lady and her sister were subjected to! To endure the language and sentiments of professed rakes, destitute of every delicate feeling, and of every spark of amiable sensibility—May heaven protect her from a connection which would infallibly render her completely miserable!

When tea was over I left the ladies there, and after doing my business at Milton return'd to Braintree; I got home a little after eight o'clock.

4TH.

The weather was extremely warm, all the forenoon.

Rambled about, upon Mr. Cranch's farm with my cousin.[1] In the afternoon, I went into the water with him: towards evening the weather began to grow more comfortable: a letter was brought me, from Mr. Belknap[2] in Boston.

[1] Terminal punctuation has been supplied.
[2] On this letter and JQA's reply of the 6th, see entry for 18 July, note 9 (above).

5TH.

Mr. Wibird preach'd this day, upon two different subjects which for him, was something very extraordinary. In the forenoon the subject was the shortness, the uncertainty and instability, of human life; occasioned by the death of one of the parishioners in the course of the last week: but in the afternoon he spoke with much animation, with great judgment, and sound reasoning, upon the excellency of the sacred writings. It was one of the best Sermons that I ever heard him preach.

After meeting Mr. Wainwright and Ben Beale, came and

drank tea with us. Mr. Wainwright is a young englishman; who to elegance of person appears to unite great softness of manners: I should from this cursory view rather judge him an amiable, than a great man.

6TH.

Down upon the water side, and along upon the marshes with my cousin all the forenoon, but we were obliged to retire before we wished. In the afternoon I wrote an answer to Mr. Belknap. I have ventured upon a step, which perhaps some persons may censure; but as the circumstances are I know not what else to do, and if I am justified in the minds, of men, possessed of candid and liberal sentiments, I feel very indifferent to whatever may be said by people of another description.

7TH.

My Cousin went to Boston in the morning, and did not return till night. I had an opportunity by the law of retaliation to discover one of his secrets: but as a secret it shall remain. This evening Emerson arrived here with Polly Smith from Lincoln, who is going to pass sometime here, and Betsey, will return in a day or two to her mamma.

8TH.

This morning Emerson went to Hingham, and I walk'd over to Weymouth, and dined with Doctor Tufts. I found Miss Brookes there and had a long conversation in order to remove from her mind some impressions very unfavorable to me, which a classmate of mine was so kind as to raise, by telling her a number of absolute falsehoods.

There are among mankind numbers who have such a trifling defect as to propagate such fictitious stories which are calculated only to ruin the character of a person for whom they profess uncommon friendship. And yet I have seen many a good soul, with more benevolence and sincerity, than knowledge of human nature, complain, that he had been injured without ever giving any cause, that misrepresentation had been employed to destroy his reputation, and break out with the utmost indignation against a man, who was capable of what he would call, so *base* an action. But the man who expects that all mankind, or the circle in which he moves will treat him according to his real merits, must have very little experience in the ways of men. It is not worth while I think, upon such occasions to make a noise about a trifle: but say with the Poet

> To virtue only, and its friends, a friend,
> The world beside may censure or commend.

If the good opinion of the world can be obtained in an honorable manner, it is not to be slighted: but the roar of the million would be dearly bought by one unjust, or ungenerous action.

At about 4 o'clock I mounted my horse, and rode to Braintree, where I found a numerous company of gentlemen and Ladies from Boston, who had dined there. It was almost half past 6 when I left my uncle's house, and at 9 I arrived in Cambridge. I found my classmate Packard here, and lodg'd with him.

9TH.

I breakfasted this morning with Mr. Andrews, and after breakfast called upon Jack Forbes; in their company I past my time away till near eleven o'clock. I then mounted, and after stopping a few minutes at Medford, I proceeded, and at about 2, arrived at the tavern in Wilmington, where I found my two brothers who were returning from Haverhill: both of them much pleased with their tour.

Between 4 and 5. we parted, they went towards Cambridge, and I came on to Haverhill, where I arrived, at about 8 in the evening.

10TH.

Spent the whole of the forenoon at Mr. Thaxter's office. Dined at Mr. Shaw's. In the afternoon I went down to Mr. White's, and found Leonard just going to ride out with his mother. Mr. White went with her himself, and Leonard remained with me. I passed the evening there till almost 9 and then return'd to Mr. Shaw's. Mrs. White is very unwell, and Mrs. Bartlett carries a very heavy burden about with her.[1]

[1] Mrs. Bailey Bartlett, Leonard White's sister, was pregnant (Haverhill, *Vital Records*).

11TH.

This forenoon, I took a ride with Mr. Shaw, to see my class-mate Welch, who lives about four miles from hence. After I return'd, I called in, at Mr. Bartlett's, where I found Mr. and Mrs. Dalton, with their two eldest daughters, and Miss Hazen. They all dined at Mr. White's, and in the afternoon all returned to Mr. Dalton's seat at Newtown.[1] The eldest daughter is very much as she was two years ago, blooming as a rose, and, they say, in a fair way to be married. The younger has grown since I last saw her, and appears to better advantage. Miss Hazen appears to have altered but very little since the Time when I lived here with her: she is indeed now two years older, and must necessarily possess more prudence and steadiness; but her manners are still the same. I passed the evening with White and returned home just before 9.

[1] That is, Newbury.

12TH.

Mr. Tappan,[1] from Newbury preach'd here the whole day. Both his sermons were doctrinal, but very ingenious. This gentleman is much celebrated in this part of the Country, for his abilities, both natural and acquired. I was much pleased with the little conversation I had with him in the course of the day: but his public speaking is far from being graceful. Elocution indeed has not till very lately been considered, as claiming a right to much attention in the education of youth; and consequently there are but very few preachers who had finished their education before the last war, that make any figure at all, as speakers: and even those who are acknowledged to be men of great genius and learning, are with respect to the delivery far inferior to many modern preachers, who have not half their talents.

[1] David Tappan was minister from 1774 of the Third Parish of Newbury, and from 1793, Hollis Professor of Divinity at Harvard (Sibley-Shipton, *Harvard Graduates*, 17:638–645).

13TH.

I intended to have gone this day to Newbury-Port, but the weather was so excessively warm, that I determined this morning to omit going, till to-morrow. I paid a visit to Judge Sargeant in the forenoon and spent a couple of hours there. Conversed upon political subjects. Saw Mr. Thaxter a few minutes. After dinner I went with Mr. and Mrs. Shaw, to see my classmate Eaton, but he was not at home. On our return we stop'd at Parson Adam's, but neither was he to be found so that we then came home, and I passed the evening with my uncle.

14TH.

It was so warm again this day, that I did not set out from Haverhill, till between 3 and 4 in the afternoon. On the road I met at different times Mr. Tappan, Stedman and Thompson, and Tom Hooper. I arrived at Mr. Tufts's in Newbury-Port, just before sun-set. I did not enter the town with the most favorable impressions: about three weeks hence I am to become an inhabitant of the place; without friends or connections, I am to stand on my own ground, and am in all probability To live here three years; whether agreeably or, not time only must discover; but the presages within my breast are not such as I should wish realized.

15TH.

In the forenoon I went to see Mr. Parsons, and inform'd him that I should probably attend at his office in about three weeks: Stedman and Thomson are there now, but the former of these will leave the office, by the latter end of next month. My classmate Putnam has applied for admission, and intends, I am told to enter the office in November. Two at once would be full sufficient, but if there are half a dozen it cannot be helped. I went accompanied by Stedman, and paid a visit to Miss Jones, the young lady who was at Mr. Wigglesworth's when Bridge, and I boarded there, last winter. She looks very unwell, and they fear she is in a consumption.

Dined at Mr. Tufts's, and soon after dinner I went to see my friend and Classmate Little. I found Thomson there, but he soon after proceeded on his way to Wenham. We had several smart showers in the course of the afternoon. Just before dark I return'd to Mr. Tufts's at the port. In the evening, between 9 and 10, we had a very heavy shower, with a violent gust of wind.

16TH.

I went again this forenoon to see Miss Jones, and offered to call in the afternoon and take a letter for Miss Wigglesworth, but when we set out I entirely forgot my promise, and did not recollect it till I had got some way out of town. Mr. Thaxter arrived in town this morning, and dined at Mr. Tufts's.

In the forenoon I engaged a place where I am to board; which is at a Mrs. Leathers's.[1] It is not so convenient as I should wish; but I must put up with it for a Time, and when I get here I shall be able to look out for myself.

Soon after dinner, I set off in company with Mr. Thaxter; stopp'd a few minutes at Mr. Dalton, where I found a large company from town, and arrived at Haverhill at about sun-set.

[1] Mrs. Martha Leathers, widow of Newburyport shipwright Joseph Leathers, in whose house JQA lodged until September 1788. JQA described her as "a good old woman, who even an hundred years ago would have stood in no danger of being hang'd for witchcraft: she is however civil and obliging, and what is very much in her favour, uncommonly silent so that if I am deprived of the charms, I am also free from the impertinence of Conversation" (Currier, *Newburyport,* 2:262–263; JQA to AA, 23 Dec., Adams Papers).

17TH.

At home all the forenoon, reading Tom Jones, one of the best novels in the language. The scenes are not only such as may have taken place, but they are similar to such as almost every person may have witnessed. This book cannot lead a person to form too favorable an opinion of human nature, but neither will it give a false one.

Pass'd the afternoon and part of the evening at Mr. White's. The papers of this day, give an account of a violent hurricane, which did a vast deal of injury in the towns of Framingham, Sudbury, Marlborough and some others in the County of Worcester; on wednesday in the afternoon. It was not perceived in these parts of the Country, where there were only two or three heavy showers of rain in the course of that day.

18TH.

This forenoon I took a ride, with White, to see our class mate Eaton. We spent about an hour with him and return'd before dinner. Dined at Mr. White's, and the afternoon went to see his pearl ash works: the sight of these and the account of all the process in making pot and pearl ash, was pleasing because it was new. Leonard complains very much of the stagnation of business; and indeed commerce, as well as the other professions, offer but a miserable prospect to young persons: it is however to be hoped, that the scene will brighten within a few years. And when we have nothing more substantial to support us, we must place our dependence upon hope.

When I return'd home, I found Mr. Shaw gone to Newbury; where he is to preach to-morrow for Mr. Kimball.

19TH.

Mr. Kimball[1] preach'd a couple of practical discourses, the subjects of which I liked better than those of Mr. Tappan, last Sunday: his manner of treating his subjects though good was not I think equal to that of the other gentleman.

After meeting I convers'd with him, chiefly upon political topics. He has a most tremendous frown and appears upon so short an acquaintance, to be possess'd rather of a peevish, difficult temper; which I judge not from his conversation but his countenance; and I am inform'd that this opinion is not erroneous. It was almost Sun-set when Mr. Shaw came home. Leonard White pass'd part of the evening here, and I took a walk with him down upon the banks of the river. The weather very fair, but looks as if it would not continue so, long.

[1] Rev. True Kimball was minister of the Second Church in Newbury, now the First Church in West Newbury, 1782–1797 (Joshua Coffin, *A Sketch of The History of Newbury, Newburyport, and West Newbury, From 1635 to 1845*, Boston, 1845, p. 370).

20TH.

I had some thoughts of leaving Haverhill this morning; but it rain'd all the forenoon; and as I am not in any particular haste, and my friends here are still willing I should remain with them: I determined to defer my departure a day or two longer. I staid at home the whole day. Mr. Thaxter spent the evening with us. He finally declared that he intended if no unforeseen event should take place, to be married before next December, and I am heartily glad of it.

21ST.

Hazy weather again all the forenoon.

I went and pass'd an hour with my friend White before dinner. Spent the afternoon with Mr. Thaxter at his office. Mr. Dodge was there, a great part of the Time. We conversed upon various subjects. Mr. Thaxter whose feelings are very warm, express'd his sentiments quite openly with respect to a gentleman, whose political conduct has been of late somewhat suspicious. I drank tea at Mr. B. Bartlett's: Parson Smith with his lady, Captain Willis and his wife were there and Mr. and Mrs. Lee from Cambridge. It was the first time I had ever been in company with Mr. Lee. He has, I am told much more show than solidity. He does good however with his fortune; and this is meritorious, though the motives by which he is actuated, may not be the most noble and generous.[1]

Return'd home at about 7 o'clock, and received an invitation from Judge Sargeant, which will detain me here one day more.

[1] Joseph Lee, the Cambridge merchant and investor whose appointment to the Mandamus Council in 1774 and dramatic resignation from that body in the face of a mob marked him as a loyalist in the eyes of many. After the start of the Revolution Lee was dropped as a judge from the Middlesex co. court of common pleas, but his property was not confiscated (Sibley-Shipton, *Harvard Graduates,* 8:592–598).

22D.

Dined at Judge Sargeant's, with Mr. and Mrs. Shaw. Mr. Porter and his lady are there upon a visit from Rye: with a child about six weeks old, which forsooth immediately after dinner must be produced, and was handed about from one to another; and very shrewd discoveries were made of its resemblance to all the family by turns, whereas in fact it did resemble nothing but chaos. How much is the merciful author of nature to be adored for implanting in the heart of man a passion stronger than the power of reason, which affords delight to the parent at the sight of his offspring even at a Time, when to every other person it must be disgusting. Yet it appears to me, that parents would do wisely in keeping their children out of sight at least untill they are a year old, for I cannot see what satisfaction, either sensual or intellectual can be derived from seeing a misshapen, bawling, slobbering infant, unless to persons particularly interested.

We drank tea likewise at the judge's, and return'd home between 7 and 8 in the evening.

Leonard White came up to give me a letter for his chum.

23D.

I left Haverhill this morning at about 9 o'clock; and at 12 arrived at the tavern in Wilmington, where I dined. At about 2 I again set off, and got to Cambridge a little before six. I came through Mystic and called at Mrs. Tufts's,[1] to see my friend Freeman, but he was gone to Boston. When I got to Cambridge I found great alterations had taken place since I left College, Mr. Reed, and Mr. Burr have resigned, and likewise the librarian. Mr. Webber and Mr. Ware, were chosen as Tutors, but Mr. Ware declined accepting as he has an unanimous call to settle at Hingham, and will probably soon be ordain'd. Mr. Abbot has since that been chosen, and Mr. I. Smith was elected librarian, but has not yet accepted.

I passed the evening at several chambers among my old acquaintance, Phillips, Clarke, Lincoln, and my classmate Packard; the only one now in town. Indeed it seemed extraordinary to walk through the college yard and the town, finding scholars every where, yet without seeing one of those with whom I was the most closely connected. It made me quite dull.

[1] Probably Elizabeth Hall Tufts (1743–1830), the second wife and widow of Dr. Simon Tufts, an older brother of Dr. Cotton Tufts and a cousin of AA.

24TH.

I lodg'd last night with Lincoln, the senior, whose chum was out of town. Breakfasted this morning with Mr. Andrews, who returned from Hingham last evening. I visited Mr. James and Doctor Jennison: both were very polite. The Doctor informs me, that several material alterations are about to take place, with respect to the plan of studies pursued here. Doddridge, is to be put entirely into the hands of the theological professor, which is its proper place, and some attention to History is to be called forth by the recitations on Saturday mornings. The mathematics will be taught in better order than they have been heretofore, and indeed it always appear'd absurd to me, that Sophimores should study Euclid, and learn common arithmetic after they commence Juniors. Henceforth arithmetic, with some little practical geometry, surveying, trigonometry &c are to be taught them before they begin upon Euclid—All the changes, which the doctor mentioned, will I think be for the better.

Dined with Mr. Andrews, and passed the afternoon at college.

Just as I was going in to prayers, I was stopped by a couple of french officers from on board the fleet now lying in Boston Harbour. They desired to see the colleges. I waited on them into the library, the museum and the philosophy chamber. After they had satisfied their curiosity, they set out for Boston, and I for Braintree. It was between six and seven o'clock before I got away, at about nine I arrived at Braintree, where I found all my friends well.

25TH.

In the forenoon I went to Weymouth, to return Dr. Tufts's horse. Dined at the Doctor's, and pass'd the afternoon there. Walk'd leisurely home, and arrived at about Sun-set.

This morning Mrs. Cranch and her son, went to Boston. My Cousin intends to read law with Mr. Dawes, and will enter his office next monday.

Very damp, sultry weather.

26TH.

I did not attend meeting this day—Employ'd myself chiefly in reading and writing. Mr. Weld preach'd for Mr. Wibird, and dined here. Miss Street and one of Captn. Beale's sons, with Mr. J. Warren dined with us likewise. In the evening Mrs. Cranch and Dr. Tufts return'd from Boston. My uncle Smith has been for some time very ill of a complication of disorders. The Doctor thinks he is at present better than he has been, but that the symptoms are yet dangerous.

Up late in consequence of an afternoon nap: read some poetry and some prose, in a cursory manner.

27TH.

I employ'd myself in the forenoon with making some necessary preparations before my final departure for Newbury-port. In the afternoon I accompanied the ladies to Mrs. Quincy's. Miss

Nancy has been very ill, and is much thinner than when I saw her last. She is however recovering.

Pass'd an agreeable afternoon, and return'd home just after dark.

28TH.

Rode out in the morning with Mrs. Cranch. It rain'd hard all the afternoon—chilly north-east wind. The fruits of the earth are at this time extremely backward, on account of the little heat, and the great rains that have prevailed this summer. The productions of our lands require frequent, rather than plentiful rains, and great heat, as the summers are so short.

29TH.

Rain'd in the fore part of the day but cleared up in the afternoon: I went with my gun down upon the marshes; but had no sport. Game laws are said to be directly opposed to the liberties of the subject: I am well perswaded that they may be carried too far, and that they really are in most parts of Europe. But it is equally certain that when there are none, there never is any game: so that the difference between the Country where laws of this kind exist, and that where they are unknown, must be that in the former very few individuals will enjoy the privilege of hunting, and eating venison, and in the latter this privilege will be enjoy'd by nobody.

30TH.

Staid at home the whole day. Doctor Tufts was here in the morning, on his road to Boston, and in the evening on his return. I took a nap in the afternoon, and had a strange dream. I cannot conceive where my imagination ransack'd the ideas, which prevailed at that time in my mind. This part of the action of the human soul, is yet to be accounted for: and perhaps has not been scrutinized with so much accuracy as it might have been.

In the evening I read about one half of Mr. Jefferson's notes upon Virginia,[1] and was very much pleased with them. There is a great deal of learning shown without ostentation, and a spirit of philosophy equally instructive and entertaining.

[1] *Notes on the State of Virginia; Written in the Year 1781, Somewhat Corrected and Enlarged in the Winter of 1782 . . .,* [Paris, 1784–1785], and subsequent editions.

31ST.

A very warm day. Rambling all the morning; I met a couple of french officers gunning on my uncle's farm. In the afternoon I went with the ladies, to see my Grand-mamma: return'd at about dusk; and closed the last day, which I proposed to spend in Braintree for some time.

SATURDAY SEPTEMBER 1ST. 1787.

Between 9 and 10 o'clock this morning I departed from Braintree with Mrs. Cranch: we got to Mr. Foster's at about 12. I went to Mr. Dawes's office, where I found Cranch and Forbes. Dined with the former at Mr. Foster's. Stroll'd about town all the afternoon and just before Sun-set: I took a walk to Cambridge: where I arrived at about 8 o'clock.

2D.

Attended meeting all day. Mr. Hilliard preach'd; much in the old way. The meeting house however did not look as it was wont. The same deficiency I found there, that I had perceiv'd, in the colleges, and every where in this Town. All my classmates gone. I dined at Mr. Wigglesworth's with Packard. Peggy appears as amiable as ever.

I pass'd the evening with my brothers, and lodg'd with Tom.

3D.

I pass'd about an hour, before dinner with Mr. Winthrop, the late librarian. He is much of a politician; his opinion with respect to the situation of the country is always favorable.

Dined with Mr. Andrews. Lincoln, the senior was there; a young lad of good abilities, and of great application: In the afternoon I met a couple of french officers in the College yard; who wish'd to see the library and museum; but the butler was not to be found; and they were obliged to defer the gratification of their curiosity, to some future opportunity. In the evening I sat about an hour in my brothers' chamber. A number of Junior's were collected in a chamber near there, and were enjoying all the pleasures of conviviality: it brought to my mind the frequent scenes of a similar nature, at which I was present, a short time ago. An involuntary sigh arose in my breast; I left the chamber to put a stop to melancholy recollection, and, went to the butler's room: I found Mr. Stedman, and Mr. Andrews with him, and pass'd the remainder of the evening very agreeably. Stedman and Harris exerted their talents at telling stories, and diverted us very much: between 9 and 10, I retired with Mr. Andrews and lodg'd with him.

4TH.

After breakfast I return'd to College, and on the way stopp'd at the President's. He was not at home, but Mrs. Willard desired me to take a letter for Sophy, who is now on a visit at Newbury-Port. At about 10 o'clock I went with a number of scholars in the stage carriage, for Boston: just as we were going off we met Cranch who had walk'd up from Boston expecting there would be a meeting of the ΦBK this forenoon, but as it is deferr'd till to-morrow, he return'd with us.

I attended Court, but there were no causes of any great importance argued.

Dined with Mr. Dawes, in company with Mr. Gardiner, who was once an orator on the 4th. of July. He is an original character, but shows much more wit in his private conversation, than in his public performances.

I had engaged a place in the stage to go to Newbury Port tomorrow, and I found some difficulty to disengage myself: however another person applied in the afternoon, and I retain'd my place for Friday.

Passd the evening at Mr. Smith's, with Mr. and Mrs. Otis, and Dr. Welch and his lady; lodg'd with my cousin at Mr. Foster's.

5TH.

Took an early breakfast, and walk'd with Cranch to Cambridge. We got to Packard's chamber, just after 9 o'clock. There was a meeting of the ΦBK. The president and vice-president being both absent, Mr. Andrews presided for the meeting: a number of new regulations were introduced; the resignation of the president was read and accepted. Just before 12 The officers for the ensuing year were ballotted. Mr. Ware, (who arrived just before the choice) was elected president; Mr. Harris vice-president; Abbot secretary, and Phillips treasurer.

Immediately after this business was finished, we walk'd in

procession to the chapel, preceded by the two orators. (*Lowell* and *Freeman*.) Freeman gave us an Oration containing miscellaneous observations, without any professed subject; and this like all his other performances was extremely well written, and equally well deliver'd. *Lowell*, gave us an encomium upon history, which contained a number of very good observations, but his delivery was not without a share of that affectation, which if I may so express myself, is natural to him. The students attended very generally except those of the Senior class; who kept off, from a spirit of envy, all except Dodge.

We return'd to the butler's room, and soon after proceeded to Mr. Warland's, where we had an excellent dinner provided for us. Besides the members, of the present senior class, there were present Mr. Kendall, and Mr. B. Green, Mr. Ware; Mr. Andrews, Mr. Harris: Packard, Cranch, Freeman, and myself: after passing a couple of hours, in friendly mirth and festivity, at three o'clock, we adjourn'd again to Packard's chamber, where we voted to admit Mr. *Bancroft,* a minister of Worcester; Mr. *Packard* of Marlborough, and Dr. Barker of Hingham, as members of the Society without the usual forms. On account of the Dudleian lecture we adjourn'd the meeting till five o'clock; when we again met, but there being no further business, the meeting was then dissolved.

The lecture was preach'd by Doctor Howard. The subject was natural religion and his text was from   [1] And we also are his offspring. The sermon was replete with sound sense, and a wholsome doctrine, as all the sermons that I ever heard from this gentleman, have been.

In the evening I called at the president's and at Mr. Wigglesworths', and took their letters for Newbury-Port. Lodg'd at college, with Clarke.

[1] Acts 17:28, but left blank in MS. The lecture was given by Simeon Howard.

6TH.

This morning after breakfasting with Mr. Andrews I walk'd leisurely to Boston. Just before I left Cambridge the parts for exhibition were distributed: Charles has a dialogue with Emerson: the circumstance gave me more pleasure than any allotment that I ever had, myself.

As soon as I arrived in Boston, I immediately went to Court, and found them engaged upon the trial of one John Shehane for burglary. The attorney general[1] began, in behalf of the common-wealth. He examined his witnesses and said but little, observing that he should wait to see what defence the counsel for the prisoner, had to make.

Mr. Wetmore[2] spoke first for the prisoner; at the first outset, he attempted to address the passions of the jury, Mr. Dawes who sat next to me observ'd that this was a bad omen. The pathetic he said should always be reserved for the latter part of the plea: a man should gradually grow warm (said he) as he advances in his subject; like a wheel, which acquires heat by rolling.

The evidence which Mr. Wetmore produced, was very favorable to the prisoner. If true it proved an *alibi;* and it proved likewise that Shehane, had bought the articles, which he was charged with stealing: but they told so many different stories, and the attorney general produced such evidence, that they were perjured; that I think no stress could be laid upon it.

Mr. Tudor spoke much at length in the afternoon; and very ably: Mr. Paine, closed for the Commonwealth, at about 7 in the evening. All the judges (there were four present) appeared to be of opinion that the prisoner was guilty. At half past 8, the jury was pack'd,[3] and the court adjourn'd for an hour: but the jury had not then agreed upon a verdict; upon which the court adjourn'd till 9 o'clock to-morrow morning.

I was so entirely engaged the whole day in hearing this trial, which was very interesting; that I had no time, to go any where else. Between 10 and 11 at night I carried my bundle to Mr. Colman's, from whose house the stage setts off, and I took a bed there, in order to be ready to go very early in the morning.

[1] Robert Treat Paine, attorney general from 1777 to 1790 (Sibley-Shipton, *Harvard Graduates*, 12:462–482).
[2] William Wetmore, a Boston attorney (same, 17:447–451).
[3] In this sense, sent out to deliberate upon a verdict.

7TH.

At three in the morning I was roused, and got into the carriage in company with, a merchant of Portsmouth, and a Sea captain of Newbury-Port; lately arrived from South Carolina. Nothing very interesting occurred in the course of our Journey. We dined at Ipswich and reach'd Newbury-Port, between 2 and 3 in the afternoon. After taking possession of my room, at Mrs. Leathers's; I went to Mr. Parsons's office, where I found Thomson, and Townsend. I soon went to see my friend Little, whom I found at Dr. Swetts',[1] I pass'd an hour there, and then went, with Little, and deliver'd the chief of the letters with which I was charged. Little came home with me to my lodgings and pass'd part of the evening with me. As I was up so early in the morning, and was somewhat fatigued with my Journey, I retired early to bed.

[1] Dr. John Barnard Swett, a Newburyport physician (Sibley-Shipton, *Harvard Graduates,* 17:635–638).

8TH.

I arose in the morning quite refresh'd, and immediately after breakfast went and took my station in the office. I began upon the first volume of Robertson's history of Charles the V. which Mr. Parsons recommended as containing an account of the feudal institutions, from which were derived many of the laws which are now established in different parts of Europe.

I have already read the book; but thought it would be best to peruse it again.

I was no where this day, except at the office and my lodgings.

Saturday evening: rather tedious.

9TH.

I did not attend meeting this day for several reasons. At home the whole day; it was extremely long and tedious. I amused myself with reading in the first volume of Blair's lectures: I have already perused the work; but I think it deserves a second reading.

Retir'd early to bed, merely from *ennui.*

10TH.

Attended at the office the whole day. Continued Robertson. Thomson engaged this morning to take the charge of one of the town schools, for a year. It will interfere very much with his attendance at the office. His father, who is very rigid in his religious opinions, and probably entertains an unfavourable idea of the profession of the law, is very averse to his son's engaging in it; and takes every opportunity he can, to discourage his son from the study; and it is supposed he took this method among others to draw off his attention from this pursuit: but he will certainly fail in the attempt, and I doubt whether Thomson will keep the school, more than half the year through. In the afternoon we walk'd to Mr. Atkins's,[1] and found Mr. John Tracy with him: we pass'd part of the evening at Mr. Tracy's house: I there met with a french gentleman with whom I convers'd about half an hour. Return'd home between 8 and 9 in the evening.

[1] Dudley Atkins Jr., a Newburyport justice of the peace at this time (Essex Inst., *Hist. Colls.*, 85:160 [April 1949]; *Fleet's Pocket Almanack and Massachusetts Register*, 1788).

11TH.

Thomson began his attendance upon the school this morning, and attended at the office, all the leisure time he had: if he should make a practice of this it must necessarily be essentially injurious to his health. I Dined this day with Townsend and pass'd the evening at home in reading and writing.

12TH.

Training day for the alarm list. From 16 to 60 years the inhabitants of this Common-wealth, are subjected to the duties of militia-men: As a student of Harvard University, I shall be exempted for three years: for all the sons of Harvard are considered as students at that seminary untill they commence masters of arts.

This forenoon I finish'd the first volume of Robertson's Charles V. and as I read now in connection with my studies, I shall not proceed with the other volumes. In the afternoon I took up Vattels' law of nature and of nations.[1]

[1] Emmerich de Vattel, *Le droit des gens; ou, principes de la loi naturelle, appliqués à la conduite et aux affaires des nations et des souverains*, Leyden, 1758, and subsequent English translations. Presumably in this and other cases, JQA was using Parsons' law books. The copy known to have been owned by an Adams at this time was a French edition, Amsterdam, 1775, given to JA by C. W. F. Dumas in 1781.

13TH.

Dined with Dr. Kilham[1] at Mr. Carter's.[2] This is a very friendly, obliging old gentleman, about 73 years of age, as I collected from his conversation: he is very sociable, and is a great genealogist. He gave me a much more circumstantial account of my ancestry, for four or five generations back, than I had ever known before, and I am told he can give the same kind of information to almost any body else. He has two sons with him, both I believe between 25 and 30 years old and one daughter: one of his daughters was married in the beginning of the summer, to Mr. W. Smith of Boston:[3] and his eldest son, proposes to be married in the spring to Miss Eppes Cutts, who has made her appearance heretofore in this journal. Her sister, Miss Nancy Cutts is now upon a visit at Mr. Carter's, and dined with us. I think she is handsomer, and that her manners are easier than those of her Sister. How the comparison might be, in mental qualifications I am not able to decide. I was alone this afternoon in the office, as Townsend and Thomson, were both gone to see the manoeuvres of the four companies of militia of the train band, who were this day forming themselves for soldiers.

In the evening I pass'd an hour at Mr. Tufts's. Mrs. Tufts is very unwell.

[1] Dr. Daniel Kilham, Newburyport apothecary and fellow boarder with JQA at Mrs. Martha Leathers' and a representative in the General Court (Russell Leigh Jackson, "Physicians of Essex County," Essex Inst., *Hist. Colls.*, 84:83 [Jan. 1948].

[2] Nathaniel Carter Sr., a wealthy New-buryport merchant (Cecil Hampden Cutts Howard, "Thomas and Esther (Marlowe) Carter and Their Descendants," same, 65:502–503 [Oct. 1929]).

[3] Boston merchant William Smith, JQA's cousin, married Hannah Carter (same).

14TH.

The weather for this week past has been from day to day alternately very warm and very cold. These sudden transitions, which in this Country are very common, are almost too powerful for our constitutions: to foreigners they are almost intolerable, and I believe even the inhabitants, who from their birth have been used to them, suffer more from them than they are aware. This forenoon I received a letter from my friend Forbes,[1] enclosing one for Miss Jones, and in the evening I called and delivered that which was consigned to my care. Mr. Parsons arrived just before dark from Boston, and was the bearer of a short letter from Cranch.[2] The supreme court have adjourn'd from Boston till some time in December. *Shehane* the fellow whose trial I attended, was found guilty, and is now under sentence of Death. But all the prisoners who were convicted of treason have received a full and free pardon:[3] is it much to the credit of our government that a man who has stole 30£ worth of plate should die for the offence, while others commit treason and murder with impunity?

I pass'd the evening and supp'd with Townsend. We amused ourselves by playing back-gammon. At about 10 I retired home.

[1] Not found.
[2] Not found.
[3] Here JQA is referring to the treatment given to the Shays rebels.

15TH.

Dined with Townsend and Thomson at Mr. Parsons's. I finished this day the first volume of Vattel. The first book treats of the duties of a nation with respect to itself: the second of its obligations towards others. His sentiments and principles appear to be dictated by good sense and real virtue. They appear all to derive from that law of nature, which every person of common sense and common honesty must wish to prevail, Do as you would be done by.

Mr. Parsons endeavoured to perswade Thomson to give up his school; he told him it would infallibly either murder his health or his studies: he himself had tried it for two years and it had almost ruin'd him.

My trunks at length arrived from Boston, and I shall at least have more convenience than I have as yet had here. Little pass'd the evening with me at my lodgings; and his company is always agreeable.

I received a letter from Braintree.[1]

The french fleet have received orders to sail immediately for Brest, and it is added they are enjoined to avoid all english fleets'. It is conjectur'd that the affairs in Holland are now arrived at a crisis, and it is not improbable that England and France will support the opposite parties.[2]

[1] Not found.
[2] A reference to the ongoing struggle between the Dutch Patriots and the Prince of Orange (the Stadholder) in the Netherlands. The Patriot Revolt had achieved an alliance with France in 1785 and had deprived the Stadholder, the country's hereditary ruler, of certain powers. The English, who sided with the Stadholder, and the French managed to avoid open conflict. Through the military intervention of the Stadholder's brother-in-law, Frederick William II of Prussia, culminating with the surrender of Utrecht on 16 Sept., Great Britain and the Orangists regained predominance in Holland. The French fleet sailed from, not for, Brest (Simon Schama, *Patriots and Liberators: Revolution in the Netherlands, 1780–1813*, N.Y., 1977, p. 100–132).

16TH.

I took a walk this morning as far as Dr. Tucker's[1] meeting house; but it was to little purpose, unless the exercice of the walk was sufficiently beneficial to me to compensate my trouble: for Mr. Kimball happened to preach; and delivered the same sermon, which I heard him read at Haverhill four weeks ago. As I did not incline to hear the afternoon sermon twice, I attended at Mr. Carey's:[2] this gentleman is a good preacher; but appears extremely indolent: his manner is also far from being graceful. After meeting I went with Dr. Kilham to his shop; and he lent me a number of Pieces of good music. He has a very pretty taste in this art, though he does not perform upon any instrument. Just before dark I took a walk with Townsend, and called in at Mr. Atkins's. He himself was not at home: his mother and Sister were. Mrs. Atkins is a very sensible, agreeable old lady, whose conversation unites the vivacity of youth, with the sound judgment of experienced age. Her daughter appears to be about 20. She may be more, or less, for near that period of life the countenance retains nearly the same appearance longer perhaps, than at any other age: she has fine eyes, and a very pleasing symmetry of features; but not an handsome set of teeth. We past about an hour there; Townsend stopp'd at my lodgings and tarried the remainder of the evening here.

I received a couple of letters from Cambridge:[3] one from Packard, and the other from Clarke, who is now a senior.

Retired late.

[1] Rev. John Tucker, minister of the First Congregational Church of Newbury (Sibley-Shipton, *Harvard Graduates,* 11:78–89).

[2] Rev. Thomas Cary, minister of the First Congregational Church of Newburyport (same, 15:29–33).

[3] Neither letter found.

17TH.

Three of us in the office were employ'd the whole day, in taking copies of the writs which are to be entered at the next Court; which will sit in this town next week. General Freeman pass'd through Town this day, and came to visit Mr. Parsons. In the afternoon I took a walk with Little. At home all the evening. Weather very cold.

18TH.

We had some more writing to do this forenoon. Mr. Parsons, went to Exeter, where the supreme court for the State of New-Hampshire are now sitting. At 12 o'clock, I attended Townsend before Mr. Justice Tracy. One M'Intier had prosecuted a Sarah Bayley for defamation in saying that he was a thief. The parties could not agree: they had not their evidence ready, and the court was adjourned till three o'clock. Townsend and I dined with his worship: Mrs. Tracy is an agreeable woman: still handsome; but with her share of Vanity: at three o'clock the Court was again opened: the parties had agreed to compromise the matter, and Bayley is to pay the costs: neither of them I believe could be easily defamed, but had the case been tried I suspect the plaintiff would have recovered damages. After this weighty affair was brought to a conclusion, I took a walk with the Squire and Townsend, about 3 miles out of Town to one Sohier's; where we eat a couple of fine musk-melons; it was dark before we got back to Mr. Tracy's. We stopp'd there, and play'd backgammon, about two hours; after which Townsend and I returned to our homes.

19TH.

The equinoctial storm, which has been gathering in the heavens for a week past, has now appeared, with all its violence and rage. Stedman arrived in town last evening, and has attended in the office this day. He brought me no letters from Cambridge, but left all friends well: we had a violent debate in the office, between Stedman and Townsend upon a point of law. The contest began by a difference of opinion between Townsend and me. Stedman was on my side of the question, and the dispute soon center'd in them; books were produced and authorities brought which both parties declared to be plump[1] in their favour respectively.

Townsend at last finding three against him, (for Thomson had sided likewise) got out of patience, and hinted to us, that we could not understand the meaning of the terms, as we had been so short a time in the office: so we left him to battle it with Stedman. An appeal was agreed upon to Mr. Parsons: Townsend however after shifting his ground several times, at length discovered that there was nothing in the case but a misunderstand-

291

ing of words; and appears at present to give up the point. But he is fond of these debates, and fonder of his own opinion. Thomson did not appear in the afternoon: this however was quite peaceable: The weather was such as rendered a fire in the office, very comfortable. I was at home all the evening, reading Rousseau's confessions.[2] This is the most extraordinary book I ever read in my life.

[1] Without qualification or uncertainty (*OED*).
[2] The Geneva, 1782, edition in two volumes is at MQA.

20TH.

I expected this morning when I waked up, to hear the winds whistle and the tempests roar: but all was still and calm: the storm was violent but short. We were pretty still this day at the office; but four at a time, is certainly too many. Some one or other of us, is talking almost all the time, and consequently, reading does not proceed rapidly.

Little came and pass'd half an hour with me in the evening: but was engaged for the remainder of it.

I copied some extracts, and wrote a letter.[1]

[1] Not found.

21ST.

Quite still in the office this day. I read a good deal.

This afternoon Amory[1] arrived; and thus we are all five here.

I called at Mr. Carter's and desired him to take charge of a letter to W. Cranch.[2]

I pass'd an hour or two with Mr. Tufts.

A very beautiful evening.

[1] William Amory, who briefly practiced law in Boston and Salem after leaving Parsons' office the following spring (*Fleet's Pocket Almanack and Massachusetts Register*, 1789, 1791).
[2] Not found.

22D.

This forenoon I finish'd Vattel. The third book treats of War, and the fourth of Peace; much in the same manner as he treats the other parts of his subject. "Honesty is the best policy," says nature; and so says Vattel.

Mr. Parsons returned from Exeter before dinner. I intended to have gone to Haverhill this afternoon, to spend the Sunday there: but the weather was such as threatened a storm; and I gave up my plan. I went up with Townsend, Stedman, Amory and Stacey[1] to Sohier's tavern about three miles out of town, where we had some fine melons. We return'd in the dark: I pass'd the evening, and supp'd with Townsend.

[1] George Stacey was apparently also studying law in Newburyport, perhaps with Theophilus Bradbury. Stacey practiced briefly in Biddeford, Maine (MH-Ar; George Folsom, *History of Saco and Biddeford, . . . Maine . . .*, Saco, 1830, p. 302).

23D.

Attended upon Mr. Carey the whole day. His manner is not very agreeable; but his stile is much better than common.

Townsend called here in the evening.

Amory set off this morning for Boston. They say it is impossible for him to stay three days at a time in one place. He has been absent 6 or 8 months, and promised Mr. Parsons some time ago that he would come, and be very steady all through the winter. He arrived here on friday, has not yet been ten minutes together at the office, and now is gone again. He is gone however upon business, and intends to return to-morrow.

24TH.

Townsend went to Topsfield to hear a cause tried before a justice. Stedman has been hunting all over the neighbourhood for his horse, who disappeared on Saturday. Thomson has an whole week respite from his school; but did not come to the office in the afternoon: I was there alone: Amory return'd from Boston between 4 and 5, and at about 6 set off for Exeter. Tomorrow he goes to Portsmouth and Wednesday morning he intends to be here again.

Amidst the noise of the Office, which was greater than usual because this is the last day, before the sitting of the court of common-pleas in this town, I made out however to read about 80 pages of Blackstone's Introduction, and making a few extracts.[1] I copied others in the evening till quite late; and at this moment my fingers are so fatigued with writing, that I positively, must throw by, my pen.

[1] William Blackstone, *Commentaries on the Laws of England* . . ., 4 vols., Oxford, 1765–1769, and subsequent editions. JQA's extracts have not been found.

25TH.

I have given up all pretences to study any more this week. The Court of Common-pleas sits here; and I shall attend that. It was near one o'clock this day before they met and then they immediately adjourn'd till the afternoon. I was there after dinner. Nothing was done but calling over the actions. Judge Greenleaf[1] gave a very short charge to the grand Jury, in which he observed to them, that frequently persons were charged, by malicious enemies, of crimes whereof they were entirely innocent; and he recommended to them to be upon their guard, so as not to be deceived by false accusations, of that nature. The court adjourned by five o'clock. I went and took a walk with Mr. Symmes and Townsend. Symmes was sworn in at the Court of common-pleas, this time last year: but has not I believe an immediate prospect of making his fortune in the profession. I was with Townsend at his lodgings till between 7 and 8 o'clock.

Mr. Bradbury[2] this afternoon told me a piece of news which shock'd me exceedingly. That Sam. Walker was rusticated; and for a crime, which is the more infamous, because it can be attributed neither to youthful levity, nor to the extravagance of ebriety.[3]

[1] Benjamin Greenleaf, chief justice of the Essex co. court of common pleas and father-in-law of Theophilus Parsons (Sibley-Shipton, *Harvard Graduates*, 13:86–90).

[2] Theophilus Bradbury, a Newburyport lawyer, in whose office Theophilus Parsons had studied law (same, 14:143–146).

[3] Several days earlier Walker had been found guilty of stealing money and a shirt from another student's room. He served out his year of rustication and in Sept. 1788, after a humble confession, was restored. He eventually graduated in the class of 1790 (MH-Ar:Faculty Records, 5:270–271, 319–321).

26TH.

Attended court the whole day. Little was done in the forenoon except calling over the cases. But in the afternoon, a cause was tried by Jury, between one Smith and James Brown. Smith had attached certain lands as the estate of Brown's father, to satisfy a debt due to him: Brown claim'd those lands, as his property, and produced in court two deeds, by which his father had made over the lands to him. The question to be tried by the Jury was, whether those deeds were valid, or whether they were given merely to evade the payment of the father's debts and in order to secure himself a maintenance during the remainder of his life. Mr. Parsons for the plaintiff proved, that for the real estate of the father, which at that time was assessed at £450. James had only allowed him about 230, and that the chief of this was by paying debts for which he had been previously bound with his father. Mr. Sullivan[1] for the defendant, endeavoured to show that such deductions were to be made from this estate as would reduce it to about 280£, and that some other charges ought to be added, to what James had allowed his father, which would make his contract quite equitable. The pleadings were very interesting, and it was after 7, in the evening, before the case was given to the Jury.

The Court then adjourned till the morning, at 9 o'clock.

[1] James Sullivan, former superior court judge, legislator, newspaper polemicist, and later governor of Massachusetts (Sibley-Shipton, *Harvard Graduates*, 15:299–322).

27TH.

The jury upon the case of Smith and Brown, gave their Verdict in favour of the Plaintiff, and declared the deeds fraudulent. The next Jury case which came on, was between William Bartlett and Daniel Dodge both of this Town. Dodge who is a Mason, engaged to build and plaister a brick house for Bartlett at a certain price, in the year 1778. In the course of his doing the work, the paper currency, depreciated considerably, and the question now is, whether Dodge is to be held to the original sum, or whether, the monies he received at different times is to be reduced by the scale of depreciation at those times. Parsons was for the plaintiff, Bradbury for the defendant. Parsons in the midst of his plea, broke off and proposed to leave the matter to a reference.[1] The parties agreed, and the Jury, after being employ'd four or five hours upon this cause, were entitled only to half-fees. However they were probably gainers by the circumstance, for the case was so difficult and intricate, that they would have found it very difficult to agree upon a verdict.

After this was over two negroes, and two white men were arraigned for different thefts; all of them pleaded guilty; and were sentenced to whipping, hard labour &c. At about dusk the court adjourned to 9 in the morning. I dined at Mr. Tufts's. Thomson,

Little, and Putnam passed the evening with me. Putnam came to apply again for admission into Mr. Parsons's office. There was a bar meeting this evening, and the matter was to be laid before them, I saw Mr. Thaxter after the meeting was over, but he would not tell me what their determination was.

¹ That is, to submit their dispute to an arbitrator or referee, a practice often followed in cases involving difficult factual issues or large quantities of evidence (JA, *Legal Papers*, 1:xliii).

28TH.

I learnt this day that the bar determined last evening to abide by the rule, which they had adopted some years ago, which was that there should not be more than three students in an office at once. Putnam therefore cannot be received by Mr. Parsons. I understand he has this day applied to Mr. Bradbury, who will receive him immediately. Court sat all day, but finally adjourn'd this afternoon, till next April, when they will sit at Ipswich. There was one trial by Jury this forenoon. It was between Parson Murray¹ of this town, and the inhabitants of Salisbury: One of the people of Salisbury attended always at Mr. Murray's meeting; but was assessed in his own town: the question was whether his tax should be paid to Mr. Murray, or whether it should go to the support of the minister of Salisbury. The jury brought in a verdict, in favour of Mr. Murray; a similar case has two or three times been determined in the same manner; I think very improperly; and so thinks Mr. Parsons.

In the afternoon, a man was convicted of stealing a couple of sheep; for which he was fined 30 shillings. Parsons, said in England he would have been hung, but I a little doubt. I dined at Mr. Carter's. Mr. and Mrs. Smith from Boston were there. Mr. Smith brought me a letter from W. Cranch,² which gives me an account of the rustication of Walker. The circumstances are much to his disgrace. I had likewise a letter from my father, and one from my mother, of the 18th. and 20th. of July.³ Some letters are yet remaining. Little was with me about half an hour this evening.

¹ John Murray, minister of the First Presbyterian Church, Newburyport (Weis, *Colonial Clergy of N.E.*).
² Not found.
³ AA to JQA, 18 July; JA to JQA, 20 July (Adams Papers).

29TH.

I attended at the office the whole day, and resumed Blackstone, whom for three or four days, I had laid aside. I did not however read a great deal. In the evening I took something of a long walk with Townsend; and as I return'd stopp'd to sup; upon the birds, which Amory and Stacey, had been hunting for in the course of the day. There were three other gentlemen there, Mr. Coffin, Mr. Winslow, and a Captain Cochran. We got to singing after supper, and the bottle went round with an unusual rapidity, untill, a round dozen had disappeared. I then thought it was high time to retreat, and with some difficulty slip'd away from those of the company, who appeared to be the most inspired, and took a walk with Townsend; it was after one in the morning when we got to my lodgings: after setting there about an hour and smoking a pipe or two we both went to bed.

30TH.

Although I had not last night, been guilty of an excess so far as to be intoxicated, yet I had not sufficiently consulted what my feelings would be this day, to be entirely prudent. I therefore arose this morning, with a very disagreeable head-ache, which continued the whole day. I could neither attend meeting nor read, nor write; and pass'd the day with much tediousness. In the evening however I took a walk with Townsend; and after returning, pass'd an hour at Mr. Tufts's.

MONDAY OCTOBER 1ST. 1787.

I have not yet got over the consequences of our frolick on Saturday evening. Three whole evenings I have by this means entirely lost, for I cannot yet write with any comfort. How inseparably in all cases of intemperance, is the punishment allied to the fault!

Stedman went this day for Portsmouth, will return here tomorrow, and take his final leave on Wednesday. He is going to open an office at Cambridge, where I heartily wish him success.

In the afternoon I went with Townsend and Thomson and Little, up to Sohier's, and had the usual fare. We return'd leisurely in the evening. I was too much fatigued to write much; having withal a little of the head ache. Putnam arrived in town this afternoon; and I suppose will enter Mr. Bradbury's office immediately.

I shall find I believe very much the want of Mr. Parsons's presence, when he goes off. His attendance upon the genl. Court, will engross his time very much. Next week he will go to Boston, and will be gone I suppose nearly two months. There are a thousand questions which I shall want to propose to him from time to time; but which I shall be reduced to find out by my own industry, and what assistance Townsend and Amory can give me.

2D.

I have at length recovered my usual tone, and have been able this day to attend to business with as much satisfaction as common. Stedman came back from Portsmouth this afternoon: in the evening I carried a packet of letters to his lodgings, for Cambridge.

I began to copy off, not a small volume, of forms for declarations.[1] This is a piece of drudgery, which certainly does not carry its reward with it. But it is a necessary piece of work, for which reason I think the sooner it is finished, the better. I was in hopes before I came here, that I should have time for reading books of entertainment: but after passing eight hours a day in the office, and spending four more in writing minutes, and forms at home, I am not husband of time sufficient to set any more apart for any kind of mental application, and indeed if for three years I can proceed with as much industry, as I have done since I entered the office, the de—l [devil?] will be to pay, if I have not some stock of law. Health is all I shall ask.

[1] A collection of various pleading forms used by a plaintiff's lawyer in actions at law. These and other pleadings were often copied by law students to serve as models for future drafting. JQA's volume of forms has not been found.

3D.

Continued in the first volume of Blackstone. In the course of my reading this day; I came across a paragraph, which surprized me; it was this. "It is a principle of *universal law*, that the natural-born subject of one prince, cannot by any act of his own, no, not by swearing allegiance to another, put off or discharge his natural allegiance to the former: for this natural allegiance was intrinsic, and primitive and antecedent to the other: and cannot be devested without the concurrent act of that prince to whom it was first due."[1] I enquired of Mr. Parsons his opinion upon the subject. He said that if instead of universal law, it was *common law* the assertion would be just; but that in his opinion, by the law of nature every man had a right to put off his natural allegiance, for good cause, and this I think much more reasonable, than to say, that a man is obliged to serve and assist his sovereign however cruel tyrannical and unjust he may be. The doctrine of Blackstone must I think imply that of passive obedience; which is not now to be refuted. It may indeed be said that every unjust act, is a tacit consent to the discharge of the subjects allegiance; but this is straining the meaning of words, a great length; and I think it is much the best to cut the gordian knot, as Mr. Parsons did.

I wrote along in the evening till late.

[1] *Commentaries on the Laws of England,* 11th edn., 4 vols., London, 1791, 1:369–370.

4TH.

I this day concluded the first volume of my author: and employ'd all the afternoon in copying from it, under heads. As Parsons goes to Boston next week and will stay there so long, that I shall probably finish the book I am now reading before he returns; I enquired of him, what would be best to take up next. He recommended, Sullivan's lectures, then Wright's tenures, and then Coke Littelton.[1] This evening I was at Mr. Tufts's; present at the marriage of his daughter Dolly to Mr. Geo. Odiorne of Exeter. Mr. Cary perform'd the ceremony. I staid there to supper, but came away soon after that, as I spent my time rather tediously. Mercy Brooks from Medford was there: she is one of the very few unmarried women, with whom I can be sociable, after a short acquaintance: whether it is owing to some peculiarity of circumstances, or of character I know not, but the fact I am sure of.

Two pages since I return'd is quite decent, I can now fairly close my book.[2]

[1] Francis S. Sullivan, *An Historical Treatise on the Feudal Law, and the Constitution and Laws of England . . . In a Course of Lectures Read in the University of Dublin,* London, 1772; Martin Wright, *Introduction to the Law of Tenures . . .,* London, 1729; Edward Coke, *The First Part of the Institutes of the Laws of England. Or, A Commentary upon Littleton . . .,* London, 1628, and subsequent editions. A copy of Sulli-

van's *Lectures,* containing the bookplate of JQA and the signature of JA on the title-page, is at MQA.

² Presumably JQA wrote his entries for 3–4 Oct., which appear on two pages in the Diary, after returning from Samuel Tufts' house.

5TH.

After writing a few lines in my common place book,¹ I took the second volume, of Blackstone, which treats of the rights of things. I did not read much, and with the extracts which I make, I shall not be able to proceed with very rapid progress. Thomson notwithstanding he keeps schools holds an equal pace with me. However he reads in the evening, while I am employ'd in copying off the forms. This he has already done, having been more than four months in the office. I dined at Mr. Tufts's. The new married pair appeared quite calm and composed, though they looked as if they had been broken of their rest. Whether it be really so is well known to those whom it may concern. In the afternoon before it grew dark, I went down with Thomson, and found Putnam; with him we went to Dr. Swett's and found Little. From thence we retired very abruptly, and went home with Moses. We spent the evening there and supped, after which we all returned respectively to our homes: here I sat a few minutes with Dr. Kilham, my very worthy fellow boarder; and then retired to my room; where, what with copying forms, and what with relating the business of the day, I have almost brought it to 1. in the morning.

¹ Not found.

6TH.

I alter'd my plans of study, and determined to copy forms in the day time because, I can do it notwithstanding all the noise that may be going forward in the office, and read at my own lodgings. I extract a great deal, and am almost tired with it, but Mr. Parsons advises me by all means not to give it up.

In the evening I received a long letter from my Sister,¹ and likewise one from W. Cranch.²

¹ Probably AA2 to JQA, 10 June–16 July (Adams Papers).
² The only extant letter at this time from Cranch, dated 5 Oct., was probably the one JQA received on 9 Oct. (Adams Papers).

7TH.

I attended at Mr. Carey's meeting, all day. In the forenoon he was quite severe upon all persons who either did not attend divine services so steadily as they might, or who being at the house of the Lord do not behave with proper decorum and respect. No person said Mr. Carey who is going into the presence of an earthly prince, will appear in a loose, neglected, attire; as it would be considered as a mark of contempt, and as an insult to the dignity of the sovereign. Hence he deduced the necessity of a serious, devout, attentive mind, at times when we go more immediately into the presence of god. His conclusion, were it placed as a distinct proposition, no one I presume would deny; but his perfectly stale and hackney'd allusion, is in my opinion not only false, but impious. I would ask Mr. Carey's, why, it is necessary to appear with such an accurate precision of dress at the Court of an earthly prince? What other cause can be assigned for the importance of a thing so very indifferent in itself, but the ridiculous vanity and fantastic foppery of the great? It is impossible to deduce an argument from similarity of effect, unless a like similarity of cause exists, and in this case, the supposition is not to be made.

In short if our preachers in general, would not take so much pains as they do, to prove facts which no man in his senses can deny, they would save themselves much exertion of thought, without injuring their reputation's.

In the evening I went with Dr. Kilham, and past an hour or two at Mr. Carter's: the family are all of them exceedingly agreeable: Miss H. Emery was there a young lady with a beautiful countenance, an elegant person, and (I am told) an amiable mind. What more could any person wish to find in a female? A fortune?—Ah! can a vile metal drag'd by the hands of slavery from the bowels of the earth, be put in competition with charms like those. The wretch who could harbour the idea, deserves to be barred forever from the pleasures of friendship and of love.

8TH.

Attended at the office; and wrote diligently, all day. Cold weather coming on apace. Thomson and I had some conversation, before we left the office at night. He is in low spirits, and sees gloomy prospects. I hope he will realize more happy ones, for he is an amiable worthy youth, with a clear head and a sound heart. From the office we went to Putnam's lodgings. There Sam, and I, play'd, to-gether, he on the violin, I on the flute, for a couple of hours. After which, we sat with him till 9 o'clock, and then respectively retired.

I sought my bed quite early this evening. I cannot study now much in my own room for want of a fire.

9TH.

I received a short letter from W. Cranch.

I make a pretty rapid progress with my book of forms, and if I am not interrupted, I hope to finish it by the latter end of next week which will take one heavy load from my shoulders: Putnam came to our office this afternoon; he and Little pass'd the evening with me. I intended to walk with Little but found it was raining hard. I proceed very slowly with Blackstone.

10TH.

A very fine day. Amory and Townsend with a number of other lads went out of town this afternoon upon a party: But I did not feel disposed to join them. Thomson spent part of the evening with me.

11TH.

This afternoon I took a ride with Dr. Kilham, as far as Newtown to see Mr. Dalton, but neither he nor his lady were at home. We rode a mile or two beyond that, and returned just after dark: that road is very good and the prospects all around are very beautiful; but the leaves begin to fall, and the year appears to proceed rapidly on a decline. Amory was with me part of the evening.

12TH.

The day pass'd as usual, except, that I had some political chat with Mr. Parsons. He favours very much the federal constitution, which has lately been proposed by the Convention of the States. Nor do I wonder at all that he should approve of it, as it is calculated to increase the influence, power and wealth of those who have any already. If the Constitution be adopted it will be a grand point gained in favour of the aristocratic party: there are to be no titles of nobility; but there will be great distinctions; and those distinctions will soon be hereditary, and we shall consequently have nobles, but no titles. For my own part I am willing to take my chance under any government whatever, but it is hard to give up a System which I have always been taught to cherish, and to confess, that a free government is inconsistent with human nature.

13TH.

Captain Wyer was in the office this afternoon, a couple of hours; very zealous for the new Constitution. Was desirous of having a town-meeting, to instruct their representatives upon the occasion. Quite enthusiastic, and so are many other people. This afternoon I went, and requested the favor of waiting upon Miss Jones, to the ball next monday; she will go if her health will permit. Little pass'd the evening with me. There was a very brilliant northern light.

14TH.

I wrote two long letters this day. One to J. Forbes,[1] and the other to W. Cranch.[2] Went with Putnam in the afternoon to Mr. Tucker's meeting, and was much pleased with the doctor's preaching. Putnam spent an hour or two with me after meeting.

[1] Not found.
[2] Owned by Miss Margaret DuBois of New York in 1957. A transcript, possibly in the hand of Mrs. JA2, is in M/CFA/31, Adams Papers, Microfilms, Reel No. 327.

15TH.

Rather dissipated the whole day. Could not study with proper attention, and indeed gave the matter up in the afternoon. At about 7 o'clock we met at the dancing hall, and from that time till between 3 and 4 in the morning we were continually dancing. I was unacquainted with almost all the company, but I never saw a collection of ladies where there was comparatively so much beauty. Two or three gentlemen got rather over the bay; but upon the whole the proceedings were as regular and agreeable as might be expected. Little lodg'd with me, and the Clock struck four, just before we went to bed.

16TH.

We rose at about nine o'clock. Dr. Kilham, was just going to take his seat in the Stage for Boston. The Dr. represents this town in the genl. Court; and goes to Boston now, to attend at the Session, which opens to-morrow. I was at the office in the fore-noon, but could not attend much to any study. I took a walk with Townsend. Return'd again to the office, and just as I had got ready to sit down to business, in came W. Cranch and Leonard White from Haverhill: who insisted upon it that I should go there with them this afternoon; and in such a positive manner that I could not deny them. They dined with me at my lodgings, and at about four in the afternoon, we all mounted our horses for Haverhill. The wind was very high, and scattered the dust so much that the riding was very disagreeable. We drank tea at Russell's, and were almost half an hour crossing the river, though the wind had considerably abated. At about seven we got to Mr. Shaw's house. Miss N. Quincy, and Miss B. Cranch came in from Mr. Duncan's soon after. Mr. James Duncan, invited, W. Cranch and me to dine with him to-morrow. The troop of horse, of which he is 1st. lieutenant are to parade in the morning, and he makes an entertainment for them.

It was past 11 this evening when we retired.

17TH.

This day a regiment of foot, and a troop of about 60 horse-men paraded, and were review'd by Genl. Titcomb. The weather was rather disagreeable, though not so windy as it was yesterday. One of the foot companies was drest in the rifle uniform. That of the horse was red faced with green: the horses in general were good, but the company has not been formed long, and are not yet perfect in their exercices. We dined at Mr. Duncans. I chatted with Mr. Symmes upon the new Constitution. We did not agree upon the subject. While we were talking Mr. Bartlett came in, and was beginning to attack me. I told him I wish'd to change the subject; as I felt utterly unequal to the task of opposing two persons of whose judgment I had so high an opinion, as Mr. Symmes and Mr. Bartlett. Bartlett laugh'd and said I was very polite. "Adams," says Symmes, "you shall go home with me, and take a bed to-night." And I found that France is not the only Country where *Yorick's secret*[1] has its influence. We walk'd up the hill where the regiment was parading in the afternoon; but the weather was so cold that I return'd back some-time before they finish'd. The general was drest and mounted rather shabbily: he has never been employd in military life; and nobody knows how he came to be a major general.

Pass'd part of the evening at Mr. White's.

Found Mr. Allen, and Mr. Tucker at Mr. Shaw's: they staid till about 9 o'clock; and then return'd to Bradford.

[1] That is, flattery (Laurence Sterne, *A Sentimental Journey through France and Italy,* in *Works,* 10 vols., London, 1788, 5:210).

18TH.

We dined this day at Mr. Bartlett's. Captain Wier, was there, and Miss S. McKinstry, who is upon the point of being married to Major Starke, and Miss Barrell, a young Lady from Boston whose countenance indicates misfortune. She had a lover, who forsook her upon discovering that she had not a fortune as he had expected. Townsend came into Town yesterday with Miss P. Greenleaf; and return'd this afternoon to Newbury.

The young ladies drank tea at Judge Sargeant's. I spent the evening till between 8 and 9 o'clock at Mr. White's.

I had in the course of the day, and have had every day since I came here a great deal of conversation with Mr. Shaw concerning Sam Walker, who still persists in declaring himself innocent, though every one who is acquainted with the circumstances, must be as fully convinced of his guilt, as if he had seen him do the deed himself: Mr. Shaw was much afflicted. He had great expectations from Walker, who had been his pupil, and whose reputation would in some measure have reflected honour upon his instructor. But "how art thou fallen Lucifer, son of the morning"![1]

[1] A partial rendering of Isaiah, 14:12.

19TH.

W. Cranch, and the two young ladies set off this morning for Boston. The weather is much milder for them than it has been for several days past.

I spent the forenoon with Mr. Thaxter at his office. He is to be published[1] next Sunday.

Dined at Mr. Shaw's. Just after dinner Mrs. Allen came in from Bradford, and inform'd us of Deacon Smith's death.[2] He died on Tuesday morning. The news came by Dr. Williams, who lodg'd at Bradford last night.

Between 3 and 4, I set out to return home, and overtook, F. Bradbury and Winslow in a chaise going the same way. At about half past five I got home; and went and pass'd the evening with Townsend. Amory is quite unwell. Return'd this day from Portsmouth.

[1] That is, his marriage banns with Elizabeth Duncan, of Haverhill, were to be published.

[2] Deacon Isaac Smith, of Boston, JQA's great-uncle, who died on 16 Oct.

20TH.

I was more attentive at the office than I expected to be between two sallies. I had determined before I went to Haverhill, not to go so far as Boston till the spring; but I have now altered my resolutions, and shall go from hence next monday, for a fortnight. This is not the way to acquire the science of the law, but dissipation is so fashionable here that it is necessary to enter into it a little in order not to appear too singular, and as Mr. Parsons will probably be absent for three weeks to come, I know not that I can take a more eligible time for a vacation.

21ST.

I attended Mr. Carey in the forenoon, and went with Putnam to hear Dr. Tucker in the afternoon. He is a very good preacher, but the generality of his hearers look, as if they were form'd of the coarsest clay. A number of female figures in particular seem to charge nature with having made gross mistakes.

I passed the evening till almost 9 o'clock with Putnam. Townsend took me from there and carried me volens nolens to sup with him. I intended to have written a great deal this day, but all my schemes vanished with the fleeting hours, and I must now refer this matter, till I return from my intended Journey.

22D.

The weather yesterday did not look promising, but is this day very clear, and for the season uncommonly warm. At about half past nine I mounted my horse, and Townsend said he would take an airing and ride a few miles with me: the pleasantness of the weather led him on till he finally agreed to go as far as Haverhill, intending to return in the afternoon. We rode part of the way with Sohier, the Collegian,[1] who was on his way to Groton; and we got to Haverhill just before twelve o'clock. I found Mr. and Mrs. Shaw had set out this morning for Hingham. At twelve we went to Mr. Thaxter's lodgings, and found fifty or sixty people heartily at work, in which we very readily joined them.[2] At about 2, there were 18 or 20 left who sat down to a table covered with "big bellied bottles." For 2 hours or more Bacchus and Momus joined hands to increase the festivity of the company. But the former of these deities then of a sudden took a fancy to divert himself, and fell to tripping up their heels. Momus laugh'd on, and kept singing, till he finally grew hoarse and drowsy, and Morpheus to close the scene sprinkled a few poppies over their heads, and set them to snoring in concert. This is I believe the first time that I have dived any depth into the pagan mythology since I undertook the direction of these very interesting memoirs. I have always had the precept of Horace in my mind.

Noc Deus intersit nisi dignus vindice nodus.[3]

and I trust the gentle reader will not think I have in this instance violated that rule. But to return to plain insipid narration, by five o'clock they were all under the table except those who had been peculiarly cautious, and two or three stout topers. I had been very moderate, yet felt it was necessary to walk, and take the air. I rambled with Leonard White, over the fields, and through the streets till near 7 o'clock. Then went home with him and after passing a couple of hours in chat, retired quite early to bed.

[1] William Sawyer, Harvard 1788, of Newburyport (Currier, *Newburyport,* 2:292).

[2] Presumably to celebrate the marriage banns announced the day before for Thaxter and Elizabeth Duncan.

[3] "Nec deus intersit, nisi dignus vindice nodus inciderit," *De Arte Poetica,* lines 191–192: "And let no god intervene, unless a knot come worthy of such a deliverer" (Horace, *Satires, Epistles and Ars Poetica,* transl. Fairclough, p. 466, 467).

23D.

Rose at about 8 this morning, and felt no inconveniency from the scene of yesterday. Townsend, who got so much engaged as to give up all thoughts of returning last night to Newbury-Port, breakfasted with us this morning; and then mounted his horse.

It was a little after nine, when I started from the opposite shore of the river, and it was about twelve when I got to the tavern in Wilmington. Mr. Thaxter, and Miss Duncan, and her brother James, a Mr. Howe, and two or three other ladies dined at Wilmington. The landlord is opposed to the proposed Constitution. I stopped about a quarter of an hour at Medford to see my friend Freeman, and delivered him a couple of letters. I expected to have seen him at the ordination to-morrow, but his school retains him at Medford. We got into Boston just before Sunset. We stopp'd an hour there to get dress'd, and take a dish of Coffee. It was quite dark before we got out of Town; and we arrived at Braintree between 8 and 9. We found that the young ladies and all the company that was disposed to attend the ordination[1] had gone to Hingham this afternoon. I was very much fatigued. I once before rode this journey in a day; (v: p: 25)[2] and was still more fatigued, but that was in the middle of Summer, when the weather was very warm, which made it more tedious to ride on horseback.

Kirkland and my brother Tom were both here, and could not go on to Hingham for want of horses.

It was almost 11. before we retired.

[1] The ordination in Hingham of Henry Ware, JQA's former roommate at Harvard.
[2] Entry for 5 Aug. 1786 (above).

24TH.

At about 10 this morning I set off for Hingham. Mr. Thaxter and Miss Duncan, went somewhat earlier. I got there between 11 and 12, and went immediately to the meeting house: it was very much crowded, and I found great difficulty to get in, I finally obtained however a very good place. They began by singing a good anthem extremely well. The first prayer was made by Mr.   .[1] Mr. Hilliard then preach'd a sermon from II Corinthians, I, 24. Not that we have dominion over your faith but are helpers of your joy.[2] He delivered his Sentiments very freely though many of them were in oppositions, to the prevailing customs. It was the best sermon I ever heard him preach, and upon this occasion it was natural that he should exert himself. Mr.   [3] gave the charge; Dr. Hitchcock made the ordaining prayer, Mr. Shute gave the right hand of fellowship, and Mr. Haven made the last prayer.[4] The ceremonies were then concluded by another anthem as well perform'd as the first. From thence the company retired, I went to pay my compliments to Mr. Ware, my old chum; and to tell him how happy I am to see him so well settled already. I intended to dine there but was called away with Mr. Gannett by Mr. Caleb Thaxter, where we went and dined. There were between thirty and forty persons at table, but chiefly young gentlemen. After dinner we had two or three songs and then walk'd. We went to Coll. Rice's,[5] where we found a similar company, smoking and singing.

We rambled about till almost seven o'clock; and I then went to Mrs. Derby's Hall, where, it was said there was to be a dance. We found here a scene of confusion similar to that which we had last spring at Sandwich:[6] however by a manoeuvre, which pack'd off about one half of the company, our numbers were so much reduced, that we were able to maintain a degree of order and regularity. I was so lucky as to draw Miss S. Smith of Sandwich for a partner, and danced with her, a great part of the evening. It was between two and three in the morning before we broke up. I then went to Coll. Thaxter's,[7] supp'd and, at about half after 3, went to bed with Charles.

[1] Left blank in MS.

[2] Timothy Hilliard, *A Sermon Preached October 24th, 1787, at the Ordination of the Rev. Henry Ware, to the Pastoral Care of the First Church in Hingham,* Salem, 1788.

[3] Left blank in MS; the charge was given by Rev. John Brown, minister of the First Congregational Society of Cohasset (same, p. 26).

[4] Probably Rev. Gad Hitchcock, minister of the second parish of Pembroke (now Hanson); Daniel Shute, minister of the Second Congregational Church at Hing-ham; probably Jason Haven, minister of the First Congregational Church at Dedham (Sprague, *Annals Amer. Pulpit,* 8:29–31; Hilliard, *Sermon,* p. 27; Weis, *Colonial Clergy of N.E.*).

[5] Col. Nathan Rice, one of JA's former law clerks (JA, *Legal Papers,* 1:cviii).

[6] See entry for 18 April (above).

[7] Col. John Thaxter Sr. (1721–1802), uncle of AA by marriage to Anna Quincy, and father of John Thaxter Jr. (*History of the Town of Hingham, Massachusetts,* 4 vols. in 3, Hingham, 1893, 3:232).

25TH.

The town is not so much crowded this day; as it was yesterday. That Class of people which is called by some persons the *rabble,* (by which word is meant people, who have neither a fortune nor an education at our university, *alias* a liberal education) went off chiefly last night: and there now remains nothing but the *genteel* company, or otherwise people who have no business, to call them from scenes of dissipation. I walk'd in the morning with Mr. Ware, and Coll. Rice down to the landing place where I found a number of people employ'd in preparing fish. There is some little business of this kind done here.

After returning into Town I saunter'd about till dinner time.

Foster, Learned, and Vose with his Sisters went away before dinner. Dined at Coll. Rice's. The Company was not large; the character that I remarked the most was a Captain Clap, who is all, soldier. He appears to delight in whatever is military; Coll. Rice's son, a lad of 7 years old, committed some little impropriety; "You rogue," Says Clap, "nothing but your age can excuse and protect you." Who but a genuine Son of Mars, would have thought of correcting, in that manner a boy of 7 years?

It was proposed that we should have another dance this night, and Blake and Perkins a couple of young fellows, both strangers in town, undertook to be managers. We drank tea, a number of us, at Mr. Caleb Thaxter's, and at about 7, went again to Mrs. Derby's Hall, where a partition between two chambers had been taken down which made it much more convenient than it was the night before. There were about 30 gentlemen and forty ladies: about 20 couples could stand up at once, and the rest amused themselves either with conversation, or with playing at cards. Between 2 and 3, we broke up, and I retired with our young ladies. We sat about half an hour at Col'l Thaxter's, and I then went to bed. But a number of the lads, after conducting their ladies home retained the music, and went a serenading all over the Town; till day-light.

26TH.

We went and escorted a number of ladies to the packet: and by eleven o'clock, almost all the company was gone, and the town look'd as solitary as a deserted village.

I took a walk with Mr. Q. Thaxter,[1] and Mr. Andrews down to Genl. Lincoln's Mills. It was half past twelve before I got back to Mr. Thaxter's. Of all the company that had been there Charles and I, only remained at dinner.

At about 2 we mounted, and arrived at Mr. Cranch's in Braintree at about half after three. The young ladies had got home before dinner, and were much fatigued. I was not so much so, as I expected to be, from keeping so constantly on the go, since the beginning of the week. In the beginning of the evening Judge Sargeant came in; he came from Taunton where the supreme Court have been sitting this week, and completed their business last evening.

¹ Quincy (1762–1837), brother of John Thaxter Jr. and cousin of AA.

27TH.

Judge Sargeant, went away this forenoon proceeding on his way to Cambridge.

Tom went to Lincoln. In the afternoon, I went with Charles and Kirkland to see my uncle Quincy.

Mr. Wibird was here in the evening.

28TH.

I attended upon Mr. Wibird in the forenoon. And pass'd the afternoon down at my father's library. W. Cranch came from Boston last evening, and returned there to'night after meeting. I was very much entertained in reading some journals of my father's, from 1769, to 1776.

29TH.

At about 10. o'clock Mr. Thaxter came in from Hingham on his way to Boston: he stay'd but a few minutes, and I set off with him. We got into Town before one. I dined with Miss B. Smith,¹ who still lives in the house that was her father's. Mrs. Cranch was there, and went for Braintree soon after dinner. I went and spent the evening with Dr. Kilham at his lodgings: he has made himself rather unpopular, by opposing the submission of the federal Constitution, to a State Convention, and I think he is perfectly right, in preferring his independency to his popularity.

¹ Elizabeth (1770–1849), daughter of Isaac Smith Sr. and cousin of AA.

30TH.

Sauntered about town, the chief part of the day: attended in the gallery of the house of representatives but there was no matter of any great importance before them. Dined at Deacon Storer's with Mr. Thaxter, who is very busy in making preparations for his marriage. I drank tea at Mr. Dawes's, and pass'd the evening at Mr. Foster's with Dr. Tufts. Lodg'd at Mr. W. Smith's.

31ST.

Saw Charles in Boston, on his way to Cambridge, as the vacation closes this day. At about noon I set out for Cambridge myself. The supreme Court sits there this week. I dined and lodg'd at Judge Dana's. I attended the Court in the afternoon, but no case came on, of any consequence. Saw Stedman there. He has not yet opened an office, but proposes to do so very soon. The House of Representatives this day rejected a report of a Committee, for erecting a bridge over Beverly ferry, in the evening I called at Mr. Wigglesworth's and pass'd an hour. Peggy is as sociable and agreeable as ever.

Here endeth the second Volume.

1787.

Heu mihi praeteritos referat si Jupiter annos![1]

[1] "O if Jupiter would bring me back the years that are sped," *Aeneid*, Bk. VIII, line 560 (transl. H. Rushton Fairclough, 2 vols., London, 1930, 2:98, 99).

Paris.   J. Q. Adams. Aug: 20th. 1783.

Ephemeris.

Vol: III.[1]

1787.

[1] Titlepage of D/JQA/12, the third of three leather-bound blank books that JQA presumably purchased in Paris on 20 Aug. 1783. For a fuller physical description of these volumes, see the note for the titlepage of D/JQA/10, *ante* 1 Jan. 1785 (above). This Diary volume contains entries from 1 Nov. 1787 to [24 Aug.–2 Sept. 1788], followed by scattered entries, twelve for September and five for Oct. 1788, and thirteen for Sept. 1789. See entry for [24 Aug.–2 Sept. 1788], note 1 (below). The volume concludes with line-a-day memoranda for Aug. through Dec. 1788, and all of 1789 and 1790, copied over from the later Diaries 13, 14, and 15.

THURSDAY NOVEMBER 1ST. 1787.

I attended in the morning, and in the afternoon at the setting of the supreme Court. Judge Dana, took his seat, for the first time since his illness; from which he has not yet, and I fear never will entirely recover. I dined at his house, and pass'd the evening with my old Clasmate Sam: Williams. The Cases before the Court were not very interesting, except one, which was so intricate, that I could not entirely comprehend it. Sullivan and Lowell spent their lungs, for three or four hours upon the cause, and it was 8 in the evening before it was given to the Jury. Sullivan asserted that in the Courts in this Country it was customary to take parol evidence, in preference to matter of record. This bare-faced falshood, was noticed by all the Court. Sumner[1] shook his head. "You are totally mistaken Mr. Sullivan" said Cushing. "They have done so" said Sullivan; "Then" said Sewall, "I hope they will never do so again." This is not an uncommon practice of Sullivan's; and when the whole Court are thus loudly against him he does not appear in the least abashed, but appears to display a countenance which never knew a blush.

I lodg'd at Packard's chamber.

[1] Increase Sumner, a justice of the Supreme Judicial Court (Sibley-Shipton, *Harvard Graduates*, 16:531–538).

2D.

I breakfasted this morning with Stedman. A number of the lawyers were there; rather nettled at a bill now before the Senate, for the better regulating the fees &c of attorney's and practitioners. The Committee by whom it was drawn up, and presented, was composed of those persons who for these two years past have been the most violent of the Community, in their antipathy to lawyers.[1]

Blessed Times! I was so much engag'd this forenoon in other matters, that I could not attend at the Court. I called at Mr. Dana's and at Mr. Wigglesworth's, and took their letters for Newbury-Port. Dined at Mrs. Forbes's. Jack, and his brother James, arrived from Boston, just before dinner. It was almost 5 o'clock, when I got on my horse; and took leave of Forbes and Packard. Just after dusk, I got into Boston. Went to Mr. Dawes's, and found Wm. Cranch with whom I went and pass'd the evening at Dr. Tufts's lodgings.

Lodg'd at Mr. W. Smith's.

[1] In Feb. 1787, in the aftermath of Shays' Rebellion, the Massachusetts legislature lowered court and attorney fees, an important cause of complaint among the rebels. When legislators attempted to enact further reductions at this time, the

lawyers were able to gather enough support to defeat the measure (Gerard W. Gawalt, *The Promise of Power: The Emer-* gence of *The Legal Profession in Massachusetts, 1760–1840*, Westport, Conn., 1979, p. 65).

3D.

Between 8 and 9 this morning, I cross'd Charlestown, and Malden bridges. I rode, as far as D'anvers before I stopp'd. There I found Mr. W. Parsons and his wife, Mr. T. Parsons, and Mr. J. Tracey. They started from thence before me, but I, came up with them again in Ipswich, where we dined at Homan's tavern. Parsons was quite witty, but strained rather too-much for it as he frequently does. "John," said he to Tracey "who made you adjutant general?"—"Mr. Bowdoin."—"Strange! how the wisest men, will err sometimes!...."[1] This kind of wit may I think be compared to a sky rocket, which spends all its force in hissing, and then disappoints us, with such a weak explosion that it can scarcely be heard. But wit to be pleasing, must, I think be unexpected, like the lightening which flashes in our eyes. From Ipswich I rode in Company with them to Newbury, and at about Sun-set I return'd my horse to his owner. I met Thompson in the street, and went with him to Putnam's lodgings. He stay'd only a few minutes, but I tarried there till almost 9 o'clock, when I came home and retired to bed.

[1] JQA's ellipses.

4TH.

I was so much fatigued in consequence of my yesterday's ride that I did not attend meeting. I wrote some lines at home, and finished reading the first volume of Buffon's theory of the earth.[1] I am exceedingly pleased, with the style, and manner of this writer. It is concise, nervous, and elegant. The theory I cannot properly judge of till I get through the other volume.

[1] Georges Louis Leclerc de Buffon and others, *Histoire naturelle, générale et particulière, avec la description du cabinet du roy*, 44 vols., Paris, 1749–1804.

5TH.

I attended at the Office. Amory was there. Return'd yesterday from Salem. Townsend went to Boston last week, and has not yet return'd. In the afternoon, we attended the funeral of Mrs. Davenport a sister of Mr. Parsons. She died of a consumption a few days since. Little, and Thomson pass'd an hour with me in the evening, after which, I went with the latter to Mr. Atkins's. Thomson was much affected, on hearing of the death of one of his school-boys; who died of the Scarlet fever, after a very short illness.

I cannot write yet in the evening, for want of fire.

6TH.

Mr. Parsons went this morning to Salem, where the supreme Court sits this week. I pass'd this evening with Thomson at the office and had a great deal of Conversation with him upon diverse subjects: I feel my attachment for this young gentleman daily increasing: the more I become acquainted with him, the more my expectation of enjoying great benefit, and satisfaction from an intimacy with him increases. Indeed I have hitherto had reason, to think myself fortunate, in my fellow students, who are all very agreeable although, their dispositions are essentially different.

I pass'd an hour this forenoon very sociably with Miss Jones.

7TH.

Quite industrious this day in copying forms. Alone in the office a great part of the day. Amory, even when he is in town, is not very attentive at the office. I pass'd the evening with Putnam.

8TH.

Finished my book of forms, and wrote an index to them. So that henceforth, I shall be able to attend more steadily to Blackstone. Townsend return'd this morning from Boston.

9TH.

Amory went to Salem this afternoon. They have a ball there this evening, said to be given to the Court. Amory went to attend it. I pass'd the evening at Mr. Bradbury's, where we play'd a number of tunes in concert, besides a cheating game of cards. I got through the theory of the earth. I am more and more pleased with the author. One part of his theory is merely hypothetical, and might perhaps be called extravagant. He supposes the earth, and the other planets were originally a part of the Sun, and that they were sever'd from it by the shock of a comett. Yet even in this part his reasoning is very ingenious; the other part of his theory is founded upon facts; he lays very justly much more stress upon this, and his arguments are very strong and convincing. He supposes that the continents and islands which are now inhabited, were covered by the waters of the ocean, and that they will be so again: that at some future period the Alps, the Pyrenees, and the Andes, will be at the bottom of the sea, and that the earth now beneath the atlantic, and pacific oceans, will be the abodes of men, adorned, with splendid cities, and crowned with venerable forests. The phenomena, from which he deduces his strongest, arguments are the continual motion of the Sea from east to west, the correspondent angles of mountains, the horizontal, and parallel position of the different strata of earth, and the innumerable quantities of sea shells and other marine productions, found in all parts of the earth, at a considerable depth under-ground....[1] If the author is some times mistaken, he is certainly every where philosophical.

[1] JQA's ellipses.

10TH.

Attended at the office as usual, and read Blackstone: passed the evening with Putnam at his lodgings. Began to read Buffon's natural history of man.

11TH.

Attended meeting, with Townsend, the whole day at Dr. Tucker's: much pleased with this gentleman as a preacher. Little came home with me: in the evening Williams came in: from Salem yesterday. We went with him to Putnam's, and finished the evening.

12TH.

I had some writing, which I wished to do this day, and I therefore did not attend at the office. Williams and Little dined, and past the afternoon with me. Townsend came in, just before dark: I went with him and spent an hour or two at Mr. Atkins's. This family is very agreeable: Mrs. Atkins, is a sociable, cheerful, sensible old lady; Miss A. is handsome, and a favorite of Townsend's.

I went home with Townsend and supped there. The evening was excessively dark.

13TH.

Williams set out this morning for Cambridge. I at length got me some wood, and had a fire in my chamber, which will enable me hence forth to study more in the evenings. Thompson was with me an hour or two this night.

14TH.

I find I am getting fast into the same unmeaning dull sameness, which has frequently abbreviated the space of a day in these pages. Study does not consist merely, in acquiring the ideas of others but, it is necessary by reflection to endeavour to form some for ourselves: But I am fearful, that I have not yet acquired sufficient knowledge, to derive much advantage from my own speculations. Ars longa, vita brevis, is a maxim, the truth of which I am experiencing daily more and more. There is not one art or science, in which I have any degree of proficiency, and I have now undertaken the study of a profession, which alone ought to employ all the time I can devote to study, for twenty years to come. My eyes and my health begin to fail, and I do not feel that ardor for application, which I should have, to be a man of science. In short the more I do, the more I find to do; and it is almost discouraging, to see one's labour increase, as we proceed in it.

15TH.

Amory, and Thompson went upon a dancing party yesterday. They invited me to join them, but I did not feel disposed. This afternoon I went with Townsend, and attended Mr. Spring's[1] lecture. I was much better pleased than I expected to be with this gentleman's preaching. His sentiments are extremely contracted, and illiberal, and he maintains them with the zeal, and enthusiasm of a bigot, but his delivery is very agreeable, and I believe his devotion sincere; although I shall never be a convert to his principles, I will not condemn them as impious and heretical. Little, Putnam, and I, spent the evening with Thomson, at his father's. A letter from W. S.[2] was canvassed; it was stiff, inelegant and trivial. I gave this as my opinion, and although they charged me with being prejudiced against the writer, yet I found, their sentiments on this point agreed perfectly with mine.

[1] Rev. Samuel Spring, minister of the Third Religious Society in Newburyport (Sprague, *Annals Amer. Pulpit,* 2:85).
[2] Presumably from William Stedman.

16TH.

I finished the second volume of Blackstone, and began upon the third which treats of private wrongs. And this evening I got through Buffon's natural history of man, which is still more entertaining than the theory of the earth.

17TH.

I set out for Haverhill between 3 and 4. this afternoon, and arrived at Mr. White's, a little after 5. Leonard was at my lodgings last Tuesday, and made me promise I would stay with him the next time I should go to that town. I was inform'd of Mr. Thaxter's marriage. Last tuesday was the day, when he departed the life of a bachelor, and was ushered into a new kind of existence. His friends had expected it would not be till next tuesday, but he fairly gave them the slip.

I went up to Mr. Shaw's this evening, and spent an hour. Lodg'd at Mr. White's.

18TH.

In the forenoon I attended at Mr. Smith's meeting: he preaches without notes, and like all the preachers, who make a practice of this, that I ever heard, often repeats the same sentiments. In the afternoon I went to hear Mr. Shaw. After meeting I went up there and pass'd part of the evening. Mr. Redington and Captain Marsh and Deacon Eames were there.

19TH.

I lodg'd at Mr. White's again last night; went this morning up to Mr. Shaw's and past an hour; and between 10 and 11, Set off for Newbury-Port. Got home at about 1. Called at the office. Found Amory was gone to Salem for a week. Mr. Parsons says, he will spoil himself in spite of any thing that can be done. Townsend dined with me. We were not much in the office, in the afternoon. Little spent the evening with me.

Rather unwell.

20TH.

Proceed slowly in the third volume of Blackstone. As this is the most important author of all those that will occur, I make large extracts from him, which takes me up so much time that I cannot read above twenty or thirty pages in a day. Townsend pass'd the evening at my lodgings. Dull weather. This afternoon there was a town-meeting for the purpose of choosing members to represent this Town in the State convention which is to meet in January, and canvass the proposed federal Constitution. The persons chosen were Mr. King, Judge Greenleaf, Mr. Parsons, and Genl. Titcomb. They are all in favour of the constitution, and the town appears to be very unanimous for it.

21ST.

I this morning requested of Mr. Parsons his opinion, whether it would be most advantageous for me to pursue, the professional study in those hours, when I should not attend at the office; or whether it would be best to devote those of my evenings, which I shall pass at my own lodgings, to other purposes, and a diversity of studies. He answered by observing, that I could not attend to any useful branch of Science, in which I should not find my account; he would rather advise me, to read a number of ethic writers: it was necessary for a person going into the profession of the law, to have principles strongly established; otherwise, however amiable, and however honest his disposition might be, yet the necessity he is under of defending indiscriminately, the good and the bad, the right, and the wrong would imperceptibly lead him into universal skepticism. He advised also Quinctilian, and the best writers upon Christianity; He himself, he said, was convinced of the truth of the Christian religion; he believed revelation, and it was his reason, that had been convinced, for he entered upon the world rather prejudiced against revelation.

It stormed in the afternoon, I pass'd part of the evening at Mr. Parsons's, and the remainder with Townsend at his lodgings.

22D.

Weather remarkably mild for the Season: I have been rather unwell for a week or 10 days back, which prevents me from applying myself with so much assiduity as I should wish to.

I passed this evening with Thompson and Putnam at Little's. We were very sociable, and cheerful. At 9 we return'd to our respective homes. The weather before this, had cleared up, though in the afternoon it had threatened to be stormy.

23D.

The events of the day were quite uninteresting. I had however an opportunity to observe the effects of the Passions. How despotically they rule! how they bend, and master, the greatest and the wisest geniuses! T'is a pity! 'tis great pity! that prudence should desert people when they have the most need of it. Tis pity, that such a mean, little, dirty passion as envy, should be the vice of the most capacious souls. Human Nature, how inexplicable art thou! Oh, may I learn before I advance upon the political stage, (if I ever do) not to put my trust in thee! This grave apostrophe, with the lines that precede it may be mysterious to you sir, but if so, remember that it is none of your business. And so I wish you good night.

24TH.

I went in the forenoon, and exhibited my complaints to Dr. Swett, but he told me, they were not worth speaking of; and so I will e'en let them take their chance.

This afternoon Townsend, and I, went down to Mr. Tracey's, upon a disagreeable piece of business, but which we got through quite comfortably. Ben Hooper called on me in the evening. I have again begun upon Gibbon's roman history, and hope, I shall this time go through.[1] I read the first volume last Spring; but at that time my avocations were so numerous, that I could not proceed in reading the book. I admire the style, and in general the Sentiment, though I think there is sometimes an affectation of wit in the one, and sometimes a glaring tinsel in the other, which are far beneath the majestic simplicity of nature.

[1] JQA's 32 pages of MS notes from his rereading of Gibbon, begun on 19 Nov., and 54 pages of sources used by Gibbon, undated but presumably made at the same time, are in M/JQA/46, Adams Papers, Microfilms, Reel No. 241. In addition, there are random notes from Gibbon on blank pages in the almanac JQA used for his line-a-day Diary from 11 Jan.–31 Dec. 1788 (D/JQA/13, same, Microfilms, Reel No. 16).

25TH.

I thought I was too unwell to pass two hours in a cold meeting house this forenoon, and staid at home. In the afternoon I ventured out, and went with Townsend to Dr. Tucker's meeting-house; but finding there was no service there, we went to church. Parson Bass,[1] is not much of an orator, and was rather negligent in treating common place topics, in common place language. Drank tea at Mrs. Hooper's,[2] and pass'd the evening at Mr. J. Tracy's. Captn. Fletcher was there. Tracy was quite warm upon the subject of the late election. He is a militia officer, and possessed very strongly of the esprit de corps. He was offended that Genl. Titcomb, should come in the last of the four members for this town, and in the course of conversation went rather beyond the bounds of prudence.

[1] Rev. Edward Bass, rector of St. Paul's Episcopal Church in Newburyport (Sibley-Shipton, *Harvard Graduates*, 11:340–359).

[2] Mrs. Mary Harris Hooper, wife of the loyalist Joseph Hooper, and landlady of JQA's fellow law student Horatio Townsend (same, 15:404–406).

26TH.

I took an additional cold, yesterday, and am still more unwell than I have been. I pass'd the evening at my lodgings; reading Gibbon, and translating a piece from the french.

27TH.

Better than I have been for these ten days past: all the time again at the office, or at my own lodgings. It is of great advantage to us to have Mr. Parsons in the office. He is in himself a law-library, and a proficient in every useful branch of science. But his chief excellency is, that, no student can be more fond of proposing questions than he is of solving them. He is never at a loss, and always gives a full and ample account, not only of the subject

II. THEOPHILUS PARSONS
See page xiii

proposed, but of all matters which have any intimate connection with it. I am perswaded, that the advantage of having such an instructor is very great, and I hope I shall not misimprove, it, as some of his pupils have done. Where nature is deficient, application must supply her place, and if Nature is liberal, there is so much more reason, for turning her partiality to advantage, for

> Nature never lends
> The smallest scruple of her excellence
> But like a thrifty goddess she determines
> Herself the glory of a creditor
> Both thanks and use.[1]

[1] *Measure for Measure,* Act I, scene i, lines 37–41.

28TH.

Finished the third volume of Blackstone, and began upon the fourth, which is upon public wrongs. Took something of a long walk with Thompson. He, and Little and Putnam passed the evening with me. Mr. and Mrs. Smith came into Town this evening, and brought me a bundle.

Mr. Parsons after making much difficulty has finally consented, that we should pass the evenings till 8 o'clock at the office, At Townsend's importunity. It will make at this Season a large addition to the time which we employ in the professional studies, though I do not know that it will be of any great advantage to me.

29TH.

Thanksgiving day: between 8 and 9 o'clock this morning I set out for Haverhill and got to Mr. Shaw's a little before eleven. I attended meeting: Mr. Shaw preach'd a long sermon, and a good one. Mr. Parker[1] and his wife dined with us: I did not admire them, the woman particularly; she has a hard masculine countenance, and black eyes, which express as much softness as those of a tyger. But she is a very good woman: only has rather too much temper, or as it is called in New-England too much *stuff.* I went down to Mr. White's in the evening, but Leonard was not at home: I was going to Mr. Duncan's, but met all the younger part of the family, in the street. I found Leonard White at Mr. Shaw's, and Mr. Flint who came this day from Lincoln.

[1] Benjamin Parker, formerly minister of the Fourth Congregational Church of Haverhill (Sibley-Shipton, *Harvard Graduates,* 10:220–222).

30TH.

I passed the forenoon with Leonard, who has been making two or three unsuccessful attempts to make phosphorus; his glass vials melt in the process.

Dined at Mr. Duncan's. Mrs. Thaxter has got two or three wrinkles on her forehead. I went to see the house in which they are to live. Pass'd the afternoon with him. His honey moon is not yet past. I was at Mr. White's in the evening.

SATURDAY DECEMBER 1ST. 1787.

I dined at Mr. White's; after dinner I went to Mr. Shaw's, stay'd about an hour, and just before Sun-set, departed for New-bury-Port. I got into the town just as the clock struck seven. Pass'd the evening with Putnam; and came home at about 9. I found Dr. Kilham, at home: he return'd from Boston on Thurs-day; and although his conduct during the late session of the general court, upon the subject of the proposed continental constitution, has not met with the approbation of his constituents in general,[1] yet I think he is very much to be applauded for that in-dependance of spirit, which disdains to sacrifice, a sentiment, to the breath of popularity. But men are too apt to suspect the motives of those with whom they differ in sentiment, and although in this Country religious bigotry is almost entirely done away, yet the same principle, in another garb, appears in all our politi-cal manoeuvres.

[1] On 24 Oct. Kilham had spoken in opposition to a resolution calling for a ratifying convention in Massachusetts (*Massachusetts Centinel*, 27 Oct.). For some Newburyport reaction to the speech, see the *Massachusetts Centinel*, 7 Nov.

2D.

I attended Mr. Carey's meeting this afternoon, and in the evening I went to Mr. Carter's. Mrs. Smith and Miss Betsey return to Boston to-morrow. Mr. Smith went yesterday. Miss Emery, and Miss Sally Jenkins, were at Mr. Carter's this evening.

3D.

Mr. Moore breakfasted with us. Mr. Parsons is quite unwell, and has been so for two or three days past. This evening White called at the office; he came from Haverhill this day. He passed the evening, and lodged with me. Townsend, Thomson and Putnam were like wise here in the evening. I feel neither the inclination nor the power to expatiate, upon the events of the day, which were very uninteresting.

4TH.

White returned this morning to Haverhill. At the office all day. Mr. Parsons still very unwell—somewhat vapourish: fears he has the distemper which is now very prevalent in the town.

5TH.

I pass'd the evening with Little and Townsend at Miss Cazneau's. We play'd Commerce,[1] and whist: but it was dull work. Miss Cazneau, has nothing in her person to recommend her, but a very good shape; her complexion is very dark, and not very clear. No feature of her face is peculiarly agreeable, and her eyes are rather unfavourable to her. A capricious, passionate, imprudent character is stamped upon her behaviour. She displays rather too much levity, and a trifling, *uninteresting* vanity is conspicuous. I call it *un*interesting vanity, because there is a certain kind of vanity, that I have observed in some women, which is exceedingly interesting, and which is sometimes productive of such pleasing manners, that I should be at a loss whether to call it a foible or an accomplishment. Miss Tucker, who likewise passed the evening there, is fair, rather too large for gentility, with a countenance, which has not sufficient animation or expression to be very strikingly agreeable. Her manners are pleasing; if I could find fault with any part of them; it would be with the appearance of an affectation of *softness.* This defect is not uncommon; but however amiable a real sweetness of disposition may be, this appearance of it in the manners is not calculated to win my heart. However if I were to judge of the tempers of these two ladies from their behaviour this evening, I should pronounce the latter, infinitely, the most amiable of the two. I came home at about 9. in the evening.

[1] A game of cards characterized by exchanges or bartering (*OED*).

6TH.

Spent the evening with Thompson and Little, at Putnam's lodgings. We conversed upon a diversity of subjects. Law, Physic, History, poetry, religion and politics, by turns engaged our attention. These meetings renew the recollection of those happy scenes, which we have all gone through in college; and in this manner, I now pass some of my most agreeable hours. But after I came home this evening: and after reading, an hour or two, I felt a depression of spirits to which I have hitherto been entirely a stranger. I have frequently felt dull, low spirited, in a manner out of tune; but the feelings which I now experienced were different from what I ever knew before and such, as I hope I shall never again experience: they kept me awake a great part of the night, and when I finally fell asleep, they disturbed my rest by the most extravagant dreams.

7TH.

Mr. Parsons, has recovered in a great measure from his illness: so that he was the chief part of this day in the office. I spent the evening in part with him. Play'd Backgammon, and draughts. At the former of these games he beats me; at the latter I beat him. I should suppose him to be a great proficient, at those games which require reflection, and a train of reasoning, which is very much the case with draughts; but much of this skill depends entirely upon practice in which he is deficient. I was fatigued for the want of proper rest, last night, and therefore went to bed, quite early; that is by ten o'clock.

8TH.

Amory went to Ipswich this afternoon. He cannot yet get entirely over his old habits. He intends however to come back this evening.

I went with Townsend to see Mr. Atkins, but did not find him at home. His Mother and Sister have both been ill of the putrid throat distemper, and are not yet wholly recovered. Townsend came home, and sat an hour with me. We conversed upon several topics, but chiefly upon Ambition, that virtue or vice, according as it is directed. We did not perfectly agree upon the subject, though our sentiments were not very different.

In the evening I wrote, and among others brought myself down to the present hour in this book, which I have not done before for these last two months.

9TH.

Attended Dr. Tucker's meeting in the forenoon. He gave us an excellent sermon upon the story of Haman, from which he drew a number of very rational reflections upon the evils of pride, haughtiness and a revengefull disposition. In the afternoon I went and heard Mr. Carey. Townsend called upon me in the evening, and I went with him to Mr. Atkins's where we stay'd about an hour; after which we went to see Thompson, who is quite unwell. We sat half an hour, below with Mr. Thompson. Parson Spring was there; and we conversed upon the topic which is now prevalent. The federal constitution. I came home early and wrote a long letter to W. Cranch.[1]

[1] This letter, dated 8 Dec., was owned by J. Delafield DuBois of New York in 1957; a transcript, possibly in the hand of Mrs. JA2, is in M/CFA/31, Adams Papers, Microfilms, Reel No. 327.

10TH.

This forenoon Townsend, sat off for Boston. Mr. Parsons intended to have gone likewise, as the supreme Court, sits by adjournment, there this week. But he was so much troubled with an ague in his face, and the tooth ach, that he could not go.

I pass'd the evening with Little at Dr. Swett's. Mrs. Swett is a pretty woman; and agreeable: not endow'd I believe with great strength of mind; not much of a reasoner nor much of a patriot, and professes to know nothing of politics, which she supposes to be entirely out of the sphere of the female sex.

It would perhaps be as well, if all women thought so, and conducted upon the principle: yet I wish even females to feel some interest in the welfare of their country.

The Dr. is a man of learning, and ingenuity. He went through a course of professional studies in Scotland, and has travell'd in different parts of Europe, but he has a mean idea of human nature, and I should not wonder if all physicians had: for they are incessantly conversant with the physical defects and infirmities of mankind: they see humanity in a state of humiliation, and it is no wonder if they have no idea of its glory.

11TH.

Reading Blackstone all day; and I pass'd the evening, at the office till eight: after which I went and past an hour with Putnam. F. Bradbury was with him. We had some conversation upon the stale topic of self love and disinterested benevolence. A subject, upon which I have very frequently conversed, with many different persons: and notwithstanding every thing that I have heard said upon the subject, I still retain the opinion which I adopted when I first reasoned upon it. I will not venture to say there is no such thing as disinterested benevolence, but I must say that after searching as deeply as possible into my own mind, I cannot find a trace of it there.

Talk'd with Doctor Kilham upon the federal constitution; the elections which have hitherto been made in different parts of the State, appear to be generally favorable to it.

12TH.

This day I finished reading the fourth and last volume of Blackstone's Commentaries. This is one of the most important books in the profession, and I have comparatively speaking taken more time in reading it, than I probably shall, for any other book: yet I am very far, from being master of it. And I intend before the end of my three years, if I should live and have my health, to go through this book once or twice more. I began in the afternoon upon Sullivan's Lectures, and read a few pages; but not sufficient to get an idea of the merits of the book. Thompson, has so far recovered, that he was at the office in the afternoon.

I pass'd the evening at my own lodgings, reading, and writing.

13TH.

The repetition of the same events, from day to day, is the only variety which can supply materials for this record of my transactions. Conversations, are seldom interesting. New characters seldom arise, and I am employed more time in thinking what I shall say for one day, than I am in writing the occurrences of a week. Fertility of imagination, might supply the deficiency of materials, but my soil produces no spontaneous fruits.

I passed this evening with Thompson: his father was taken very ill this afternoon with a nervous disorder, and was so sick that we broke up our assembly before eight o'clock.

14TH.

I was about an hour with Dr. Kilham at his shop, Immediately after dinner; I took up one of the volumes of Junius's Letters,[1] and carried it with me to the office; I read the whole afternoon, and was interrupted only by the shadows of the evening. I called upon Little, and brought him home with me, to my lodgings: we pass'd a very sociable evening together: after he was gone I took up again my volume of Junius, and just before I finished it, the midnight Clock reminded me, that the hour of retirement was again come round. This hour, and that of rousing from the night's repose are equally disagreeble to me. My mind seems in this respect to partake of the vis inertiae of matter. I cannot possibly rise early, and I am obliged to run forward into the night for those moments of contemplation, and study which perhaps would be more advantageously taken before the dawn of day.

[1] A collection of letters, written between 1769 and 1772, attacking the British ministry, 2 vols., London, 1772. The authorship of these letters has been a source of debate, having been attributed to several dozen different writers.

15TH.

A violent North-west wind, blew, the whole day, but we have no snow yet. Dined with Amory at Mr. Farnham's.[1] Mr. J. Greenleaf, and Mr. J. Carter were the Company besides the family. I saw Mrs. Hay, whom I had not before seen these three years. We did not pass the afternoon there, as Amory was called away soon after dinner. I went for about an hour to the office, and spent the evening with Putnam; who has lately taken a great fancy to digging in metaphysical ground: though he is not perfectly acquainted with the nature of the soil. He has drank just enough of the pierian spring to intoxicate the brain, and not sufficient to sober him again.[2]

[1] William, the second son by that name of Newburyport lawyer and tory sympathizer Daniel Farnham (Currier, *Newburyport,* 2:229–232).
[2] "An Essay on Criticism," lines 215–218.

16TH.

I waited upon Parson Cary this forenoon, in expectation of much edification; but he gave us a more indifferent sermon than usual; which in addition to the weather's being very cold, prevented me from going in the afternoon: instead of which I read three or four of Yorick's sermons; Townsend, who returned last night from Boston; was here all day: in the evening I concluded the first volume of Gibbon's history. The two last chapters which treat of the rise and progress of Christianity, are written neither with the indulgence of a friend, nor even with the candor, and ingenuous openness which an enemy ought ever to show. The sentiment, however with which he concludes the volume is a melancholy truth; and it is to the immortal honour of the present age, that no new religious sect, can gain ground, because it cannot find a persecutor.

17TH.

I have continued reading in Sullivan's lectures. The book is entertaining, and the author so far as he goes appears to be master of his subject. In general he is perspicuous and intelligible, but the Treatise is rather historical than professional: it was a posthumous work, and therefore probably much more imperfect, than it would have been, had the author himself given it to the public. The style is rather harsh and inharmonious, and there are many inaccuracies even of grammar, which are probably nothing more than errors of an uncorrected press. Townsend and I pass'd the evening in the office till about 8, after which I went in and play'd with Mr. Parsons at back-gammon about an hour.

18TH.

Passed the day at the office; Townsend and Thompson were there in the evening.

The question, what am I to do in this world recurs to me, very frequently; and never without causing great anxiety, and a depression of spirits: my prospects appear darker to me, every day, and I am obliged sometimes to drive the subject from my mind, and to assume some more agreeable train of thoughts. I do not wish to look into futurity; and were the leaves of fate to be opened before me, I should shrink from the perusal. Fortune, I do not covet. Honours, I begin to think are not worth seeking, and as for "the bubble reputation," though deck'd with all the splendors of the rainbow, yet those very splendors are deceitful, and it seldom fails to burst, from the weight of the drop which it contains.

19TH.

I spent my time this day, in the same manner that I did the two last. I came home to my lodgings at about 8 in the evening, and not being disposed to study, felt quite dull. When Dr. Kilham is not at home, I am entirely without company; for my landlady is in fact a good woman, but merely a good woman.

20TH.

The cold weather appears to be for setting in seriously; and indeed it is high time that it should. It snow'd some part of the day. Just after dusk, I walk'd with Thompson and Putnam to Little's home in Newbury, but he was gone to attend the ordination at Byfield. We return'd, and the lads pass'd the evening quite sociably with me, till 9 o'clock. Captain Wyer was here in the evening. He was he says, an enthusiast for liberty in 1775, but finds it all a farce; he is now, no less an enthusiast; and he may chance to find his present object, which is different enough from Liberty, more tragical, than merry. I finished this day with Sullivan's lectures; and am not displeased to have gone through it.

21ST.

I read through Wright's short treatise upon the feudal tenures. I found nothing in it, but what I had before read upon the subject in other writers. In the beginning of the next week, I shall take up Coke upon Littleton, Which seems to be the great magazine for law knowledge but it is one of those unlucky folio's, which appear so formidable to many students in the profession. I set myself down, for three months at this book.

22D.

I pass'd the day as usual at the office; but there was scarce a half an hour at a Time, without some visitor who entered into conversation with Mr. Parsons, and prevented us from paying any attention to our books. This is too frequently the case, and much of our Time is lost in that manner, luckily this was to me a leisure day, and I only made a few extracts from Blackstone.

Little pass'd the evening with me.

Weather quite moderate.

I should wish in order to give some kind of variety to these pages, to bring in the aid of something more, than a mere insipid narrative of my journeys from the office to my lodgings, and from my lodgings to the office. I have heretofore made free plunder with the characters of persons with whom I had any connections, but on many accounts I have found this a dangerous practice: for as I cannot keep these volumes so secret as I should wish to, and as the models may by some measure get access to the picture, I am obliged either to forfeit my sincerity, even towards myself, or to run the risque of making enemies. My disposition has prompted me to prefer the latter evil and I have sometimes experienced the disadvantages of committing my real opinions to writing. I have been thinking whether the method of recording observations, without exemplifying characters, would not be equally agreeable to me without being dangerous. If my observations are collected from a concurrence of facts, and if they should be upon subjects of any consequence, I might in that manner pluck the rose, without pricking my finger with the thorn. I believe I shall endeavour, though not immediately to practice upon this plan.

23D.

I went this forenoon to hear Parson Murray preach. He expatiated somewhat largely upon the seventh commandment. I was not very much pleased with him. His voice is clear and strong, and his delivery agreeable: but I have heard even extempore speakers preach more to my satisfaction. His arguments against a crime which must meet with general abhorrence, were not I think the most forcible that might have been brought, and he extended it further than I thought reasonable. I did not attend meeting in the afternoon. We finally have got a violent snowstorm; which begun this morning, and has been acquiring force the whole day.

24TH.

Began upon Coke-Littleton, and read about a dozen pages. Pass'd about an hour in the evening with Mr. Parsons, playing back-gammon.

I have often wondered at the blind, unreasonable affection, which Nature has given to parents for their Children. It is so un-accountable upon any principle of ratiocination, that I have thought it was the effect of mere instinct totally independent of the mind. This conjecture is in some measure confirm'd, by the tender affection, which appears universally to influence the brute creation for their young. But it is humiliating that man should be directed by the same mechanical impulse, and there-fore with that vanity, which is perhaps the greatest characteris-tic which distinguishes him from the rest of the animal world, he has converted an involuntary attraction into an amiable vir-tue. The tender affection which a child owes to his parent, is ra-tional; it proceeds from the best of motives, from gratitude for obligations received. Even The fondness of Lovers, although it is said to be a species of folly, yet is founded upon a mutual benefit, and may be so directed as to be perfectly reasonable; but in this attachment to a man's offspring, all appear to be equally faulty; all equally thoughtless. The infant son of Alcibiades, governed the world: and the power of any other child, is limited only by the situation of the parent.

I would proceed to speculate, but the midnight Clock re-sounds, and calls me away. Ars longa, vita brevis.

25TH.

Christmas day. Parson Bass, preached a sermon, but I did not go to hear him. I dined with Townsend, and pass'd the afternoon there. At about dusk, I took a long walk with him, and then re-turned to my own lodgings. The Dr. this day took a ride out of Town. In the evening I fell to speculating upon political sub-jects. I regret exceedingly that I have so little time, at my own disposal. A thousand subjects call my attention, and excite my curiosity: most of them I am obliged to pass from without notic-ing them at all; and the few to which I can afford any leisure, only lead me to regret, that I cannot go deeper. The tedious study of a profession, which requires indefatigable industry, and in-cessant application, is alone sufficient employment. But the arts and sciences in general, and in particular the liberal arts must not be neglected.

I suspect I shall soon drop this journal.

26TH.

Office as usual. Dr. Kilham, returned to Town this evening. I passed an hour or two with Mr. Tufts.

The most amiable of the roman Emperors, at the close of a day, which had presented no object upon which he might exert his benevolence, exclaimed "I have lost a day." To a man placed in a situation which enabled him so eminently to be useful to his fellow creatures, it must really be a misfortune, that one day should pass over without offering him an opportunity, to display his virtues: but as this was his peculiar duty in his sphere of life; so has every individual, (however humble the tenor of his way may be,) his own; and every day to him is lost which does not render him more capable of fulfilling the duties for which he was created. Such however have been many, many of my days, and even this among the rest was so barren, both of occurrences, and of observations, that unless I had recollected that circumstance I should have had nothing to say.

27TH.

St John's Day. An entertainment for the Society of free-Masons.

In consequence of Stacey's exertions, we had this evening a good dance. There were only thirteen gentlemen and fifteen ladies. The diversion was general, and the company spirited: upon such occasions there is almost always somebody who makes peculiar amusement for the rest of the Company. A Captain Casey, was this evening as singular as any of the gentlemen. As a Mason, he had the generosity of his heart, at dinner, rather than the reflections of prudence, and as this like most virtues increases by being put in action, he had not laid any illiberal restraints upon himself in the evening; it increased exceedingly his activity, and after all the Company had done dancing, he retained vigour to walk a minuet, and to skip in reels. In all this there was nothing but was perfectly innocent; yet so fond are the sons of men, to remark their respective foibles, that the Captain, was not totally exempted from the smiles of the company. This was the most particular circumstance that took place. In general, I was much pleased. It was between four and five in the morning before we broke up. Putnam came and sat an hour with me and Little, in garrulous conversation. A Little after the Clock struck five, Putnam went home; and I much fatigued retired to bed.

28TH.

We rose, between ten and eleven in the forenoon. Little took a breakfast with me; after which I went to the office; but felt entirely incapable of doing any thing serious. I pass'd the time therefore till dinner in idle chat. In the afternoon I passed an hour with Dr. Kilham; and again repaired to the office, with as little success as ever. In the evening, all the gentlemen who were last night at the dance, were at Putnam's lodgings. We drank and smoked, and sang there till nine o'clock; but notwithstanding a forced appearance of hilarity was kept up, there was in fact no real mirth. All were fatigued by the last night's siege, and unable to bear another, such as the inexhaustible spirits of Amory, would have relished. At nine therefore we retired, and not long after I got home, I went to bed.

29TH.

Not entirely recovered yet from the fatigue of Thursday night, but could in some measure attend to reading. Mr. Parsons's students all dined with him. Master Moody[1] from Byfield, with a son of Dartmouth by the name of Parish were likewise of the Company. Mr. Parish[2] has to perfection the appearance and manners, which have distinguished all the young gentlemen from that seminary, with whom I have had any acquaintance. The same uncouthness in his appearance; the same awkwardness in his manners, and really I am not illiberal if I add, the same vacancy in his countenance. That a man should not at the same time make a scholar and a fine gentleman, that the graces and the muses should refuse to reside in the same mansion, is what I have never thought strange; that they seldom unite is at once my sorrow and my consolation; but the students of Dartmouth, appear determined, to raise no rivalship, between these sets of Sisters, and therefore discard them all. Mr. Moody was extremely full of high flown compliments; the grossest the most fulsome, flattery was incessantly in his mouth. Every virtue and every accomplishment he lavished away upon the company, with so little consideration that he seemed to forget that modesty was in the list. He went off however very soon after dinner.

By G. Bradbury, I received a couple of letters from Cambridge,[3] which gave me no agreeable news. Bradbury was with me, in the evening; he relieved me in some measure from my fears. The Colleges it seems in the course of the last quarter have been in great confusion and the students are much irritated.[4]

[1] Samuel Moody, the first master of Governor Dummer Academy in Byfield, Mass. (Sibley-Shipton, *Harvard Graduates,* 12:48–54).

[2] Elijah Parish, who served as minister at Byfield, Mass., from 1787 to 1825 (Sprague, *Annals Amer. Pulpit,* 2:268).

[3] This may include Nathaniel Freeman's letter to JQA, 22 Dec. (Adams Papers), the only extant letter from Cambridge for this period.

[4] See note for entry of 2 Feb. 1788 (below).

30TH.

Attending meeting the whole day at Mr. Carey's. Dined at Mr. Hooper's[1] in company with Mr. Symmes, who return'd in the afternoon to Andover. In the evening I walkd with Dr. Kilham to Mr. Carter's; found nobody at home. We then went and pass'd the evening with Mrs. Emery. The conversation was agreeable, tho' not extremely interesting.

[1] Stephen Hooper, a merchant with interests in Newburyport and Newbury (Sibley-Shipton, *Harvard Graduates,* 15:53–56).

31ST.

In the Evening I went with Townsend, to see Miss Cazneau, and to fulfill a promise, of playing on the flute for her; which I made some weeks ago; and renew'd last Thursday. The character of Miss C. I propose to delineate at a future period; if I should continue to draw any.

At eight I left her and pass'd the remainder of the evening at Mrs. Hooper's.

The night, which puts a period to the revolving year, always presents to my mind a crowd of the most serious reflections. But none are more important than those upon the shortness of human life. A twentieth part of the days of man has nearly elapsed since, I began this journal; yet, how uninteresting the events! how much of that period lost! how much mis-spent! But revert the question: how much employed to make me wiser, better and more useful? Ah! how shall I answer?

TUESDAY JANUARY 1ST. 1788.

Pass'd the day and evening at the office. Read at my own lodgings till one o'clock in the morning.

I feel every day a greater disposition to drop this nonsense. It takes up a great deal of my time, and as it is incessantly calling upon me, I can never have any respite: in the extreme cold of winter I have no convenience, for writing, and was it not for the pleasure of complaining to myself, I believe I should have done long ago. I often get in arrears and then I have as much time to recollect, the circumstances of one day, as at other times I have to write for four. These inconveniences however are most prevalent in the severity of the winter Season. As I have got so far through this, and more particularly as I have now begun the year, I will make an effort to carry it on for one more revolution of the Sun, and if I then feel as averse to writing as at present, I will e'en stop, at least while the events in which I am concern'd are as trivial, as they are at present. One consideration upon this subject, at least affords me some satisfaction: it is that when I look back in these volumes, and peruse, the temporary productions of my pen; I am at least able to say, at the close of the day; that day I did something.

2D.

In the beginning of the evening, Putnam called at our office, and invited me to go with him and pass a couple of hours at Mr. Frazier's;[1] after debating with myself some time upon the subject, I determined finally to go. We found there a number of young gentlemen and Ladies. After we had sat a little while the infallible request to sing made its appearance. One could not sing, and another could not sing, and a total incapacity to sing, was declared all round the room. If, upon such occasions every one would adhere, to his first assertion, it would be very agreeable; at least to me: for in these mixt companies when the musical powers are finally exerted, the only recompence, for the intolerable tediousness of urging, generally is a few very insipid songs, sung in a very insipid manner. But the misfortune is, that some one always relents, and by singing furnishes the only materials for a conversation, which consists in intreaties for further gratifications of the same kind.

When we had gone through this ceremony, and had grown weary of it; another equally stupid succeeded; it was playing pawns: a number of pledges were given all round, and kissing was the only condition upon which they were redeem'd. Ah! what kissing! 'Tis a profanation, of one of the most endearing demonstrations of Love. A kiss unless warm'd by sentiment, and enlivened by affection, may just as well be given to the air, as to the most beautiful, or the most accomplished object in the Universe.

After going through this likewise, as if the Pope had done us any injury, nothing would do but we must break his neck.[2] It is the fate of the poor representative of St. Peter, to be abused at this day. But we were peculiarly cruel, for we persecuted him without any kind of advantage to ourselves. Thus we pass'd the heavy hours till about 10 o'clock, when we all retired.

I did intend to mention the young ladies that were present, and give my sentiments upon their persons and manners; but this day has already usurp'd more than its proportion of the volume, and I will take some other opportunity for delineating: for the present I will quit the pen.

[1] Moses Frazier, Newburyport shipowner and town officeholder (Currier, *Newburyport,* 1:678, 679, 687; Essex Inst., *Hist. Colls.,* 70:200 [April 1934]; 71:360 [Oct. 1935]).

[2] "Break the Pope's neck" was a game. In Virginia, players formed a semicircle and from their number one was chosen Pope and the others were friars. As the game proceeded, the players found "great Diversion in the respective Judgments upon offenders" who were finally "dismissed" (Philip Vickers Fithian, *Journals and Letters, 1767–1776,* ed. John Rogers Williams and others, 2 vols., Princeton, 1900–1934, 1:65).

3D.

Pass'd the evening at Little's in Newbury. A Mr. Coffin, who graduated two years ago, at Harvard, was there. We spent our time in sociable chat, and in singing; not such unmeaning, insignificant songs, as those with which we killed our time last evening; but good, jovial, expressive songs such as we sung at College, "when mirth and jollity prevail'd." One evening of this kind gives me more real satisfaction than fifty pass'd in a company of girls. (I beg their pardon.)

4TH.

Nothing—It would be a fine theme to expatiate upon. It has been well expatiated on. When I look around me, and see the vices, the follies, the errors of my fellow creatures, when I look into myself and enquire, into the springs and motives of my actions, when I look forward, and ask, what am I to do, what am I to expect, an involuntary sigh, acknowledges that *nothing,* is the only answer. In the physical world, what are sensual gratifications, what is the earth, and all it contains, what is Life itself—nothing. In the moral world, what is honour, what is honesty, what is religion?—nothing. In the political world, what is Liberty, what is patriotism, what is power and grandeur?—nothing. The universe is an atom, and it's creator is all in all. Of him, except that he exists, we know nothing, and consequently our knowledge is nothing.

Perhaps the greatest truth of all is, that for this half hour, I have been doing nothing.

5TH.

I have this week been reading Cecilia,[1] a novel of some reputation; it was written by a Lady, and does not exhibit that knowledge of human nature, which is the greatest excellency, perhaps of novels. Some of the characters however are well drawn; they are generally exaggerated, and appear rather too strongly marked for perfect imitations of nature. The characters of Miss Larolles and of Meadows, appear to me, original, and true: that of Lady Pemberton, is pleasing, but merely an imitation. The story in general is well told, and the interest is preserved; but in many places probability is not sufficiently consulted, and the repetitions of the mistakes at Belfield's lodgings, become tedious, and wearisome; the catastrophe is not just as I should wish it, yet perhaps it is more judicious than it would have been to have preserved her fortune. If the book, was made shorter by two volumes, I think it would be much better than it is; but even now it is infinitely superior to the common herd of novels, which are mere nusances to Literature.

I passed the evening quite in a solitary way at my own lodgings. The weather has this week been extremely cold.

[1] Frances (Burney) d'Arblay, *Cecilia, or, Memoirs of an Heiress,* 5 vols., London, 1782.

6TH.

Heard Mr. Carey preach two sermons this day; but the weather was very cold. In the afternoon the Parson was extremely vehement; in an occasional discourse upon the renewal of the year, he complained exceedingly that the language of the people was "the time is not come." And with all his powers of eloquence, and of reasoning, he exerted to prove that the time is come. He was rather too violent: his zeal was so animated that he almost had the appearance of being vexed and chagrined. But he said he was not aiming at popularity.

Passed the evening with Dr. Kilham, at Mr. Carter's, where we had a whole magazine of antiquity. Miss Sally Jenkins was there; I was pleased with her manners: she is of the middling female size, and has a fine form, the features of her face, are regular, and were not the nose, too much inclined to the aquiline, would be very handsome. Twenty two, I should think her age; but perhaps she is two or three years younger. She conversed not much, and indeed, in the State of female education here there are very few young Ladies, who talk, and yet preserve our admiration. For my own part, the most difficult task that could be assigned me, would be, to carry on a conversation with one of our fine Ladies. The topics upon which they are able to be fluent, are so totally different, from any of those with which I have ever been conversant, that I feel the same embarassment, that I should with one, whose Language I should be wholly unacquainted with. This is not meant however to apply to Miss Jenkins, who is I hope of a different cast: perhaps I shall discover upon a better acquaintance, attractions in her, besides those of person, and they will appear the more amiable, as they are the more rare.

7TH.

In the beginning of the evening I wrote a Letter to W. Cranch requesting of him an explanation, of something he wrote me, which was plain enough to alarm me exceedingly, but not sufficiently explicit to ascertain my suspicions.[1] At eight o'clock I left the office, and went to Dr. Swett's; where I found Little very agreeably situated. He had been writing part of a Letter to Freeman. I join'd with him, and scribbled, about half a page upon the subject of Miss Cazneau.[2] I know not, but I should have done best to adopt the prudent stile of panegyric; but what is done cannot be helped; and I must run my chance of incurring the tremendous resentment of an offended female. If she should discover what I have written, my only resource would be to flatter her. This I believe would be an infallible recipe, for appeasing her.

While I was sitting with Little, the Sexton came in. "You mentioned a matter to me the other day" said he; "and I met with one yesterday; all entire. He has been there but a few years. The flesh has sunk away not much. Rather dirty, as the clods fell on him as I was digging; but it's easy to wash that away. If you want one now, you may have him early to morrow, morning." Little told him such an one would not answer his purpose, not being fresh enough. I bless'd myself for not being a student in physic, and for being exempted from an application to any art, by means against which humanity revolts.

How much is an honest and a humane physician, to be respected and esteemed! No man certainly can render himself useful to his fellow creatures in a manner, more painful and disgusting to himself, and few men, have a poorer prospect of obtaining the reward of their labours; in this Country especially.

I sat about an hour with Little, after which I retired to my own lodgings.

¹ Neither letter has been found.
² Not found.

8TH.

It snow'd all the forenoon; but as the weather kept continually moderating, in the afternoon it began to rain, and before the weather cleared up, the snow was almost gone. I went with Townsend, and drank coffee at Mr. Thompson's. His son goes to Boston to-morrow. I gave him my letter for Cranch: after we went from there, we called in at Putnam's lodgings and found Captain Noyes there. Mr. Townsend soon went away. I sat there till after nine o'clock; and heard the doleful story of the Clock upon Mr. Murray's meeting house, which the other night, kept striking without ceasing almost the whole night; and how it is an indisputable omen, foreboding the death of the Parson, who is very sick.

Superstition and bigotry, will ever be inseperable companions: and they are always the tyrants of a mean and contracted mind.

9TH.

This day our State convention is to meet in Boston for the purpose of assenting to and ratifying, the federal Constitution. The members from this Town, went for Boston yesterday, except Mr. Parsons, who will go to-morrow. The conjectures concerning the issue of their debates, are different, according to the dispositions of the speculators. Some think there will be a great majority for adopting the Constitution, while others hope, the opposite party will greatly preponderate. In the evening I play'd with Mr. Parsons at back-gammon, and was beat by him. After leaving the office, I pass'd the remainder of the evening with Townsend, at Mrs. Hooper's.

10TH.

Between eleven and twelve Mr. Parsons, went for Boston; Amory goes with him in a Chaise as far as Salem: from whence he will proceed in the Stage. I went this evening to Dr. Swett's with the Intention to pass the evening there, but neither the Doctor nor his Lady were at home; I called upon Putnam, and would have gone with him to Mr. Bradbury's; but they were all out. I met Little in the Street, he came home with me, and sat half an hour.

The convention, met at Boston yesterday. About 300 members present; They chose Mr. Hancock president, and as his infirmities are such as will probably prevent him frequently from attending, Judge Cushing was chosen vice-president. But they have not yet proceeded to business of any consequence. Nor does it appear, which party is most likely to prevail: from which we may perhaps infer that in either case, the majority will be small.

11TH.

From the office this afternoon I went with Townsend to his lodgings, and there past a couple of hours; after which I went in to Mr. Tufts's, spend the remainder of the evening, and supp'd there. I found Mr. I. Smith there, and conversed with him upon the subject of the late disturbances at college. He hinted to me, that one of my brothers, had been much irritated, and that he was suspected of being peculiarly active upon some of the late occasions.[1] I hope however there was no just ground for their suspicions.[2]

[1] See entry for 2 Feb. (below).

[2] Beginning on this date and continuing until 31 Dec., JQA also wrote in another Diary, designated by the Adams' editors as D/JQA/13, consisting of line-a-day memoranda written on blank pages in his copy of *Fleet's Pocket Almanack and Massachusetts Register for 1788,* Boston, [1788].

This leather-bound volume, measuring 3 ¼″ × 5 ½″, also contains notes from JQA's readings and lines of poetry. These entries occasionally add some small detail to the fuller entries contained in D/JQA/12. Significant additions are mentioned in the notes.

12TH.

Saturday evening. I was as usual, all the evening at my own lodgings: I spent my time in reading Gibbon's roman history, 2d volume, and now at 12 at night, upon compulsion I am to say something for myself. And I know nothing better than to testify, that at Mr. Parsons's office, I have lost a great part of this week, by conversing with him and with Townsend.

Mr. Parsons is now gone to Boston, and I hope to god, I shall not go on in this way squandering week after week, till at the end of three years I shall go out of the office, as ignorant as I entered it. I cannot, must not be so negligent: all my hopes of going through the world in any other, than the most contemptible manner, depend upon my own exertions, and if I continue thus trifling away my time, I shall become an object of charity or at least of pity. God of Heaven! if those are the only terms upon which life can be granted to me, oh! take me from this world before, I curse the day of my birth—Or rather give me resolution to pursue my duty with diligence and application, that if my fellow creatures should neglect, and despise me, at least I may be conscious of not deserving their contempt.

13TH.

This morning Townsend called on me; and invited me to go and hear Parson Tucker. We met Little in the street who turn'd about, and walk'd that way with us. When we got to the meeting house we found there was to be no service there in the forenoon, and as it was then too late to go any where else, we turn'd back and went home. Dined, with Dr. Kilham, at Dr. Swett's, and

Little dined with us. We spent the afternoon, and drank tea there. Mrs. Swett is handsome, and like most of our Ladies, is perfectly acquainted with the various forms of propriety in company, which have been established here. She has too much good breeding to know any thing upon speculative subjects, and she has a proper aversion to politics. She has however I believe a good understanding, and is infinitely superior to many of our female beauties who flutter, in all the pride, of variegated colours. After I return'd home, Thompson called and delivered me a letter from W. Cranch.[1] I went with the Dr. to see Mr. Jackson, but he was not at home, and we called in at Mrs. Emery's. This Lady and her Daughter converse more to my satisfaction than the generality of my female acquaintance. In their company my time passes away fast; and I am not often able to say as much.[2]

[1] Not found.
[2] According to his line-a-day entry for this date, JQA refers to Mrs. Parsons whom he presumably also saw (D/JQA/13, Adams Papers, Microfilms, Reel No. 16).

14TH.

Last night Mr. Parsons' family was increased by an additional daughter; Mrs. Parsons as well as to be expected. This evening I went with Townsend; in the first place to Mr. Atkins'; this too is an house, where I always visit with pleasure: as I am always sure, to meet with good sense and sociability. From thence we went to Mr. J. Tracey's, where we found three Ladies, all drest in the deepest mourning, and Captn. Farris, who lately lost his wife. Mrs. Tracey, is much such a Lady as Mrs. Swett, though there are a few distinguishing characteristics. Her husband is a singularity. But he is a justice of the peace, and deputy adjutant general of the militia; and with equal importance and dignity he wields the scales of justice, and the sword of Bellona. He frequently tells of his judicial performances, and takes pleasure in boasting that to do his duty he must see every man in the County once a year. But he is friendly and hospitable, and indeed except when mounted on one of his two hobby-horses, a very good companion.

15TH.

After passing the day as usual at the office, Townsend, came spent the evening and supp'd with me. The weather for these three or four days past has been excessive cold; but has moderated greatly this evening.

After supper I amused myself an hour or two with writing. And I have been reading two or three of Shakespear's historical plays. I believe I should improve my reading to greater advantage, if I confined myself to one book at a time; but I never can. If a book does not interest me exceedingly it is a task to me to go through it: and I fear for this reason, I shall never get through Gibbon. Indolence, indolence, I fear will be my ruin.

16TH.

It snow'd all the forenoon; but the weather continued moderating and in the afternoon, a steady rain took place of the snow: and when I came this evening from the office, the ground was covered all the way with one continual glare of ice. It was dangerous walking, and I came as much as half the way, without lifting my feet.

I spent the evening at home; writing to make good the time which I have lately lost; but I accomplished my purpose only in part.

It may be observed that I say of late, little, but of what I do in the evening; and the reason is, that the only varieties of any kind, that take place, are in that part of the day. At about nine in the morning, I regularly go to the Office, and when, I do not lose, my time in chat, with Amory or Townsend, I take up my lord Coke, and blunder along a few pages with him. At two I return to dinner. At three again attend at the office, and again consult my old author. There I remain till dark, and as Mr. Parsons for special reasons, to him best known, objects to our having a fire in the office, in the evening, while he is absent, as soon as day-light begins to fail, we put up our books, and then employ the remainder of the day, as best suits our convenience, and the feelings of the moment. I go but little into company, and yet I am not industrious. I am recluse, without being studious; and I find myself equally deprived of the pleasures of society, and of the sweet communion with the mighty dead. I am no stranger to the midnight lamp; yet I observe not that I make, a rapid progress in any laudable pursuit. I begin seriously to doubt of the goodness of my understanding, and am not without my fears, that as I increase in years, the dulness of my apprehension likewise increases. But we are all mortal.

17TH.

Putnam called at our office this forenoon, and return'd Sullivan's Lectures, which he borrow'd about a fortnight ago. I pass'd the evening till 9, with Little and Putnam at Thompson's. We convers'd upon the subject of originality. Thompson opposed my sentiments upon that head, though, I believe he does not differ very widely from me.

I told him I was fond of novelty in characters, and was even pleased with excentricity if it was not affected. I cannot bear your people, who have no characters at all. And yet I could name many young gentlemen, who being merely blest by nature with a good memory, and by art with diligence and application; bustle through the world, and even find people, who will call them men, of genius. These fellows will always secure the favour of their superiors by an hypocritical kind of modesty. They will treat their equals equivocally, and suit their conduct to circumstances: but from those whom they consider as their inferiors, they will claim the same veneration which they themselves pay to men from whom they have any thing to expect. I have sometimes been fatigued to death, with a coxcomb of this kind, in hearing him deal out for an half an hour together, a parcel of common place thoughts, with as much pomposity, as if he was all the time delivering aphorisms. And this he will do in the company of three or four women, who will all the time wonder at the immensity of his abilities. But of such an one, I can neither disguise nor conceal my contempt. His genius is imitation, and his skill is cunning. I had much rather see a person, who can invent, who can create, even though the production, should be more imperfect.[1]

[1] In JQA's line-a-day entry, he adds, "Putnam went off" (D/JQA/13, Adams Papers, Microfilms, Reel No. 16).

18TH.

This afternoon I wrote a couple of letters to send by Mr. Atkins, who goes to Boston to'morrow. One for N. Freeman, and the other from [for] Wm. Cranch,[1] and as I could not finish before dark, I ventured to stay in the office till seven o'clock. I then went with Townsend, to Mr. Atkins's, to give him the letters:[1] Miss Dashwood was there: a young Lady from Boston. She speaks thick, and quick, which is at present all I have to say of her; except that by candle-light, she looks handsome. I came home, and then went with the Doctor to Mrs. Emery's. There we found Mrs. Jackson, and Miss Fletcher. Mrs. Jackson, looks better than I ever saw her, and was in high spirits. She talk'd almost all the time, and would have talk'd well, had she not appeared rather too fond, in repeating some gentleman's speeches, to render every word, even those which are most superfluous; words which if used before women, even by a man, at least argue ill-breeding; but which the lips of every woman, ought to be ignorant of pronouncing: Miss Fletcher sat two hours, and scarcely opened her mouth. The poor girl is in love, and when her friend is absent,[2] she can utter nothing but sighs. This evening it is true, she had no chance to speak, but she was not only silent but absent. She did not appear to enjoy the conversation, and all Mrs. Jackson's wit, could scarcely soften her features to a smile.

After they were gone, we sat there about half an hour in chat with Miss Emery: she is Thompson's favorite, and in this as in many other instances, he shows the goodness of his taste.

[1] Neither letter found.

[2] Presumably JQA's fellow law student William Amory, whom Lucy Fletcher later married.

19TH.

At home all the evening. Master Moody, called to see me; "Don't you think said he, that I am very condescending, thus to come and visit you." It might be very true, considering the dignity which his years have given him: but the address was very much that of a schoolmaster, whose habits of commanding give him a prescriptive title to importance. He sat with me about an hour, and then departed.

I have been more attentive to studies this week, than I was the last. I have made considerable progress in my folio, and have got some insight, into one or two particulars, which had hitherto been involv'd in intricacy and obscurity. I have spent three evenings this week in my own room, and have in some measure retrieved my particular arrearages: The weather has been very favorable, so that I have not been forced to drop my pen from the stiffness of my fingers. The winter is already far advanced, and is now rapidly passing away. I can afford, if the severity of the weather should require it, to fall back once or twice more, and the extremity cannot I think last so long as to make me lose the thread of my adventures.

It seems as if we were fated to have no lasting snow this winter. It snow'd again all this forenoon; but so soon, as a sufficient quantity had fallen, to make good sleighing; it turn'd to rain; which I suppose, will sweep it all away again.

20TH.

I attended at Parson Carey's meeting. We had two Sermons, in continuation of a subject upon which he preached last Sunday; the excellency of Christianity. I pass'd the whole evening in writing very industriously; not a little to the increase of this volume.

It thaw'd all last night, but not so as to carry off all the snow. The streets, were like a river the chief of the day, but at about five the wind got round to the North-west, and blew with some violence. In two hours time the streets were dry, and the ice strong enough to bear a man. I think I never saw a more sudden, or a greater alteration in the weather. The wind subsided to a degree, before midnight; but left it very cold.

And now I bid adieu to my pen, and to my book.

21ST.

I began upon the third book of the first part of the Institutes and read a few pages as usual. In the evening I again look'd into Gibbon, and made some progress in his second volume. I have also been reading for these two or three days past, the letters from a Chinese philosopher;[1] which are a number of essays upon various subjects, wrought into a kind of a novel: they are entertaining, and exhibit no bad picture of english manners.

The accounts from Boston this evening are disagreeable. The opposite parties in the convention grow warm, and irritable; Mr. Dana and Mr. Gerry it is said have come to an open and public rupture.

Mr. B. Lincoln, the general's son, and Dr. Adams, son to the president of the Senate, died last week.

348

[1] Oliver Goldsmith, *The Citizen of the World; Or, Letters from a Chinese Philosopher* . . ., 2 vols., London, 1762.

22D.

This afternoon, Leonard White called on me; and sat about half an hour. He came from Haverhill, this morning, and returns to night. Between four and five I received an invitation from Putnam, and F. Bradbury, to join them for a party at sleighing. Though not particularly desirous to go I did not refuse; and at about 6 o'clock we started. We went to Sawyer's tavern, about three miles off, and there danced till between 12 and 1. The company was rather curiously sorted, but the party was agreeable. I Danced with the eldest Miss Frazier, with Miss Fletcher, and with Miss Coats.

Miss Fletcher appears to be about 20. She is not tall, but has, what is called a very genteel shape. Her complexion, is fair; and her eye is sometimes animated, with a very pleasing expression; but unfortunately she is in Love; and unless the object of her affections is present, she loses all her spirits, grows dull, and unsociable, and can be pleased with nothing. This evening she was obliged to dispense with his company; and the usual effect took place. I endeavour'd as much as possible, to bring on a conversation; but all to no purpose.

> "She sat like Patience on a monument.
> Smiling at grief."[1]

And as I found she could talk only in monosyllables, I was glad to change my partner. Miss Coats is not in Love, and is quite sociable. Her manners are not exactly what I should wish, for a friend of mine; yet she is agreeable: I am not obliged with her, both to make, and support the conversation: and moreover what is very much in her favour; she is an only daughter and her father has money.

We return'd to town a little after twelve: but the weather was not very agreeable, as it snow'd violently.

After we had carried home the Ladies, Putnam came to lodge with me. We sat and chatted about an hour and then retired to bed.

[1] *Twelfth Night,* Act II, scene iv, lines 117–118.

23D.

I took a violent cold by our party last night, and as I felt rather unwell, and extremely indolent; I did nothing at the office.

Amory very unwell with a cholic, to the great affliction of Miss F. I suppose.

I pass'd the evening at Dr. Swett's. Mrs. and Miss Cazneau were there. We had some agreeable, and entertaining conversation, but singing soon came on to the Carpet, and then the usual nonsense succeeded.

I believe I will try one of these days and see if I cannot stop the career of this same singing at least for one evening. I even got quit this time with singing once; In order not to appear singular, I was in the common way urging Miss Cazneau to sing; she told me she would upon condition that I should sing first. I humm'd over a tune; but avoided claiming the fulfilment of Miss C's promise, and so she would not sing; which happened very much to my satisfaction. A Short time before nine I left them.

24TH.

Mr. Atkins returned from Boston, but brought me no letters which is somewhat surprizing to me. The quaternity pass'd the evening at Putnam's lodging's. Little left us however at about 8 o'clock. Townsend came in soon after, and between 9 and 10, I walk'd with him. I began yesterday upon another attempt, to ascend Parnassus; and this time I am determined to take it leisurely. I have frequently made a trial of my strength in this way; but my patience has always been overcome, after proceeding but little. I have I suppose begun an hundred times to write poetry. I have tried every measure and every kind of strophe but of the whole, I never finish'd but one of any length, and that was in fact but the work of a day.[1] It is contained in a former volume of this Journal. I fear I shall end this Time, as I always do.

The convention are now proceeding in the examination of the proposed constitution by sections: but we cannot yet presume how the scale will turn.

---

[1] Presumably this was "A ballad, founded on fact," which was written into JQA's entry for 7 July 1787 (above).

25TH.

Leonard White came from Haverhill again yesterday and called to see me this morning. He informed me that both my brothers were at Haverhill. In the evening I went with him to Dr. Swett's, and pass'd an hour with Little.

I communicated to Little my design of drawing a number of female characters, but I doubt whether it will ever be any thing more than a design.

26TH.

At home as usual all the evening. Read a little in Gibbon; wrote in the same slavish way as I have done now for more than three years.

But I feel dull, and low spirited. I have neither, that insatiable ambition, nor that ardor for pursuing the means to gratify it, which not long ago, was an argument which my vanity offered my mind, to prove, that if life should be given me, it would not be, to live unknowing and unknown. I feel no extraordinary inclination for study of any kind. Putnam, reads law as fast, or faster than I do, and if there is to be no alteration in the situation of my mind; he will make greater improvements in his three years, than I shall in mine. Before the cold weather came on, I expected to derive great advantage, from the long winter evenings which were approaching. In my imagination, I had written volumes, and read books without number. Yet so totally different has been the event, that I have written scarcely any thing except what this book contains, and, though I began Gibbon three months ago, I have not got half through the second volume. In my lord Coke, I trudge along, at the rate of about 80 pages a week, and do not understand, a quarter part of that. Yet when I call myself to an account and enquire how I mis-spend my time I do not find a spirit of dissipation in my conduct. I have I believe upon an average, spent one half of my evenings this winter at home; and when I do, I almost always hear the morning Clock. I somewhat suspect, that irregularity is one great cause of my poor success, and as I am peculiarly fond of trying experiments; I will attempt soon to be periodical in my visits at home, and abroad: if this will not do, I can only submit to my fate.

27TH.

Heard Parson Carey, the whole day. In the forenoon he was intolerably lengthy, as the weather was very cold. I intended to have visited somewhere this evening, but got engaged in writing to Packard,[1] which employ'd me till ten o'clock.

[1] Letter not found.

28TH.

Mrs. Hooper's family are in great distress. Ben, was brought home dead, last night between twelve and one o'clock, and to make the misfortune as great as possible, there is every reason to suppose, that he was the wilful author of his death. He had been from Town, more than a week, and on Saturday night, he took a quantity of liquid laudanum, at Robertson's tavern in Salem; he died in violent convulsions in the course of the same night. The verdict of the Coroner's jury, it is said, was wilful self murder, but the information is indirect, and therefore not entirely to be depended upon. To his mother the shock must be dreadful. Indeed she seems to have been marked out for misfortune. Her father was formerly one of the wealthiest merchants in this Town; and her education was suitable to his fortune. She married a Mr. Hooper,[1] whose circumstances were no less advantageous, and entered, but little more than twenty years ago, upon the stage of the world, with the most pleasing prospects. But her husband, was a man of pleasure, and dissipation, and moreover, opposed to the late revolutions; wherefore he left the Country at the beginning of the late war; and went to England, where he still remains: since that time she has been reduced to the necessity of supporting herself and her three children, by taking boarders. For although several of her husband's nearest connections, are still persons of the greatest affluence, that are in the Town, yet she has never received much assistance from them

> Donec eris felix, multos numerabis amicos:
> Tempora si fuerint nubila, solus eris.[2]

She endeavoured to educate her children as well as possible: but a father's care was wanting, and indulgence is the defect even of the most accomplished women. Ben, for several years had followed the sea, and in the fall, was disappointed of sailing with

Callahan for London. He had been very dissipated and debauched: he found himself destitute of employment; his reputation lost, his means of continuing in the course of life, which he was pursuing, gone, and his resolution insufficient to reform his conduct, he determined to put an end to all the disagreeable feelings, of his mind, and to "die in the bed of honour" as he expressed it. He was scarce nineteen years old.

Such was the deplorable fate of a youth, whose disposition, was such that he would have injured no one but himself, and who might have been an ornament to society, had he been educated under the prudent severity of a judicious father.

They intend to bury him to-morrow, but it is doubtful whether the unfeeling passions of the multitude, will suffer them to make a public funeral.

My brothers Charles and Tom, came into Town this forenoon. After dinner, I took a ride in a sleigh up to Sawyer's, with three of the Bradbury's and Charles: drank tea at Mr. Tufts's. I pass'd the evening and supped at Mr. Jackson's. Dr. Kilham was there, and as usual conversed upon political subjects. Charles spent the evening at Mr. Frazier's but came and lodged with me.

¹ Joseph Hooper ended his financial problems by contracting a second—and bigamous—marriage in England. Mary Hooper, whom JQA regularly visited while living in Newburyport, sued for divorce in 1790 (Sibley-Shipton, *Harvard Graduates*, 15:404–406).

² "So long as you are secure you will count many friends; if your life becomes clouded you will be alone," Ovid, *Tristia*, Bk. I, chap. 9, lines 5–6 (*Tristia and Ex Ponto*, transl. Arthur Leslie Wheeler, Cambridge, 1959, p. 44, 45).

29TH.

It snow'd part of the forenoon; then turn'd to rain, and after making the streets very disagreeable, cleared up in the afternoon. I dined with my brothers at Mr. Bradbury's; we had some conversation upon the subject of Ben Hooper's funeral. I could not agree in sentiment with Mr. Bradbury. I told him that although I abhorr'd the action itself, as much as any one, yet after a man was dead to refuse to attend his funeral, would only be an insult upon the feelings of his friends without being any kind of punishment to him. And indeed I cannot but think that Laws against suicide, are impolitic and cruel for how can it be expected, that human Laws which cannot take hold of the offender personally, should restrain from the commission of this crime, the man, who could disregard, the natural and divine Laws, which upon this subject are so deeply imprinted upon the heart? When we consider too how easily such a Law may be evaded, how many ways a man might put a period to his own existence, without exposing himself to the severity of any law that the human fansy could invent, we can only suppose, that these punishments must fall merely upon a thoughtless youth, or upon one ignorant of the existence of such regulations. Mr. Bradbury however thinks differently and is perhaps in the right.

I pass'd about an hour in the evening with Putnam; he then went with G. Bradbury and my brothers, into a company of young Ladies, and I cross'd the street and sat till nine o'clock, with my friend Thompson. Tom lodg'd with me.

30TH.

I went up to the office, in the morning, and sat a couple of hours; but I felt restless and dissipated: I could not study, and therefore walk'd down in town and saunter'd about. Dined with G. Bradbury and Charles at Mr. Hooper's. He is very sanguine in his hopes for the adoption of the Constitution.

Pass'd the evening at Mr. Bradbury's. Dr. Smith and all his family were there. We had some music in the beginning of the evening, and afterwards play'd a number of very amusing sports, such as start; what is it like; cross questions, I love my love with an A, and a number more. My opinion of such diversions I have already given: when it was confined to a number of young persons; but that the most inexcusable levities of youth should appear in the garb of old-age is something that calls for more than disapprobation: nor will a grey hair'd trifler excite our pity merely; but must raise our indignation and contempt. Mr. Bradbury however is a very respectable man, and as this conduct has here the sanction of custom, it is not him but the manners of the times that I blame.

31ST.

The weather somewhat cold. My brothers dined with me and between 3 and 4 o'clock, we all set off for Haverhill. We got there just after five, a little fatigued. The riding was not bad but in some places the cold had not been strong enough to harden the snow; and the road was sloppy.

FRIDAY FEBRUARY 1ST. 1788.

Pass'd a great part of the fore noon at Mr. Thaxter's. He is now quite in the family way: he dined with us at Mr. Shaw's; as did Leonard White and Sam Walker. In the afternoon we rode in a couple of sleighs about 6 miles down upon the river, and return'd just after dark. The party was agreeable; but Walker was an object of great pity. He has ruined his reputation irrevocably; the fairest Life henceforward, could only heal the wound; but the treacherous scar, must forever proclaim in indelible characters, that he once fell. Nor can his dearest friends help acknowledging to themselves, that this is viewing the prospect in its fairest light. To consider the appearances such as they must present themselves to the imagination of one disposed to see objects in their most unfavorable colours, must be shocking to the feelings of every one who was once his friend. He appears to be in a perpetual state of humiliation: he can enter into no satisfaction express'd by the company in which he appears. He can enjoy no amusement, and must feel a conscious inferiority to every one with whom he associates. Yet if he can be recovered at all it must be by softening measures. And those persons who wonder why people keep company with him, and wish rather to insult him, in his distress, are in my opinion to be esteemed but little better than himself. The disposition in human nature, to sink a man that has fallen, still lower than he is, would afford one of the richest themes for a misanthropist.

2D.

I dined with Walker at Mr. Thaxter's. My brother's both dined at Mr. White's. In the afternoon, we rode again in sleighs upon the river as far as we went yesterday. We had a number of songs, somewhat in the Collegiate stile; but in order to be exemplary return'd home quite early in the evening. Mr. Thaxter lives very agreeably, and has retracted his theory with respect to matrimony: and indeed I believe our sex are not less prone than the other to profess a System, which in fact, we wholly disbelieve.

Mrs. Shaw shew me a letter which she has been writing to Walker; and I am in hopes it may have a good effect upon him. If he has any sensibility, or any principles remaining he must be affected by it.

I had with Mr. Shaw some conversation upon the subject of

the disorders which happened at College, in the course of the last quarter: his fears for my brothers are greater than mine: I am perswaded that Charles did not deserve the suspicions which were raised against him: and I have great hopes that his future conduct, will convince the governors of the University, that he was innocent.[1]

[1] On 29 Nov., after Thanksgiving dinner, a number of students engaged in a disturbance in the college dining hall in which they broke windows and furniture. All students who could not prove that they had left the hall were charged for the damages. Several students, including CA, who served as waiters in the dining hall were especially singled out for not giving evidence against their fellow students concerning the disorder and were dismissed from their jobs (MH-Ar:Faculty Records, 5:278–279).

3D.

I attended meeting twice this day. Mr. Shaw as usual had company in the evening. I conversed with Madam. Charles and Tom went out in the evening.

4TH.

This morning between seven and eight o'clock my brothers set out to return to Braintree and from thence to Cambridge, as the vacation closes next Wednesday. In the forenoon I went down to see Leonard White, who was not at home. I met him however in the street with Mr. McHard, to whose house we went and sat an hour. I dined at Mr. Shaw's, and at about 4 was on my horse. I got home by dark: though the roads were much worse, than when we went to Haverhill. I found my old Lady, had some company, but they soon went away. I pass'd all the evening at home, quite in low spirits as indeed I have been for a week or ten days past. Not even dissipation has been able to support me. My nerves have got into a disagreeable trim, and I fear I shall be obliged to pay still less attention to books than I have of late. And if that be the case I am sure I must be very ignorant, when I leave the title of a student. It seems very unfortunate that there should be no medium that a man must be a fool or an invalid.

5TH.

The weather this day has been extreme cold: I have not experienced the severity of the Season, so much since the winter I pass'd in Sweeden. I pass'd the evening with Townsend and

Amory at Dr. Smith's. The old man is very fond of telling long stories, and indeed it is quite necessary to attend to him. There are however two young ladies in the house, to whom we attend with much more pleasure. Miss Smith may be 20 years old; She is not handsome; but has a great degree of animation in her eye, and as the want of it appears conspicuous in every other feature the mixture of opposites has a singular effect upon her countenance. Her person is not elegant, nor is her taste in dress such as suits my mind: she has a satyrical turn, and is fond of being esteemed witty. So much I think I can judge from the short acquaintance I have with her. Perhaps at some future period I may be able to say more. Miss Putnam I will mention the next time I fall in company with her.

We play'd at whist about a couple of hours; after which we sung; or attempted to sing; for of all the company Amory, was the only one that could sing so as to give any kind of entertainment.

6TH.

The weather has moderated very considerably. In the evening, I walked with Thompson and Putnam, to Little's where we past the evening till 9 o'clock: Quite agreeably without ceremony or restraint.

7TH.

This day at about noon, the news arrived in this Town, that the federal Constitution, was yesterday, adopted and ratified by a majority of nineteen members in our State convention.[1]

In this town the Satisfaction is almost universal: for my own part, I have not been pleased with this System, and my acquaintance, have long-since branded me with the name of an *antifederalist*. But I am now converted, though not convinced. My feelings upon the occasion have not been passionate nor violent, and as upon the decision of this question I find myself on the weaker side, I think it my duty to submit without murmuring against what is not to be helped. In our Government, opposition to the acts of a majority of the people is rebellion to all intents and purposes; and I should view a man who would now endeavour to excite commotions against this plan, as no better than an insurgent who took arms last winter against the Courts of Justice.

This afternoon I went in company with a number of young Ladies and gentlemen of this town, upon a sleighing party. We rode about 8 miles into Newbury, and by dark return'd to Sawyer's tavern. After drinking tea, we went to dancing, and excepting supper, continued so till about mid-night. I danced with Miss Coats and Miss Smith; both of whom were very agreeable partners. At twelve we broke up, and return'd home. Thompson came and lodg'd with me. Mr. S. Cutler, came and sat about half an hour with me: he was exceedingly mortified at having overset his sleigh: some of the ladies were affronted, and some affrighted, so that in returning he had somewhat of an uncomfortable time, sweating between two fires. In the company was an Irish gentleman by the name of Hutchinson, a man of genuine wit and humour: and a person of much reading and information. He has a vessel here loading, and expects to sail for Ireland in a week or ten days.

[1] The ratification of the Constitution in Massachusetts was a crucial contest between federalist and antifederalist forces; "Had the Constitution lost in Massachusetts," according to one historian, "it would never have been ratified." With a few important exceptions, the battle was between the commercial interests along the coast and in towns bordering the Connecticut River that supported the Constitution, and the backcountry, Shaysite sympathizers who wished to defeat ratification. At the beginning of the convention, the antifederalists clearly held a majority of delegates, but eventually, enough were persuaded to vote for ratification or abstain from voting. In the contest federalists gained support by making effective use of their debating skills (their speeches were printed in newspapers throughout the state), using town meetings of ratification sympathizers to help persuade less committed antifederalist delegates, and allowing moderate antifederalists the opportunity to submit to the convention amendments in the form of nonbinding recommendations (Jackson Turner Main, *The Antifederalists: Critics of the Constitution 1781–1788*, Chapel Hill, 1961, p. 200–209).

8TH.

This afternoon the delegates from Newbury, and from this town, returned home from Convention. A number of very respectable citizens, and a number, who were not very respectable, went out on horse-back to meet the members and escort them into Town; as they came along, the bells at the different churches were set to ringing, and this noisy expression of joy, was continued with some intermissions till 8 o'clock in the evening. The mob huzza'd and one would have thought that every man from the adoption of the Constitution had acquired, a sure expectancy of an independent fortune.

I pass'd the evening at home in reading and writing.

9TH.

Mr. Parsons gave me this morning a packet of Letters, which I have been expecting these five weeks. There was however but one short Letter from Europe.[1]

In the afternoon Amory went for Salem. I took a ride with Townsend, S. Cutler, J. Greenleaf, Prout, Thompson, and three or four Ladies in a sleigh: we rode out as far as Mr. Dalton's farm: and after taking something of a circuitous rout, return'd and took tea at Sawyer's. After passing an hour we all return'd to Town. I spent the evening at Mrs. Hooper's. It was the first time I had been there since her misfortune. She bears it well, though frequent sighs rise deep from her breast. Mr. L. Jenkins was there; a good, honest, simple soul, without the least kind of harm in him. Miss Lucy Knight was there too. She has a very amiable countenance, a fine form and a benevolent disposition. Townsend says she has no sensibility, and I think her countenance wants some of that expression, which communicates the charm of sympathy to our souls. She may be possessed of many virtues, and if so will attract my esteem, and respect; but she is incapable of loving, and therefore could never be an object of love to me. A young fellow by the name of Rogers, for a year and a half paid the closest attention to her; and when it was daily expected that they would be published, he suddenly left her, and neglected her entirely; she wrote him a letter containing a dismission, and appears not to have had a disagreeable sensation upon the subject ever since. A disposition like this certainly smooths the path of life; but at the same time it certainly serves to make it narrow and contracted.

[1] These letters probably included William Cranch to JQA, 22–27 Jan.; John Murray Forbes to JQA, 19 Jan.; Nathaniel Freeman to JQA, 27 Jan.; and possibly AA to JQA, 12 Oct. 1787, the only extant letter from Europe at this time (all Adams Papers). Any others remain unidentified.

10TH.

I went with Townsend in the forenoon to hear Parson Tucker; he gave us an excellent discourse from, Ecclesiastes VII. 17. Be not over much wicked. Neither be thou foolish. Why shouldest thou die before thy time? Without alluding to the late circumstance of Hooper's death, it appeared plainly that the sermon was dictated by that occasion; and it was very well adapted; he particularly exhorted his hearers to avoid scenes of debauchery, of lewdness and intemperance, and with his usual liberality and ability, recommended the opposite virtues. I did not attend meeting in the afternoon; but wrote a little, and read a great deal as very frequently happens with me.

Townsend past the evening and supp'd with me. I have done keeping late hours. I find they are wholly incompatible with my health. I have of late, several times, after setting up at writing till one or two o'clock in the morning, been utterly incapable of getting any sleep the whole night. My nerves have got into an unhappy tone, and I am obliged to desist from continued application. My spirits for sometime have been low, and I have felt an incapacity of enjoyment, but that is now wearing off, and I am in hopes, that before long I shall again be able to resume at least as much diligence as I have been used to.

11TH.

We have had this day very little studying in the office. Mr. Parsons is so fond of telling of all the manoeuvres which they used in and out of convention, that he has given the same story to every body that came into the office through the course of the day. He mentions with great complaisance, the formidable opposition that was made, as it naturally enhances the merit of the victory. He speaks with pleasure of every little trifling intrigue, which served to baffle, the intentions of the *antifederalists;* though many of them to me exhibit a meanness which, I scarcely should expect a man would boast. Mr. Parsons makes of the science of politics the science of little, insignificant intrigue, and chicanery. These principles may possibly meet with success sometimes; but it is my opinion that fair, open and candid proceedings, add an influence, as well as a lustre to the most brilliant capacity.

I called just before dark to see Mr. Hutchinson, but he was not at his lodgings: I then went home, took my flute, and went to see Putnam: with whom I play'd a number of tunes: Frank Bradbury was there. Between 9 and 10 we both came away. I got home with some difficulty, as the walking in the streets is excessively slippery.

12TH.

In the beginning of the evening I called upon Mr. Hutchinson, and look'd over his music: he plays on the flute, and has a good collection of musical books: I found Townsend and Amory there. Between 7 and 8 I went to Mr. Bradbury's where I found a number of the young gentlemen and Ladies dancing: I took a share in the diversion, which we continued till midnight, when I return'd home. I danced with Miss Nancy Jenkins, a very pretty girl, about 17. Not entirely free from affectation.

13TH.

This afternoon I had something of a long conversation upon the subject of the ball, which is intended to be on Thursday. He had determined not to go; but upon consideration of several circumstances, which I mentioned to him, he came to an alteration in his sentiments: he was something piqued, at not having an invitation to join our party last week: but when I informed him of the reason, for which he was neglected, he was satisfied with its validity. He[1] and Thompson pass'd the evening with me; Little ought to have been of the party; but Miss Cazneau, had engaged him to go with her to Captain Fletcher's.

[1] "Thompson and Putnam with me" (D/JQA/13, Adams Papers, Microfilms, Reel No. 16).

14TH.

I attended at the office only in the forenoon; the after part of the day being employ'd in rigging for the ball.[1] I had sent a billet to Miss H. Greenleaf requesting the honor of waiting upon her. She was not engaged, and I was taken at my word; which will teach me to be sincere. It was late before I could get a carriage, and when I went for my Lady, I found, all the rest of the family were gone: which was against me again.

The ball rooms were too small. Not one quarter of the Ladies could dance at a Time. I danced enough myself, and made out to affront three or four Ladies, which is much in my favour. Townsend took cold in making the preparations for this ball, and was so unwell, that at about 11 o'clock, he went home and consigned his Lady, Miss L. Knight, to me. She being very agreeable, was upon the whole I believe, more the object of my attentions than another Lady: this cannot now be helped and whatever is, is right.[2]

Between 3 and 4 in the morning, the remainder of the company retired; Putnam lodged with me. The party was perfectly agreeable.

[1] The Federal Ball (D/JQA/13, Adams Papers, Microfilms, Reel No. 16).
[2] "And, spite of Pride, in erring Reason's spite,/One truth is clear, Whatever is, is right" ("An Essay on Man," Epistle I, lines 293–294).

15TH.

We indulged ourselves this morning till almost twelve o'clock before we rose.

I called at the office; and pass'd about half an hour there. I felt rather dissipated, and somewhat indisposed for study. In the afternoon when I called at the office, I found Mr. Wendell there. A singular eccentric character with whom I was acquainted, while I was in College, and whom I have probably mentioned before now. He still persists in his singularities, and in walking from Boston the day before yesterday froze, one of his feet.

Townsend is quite unwell; has an uncomfortable cough, and sore throat, but he went with me to visit several of the Ladies, who were of the company last evening. We first called at Captain Coombs's, where we found only Miss Nancy Jenkins. She holds her head too stiff for elegance, and has read too many novels; which render her manners rather fantastical and affected. We stopped a few moments to see Miss Coats; who was well, and we then went to Judge Greenleaf's, where we drank tea. Here were young Ladies, I had almost said innumerable: a choice, of every complextion, and probably of every disposition, among them all Miss Derby has the most promising appearance, but she, in company is reserved. The Judge talk'd about religion and politics, and Mrs. Greenleaf pass'd encomiums upon the british Constitution; but the young Ladies were all silent. We took our departure quite early, and I pass'd the remainder of the evening at Mrs. Hooper's, where I found Miss Knight and Mr. Cutler.

Learnt to play quadrille.

16TH.

The most violent snow storm, that has appeared in the course of the winter, it began in the night, and continued, all this day. In the evening it cleared up.

Townsend was not out. Amory and I dined with Mr. Parsons. Captain Hodge likewise was of the company.

I wrote a Letter in the afternoon; or rather part of a Letter to W. Cranch.[1] From the office, we went, and pass'd an hour with Mrs. Jackson; where we found Mr. Wendell, feasting upon his apples and nuts. He slept last night in Mr. J. Tracey's green house; which is entirely unprotected from the inclemency of the Season; and the better to enjoy the benefits of the open air, he stripp'd himself entirely naked. He converses in the same style, that he did a year ago; and appears to me, too consistent for a distracted person, as many suppose him to be.

We spent the remainder of the evening at Dr. Smiths. I made an apology to Miss Smith, for a blunder, which took place at the ball: she appeared plainly to be offended, but was satisfied after I had made my explanation: I know not whether to like or to dislike this girl: but perhaps Time will supply me with the means of information.

At supper Amory was excessively diverted with the appearance of a Bologna Sausage, which the Doctor introduced, and which Mr. Cutler observed would be ripe in June. After Supper I got seated next to Miss Putnam, and entered into Conversation with her. I found her inclined to flattery, a defect, not uncommon, among our young Ladies; and I answered her in her own way, as I always do. When a Lady pays me a compliment, I always consider myself indebted to her untill I return one, at least of equal value; and I am generally so good a creditor, that I pay with large interest. I have even once or twice in my life so far surpassed a Lady in that way, as to silence her, and make her ashamed of attacking me with those weapons: but I never flatter a Lady that I esteem.

[1] Dated 16 Feb. (owned by Dr. Eugene F. DuBois of New York in 1957).

17TH.

Parson Carey is very sick; and consequently we had no meeting: so I staid at home; wrote a long Letter to my friend Fiske,[1] and a page or two some ways back in this book. In the evening I went to Mrs. Hooper's to see Townsend, whom I found very hoarse, and with a bad cough. I pass'd the evening there, as likewise did Mr. S. Cutler. Within these two years Townsend has lost two brothers and a Sister by consumptions, and it is much to be feared that he himself will be subject to the same misfortune: I am in hopes however, that by their fate, he will be warn'd to take such care of himself, as will preserve his life and lengthen his days; for I feel a great degree of friendship for him.

¹ Letter not found.

18TH.

After passing the day at the Office, I went and pass'd the evening at Mrs. Hooper's. Townsend's cough hangs upon him, but he is getting better. We play'd quadrille till supper time. Miss Knight is still there; she is very handsome, and very amiable; yet not very interesting.

19TH.

Called upon Putnam after leaving the office, and passed the evening at his lodgings: I have a greater regard for this young fellow than I had when at College. He is friendly and good-natured, and pursues his studies with diligence and attention. Perhaps indeed that now the warmth of emulation has subsided, and we can in no instance be rivals neither he nor I view each other in the same light, that we did nine months ago.

20TH.

Mr. Parsons went yesterday to Boston, to attend the supreme Judicial Court.

This evening I past with Thompson, at Mrs. Emery's. Miss Smith and Miss Putnam were there. We play'd cards about an hour; after which Miss Emery play'd us a number of tunes very agreeably upon the harpsichord. I had another match with Miss Putnam at complimenting, and succeeded tolerably well.

21ST.

Mrs. Emery and her daughter were going to Exeter this morning in a single sleigh. Dr. Kilham and I after greatly debating the question had likewise determined to go: so we agreed to divide; the Doctor went with Mrs. Emery, and I with the young lady. It was just eleven o'clock when we started; and the roads were so difficult, that we did not get to Exeter till three. Nor the other sleigh till five. After sitting down my companion I went and dined, and then immediately proceeded to the meeting-house where the State Convention for the State of New-Hampshire were debating upon the subject of the federal Constitution. I found Mr. Pickering a member from Portsmouth zealously, though I cannot add very forcibly arguing for the good cause. Several other members spoke; but none of them, in my opinion much to the purpose: They have gone through the System by paragraphs: and are now considering it generally.

I found Mr. Shaw, Mr. Thaxter and a number more of our Haverhill friends there, and pass'd the evening with them at Mr. Peabody's; a friend of the Doctor's; where we lodg'd; for there was not a bed to be had at any of the public houses. We were disappointed of an assembly this evening as we expected; and the debates I really think were not worth the ride, in a cold day; but the satisfaction of riding with an amiable girl; and the novelty of the town which I never saw before, will in some measure compensate for the failure of my expectations.[1]

[1] In JQA's line-a-day Diary at the bottom of the page after the entry for 22 Feb. is a second entry dated 21 Feb.: "Mr. Atkins. Sci: fa: bail" (D/JQA/13, Adams Papers, Microfilms, Reel No. 16).

22D.

I attended to hear the debates in convention again, this forenoon. Mr. Langdon[1] began by making a motion that the Convention should adjourn to some future day: But said he would waive his motion if any gentleman had further observations to make upon the System. Mr. Atherton,[2] the leader of the opposition rose, and in a speech of more than an hour recapitulated every objection that he could invent against the constitution. He observed that *confederation* was derived from the Latin word *foedus;* and that *consolidation* was a metaphorical expression borrowed from the operations of chemistry; these were two of his most ingenious ideas, and upon the whole I think he may candidly be pronounced a miserable speaker, and a worse reasoner.

A reverend Parson Thirston[3] spoke as long, and as little to the purpose on the other side. He talk'd of France's demanding her money with the dagger in her hand; and of Britain's sending 50 sail of the line and 60,000 men to take New Hampshire But did not even attempt to support the plan, upon the fair and honourable basis of rational argumentation. When these two gentlemen had exhausted the resources of their lungs, the motion for an adjournment was again brought upon the carpet. This was the off-spring of the fears of the federal party; and was faintly opposed by the other faction, who appeared to be equally fearful of the event; though more confident in their numbers. The vote for adjournment however was carried by a trifling majority. The time and place at which they should meet again, was a subject of some conversation; but finally the third wednesday in June, and Concord were agreed upon.

We dined at Mr. Peabody's. Dr. Kilham was troubled with the impertinence of one Hopkinson, a distracted fellow, who came, and pretended to call him to an account for coming and intermeddling with concerns, in which he was not interested. A little after three we got into the sleigh, and between 6 and 7. cross'd the river from Salisbury.

I immediately went to Thompson's: I found Little there, and Putnam came in soon after: we pass'd the evening in sociable chat till 9 when I returned home.

[1] John Langdon, delegate to the Constitutional Convention in Philadelphia (*DAB*).

[2] Joshua Atherton, a lawyer from Amherst, N.H. (Joseph B. Walker, *A History of the New Hampshire Convention for the ... Federal Constitution ...*, Boston, 1888, p. 15).

[3] Rev. Benjamin Thurston, minister at North Hampton, N.H. (same, p. 9).

23D.

When I went to the office this morning I found young Pickman of Salem there. I was acquainted with him somewhat in Europe, and I believe he is mentioned in the first volume of this repository.[1] (repository!) He has been studying more than two years in Mr. Pynchon's office; and proposes now to pass five or six months in Mr. Parsons's. And I shall be very happy in this additional companion, as Townsend and Amory are both soon to leave the Town.

I pass'd the evening at home, and my friend Little spent it with me.

Wrote nothing, though it was very necessary.

[1] See entry and note for 27 Feb. 1785 (above).

24TH.

Mr. Carey is still very sick, and we had no divine service this day at his meeting. I again pass'd the whole day at home; I was tired in the evening, and took a walk as far as Deacon Thompson's; and desired Tom, to come, and pass an hour with me which he did.

I called at Putnam's, but he was not at home....[1] I wrote diligently in the course of the day, and acquired some little credit.

[1] JQA's ellipses.

25TH.

Pass'd the evening at Merrill's, with Mr. Hutchinson: and had some very agreeable musical entertainment. Mr. H. is a performer upon the flute, and has a good collection of books. He has been waiting a fortnight or three weeks for favorable winds to sail for Ireland. Captain Cazneau, and Captain Casey were there part of the evening.

26TH.

This forenoon while I was at the office I received a billet from Mr. Dalton, with an invitation to spend the evening at his house. Between six and seven I went, and was introduced into a room full of Ladies, with no other gentleman, but the master of the house. The situation was not perfectly agreeable, but I was relieved by a proposal of cards. I sat down to a game of whist with Mrs. Jones, a Lady from Boston, Mrs. Marquand, and Fanny Jenkins, who soon after resigned her seat to *Miss Dalton,* emphatically so called even by her parents which is rather unusual, but a custom which is claiming introduction. Major Greenleaf and Mr. Hooper came in before supper; which was at about ten o'clock, and which was formal, cerimonious, and consequently elegant. The company gradually retired after supper, and between eleven and twelve, Mr. Hooper gave me a place in his sleigh and I came home. The narrative is about as uninteresting as the scene. I found myself in the midst of a large company of Ladies, with none of whom I had an acquaintance sufficient to warrant an agreeable familiarity. I soon got seated at a card table, with Ladies whom I did not sufficiently admire. Mrs. Jones,[1] is young, uncommonly handsome, and having received her education in Europe, is the arbiter of taste, and propriety in the complicated science of female fashions. To be insensible to all these advantages would have the appearance of stupidity or of ingratitude; and Mrs. Jones takes every opportunity to show how free she is from such *vices*. Soon after we sat down she complained that her gloves pinched her arm excessively; and with some difficulty pulling one of them off, she exhibited, an arm, the beautiful contour and snowy whiteness of which, might fire the imagination of a sensual voluptuary, but which I unfortunately did not think of admiring till it was too late; on the forefinger of the hand; sparkled, a costly diamond, which demanded its share of observation, and perhaps in the mind of a polite spectator might revive a question often debated, upon the mutual pretensions of Nature and of art, to the superiority of beauty. Mrs. Marquand equally professes, to dictate the laws of fashion; but could not stand her ground against the irresistible power of the other Lady, who could silence her in a moment, by the resources which she drew from her English Education.

Miss Jenkins, she observed, looked very much like Mrs. *Siddons;* and if there is in fact not the most distant likeness, yet the remark might convince us that Mrs. Jones had seen that justly celebrated actress. The only particular in which she varies from the manners of the english Ladies, is in her ardent affection for her husband. He left her here yesterday being called by his business to Boston; but is expected here again to-morrow. Yet though this absence is so short, yet she could not hear his name mentioned without fetching a deep sigh: she anxiously enquired for an opportunity to send a Letter to him: and when somebody imprudently suggested that perhaps Mr. Jones would not return till Thursday; she held her handkerchief to her eyes, to conceal the involuntary tear, which was undoubtedly excited by the distressing idea.

A number of other circumstances similar to those related, concurred to form the opinion which I entertain of Mrs. Jones's character, and these anecdotes may exhibit it perhaps better than the most laboured description that I could write.

This Lady has taken so much of my time and of my volume; that I must really wait for other opportunities to speak of the other Ladies; who were Judge Greenleaf's daughters, Miss Prince, and Miss Derby; Mrs. Coffin, and Miss S. Jenkins, besides Mr. Dalton's own daughters, who tell up, well.

[1] Possibly Abigail Grant Jones, wife of John Coffin Jones, a Boston merchant formerly of Newburyport (Sibley-Shipton, *Harvard Graduates*, 17:49–54).

27TH.

Mr. Hutchinson sailed yesterday for Ireland. The weather for several days past has been quite moderate; but this afternoon blew up very cold again. I pass'd the evening with Townsend and Pickman at Dr. Sawyer's. Play'd quadrill with Mrs. Sawyer and Mrs. Hay; the family is very agreeable.

28TH.

The severity of the weather has been increasing, and is this night but little inferior to the greatest extremities of the winter. Our social club, met this evening at Little's. The walk was rather long, and bleak; but our enjoyment was sufficient to compensate for that. Notwithstanding Mrs. Jones's opinion, I confess I do not dislike clubs. I think they may be sociable and friendly without being slavish.

29TH.

A number of us spent the evening at Dr. Swett's. I play'd on the flute, an hour or so.

I have heretofore mentioned Mrs. Swett. The Doctor perhaps may come under the denomination of a reformed rake: in his youth he was wild; but he has become quite a useful man: Such instances are rare!

SATURDAY MARCH 1ST. 1788.

The weather is very severe: The month comes in like a Lion, and according to the farmer's proverb it must go out like a Lamb. I passed my evening in contemplation, and in writing at home; and have very Little to say for this day.

2D.

We had no meeting at Parson Carey's. I was employ'd in writing all the forenoon; but after dinner, went to hear Mr. Spring. The speculative sentiments of this gentleman, upon religion, are not such as I should admire. They may I think safely be called illiberal; though I am sensible such charges, are not in general very liberal. He has adopted all the fancies of the *Hop-*

kintonian sect[1] as they are called. These people while they profess to found their system entirely upon *disinterested benevolence,* by what appears to me a strange inconsistency, suppose that it may be agreeable to the general plan of the supreme being, to condemn to eternal torments all the human race except such as have experienced the effect of saving grace; The point upon which Mr. Spring continually harps; is that holiness consists in a total exemption from all selfish ideas, and that all sin originates in selfishness. I suppose he has not preach'd a sermon these ten years without introducing those favorite sentiments: his repetitions are so frequent; that they become very tiresome, to one whom they cannot convince. But his delivery is very agreeable; there is an earnestness and a solemnity in his manner which I wish I could find in preachers whose doctrines are more comformable to my ideas of truth.

[1] Named after Samuel Hopkins, minister at Newport, R.I., and a disciple of Jonathan Edwards; Hopkins' conservative religious doctrines were an important foundation of the New Divinity theological tradition in the latter part of the 18th century (Sydney E. Ahlstrom, *A Religious History of the American People,* New Haven, 1972, p. 407–409).

3D.

The weather continues extreme cold. The river is fast as low as this Town, and many persons have this day cross'd it upon the ice. Townsend set out to go with me this evening to Mrs. Emery's; but would not go in when he found there was company there. It was Judge Greenleaf's family. We play'd at cards and backgammon as usual; and between ten and eleven, I came home. Miss Prince, is not handsome, but sociable: she is generally called sensible and very agreeable; but I have imbibed an unaccountable prejudice unfavourable to her, from the appearance of her person and manners: perhaps I ought not to commit such a weakness to writing; but indeed it is a weakness from which I believe very few persons can boast of being free. Miss Derby is handsome: but her beauty is stern and forbidding: she is reserved and unsociable: her manners are not wholly exempt from the appearance of pride. But the effects of this passion, and of modest diffidence, so different from it, are similar in appearance, and when the causes of conduct, may be various the most

favourable construction is always the best. The Miss Greenleaf's ———.[1]

¹ Thus in MS.

4TH.

Doctor Kilham, went to Boston this day to attend the general
court. His opposition to the federal constitution, has made him
so unpopular in this town, that I do not expect he will be chosen
as representative at the next election, and he may I think with
this Session, take his leave of the legislative body for the present.
I passd the evening with Townsend and Thompson at Mrs.
Atkins's. The justice was not at home: between 7 and 8 o'clock,
we were alarm'd by the cry of fire; but it was extinguished, before we got to the house.

While the Doctor is absent, I shall read more than I can when
he is here: The intervals between the hours which I pass at the
office, I usually spend in conversation with him; when he is gone
I devote them to reading. I have taken up the second volume of
Gibbon, which I have for a long time laid aside; and I am determined to try again to get through this book. I have possessed it
several years, and have been all the time just about to read it, but
it has been like the hinge of Tristram Shandy's door. Never
done, because it could be done at any time.

5TH.

I pass'd the evening with Thompson and Putnam at Mr. Bradbury's. Frank came from Boston this morning, and bro't an account of the interment of his Honor Thomas Cushing Esqr. who
died last week. He has been lieutenant governor of this Commonwealth, ever since the establishment of the Constitution;
and it is probable, there will be a vast deal of electioneering intrigue, for the diverse candidates for the place.

The paper also contains an extract from the concluding Letter
of the third volume in defence of the american Constitutions,
which speaks very favourably of the System proposed by the federal Convention ... I did not expect it, and am glad to find I
was mistaken, since, it appears probable, the plan will be
adopted....[1] We play'd cards an hour or two and then amused

ourselves with music. There were several *young* Ladies present, Miss Harriet's companions; a sett that are almost always together, and who have at least more personal beauty, than any equal number of other unmarried Ladies in this town.

Miss Wigglesworth,[2] is about 17. Her stature is rather diminutive; but *smallness* is said to be one of the essential requisites of *prettiness*; Her features are regular, and her shape admirably proportioned. Her disposition is said to be amiable; but she talks very little. The greatest defect which I have observed in her is a frequent smile, which is certainly either unmeaning, or insulting. The only method I can pursue, when I catch her eye is to smile too; and by this means put her out of countenance. Thus much for the present; I will take some other opportunity to mention the other stars that form this constellation.

[1] JQA's ellipses here and above. Written by JA to WSS on 26 Dec. 1787, the letter appeared in the *Massachusetts Centinel* printed on this date (JA, *A Defence of the Constitutions of Government of the United States of America,* 3 vols., London, 1787–1788, 3:502–506).

[2] Probably Sarah Wigglesworth, the daughter of Col. Edward Wigglesworth of Newburyport (Sibley-Shipton, *Harvard Graduates,* 15:129–133).

6TH.

We met in the evening at Putnam's chamber. I did not pass my time so agreeably as I usually do these evenings. Townsend and Amory were there, and instead of devoting our hours to free and unrestrained conversation, we lost them in playing on the violin, and flute. Between 9 and 10 we retired.

7TH.

The weather begins to abate of its severity; yet people cross'd the river on the ice all this day. Townsend and Pickman this afternoon went to Salem. I was at home all the evening and Thompson spent part of it with me. He intends to quit his school, in three or four weeks; and I hope I shall then enjoy more of his company.

8TH.

I this day got through, my folio of Lord Coke, which has been hanging heavy upon me, these ten weeks. It contains a vast deal of Law learning; but heaped up in such an incoherent mass that

I have derived very little benefit from it. Indeed I think it a very improper book to put into the hands of a student just entering upon the acquisition of the profession. I am perswaded I might have spent the Time which has been employ'd in reading this book, to much better advantage, and that a twelvemonth hence I could have read it in less time and with more profit: but if this be the case how much more laborious must the study have been, when this was the only elementary book of the profession. The addition of Wood's Institutes and more especially of Blackstone's commentaries, has been an inestimable advantage of the late students in the profession.

In the afternoon I read a few pages in Blackstone and the contrast was like descending from a rugged, dangerous and almost inaccessible mountain, into a beautiful plain, where the unbounded prospect on every side presents the appearance of fertility. I read with more advantage than usual, as I was wholly alone in the office, all day. I spent the evening in my own room, uninterrupted by any intrusion. I proceed in the second volume of Gibbon, about fifty pages a day.

9TH.

Parson Carey got out to meeting this forenoon; but he was still so weak, that the effort was too great: he was scarcely able to get through the morning exercises: and in the afternoon the church was again destitute. I went to hear Parson Spring rattle away upon disinterested benevolence, and pass'd the evening at home.

10TH.

Pass'd the evening and supped with Thompson at Dr. Sawyer's. Mr. Russell was there: he came from Portsmouth this morning and returns to Boston with Mrs. Hay, to'morrow. We play'd Quadrill. Mr. Farnham took an hand; and is skilled, in all the trifling conversation of a card-table. Every one, it is said possesses[1] his peculiar excellence. Mr. Farnham's talent lies in the *science* of politeness. He understands to perfection all the nice and subtle distinctions between confidence and assurance, between ease of behaviour and familiarity, between elegance, and foppery &c. A science in which I am very ignorant, as in all others.

---

[1] That is, is acquainted with (*OED*).

11TH.

Townsend and Pickman, returned, this afternoon from Salem. Townsend, has been on to Boston and to Medfield; he brought me two or three Letters.[1] I passed the evening with Thompson at Captain Coombs's. Mr. Cutler came in, soon after us. There are several young Ladies there. The Miss Coombs's are neither of them handsome, and I have not sufficient acquaintance with them to form an accurate opinion. Fanny Jenkins is perhaps twenty one. A countenance more amiable than beautiful is her greatest personal ornament, she is not tall enough to have an elegant form, but when she smiles such a lovely disposition beams in her eyes that no one could wish her more handsome: she talks much, and tolerably well, but when a young Lady has so excellent a temper,

"Let her speak and whatever she say,
Methinks I should love her the more."

Her sister Nancy, is about seventeen. She is tall and beautiful in countenance and in the form of a person, not less sociable, but less sensible than Fanny. She has read too many novels; her expressions are romantic, and her ideas are far otherwise. Her disposition is I believe good; and a few years may cool her down, to an agreeable sensible girl: now, it may suffice to say she is young: But after all, the best object for description is Mr. Cutler. He is somewhat singular, but it requires a much longer acquaintance, to form a just opinion of the character of a man, than of a woman: the distinguishing traits are deeper and much more numerous. For which reason and some others I will defer speaking of Mr. Cutler, to some future opportunity.

[1] Among these may have been Cotton Tufts to JQA, 5 March (Adams Papers).

12TH.

I Dined with Townsend at Mrs. Hooper's. Amory went to Portsmouth on Monday, with several of his friends. They return'd this day to dinner at Davenport's. We called to see them; and sat with them drinking and singing till five o'clock, when they went for Ipswich. I pass'd the evening with Pickman, at Doctor Smith's. Townsend, went there with us, but found himself so unwell, that he went home very early. His cough has return'd, with several disagreeable symptoms. I fear exceedingly, that he is not long for this world.

We play'd whist an hour or two at Dr. Smith's and between 10 and 11. retired.[1]

¹ JQA also mentions a "Perkins" in his line-a-day entry (D/JQA/13, Adams Papers, Microfilms, Reel No. 16).

13TH.

Thompson, Pickman and Little, pass'd the eve at my lodgings: Townsend, was so unwell, that he could not come, and Putnam, went home some days since, and has not yet return'd. The office, for a week past, has been tolerably clear; and I have made considerable progress in Blackstone.

14TH.

Mr. Parsons return'd this afternoon from Boston, where the supreme judicial Court, and the general assembly are now sitting. I called with Pickman, to see Townsend, who is now confined to the house; and pass'd an hour or two with him: And for this day I have nothing more to say.

15TH.

I called this evening at Putnam's lodgings, and pass'd an hour or two with him. He went home last Sunday intending to be absent about a week; but he return'd yesterday, without compleating his visit. I told him some time ago, that I expected he would not be absent long from this town with any satisfaction to himself. He says he is happy as the day is long. He admires Newbury-Port exceedingly, and never enjoy'd himself more, than he has for the six months past. He says he is not in Love, and that is not the least reason, from which I conclude that he is. A young Lady similar in her manners, and perhaps in her disposition to him, has engaged his affections; and the schemes which he forms to be in company with her, and the manifest fondness which appears when he is with her, more than outweigh his declarations, which in cases less justifiable than the present, are not always consistent with truth.

16TH.

In the forenoon I attended at Mr. Carey's meeting. The man that appeared in the pulpit I concluded very soon, was a son of Dartmouth. All was common-place: his ideas were trifling, his language was inelegant and his manner, was an unsuccessful attempt to the florid. He apostrophised Innocence, and said she was charming. In short he appeared to me to have all the defects without one of the excellencies of a youthful irregular imagination. After meeting was over I heard his name was Oliver,[1] and that he is settled at Beverley. I had quite enough of him in hearing him once, and therefore in the afternoon I went to hear Mr. Spring, who entertained me much better, though, I am not a great admirer of his doctrine.

[1] Daniel Oliver, Dartmouth 1785, minister at the Second Church of Beverly (Sprague, *Annals Amer. Pulpit*, 2:43).

17TH.

Mr. Parsons held a court this forenoon at ten; and at the same hour I attended at Mr. Atkins's, with several actions, brought before him. Mr. Parsons in the afternoon went from home to return to Boston. I pass'd the evening at Mrs. Hooper's. Play'd quadrill as usual.[1]

[1] JQA adds, in his line-a-day entries, "Townsend unwell" (D/JQA/13, Adams Papers, Microfilms, Reel No. 16).

18TH.

I am sinking again into the same insipidity which I have so often lamented. The circumstances which daily occur, are now more than ever alike, for I not only spend the whole day in the same occupation at the office; but as Townsend is unwell, and confined to his lodgings I pass almost all my evenings with him: We have no news stirring of any kind, and as Dr. Kilham said to me, a short time before he went to Boston, "I am tired to death, of seeing one day only the dull duplicate of another."

19TH.

The weather was dull, gloomy, and part of the day rainy. Amory invited me to dine with him and Stacey and Azor Orne at Davenport's, but I did not feel inclined that way. I call'd at Mrs.

Hooper's in the evening and spent a couple of hours with Townsend. The lads who dined at Davenport's warm'd themselves so well with Madeira, that at about seven o'clock this evening, they all set out upon an expedition to Cape-Ann, to attend a ball there this night. Twenty seven miles in such weather and such roads after seven o'clock at night, to attend a ball, would look extravagant in a common person; but it is quite characteristic of Amory.

20TH. THURSDAY.

We met this evening at Thompson's. Pickman came; but rather late in the evening. Young Sawyer was there likewise: he spends the present quarter at home, by order of the college government.[1] I have not a very high opinion of his abilities; still less of his improvements, and least of all of his moral character. One thing however may be said in his favour. He is handsome in his person. His father is a very respectable, worthy man, and the family to which he belongs is very agreeable.[2]

[1] Sawyer had been rusticated since December for disorderly behavior at the college, but was restored in May (MH-Ar:Faculty Records, 5:289–290, 302).

[2] On the top of the following page in the Diary, JQA has written: "N B. this opinion of Sawyer did him great injustice. April 1790."

21ST.

I can read tolerably well when I am alone in the office, and make as much progress in one day, as I can sometimes in a week, when all the other gentlemen are here. I have read through the first volume, and have made some progress in the second of Blackstone....[1] And I read it I think with more advantage, than I did the first time; but my progress is slow; too slow.[2]

[1] JQA's ellipses.
[2] In his line-a-day entry, JQA mentions "Mrs. Hooper's. Evening" (D/JQA/13, Adams Papers, Microfilms, Reel No. 16).

22D.

Amory and Stacey, return'd from their expedition: They got to Cape-Ann at about twelve on Wednesday night, and were about two hours at the ball. On Thursday they proceeded to Marblehead, and attended at the assembly which was held there: Last Night they patrol'd the streets of Salem, serenading the houses, and came home this afternoon compleately fatigued.

Mr. Parsons arrived in town too this morning from Boston, and held a court, for taking cognizance of Mr. Atkins's actions.

Pickman, pass'd the evening with us at Mrs. Hooper's. Mr. Cutler was likewise there.

23D.

Pickman had agreed to go with me, and hear Parson Tucker preach this forenoon; but some circumstance prevented him; so I went alone. The Dr. gave us a very good sermon upon the education of children. I went home with Mr. Tracey to dinner, and Pickman soon came in. We dined and pass'd the afternoon with Mr. Tracey. This gentleman, was in the course of the war, peculiarly fortunate and accumulated, an immense fortune; but he has since been equally unluckily, and is now, very much reduced. The generosity of his heart is equal to any estate whatever: and although he has not been so prudent, as might be wish'd, yet every one who is acquainted with him, must lament his misfortunes, and heartily wish he may retrieve his affairs. We rode in to town in the beginning of the evening as the weather was rainy. We stop'd at Mrs. Hooper's. We found Miss Cazneau there; and Thompson and Putnam came in soon after. The evening was dull. Miss Cazneau, would sing; and murdered two or three songs. A specimen of Townsend's wit, set us to laughing. Mr. Parsons, set out this morning, to go to Boston, but the weather being disagreeable, he return'd home after proceeding three or four miles. I have undertaken a task[1] which possibly at some future day, may serve to fill part of this volume; but which at present takes up much of my time.

[1] JQA is referring to his poem "A Vision." See note for entry of 30 Jan. 1787 (above), and entry of and note for 28 March (below).

24TH.

I attended at Mr. Atkins's Court; and appeared to the actions. Mr. Marquand who had been summoned there, appeared, and somewhat diverted us by his impetuosity. I met young Thomas in the street who gave me some information from Cambridge.

This being the last day of service, we have been uncommonly busy in the office in copying the writs and making out records, according to the Justice's act,[1] which is useless and even troublesome on every account. I this day finished reading Gibbon's History, which I have had a long time without perusing. It has given me much information upon a part of history with which I was but little acquainted. The style upon the whole I think is elegant, but his manifest partiality against the Christian religion; is equally injurious to his character as a philosopher, and as an historian. He affects to despise those men who from a zealous attachment to their religion, have adopted the effusions of enthusiasm, as readily as the pure and indisputable relations of history; while he is himself guilty of the other extreme, which in my mind is much less excusable. Knox however is I believe too severe when he says, that this writer by a *meretricious* and *affected* stile, far beneath the native dignity and simplicity of the ancients has caught the transient applause of the public, and indeed the occasion upon which he passes this judgment renders the censure very reprehensible:[2] The reflection upon Julian's leaving Paris, was to me one of the most ingenious passages in the book: And Knox, by setting himself up as the Champion of english prejudices, cannot be quoted by a neutral person as an authority of great weight.

[1] *Perpetual Laws of the Commonwealth of Massachusetts, 1780–1800,* 3 vols., Boston, 1801, 1:146–149.

[2] Vicesimus Knox, *Liberal Education; Or, A Practical Treatise on the Methods of Acquiring Useful and Polite Learning,* 10th edn., 2 vols., London, 1789, 2:307–309.

25TH.

Copies of all the actions which are to be entered at the next Court of Common Pleas were this day sent to Salem, to be filed in the clerk's office; seven days before the sitting of the court, as the law directs: And as we have now got through the hurry of business, we have this day been very idle: Mr. Parsons has been talking all day with some one or other who came to the office: much of our time is lost in this manner; and if we complain, we are told we must learn to read without suffering ourselves to be interrupted by any noise whatever, a direction with which I believe I shall never be able to comply. And It would be much more agreeable to me, if he would receive his company in the other room, and spare us the trouble of an apprenticeship to an art which we cannot acquire.

26TH.

I took a long walk, this afternoon with Putnam, and as we came back we stop'd at Mrs. Hooper's. Townsend is still there the weather being so unsettled, that he has not ventured to go much from the house yet; He must however go in a few days to Ipswich as he is to be sworn in at that Court. We play'd quadrill. Miss Knight and Miss Phillips were there. With the latter of these Ladies I have never hitherto had any acquaintance. I went a mile with her, after ten to wait on her home, and on the way met Master Thompson, but as I returned I could not overtake him.

27TH.

I went with Pickman, Amory Stacey and Putnam to Salisbury, to see a vessel launch'd: She stuck as she went off. We dined there but the party was very far from being agreeable. A. Orne, is an habitual debauchee, who at the age of five or six and twenty has brought upon himself the infirmities of old age. He is one of those human beings whom to see is to despise. The description in the choice of Hercules[1] beautifully expresses the character.

At about five in the afternoon, I return'd with Pickman and Putnam, to Newbury-Port, and from thence walk'd up to Little's; where we found Thompson and Sawyer: we pass'd the evening agreeably; and much more to our Satisfaction than we could have done with those other Lads whom we left at Salisbury.

> "Vast Happiness enjoy thy gay Allies!
> A Youth of Follies; an old age of Cares:
> Young, yet enervate; old yet never wise;
> Vice wastes their vigour, and their Mind impairs."

[1] That is, the choice presented to Hercules by female representations of Virtue and Vice, each of whom urged him to follow the path she pointed out. JA suggested the fable as a theme for the United States seal (*Adams Family Correspondence*, 2:ix–x, 96–98).

28TH.

The weather was pleasant. Townsend rode, this day. I pass'd the evening with him: and found Miss Knight at Mrs. Hooper's. After having dismiss'd two or three inconstant suitors, she is now address'd by a Mr. Gregory from Boston, to whom she will probably soon be united.

> With all the charms of beauty richly fraught,
> Lucinda's form my fond attention caught.
> A faultless person and a lovely mind,
> I found with wonder, were in her combin'd
> Deficient only in a single part,
> She wanted nothing but a feeling heart.
> Calm and unruffled as a Summer Sea,
> From Passions gale's Lucinda's breast is free,
> A faithless lover she may well defy
> Recall her heart nor breathe a single sigh
> And should a second prove inconstant too
> She changes on till she can find one true.[1]

Such a character may be esteemed; it may likewise be beloved, for she has had more than one Lover; but their unsteadiness may possibly derive some excuse from this very disposition of her's: for my own part, I never could conceive such sentiments with respect to her, as would enable me to be inconstant.

[1] This stanza and the one recorded in the entry for 8 April (below) were later incorporated in "A Vision." This work, begun as early as 30 Jan. 1787 but not completed until June 1790, became a satirical sketch of nine young women whom JQA knew during his years in Newburyport. It remained unpublished until Dec. 1839, when *Brother Jonathan,* the weekly edition of the *New York Evening Tattler,* printed it from an MS copy. Later the poem was published in JQA's *Poems of Religion and Society,* Auburn and Buffalo, N.Y., 1853, and Currier's *Newburyport,* 2:541–547. The only known MS copy of the work in JQA's hand is in M/JQA/28, Adams Papers, Microfilms, Reel No. 223. Upon rereading the printed version in 1839, JQA regarded it as an unequaled effort. "As a Poet I have never surpassed it," he wrote; "My summit level as a Statesman, Orator, Philosopher and Proser is of about the same elevation" (William Cranch to JQA, 10 June 1790, Adams Papers; JQA, Diary, 25, 28 Dec. 1839, *Memoirs,* 10:176–177).

29TH.

I received two or three Letters for Little, and after finishing the day at the office, I went and delivered them. He went with me and pass'd the evening with Townsend: Mr. Morland came in to wait on Miss Knight home; but she preferr'd staying a day or two longer where she was. Mr. Cutler was an hour or two with us. Sometime after ten I came home.

30TH.

Parson Toppan of Newtown[1] preach'd at our meeting this day. I attended all day and was very much pleased with his ingenuity: he is quite orthodox enough, although he has contended with Mr. Spring upon some very knotty points. His delivery is not graceful, nor even agreeable; but the sound sense, and ingenuity, which appear in his sermons, more than compensate for defects which are so common.

I have read through Knox's treatise upon Education, and in general am much pleased with it. If his censures of the present times, did not sometimes border upon ill-nature, and if he had not profess'd to maintain the advantages of prejudice, and partiality I should place much greater confidence in his opinion; but his complaints in many cases are but too just, and too applicable to the manners of this Country.

[1] Probably David Tappan, minister at the Third Parish of Newbury, now West Newbury.

31ST.

Mr. Parsons held a Justice's Court for the trial of a trifling action of trover and conversion. The dispute was about 600 feet of pine boards. The witnesses on both sides were examined and after a trial of two hours; Mr. Parsons advised them to settle the matter between themselves without any judgment; which they accordingly did. The weather for a day or two past has been very mild and pleasant; verifying, the vulgar saying, mentioned at the beginning of the month. I walk'd with Putnam this afternoon and pass'd the evening with Townsend.

TUESDAY APRIL 1ST. 1788.

The Court sits this day at Ipswich. Mr. Parsons went in the afternoon, I dined with him. Pickman gone to Salem: so that for two or three days I have been wholly alone at the office: Putnam took a long walk with me; he has been amusing himself with Stacey this day by the prescriptive privilege of deceiving. The manner was imprudent, and the thing itself beneath his years: but there is a pleasure in playing the fool at times; and perhaps these are peculiarly excusable. As we returned from our walk, I stop'd in at Mrs. Hooper's to pass the last evening with Townsend. Parson Bass was there but soon went off. Amory took his usual rout; a Mr. Gartz, who belongs to Baltimore; Mr. Cutler and Thompson were with us all the evening: and we left them a little after ten.

2D.

This day Townsend and Amory finally left us and were to be sworn in to the Court of common-pleas at Ipswich. They entered the office both nearly at the same time, and have both continued here, more than three years. Their characters and dispositions, are essentially different. With Townsend I have been very intimate ever since I came to this town; but my acquaintance with Amory, has only been such as necessarily followed, from being so frequently with him. Townsend is in his twenty fifth year. His genius is very good, and somewhat eccentric. While at College, and for some time after he laboured under great disadvantages from his narrow circumstances; but for three or four years past he has been well supported, by a wealthy uncle, who has no children, and who will probably leave him something. Since he came here his studies have repeatedly been interrupted; and he has been obliged to attend for months together upon his brother, who died last summer in a consumption. The time which he could spend here was generally well employ'd. His disposition was easy and contented; rather apt to contract prejudices either favourable, or unfavorable to persons, from their first appearance; his friendships were very strong and his aversions rather severe. He was attached to his opinions, and would defend them with warmth: so that many of his acquaintance think him obstinate. But he has frequently said and I believe justly, that obstinacy consists in persevering in an opinion, without being willing to defend it when attacked; not in being unwilling to give it up without sufficient grounds to conclude it erroneous: and if his definition be true, I do not think he can properly [be] called obstinate. Upon general subjects his sentiments coincided very well with mine; but we differed very frequently in descending to particulars.

Generosity, humanity and benevolence, are the ornaments of his heart, and in short from his whole character I have such an attachment for him, that I shall regret much his leaving this Town: my anxiety for his health increases this regret; his disorder is alarming, and by so much the more as it has been peculiarly fatal to his family.

Amory I will mention to-morrow.

I took a walk with Putnam this afternoon, and as we returned Putnam urged me to go in to Dr. Smith's; to which I finally agreed: Putnam pass'd a number of high encomiums upon Miss Smith; but as soon as we went into the house I found Miss Bradbury there; which explained Putnam's eagerness. I sat and conversed till about nine o'clock, and then came off leaving my companion with his Dulcinea there.

3D.

Thompson went yesterday morning to Ipswich and returned last evening. I dined with him to day. Frank Bradbury and Putnam were likewise there. Amory and Townsend were sworn into Court yesterday in the afternoon, and immediately went on to Salem. Amory, whom I promised to mention this day is about twenty three. At a very early period of life he was engaged in scenes of intemperance and debauchery; and contracted a fondness for them, which he has not yet conquered. His imagination is lively and his apprehension uncommonly quick: but a great degree of volatility and unsteadiness, render all his reforming resolutions abortive. With any particular object before him he is indefatigably active, and industrious; but when it is once accomplished, he too often relapses into dissipation and inattention. Of almost three years and an half which have past since he entered Mr. Parsons's office, he has not I suppose spent two in this Town, and of that Time perhaps he has not employ'd one half in the office. Yet such are his natural advantages for improvement, that in the short Time which he has devoted to study, he has acquired almost as much knowledge of the Law as a common person would, who should have been attentive through the whole period. Notwithstanding his habits of intemperance he has formed a tender connection with a young Lady in this Town, who is undoubtedly firmly perswaded that he will marry her. It will certainly be a great misfortune to her, should she be disappointed: for after so long, and so great an intimacy, with a young fellow whose principles and practice, are so repugnant to the general ideas of morality, and religion; it must be supposed that any other young gentleman, would be somewhat punctilious before he would venture to pay his addresses to her. Unfortunately, the same causes, which are prejudicial to her reputation, will tend to render him faithless and inconstant. All that can be hoped is (and it is devoutly to be wished) that his native good sense, and strength of mind, will rise superior to all his youthful follies, and that of all the heterogeneous qualities which compose his character, the good only will remain. His manners and address are remarkably agreeable, and insinuating, and, he possess candour to applaud in others even those virtues of which he is most destitute. In short we may fairly say, that without an essential alteration in his course of life, he will ever be a worthless character; but that with such alterations as time and experience may very well produce, he may become one of the best and most useful men in the Commonwealth.

Dr. Kilham returned this afternoon from Boston and Mr. Parsons from Ipswich.

I took a long walk after dinner, with Putnam, F. Bradbury, and Thompson, and we passed the evening at Putnam's lodgings.

4TH.

The weather has been rather disagreeable this day.[1]

In the evening I went with Thompson and Putnam, to Mr. Bradbury's, where we found a large company. Mr. W. Parsons and his wife; Mr. Sigourney, and his enamorata and an innumerable quantity of Miss Greenleafs'. We pass'd the evening as usual: singing, playing cards &c. Mr. Sigourney, has a very good voice, and entertained the company much more than such exercises generally do.

We retired between 10 and 11 o'clock.

[1] "Rain" (D/JQA/13, Adams Papers, Microfilms, Reel No. 16).

5TH.

Rain'd again a great part of the day. Putnam pass'd the evening at my lodgings. We conversed upon a variety of Subjects. I am more pleased with him, than I was while we were, Classmates: he is not exempt from that puerility which I mentioned as constituting his character;[1] and I have sometimes seen him exert a degree of little cunning, to obtain an end, in trifles where it was totally unnecessary even to serve his own purpose; But he is good-natured, and friendly; willing and ready to oblige; easy and contented; enjoying the present, and looking forward to futurity without sufficient anxiety to embitter his happiness. I often envy him his feelings. For "who by taking thought can add one cubit to his stature."[2] The prospects of life which are before me, are by far the most frequent employment of my thoughts: and according to the different temperature of my Spirits, I am sometimes elated with hope, sometimes contented with indifference, but often tormented with fears, and depressed by the most discouraging appearances. Such reflections serve only to deprive me of my present enjoyments; after all, the events which Time is to produce, must take their course, and "sufficient surely," to the day is the evil thereof.[3]

[1] JQA's earlier sketch of Putnam is in the entry for 27 May 1787 (above).
[2] Matthew, 6:27.
[3] Same, 6:34.

6TH.

A Parson Allen preach'd this day for Mr. Carey. I went to hear him in the forenoon. His Sermon was sensible, but his delivery was quite disagreeable: his manner of speaking was so singular that several times it was with difficulty I restrained myself from laughing. I did not feel a great inclination to hear him again, and I therefore, went in the afternoon, and heard Mr. Murray. He is an orator; but if he did not betray such a consciousness of his own powers, while in the pulpit, he would be much more pleasing to me. There is no situation perhaps in which that consummate art of concealing art, is more requisite, than in the desk. Art is undoubtedly necessary in speaking to command the attention of an audience; but if that art is apparent, the solemnity of the occasion, greatly tends to increase the disgust which I always conceive, against affectation. For when a preacher appears so wholly occupied with the admiration of his own rhetorical talents; it seems he can have but little concern for the important subject, of which his eloquence is only the instrument, and which ought to be the chief, I had almost said the only object of his thoughts.

7TH.

I went with Thompson, to Mr. Atkins's, to answer to an action which we had brought before him this day.

The first Monday in April, being the day appointed by the Constitution for the choice of Governor, Lieutenant Governor and Senators The Town meeting here began at ten in the morning, and the poll was closed at four in the afternoon. Mr. Hancock and General Lincoln, had a great majority in this Town, as well as in Newbury. And a federal List of Senators; for. Fed and anti; are the only distinctions at this day. Mr. S. Adams had a ⟨great⟩ number of votes for Lieutt. Governor; but, for what reason, I cannot tell, all the influence was against him. The revolution that has taken place in sentiments within one twelve month past must be astonishing to a person unacquainted, with the weaknesses, the follies, and the vices of human nature. The very men, who at the last election declared the Commonwealth would be ruined if Mr. Hancock was chosen, have now done every thing to get him in, and the other side are equally capricious. We have not yet got sufficiently settled to have stated parties; but we shall soon I have no doubt obtain the blessing.

I pass'd an hour or two this evening with Thompson at Mrs. Emery's: and he spent half an hour with me, till nine o'clock.

8TH.

Pickman returned last evening from Salem. The votes in that Town, and in several others from which accounts have been received, are equally favorable or more so, than they were in this Town, to Mr. Hancock, and General Lincoln. I called and passed an hour or two at Mrs. Hooper's in the evening: Miss Cazneau was there. Came home early in the evening.

> Belinda next advanc'd with rapid stride
> A compound strange, of Vanity and Pride
> Around her face no wanton Cupids play,
> Her tawny skin, defies the God of Day.
> Loud was her laugh, undaunted was her look,
> And folly seem'd to dictate what she spoke.
> In vain the Poet's and musician's art,
> Combine to move the Passions of the heart,
> Belinda's voice like grating hinges groans,
> And in harsh thunder roars a lover's moans.

9TH.

Dined with Pickman and Thompson, at Mr. Parsons's upon Salmon, which begin now to be caught in the river. We did not do much business in the afternoon. I called upon Putnam, after taking a walk with Thompson, but Putnam was engaged for the evening; so that I soon came home to my lodgings.

10TH.

From the divers interruptions which we met with in the course of the day, we did but little at the office. We met this evening at Pickman's chamber: he has joined us and is regularly with us. Stacey likewise pass'd the evening with us; and Mr. W. Farnham; I agreed to go with Pickman to Haverhill to-morrow. From thence I intend in the beginning of the next week, to proceed to Cambridge; attend at the exhibition there; and then go to Braintree and spend a few days. And I shall probably meet my brothers there. I have sometimes intended to wait for my father's arrival; before I should go that way; but it is almost six months since I saw my friends in Cambridge, Braintree &c. which makes me somewhat impatient; and if I wait for my father I know not whether I shall go in one month or two: as I have been so little absent through the winter, I may venture now to indulge myself for a fortnight.

11TH.

I set out with Pickman this morning at about nine o'clock: the weather was clear though rather windy: before twelve we arrived at Haverhill. I went immediately to Mr. Shaws; and Pickman, went to the tavern to meet a carriage, which he expected from Salem; but very unfortunately he found the Carriage, had past through the Town, not more than a quarter of an hour before he got there: such disappointments, are peculiarly teazing to Lover's, and felt perhaps more keenly than greater misfortunes. After dinner I went down to Mr. White's, and was sorry to find, that Leonard was gone to Hamstead with his mother. I call'd likewise at Mr. Thaxter's, but he was not at home. I sat, half an hour with Mrs. Thaxter, who has met with a misfortune, and been very unwell for some time past.

I thence went up to Judge Sargeant's to pay a visit there; And I found Mr. Thaxter with him; I returned soon and drank tea at Mr. Thaxter's; and soon after; went back to Mr. Shaw's.

12TH.

In the forenoon I went down, and spent a couple of hours with Mr. Thaxter: the rest of the day I employ'd in reading, upon several subjects. I took up Hudibras in the afternoon, and diverted myself with it for an hour or two.[1]

[1] JQA adds, in his line-a-day entry, "Mr. Shaw's. All day" (D/JQA/13, Adams Papers, Microfilms, Reel No. 16).

13TH.

Attended meeting all day. Dined at Mr. Thaxter's with Mr. J. Duncan. And in the afternoon, after service: we took a long walk. When we return'd to Mr. Thaxter's we found Mr. Bartlett and his wife and Leonard White there. Mr. Parsons came in soon after. He is going to attend the Supreme Court, who will sit this week at Concord. The conversation soon turned upon political subjects; I knew we should have over again, what I have heard twenty times; and therefore I took a walk with Leonard White; and went home between 9 and 10 in the evening.

14TH.

I met with several impediments in the morning so that it was eleven o'clock before I cross'd the river: the weather was very good, but growing Cloudy. I got to Doctor Kitteridge's house at Andover, before one. I stop'd to see my Class-mate W. Abbot and dined there. Bowman and Wyeth were likewise there. I would say something of Mrs. Kitteridge, but it would be now a very improper time to give an account of such impressions. I left the House before three; and soon after it began to rain, and continued without intermission untill I arrived at Cambridge; I got there at about six. I rode, eight or ten miles with an Almsbury man, who is going to Concord court upon business. Mr. Parsons is engaged in his cause, and the man had a deal to say about lawyer's.

I found my brothers at our old chamber, and after sitting with them half an hour, went over, and pass'd the remainder of the evening with Packard. I found Cushman, at his chamber, and we spent the eve very sociably. Clarke had been riding in the rain as well as myself, the greatest part of the day. He came from Harvard, where he went to accompany Grosvenor, who went home very sick a few days ago.

Cushman is apprehensive that he will not be able to obtain his degree[1] before next Commencement. He tells me he has not yet preached, as had been reported: Child, Kellogg and Mead are, he says the only Classmates of ours who have yet appeared in the pulpit.

[1] Cushman had not received his bachelor's degree in the commencement of 1787 because of unpaid college bills.

15TH.

The weather was quite disagreeable, for exhibition; in consequence of which there was but little company. Phillips began the performances, with a Latin Oration. His subject was General Washington; a subject which must be inexhaustible or it would long since have been exhausted. He spoke well. *Treadwell* and *Gardner,* next came upon the stage, in a forensic disputation. Their question was something like this. "Whether mankind have any natural right to authority over one another." They quibbled about words, and said on neither side much to the purpose. Treadwell however did better than I expected of him. In the Syllogistic dispute Cutts was respondent, Blake 2. and Wigglesworth opponents. I have forgotten the question upon which they exerciced their ingenuity. Bradbury and Hooper, personated Plato and Diogenes; in a dialogue, upon the conduct of courtiers: the only fault that could be found, was that Hooper's delicacy of person, and neatness of dress, contrasted rather too much with our ideas of Diogenes, and indeed, with what he said in that Character. Paine and Shaw spoke a greek dialogue, in which I did not feel myself greatly interested; and Abbot closed with an English Oration, upon the slave-trade. The Composition was very good, and it was well spoken, though, the natural disadvantage of a weak voice, injured the effect of his delivery. I do not recollect having heard any performances upon this subject, at College, and it will afford a fruitful source for declamation....[1] The governor then arose, and made a speech addressed to the Students, in which he congratulated them upon their proficiency, and exhorted them to go on in the ways of well-doing.

The music which succeeded was but indifferent. They had no violin: and Fay their best performer, was unwell, and did not attend.

After the exhibition was over I went down to Judge Dana's, and dined in company with a number of Ladies. Stedman and Harris, the butler, dined there too. There was a Miss Patten from Rhode Island; Almy Ellery is fond of her; and I will trust to her judgment; but was it not for that I should not be much prepossessed in the Lady's favour: She is very tall, very young, and very diffident. Miss Badger I have seen before; but there are three or four Miss Clarke's of whom I have heard much said; and whom I this day saw for the first Time. They are all agreeable; and none of them handsome: Patty is the most comely, me judice.

After dinner I called at Dr. Wigglesworth's, but the young Ladies were gone over to the College, to drink tea. We went to Phillips's chamber. It was full of Company. Between seven and eight we went to Brown's Rooms, and danced till between Twelve and one.[2] I was completely fatigued, and glad that the company then dispersed. I pass'd the evening very agreeably; and after breaking up went with my Classmate Foster, and lodg'd at my brother's Chamber; where by priority of possession I still claim a right.

[1] JQA's ellipses.
[2] "Senior dance" (D/JQA/13, Adams Papers, Microfilms, Reel No. 16).

16TH.

Breakfasted at Judge Dana's. Doctor Waterhouse came, in and entertained us for some time with his quaint wit. I paid several visits in the course of the forenoon: pass'd a couple of hours very agreeably with Miss Wigglesworth and Miss Jones.[1] The latter of these two Ladies, in former times, was not with me upon so good terms as at present. I thought her capricious, and ill-natured: but of late she has been much better. I once wrote a double acrostic for her, neither part of which was true. As I did not insert them at the time I will now introduce one of them;[2] for the contrast is false and unjust. I went to see Mr. Smith, the Librarian, and also to Mr. Gannett's; where Miss Lucy Cranch, has been these two months past. The young Lovers went home this forenoon with the Miss Clarkes, And Mr. Andrews did not get back, till we had nearly dined. Immediately after dinner I mounted my horse; and got to Mr. Cranch's, between six and seven. My aunt I found was gone to Cambridge, for Lucy, and expects to return with her to-morrow. I found my friends well except W. Cranch, who has been very unwell, but is recovering.

> C—ould all the powers of rhetoric combined
> A—ssist to show the beauties of her mind
> T—he Poet's efforts would be all in vain
> H—er mind is fair, without one single stain
> A—ll the soft Passions which improve the heart
> R—eign in her breast, and every thought impart
> I—n such a breast no foible can reside
> N—o little art, for *prudence* is her guide
> E—ach moral beauty, which adorns the soul
> J—oin'd to each grace, completes her soft controul
> O—f Siren charms, the poets often tell,
> N—o goddess e'er employ'd them half so well;
> E—nvy itself must drop a tear to find,
> S—o fair a face with such a beauteous mind.
>
> Jany. 22d. 1787.

¹ JQA mentions Miss Jones and Miss Ellery in his line-a-day entry (D/JQA/13, Adams Papers, Microfilms, Reel No. 16).

² The acrostic that JQA copied into this entry first appeared in his verse composition book, M/JQA/28, Adams Papers, Microfilms, Reel no. 223. The second acrostic, which he apparently wrote down on the leaf that followed, has been clipped out of the book.

17TH.

Fast day. In the forenoon I remained at home, and spent my time in writing and reading. In the afternoon, I heard Parson Wibird. Mrs. Cranch and Miss Lucy came home this evening; a person from Boston brought us some Letters which came from Europe.¹ Callahan was to sail, about the first of this month; which will probably be extended to the fifteenth.

By this time I suppose my friends will be at Sea.²

¹ These may have included JA to JQA, 23 Jan., and AA2 to JQA, 10 Feb., the only letters for the period sent to JQA from Europe and surviving in the Adams Papers.

² John Callahan's *Lucretia,* in which JA and AA were traveling, was delayed off Weymouth, England, by winds until 27 April; the Adamses eventually arrived at Boston on 17 June. On 5 April, AA2 and her husband sailed from Falmouth in the *Tyne* packet, reaching New York in mid-May (JA, *Diary and Autobiography,* 3:214–216).

18TH.

A cold north east storm, confined us to the house all day. I read a few pages in one of Gilbert's treatises and wrote a little, likewise. The time however was spent without much improvement; Doctor Tufts was over here Yesterday and this day. He was attending upon Miss Quincy, who has been very ill in consequence of making a mistake in taking medicine, by swallowing salt petre instead of salts.

19TH.

The weather has been rather better this day than it was yesterday. I went with both my brothers on a shooting party, an amusement which I follow no where except at Braintree though, there could not perhaps be a more miserable place, for sport. Dined with W. Cranch, and my brothers at Dr. Tufts's in Weymouth; and saw Mrs. Tufts for the first Time since her marriage: last fall she was at Newbury-Port, when Mr. Odiorne, was married; and at that time had no thoughts, or at least no expectation, of changing her situation soon. But Mr. Tufts, who had always been remarkably backward, in affairs of this nature; was equally expeditious, when he was once engaged: he could not even wait, till he had got an house ready; but married immediately and lives for the present with his father. We return'd, so as to get home just before dark.

20TH.

I pass'd the forenoon at home in writing. In the afternoon, I attended meeting and heard Mr. Wibird. After meeting, I went down to view the house, which they are repairing for my father:[1] I was not perfectly pleased with it; but it now appears in a very unfavourable light: they are obliged to make the most necessary repairs very hastily expecting my father in a few weeks. I am in hopes, that after my parents return; this place will be more lively and agreeable to me than it is at present. I think I shall never make it the standing place of my residence: but I shall wish to pass much of my time here, and hope the change may be for the better.

[1] The Vassall-Borland place was an abandoned loyalist estate in Braintree. Several individuals occupied the house during the Revolution and afterward, until it was finally purchased for JA in Sept. 1787 through the agency of Drs. Cot-

ton Tufts and Thomas Welsh. Long known as the Old House, four generations of Adamses lived in it until 1927. In 1946 it was deeded to the federal government and became the Adams National Historic Site.

For additional details, consult the notes in *Adams Family Correspondence*, 3:264–266, and JA, *Diary and Autobiography*, 3:217; the Old House is illustrated in JA, *Diary and Autobiography*, 4:facing 195.

21ST.

We were again confined all day to the house, by the badness of the weather. Mr. Cranch however went to Boston. I find, as I always have found, great inconveniences in writing here, and indeed, there are no small inconveniences in thinking; I wrote however a little, and read a few pages in Gilbert's treatise of Evidence,[1] it being a Law book. W. Cranch is reading Bacon;[2] but makes no great progress in it at Braintree. It is a book which many instructors recommend to be read through in course; but Mr. Parsons says it is calculated, only to make matter of Fact lawyers; men, who without knowing the true principles upon which the Science is grounded, or the reasoning by which it is supported; will be confined in their knowlege to ita lex scripta est, and will be incapable of applying the principles to new cases, or to circumstances different from such as have already taken place.

[1] Geoffrey Gilbert, *The Law of Evidence* . . ., London, 1717, and later revised and corrected editions.
[2] Matthew Bacon, *A New Abridgment of the Law* . . ., 5 vols., London, 1736–1766.

22D.

I took a ride in the forenoon with W. Cranch. Mr. Cranch came home from Boston, and brought young Waters with him. Mr. Weld, with his wife and her Sister pass'd the afternoon here; and when I return'd from my father's Library, where I went to take a list of his Law-Books; I found Mr. Norton here: he has some thoughts of going to Menotomy to-morrow, to Mr. Fiske's ordination; and made this a stage on his way. He is paying his addresses to Miss Betsey Cranch, and will, I suppose marry her, unless some particular accident should intervene. He was ordained last fall, at Weymouth, in the parish where, my grandfather Smith was settled; and he is said to be a young man of good sense, and a good disposition.

23D.

The weather was so disagreeable, that Mr. Norton gave up the thoughts of going to Menotomy, and return'd to Weymouth. It has been very dull, a great part of this month. March was much more agreeable. My Brothers however went over to Milton in the afternoon, I intended when I came here to have returned yesterday to Cambridge; but I have deferr'd it, and shall probably still defer it till friday. On Saturday, I must certainly get home to Newbury-Port; where by my diligence I must repair the loss of time which I have sustained in this tour.

24TH.

Charles went to Boston this morning, and brought me back some letters from Europe.[1] I went in the forenoon with Miss Betsey Cranch, down to Mrs. Quincy's where she intends to spend a few days: but I did not see either of the ladies there: Miss Quincy, has in some measure recovered from the illness occasioned by a mistake in taking a medicine. I spent my time this day as I have every day since I came here, somewhat miscellaneously.

[1] See entry for 17 April, note 1 (above).

25TH.

I left Braintree between 9 and 10. and stoppd, about half an hour at Genl. Warren's, he was gone to Plymouth but Mrs. Warren was at home. The Genl.'s political character has undergone of late a great alteration. Among all those who were formerly his friends he is extremely unpopular; while the insurgent and antifederal party (for it is but one) consider him in a manner as their head; and have given him at this election many votes for lieutenant governor. Mrs. Warren complained that he had been abused shamefully, and very undeservedly; but she thought me too federal to talk freely with me.

I called for a few minutes at George's Office, which he has lately opened. I got to Cambridge, a little before one, and called at the Butler's room: where I found Mr. Ware, and Packard. Dined at Judge Dana's. Miss Jones was there, and agreeable as usual. In the afternoon, I went to Dr. Williams's. Sam has been gone about two months to Sea; Jenny is still losing her beauty, and will soon, have none to lose.

I was at Abbot's chamber an hour or two. And return'd to Mr. Dana's with Packard to tea. Stedman, and Harris, and my very good friend and Classmate O. Fiske, pass'd the evening there; and it was uncommonly sociable.

I had promised Pickman to meet him this day in Salem, but was prevented by the weather as it rain'd all the afternoon.

I forgot to mention, that my Classmate Harris dined with us at Judge Dana's. He came a day or two ago, from Worcester, where he is now keeping school. It was feared, that he was in a decline, but I think he looks better than he did when we left College.

26TH.

Between five and six this morning, I left the judge's house, with Mr. Andrews who is going to preach at Newbury-Port. We stopp'd at the Colleges, to take their Letters, but they had not risen. The Clock struck six, as we went out of the College yard. We breakfasted at Newells tavern, and got into Salem at about ten o'clock: I paid a visit to Mr. Read; he is going to be married; and to a young Lady with a large fortune, which is rather surprizing.

I met Pickman in the street, and went home with him. After sitting a few minutes we walk'd about the Town; I went to see Miss Hazen; who appears just as she did two years ago. Dined with Pickman; and at about two o'clock Andrews called me, to proceed. The weather was so windy, and the surf so great that we had some little difficulty in getting over Beverley ferry. We arrived in Newbury-Port at about seven. I went and pass'd a couple of hours with Putnam. I then came home, and soon retired as I was exceedingly fatigued, and felt very stiff.

27TH.

I attended meeting all day, and heard Mr. Andrews. He speaks very well, and his composition was I believe generally pleasing. I sometimes think that he mistakes his genius, and imagines that his fansy is lively and his first thoughts the best; while in truth his conception is naturally slow, and he ought to study greatly his writings. He was this day very brilliant in his expressions, and flowery in his periods, but his thoughts were rather too much in the common run, and this fault, I have frequently observed, in his pieces.

In the beginning of the evening, I called at Mr. Tufts's, to give him a watch which I brought for him; I spent the remainder of the evening and supp'd at Deacon Thompson's. Walk'd with Mr. Andrews up to Mrs. Farnham's, where he lodges; he proposes to return to-morrow to Cambridge.

28TH.

Dull weather. Wind Northeast. It began to rain a little after noon, and continued all the rest of the day. I pass'd the evening at Dr. Swett's. We play'd whist, and I was somewhat unfortunate. Little came home and lodg'd with me; the weather being so bad, that he could not conveniently go to Newbury.

29TH.

The weather this day was tolerable. I went in the evening with Thompson to Captain Coombs's, where we found the young Ladies. Polly Coombs, is very sick; they fear in a Consumption. Nancy Jenkins too has been unwell, and still looks thin. Mr. Farnham and J. Greenleaf were there; and Mr. Cutler. We had singing as usual.

30TH.

Very agreeable weather. After we had done at the office, I took a long walk with Thompson.[1] We then went to Mrs. Emery's where we found Miss Roberts. We there pass'd a couple of hours, and from thence went to Mr. Frazier's. We found ourselves in the midst of a large Company of young folks. All the College lads, and all the young Misses of that sett. We past about an hour with them, and then without much reluctance left them.

[1] JQA notes in his line-a-day entry that he "could not study" (D/JQA/13, Adams Papers, Microfilms, Reel No. 16).

THURSDAY MAY 1ST. 1788.

Pickman returned this afternoon from Salem. The Club were in the evening at my room: Young Fowle, Thompson's poetical Class-mate spent the evening with us. Pickman went off quite early. He attended a ball in Salem, last evening, and what with the fatigue of dancing, and that of riding this day he was tired out.

2D.

After passing the day at the Office, I stroll'd with Pickman, as far as Sawyer's tavern, where we stopp'd and took a dish of tea. When we set out to return there was a little sprinkling of rain, which we thought was not sufficient to stay our progress: but it kept continually increasing till it became quite a smart rain, and by that time we were so much soak'd that we concluded the sooner we should get home would be the better. As soon as I got home I was obliged to change from head to foot. Pickman said, it was one of the agreeable rubs of life.

3D.

I this day got through the 4th. volume of Blackstone's Commentaries a second time, and I imagine I have derived no less benefit from a second perusal, than I did from the first. I have been longer about it than I wish'd, but the interruption of an whole fortnight by a Journey prolonged the time which I took for reading this book, greatly.

In the evening I took a long walk with Pickman and Thompson, and as we were returning, we met Mr. Andrews who was coming from Cambridge.

Nothing new. Dull weather.

4TH.

I heard Mr. Andrews preach, his sermons were both very short; but better I think than those he delivered last Sunday; his text was, "If they believe not Moses and the prophets, neither would they be perswaded though one rose from the dead." Pickman observed, that there was a Sermon of Archbishop Tillotson, from the same Text, and the similarity is such as proves that Mr. Andrews had read it; though not so great as to charge him with plagiarism. However, the people in this Town, are so bigotted that a Man of Mr. Andrews's liberal religious sentiments will not be half so popular a preacher, as one who would rant and rave and talk nonsense for an hour together in his Sermon. I wrote a long Letter to my brother Tom;[1] which I gave to Mr. Andrews; with whom I pass'd the evening at Mr. Bradbury's. Dr. Sawyer, and Mr. Farnham, were likewise there. Parson Carey is still very unwell, insomuch, that there are but little hopes of his ever recovering, so as to attend constantly to the duties of his profession. Mr. Andrews is engaged to supply our pulpit three Sundays more. After which he is under other engagements till Commencement.

¹ JQA to TBA, 3 May (Adams Papers).

5TH.

I began this morning at the Office upon Foster's Crown Law,[1] a book admirably written I am told, and notwithstanding the barrenness of the subject as entertaining as it is instructive. I pass'd an hour in the beginning of the evening at Mrs. Hooper's and then went with Thompson to Mr. S. Hooper's. Miss Roberts was there; I think I have already mentioned this Lady; she is uncommonly sensible, and if she has not the advantages of youth and beauty, neither is she chargeable with its thoughtlessness, and nonsense. Mr. Hooper as usual, talk'd rather more of himself, than of any body, or any thing else; but was very complaisant.

¹ Michael Foster, *A Report of Some Proceedings on the Commission of Oyer and Terminer and Goal Delivery . . . To Which are Added Discourses upon a Few Branches of the Crown Law,* Oxford, 1762. A copy is in JA's library at MB.

6TH.

In the beginning of the evening, I took a walk with Pickman, up to Mrs. Atkins's. We found only the old Lady at home; and she was so unwell, that we supposed Company would not be very agreeable to her; and soon came away: we met Thompson just as we were coming out; he turn'd about and came back with us.

I have little to say. That part of my Time which is best improved is productive of nothing, which may properly be recorded here; and as these volumes, or the greater part of their contents, are only an account of the occurrences of my idle hours, they must be proportionably trifling and insignificant. While I was in College these books were useful, as they contained copies of all my compositions, which I wished to preserve; but since I graduated, I have scarcely composed any thing, and indeed I have been much too negligent in that respect; but with so many other objects to engross my attention and employ my time, I have perhaps some excuse.

7TH.

The weather was very fine; I took a long walk in the evening with Thompson and Putnam. Thompson left us, and went to see Parson Spring. Putnam came home, and past the remainder of the evening with me. I have used myself for several days past to rise very early, and should wish to do so through the Summer: but my propensity to sleep is so great, that it is almost always impossible for me to awake so soon as I wish.[1]

[1] In his line-a-day entry, JQA refers to Michael Foster's *Discourses upon a Few Branches of the Crown Law* (D/JQA/13, Adams Papers, Microfilms, Reel No. 16).

8TH.

The town met this afternoon to make choice of representatives for the ensuing year. Jonan. Greenleaf Esqr. Theop Parsons Esq. Captn. W. Coombs, and Mr. Jonan. Marsh, were the persons elected. We met in the evening at Putnam's lodgings. Stacey desired to join the Club, and was accordingly received. Little did not come; and as we began to be impatient we sent over to Dr. Swett's for him. But they sent us word that he was gone to be inoculated for the small pox. This disorder was introduced by a mistake of Dr. Smith; in consequence of which a number of persons have been inoculated, and removed to the Pest house. Little went without leave or licence; and is liable to prosecution for so doing;[1] but in his circumstances I think he was very excusable in running the risk.

[1] Although the town of Newbury on 8 May had authorized the use of the hospital in "Common Pasture" for inoculation, the selectmen of Newburyport promptly declared that the use of the building for inoculation was illegal and a threat to public health. On 16 May the town voted that those who inoculated others or were themselves inoculated should be prosecuted (Currier, *Newburyport*, 1:75).

9TH.

Violent North-east storm, all day.
We all dined with Mr. Parsons. Thompson pass'd the evening

with me. This storm gives me some anxiety, as possibly Callahan may be now upon the Coast. I would hope however for the best.

10TH.

The storm continued all this day, and rather with increasing violence. Thompson and I again dined with Mr. Parsons.

I passed the evening with Putnam at his lodgings: I this day got through Foster, and have been more pleased than with any professional book I have hitherto read; not even Blackstone excepted. The subject indeed being the pleas of the Crown, is not so immediately connected with a young lawyer's practice as many other books; but as Foster always ascends to first principles, his reasoning, may by analogy apply to very different branches. The style is nervous and elegant suitable to the dignity of the author; and the "pride of virtue," as he himself expresses it, shines forth in every page of the performance. What increases greatly the pleasure with which this book is read, is that the writer appears, not only a learned and judicious lawyer, but an excellent man. The encomiums which he justly bestows upon Sir Thos. Abney, are said to be applicable in a still more eminent manner to himself. And after all, the virtues of the heart have a greater claim even to our veneration and esteem, than all the splendid appendages of genius. The compliment which Thompson pays to Pope,

> For though, not sweeter his own Homer sings,
> Yet is his Life the more endearing song,[1]

is more to his Honour than the most laboured panegyric, that ever was composed, of his talents.

I have undertaken to read Hume's History of England again: It is almost seven years since I read it, and the connexion of important events in that kingdom has almost been obliterated from my memory.

[1] James Thomson, *The Seasons: Winter,* lines 553–554.

11TH.

I attended meeting to hear Parson Barnard of Salem. He gave us two very excellent Sermons. And his prayers were admirable; which is something very uncommon. I am told indeed that he regularly composes this part of the service; as well as his Sermons; an example worthy of imitation. His address for Mr. Carey, was tender and affectionate, and the manner in which he spoke it was truly affecting.

Thompson and Putnam pass'd the evening with me.

12TH.

I have been quite unwell, these two or three days past; a disorder recurs with which I have been troubled in the Spring, the two years back; and it is more inconvenient this time than it ever has been before.

At Mr. Parsons's recommendation, I have this day taken up Hawkins's pleas of the Crown.[1] I think I should not now have selected this book, had it been left at my option. This branch of the Law, will be of no service to me, within these seven years, and there are many subjects which will be more immediately necessary. The theories relating to civil actions, will surely be sufficient to employ all my time for the remainder of my three years, and I shall certainly have enough leisure time afterwards to acquire a competent knowledge of the criminal Law, before I get to the supreme Court, if I ever do. However Mr. Parsons must know better than I, what is to be done in this case; and I therefore cheerfully submit to his directions.

I took a long, solitary walk this evening, and then came home, and amused myself, for a half an hour, with my flute.

[1] William Hawkins, *A Treatise of the Pleas of the Crown* . . ., London, 1716. A copy is in JA's library at MB.

13TH.

I took a walk with Pickman up to Sawyer's tavern, and drank tea there. The evenings are now so short that it was nine o'clock before we got back. Our Future prospects in life were the Subject of our conversation. The appearance before him is very fair: his father is a man of large fortune, which although divided among several children, gives each of them a sum sufficient for starting forward: He will now in a few months be ready to enter upon the profession: he is paying his addresses to a young Lady whose fortune will probably be amply sufficient; and from appearances I should judge he will be married ere long. Yet even he is anxious for his future welfare; and how much greater reason

402

have I to look forward with terror. I have two long years yet before me, which must be wholly employ'd in Study, to qualify myself for any thing. I have no fortune to expect from any part, and the profession is so much crowded, that I have no prospect of supporting myself by it for several years after I begin. These are great causes of discouragement; but my only hope and comfort is, that diligence, industry, and health may overcome them all.

14TH.

I walk'd with Thompson up to Mrs. Atkins's. The old Lady is gone to Boston to spend a fortnight. Mr. and Mrs. Searle were there; and Mr. Atkins came home soon after. Atkins is a man of abilities; but of strong passions; and as he was cramped in his youth, by his penurious circumstances, his disposition was soured, and he is now excessively irritable, and his natural frankness has degenerated to the unfeeling bluntness of a cynic. He has now the expectancy of a considerable fortune, at the decease of an aged relation; and it is to be hoped that when that circumstance takes place, it may soften his temper and reconcile him more to his fellow mortals.

I still continue quite unwell; it has had one good effect at least; that of making me rise early for several days past.

15TH.

Club met this evening at Pickman's. All there but Little, who is going through the small pox. Mr. Farnham was there; the evening was agreeable. Pickman left us at half after eight, to call on a Lady, who came this afternoon from Salem. After nine we took a walk of a mile or two before we retired; just as I got home I met a number of people; who had just come from the town-house, where it seems they were entertained with a concert this evening.

16TH.

Took a walk after leaving the office, with Thompson and Putnam. We were for calling in at Mr. Frazier's, to see the young girls, but upon the presumption they were not there, I would not stop; accordingly we proceeded. Thompson left us: Putnam, was very impatient, but just as we had turn'd the corner into high street, both Miss Frazier's, and Putnam's own Harriet appeared. He was as happy as present enjoyment can render any one. We walk'd with the girls, and after conducting them home, took our leave. Putnam afterwards called to see me. He had no idea of meeting the girls, nor did he even suspect, that Harriet could be with them. The most exceptionable part of this young fellow's character, is a spirit of deception, a disposition to be cunning, even in the most trifling occurrences of life: in which a complicated policy, would require an appearance of the greatest candour and frankness. He is deeply smitten with his Harriet; every look, and every action afford demonstration strong of this. Yet he pretends to deny it. He is sure to meet her every evening; and yet he boldly declares that it never happens but by accident. Upon this subject it is true his friends have no right to catechise him; but he himself leads the way by making declarations, which any person of common sense, and any ways conversant with him, must know to be totally repugnant with the truth. We laugh at him for this conduct, but he does not appear sensible, how much it lessens our esteem for him. And he still attempts to carry on a deception, which we have told him was long since detected.

17TH.

Dined at Judge Greenleaf's with Pickman and Thompson. Two Miss Dalton's were there; and Miss Deblois a young lady whose brother is paying his addresses to the eldest Miss Dalton. Miss Deblois has been much celebrated, as a beauty; and she may still be called very handsome: though she be as much as 27. She is sociable and agreeable: Though she is not yet wholly destitute of that kind of vanity, which is so naturally the companion of beauty. She puckers her mouth a little, and contracts her eyelids a little, to look very pretty; and is not wholly unsuccessful. The Miss Dalton's, as usual talk'd more about themselves and the family, than any thing else. The eldest is said to be blest with a very amiable disposition, and as for Polly, Miss Deblois said, she made her laugh yesterday beyond measure, and it is well she has the talent of exciting laughter, in others; for unless her countenance very much belies her she is seldom, guilty of such a trick herself. Judge Greenleaf's daughters', are always so much addicted to silence, that although I have been in company with them a number of times, I know not what opinion to form of them.

In the afternoon I took a long walk with Thompson and Putnam. The weather was very dull and disagreeable. Thompson stopp'd at Mrs. Atkins's. I pass'd the evening with Putnam at his lodgings.

18TH.

Mr. McKeen of Beverley preached at Mr. Carey's this day. I attended to hear him. His discourses were, though sensible, calculated to please the generality of the audience; I did not like them so well as those of Mr. Barnard, the last Sunday. After meeting Pickman called upon me, and I went up with him to see Mr. Jackson, where we drank tea, and pass'd the evening. Mr. McKeen, and Mr. Farnham were there; but went away soon after tea. Miss Wendell was likewise with Mrs. Jackson. She is not handsome, but is said to be very amiable. A little after nine I came away; Pickman still remaining there.

19TH.

Began upon the second book of Hawkins. The first treats of all offences, against the public; and this of the punishments to which they are liable.

I walk'd with Thompson in the evening: we called at Mrs. Hooper's, and pass'd an hour there; after which we went to Mr. Carter's. Miss Polly goes to Boston to-morrow.

20TH.

Mr. Parsons had the frame of his House raised, and was consequently very busy. Walk'd with Pickman. We met Thompson, and all went to see Mr. N. Carter who was lately married. His wife is not quite so stiff in her manners, as she used to be, a year and an half ago; but she has already adopted other airs; and appears no less affected than formerly. De gustibus non est disputandum; There's no disputing about the choice of a wife. Nancy Cutts, Mrs. Carter's sister, appears much more agreeable; and upon the whole I think her the handsomest of the two: however Mrs. Carter was abundantly complaisant, and we pass'd the evening tolerably.

21ST.

I walk'd with Pickman in the evening to Sawyer's; where we drank tea; and made it almost ten o'clock before we got home. I then went up with my flute to Stacey's lodgings, our general head quarters. About a quarter before twelve, Stacey, Thompson, Putnam, with a couple of young lads by the name of Greenough and myself sallied forth, upon a scheme of serenading. We paraded round the Town, till almost four in the morning; the weather which was not very agreeable, when we first set out: and was growing worse continually: at length it began to rain smartly; upon which we all separated; and respectively retired.

22D.

I was up before eight, and had not slept well, even the short Time I was in bed; I felt stiff and unfit for almost every thing. I read but little at the Office; and omitted one thing, which for three weeks past has claimed my attention, very constantly: The Club, were at my lodgings this evening; Stacey however went away somewhat early; to meet some of his friends from Andover, and we were all too much fatigued, by the last night's jaunt, to be very sociable, or gay. At nine we separated as usual.

23D.

Continual North east winds have prevailed for a week past. This evening, I past, with Thompson at Captain Coombs's. We found Mr. Porter and Mr. Kellogg, two young Parsons there. The evening was tolerable; and something more. Fanny Jenkins was as easy, as good natured, as talkative as usual. Jenny Coombs is sensible and clever. Her Sister Polly it is feared, is in a consumption: a disorder by which Captain Coombs has already lost two of his children....[1] Poor, miserable beings we are! Dependant for our happiness, not only upon our own conduct, but equally upon the caprices of fortune, and the casual occurrences of a day. What must be the feelings of a Parent, who after rearing a numerous family of promising children, just as they are entering upon the Stage of Life; and when he begins to reap the rewards for his pains in educating them, by being witness to their usefulness in the world; when he fondly hopes to leave them in the enjoyment of prosperous circumstances; to see them drooping, and dying under the operation of a long, lingering disease, in which the terrors of death are increased, by its slow and gradual approaches. Yet, this is the situation of many Parents. And if the causes of misery are thus distributed, as well to the virtuous and the good, as to the abandoned and unprincipled, what is the lot we have to expect in the world? I look forward with terror; and by so much the more, as the total exemption from any great evils hitherto, leads me to fear, that the greatest are laid up in store for me.

[1] JQA's ellipses.

24TH.

Pickman went to Salem this morning. In the evening, I took a long walk with Thompson, down towards Newbury Bridge, in hopes of meeting Mr. Andrews; we were however unsuccessful. When we returned, I stop'd and past an hour with Putnam. He told me they had received a letter at Mr. Bradbury's from Andrews informing them, that his health, would necessarily prevent him, from coming to-morrow, but that he will send somebody if he can to supply his place.

25TH.

Mr. Webber preach'd here, for Mr. Andrews; and I was much pleased with his discourses. They were quite argumentative; and his manner of reasoning was such as shewed him to be an acute metaphysician. He has always had a peculiar attachment to mathematical studies; and has acquired great knowledge in that branch of Science, which has at the same time habituated him to a degree of precision in his reasoning, which few people possess. After meeting this afternoon Putnam called at my room, and urged me to go to Mr. Spring's, where it seems they were not contented with two Services, but were going upon a third. Putnam went I believe, rather from the motive of seeing certain young Ladies there, than from an excess of piety. But as I wished to write a Letter to W. Cranch, and as Mr. Parsons will go for Boston early to-morrow morning, I declined going with Putnam. After writing my Letter[1] I went and took a long walk quite alone the weather being very fine; and as I return'd I stopp'd an hour at Mrs. Hooper's. Thompson came in soon after me.

We walk'd again, and as we were passing before Mr. Frazier's door, the young Ladies were standing there: we stopp'd, and went in. Mr. and Mrs. Frazier return'd home, a few minutes after; with Miss Phillips of Boston; a Lady whom I saw at Hingham last fall; who has play'd the coquette, for eight or ten years past, with a number of gentlemen, but who has now a prospect of being married shortly. We soon came away; Thompson pass'd an hour at my lodgings.

¹ Letter not found.

26TH.

In the afternoon, I took a walk with Thompson, to see Little. He has the small pox full, upon him at this time.¹ We returned, and I pass'd the evening at Mrs. Emery's. Judge Greenleaf's daughters, and Miss Smith and Miss Wendell were there. The evening was not agreeable; there was too much ceremony and too little sociability: we conducted the Ladies home, and retired.

¹ JQA was inoculated in July 1776, along with his mother, sister, and brothers (*Adams Family Correspondence*, 2:45–46).

27TH.

Mr. Jackson, sent one of his sons to inform me, that he heard last evening at Beverly, that Callahan had arrived, in Boston. The report I find is all over the Town; and I have received the congratulations of almost all my acquaintance here.

This evening, by means of an accident which was contrived in the morning a number of gentlemen and Ladies happened to meet, at Mr. Brown's house, where we danced till about twelve o'clock. The weather was rather too warm; otherwise the party was agreeable. We often changed partners. And as there were several more Ladies than gentlemen; one or two of the young misses, thought they were not sufficiently noticed, and so much mistook the intrinsic value and importance of their resentment, as to display it, in a manner, which raised an involuntary smile: involuntary I say; because no one surely could willingly smile at the resentment of a Lady. I escorted Miss Newell home; and then retired likewise, myself.

28TH.

Election Day. And there is not a poor Devil, who has lost his election, in the Commonwealth, that feels half so much vexed, and disappointed as I do. After enjoying the satisfaction of supposing my friends all arrived safe; I find this day that the report was without any foundation. That Callahan has not arrived, and has not even been spoken with, as has been said.

I walk'd in the evening with Stacey, and called afterwards, for half an hour at Mrs. Hoopers.

29TH.

Club at Thompson's this evening. Putnam inform'd us, he must leave us at a quarter before nine. I told him he must make no appointments for Thursday evenings. It was no appointment he said; but he was under an indispensible obligation to write a letter this evening: accordingly he left us. At nine we likewise came away. I took a walk with Stacey in high street, with the expectation of meeting Putnam; nor were we disappointed. He was walking home with the young Ladies, that he is generally most attentive to.

After we had ascertained the matter sufficiently, we continued a walk, and, I came home at about ten. I found a bundle, for me which Mr. Carter brought from Boston, but there was no Letter with it.

30TH.

I called this morning at Mr. Bradbury's office, and affronted Putnam by rallying him upon his deception last night. In the afternoon I walked with Thompson: we overtook Mr. J. Tracy and his Lady; and accompanied them. As we were passing by Mrs. Atkins's she arrived, with her son from Boston. We stopp'd there a few minutes. Genl. Lincoln is Lieutt. Governor, &c.

We spent the remainder of the evening at Mr. Carter's with the old gentleman; as none of the young folks were at home.

31ST.

Finished, this forenoon with Hawkins. Dined at Mr. N. Carter's. As did Mr. Farnham and Thompson: called at the office in the afternoon; but did nothing. Walk'd with Thompson.

Went in to Mrs. Hooper's and drank tea there. Miss Emery was with her. I soon came out and left Thompson there. I took a solitary walk of two or three miles into Newbury: was surprised by the rain, and quite sprinkled before I got home. We have had a great deal of rain this Season, but very little warm weather. Fruits rather backward.

SUNDAY JUNE 1ST. 1788.

Mr. Allen preached for us this day; and I attended to hear him. His Sermons are judicious and sensible; but his manner of delivering them is very disagreeable.

In the evening I took a long walk with Doctor Kilham; and pass'd the remainder of it at home.

2D.

Pickman returned this day from Salem, where he has been for ten days past.

I began to read Wood's Institutes;[1] a book written upon a similar plan, to that of Blackstone; but much inferior in the execution.

I took a long walk this evening alone, musing and contemplating upon a subject which at this time engrosses all my attention.

[1] Thomas Wood, *An Institute of the Laws of England; Or, The Laws of England in Their Natural Order, According to Common Use . . .*, London, 1720.

3D.

I walk'd with Thompson a mile or two in Newbury. The prospects on that road are delightful; and I am more pleased with that walk than with any other near this town. We went to Judge Greenleaf's. Mrs. Hodge and Mrs. Parsons were there. We past the evening as usual at that house. The judge was very sensible and sociable; Mrs. Greenleaf was very agreeable; and all the daughters sat like just so many young misses, whose mamma, had told them, that little girls must be seen and not heard. The judge to strangers appears to be quite a soft and complacent man; but his family regulations are rather despotic: this circumstance takes off much of the pleasure of visiting there, which would otherwise be great; for his conversation and that of his Lady are quite entertaining.

She asked me if I had not been greatly disappointed last week; I told her I had, and that it had been a subject of much vexation to me. The judge said it was well. He always wished that his young friends might meet with disappointments and misfortunes; and the greater the better, if they were not such as to debilitate the mind. It was best to be enured to misfortunes in early life; sooner or later they would come; and it was much best to be prepared for them by experience.

Thompson came home and supp'd with me.[1]

[1] In his line-a-day entry, JQA refers to "Wood." Presumably he continued his reading of Thomas Wood's *Institutes* that he had begun the previous day (D/JQA/13, Adams Papers, Microfilms, Reel No. 16).

4TH.

Walk'd into Newbury in the evening with Thompson;[1] and we returned through Joppé,[2] by a different route from that which I usually come. We past an hour at Mrs. Emery's. Her daughter is very amiable, though not handsome. She entertained us sometime by playing upon the Harpsichord. Mr. J. Greenleaf was there; it is reported that he is paying his addresses there. The dispositions of the persons are not sufficiently congenial to render either of them happy, and I should therefore wish that this report, like most others of the same nature may prove an idle surmise without any foundation.

[1] "Tolerable weather" (D/JQA/13, Adams Papers, Microfilms, Reel No. 16).
[2] Joppa, a small fishing village on the Merrimack River, east of Newburyport in Newbury (John J. Currier, *"Oulde Newbury": Historical and Biographical Sketches,* Boston, 1896, p. 218–219; Currier, *Newburyport,* 1:151).

5TH.

We met in the evening at Stacey's lodgings. Putnam was not present. At about seven we received a letter from him which for its singularity I am determined to preserve.[1] And after I came home[2] I wrote him an answer which is likewise here inserted, and which I shall send him to-morrow.

Messrs. Stacey, Thomson and Adams
   or to any one of them.   Present.
Gentlemen   Newbury-Port June 5th. 1788

You doubtless recollect the conversation which passed at our office, the evening after our last club night. It will be needless for me again to go over the same ground; let me just observe "that at the time I left you, I neither wished or expected to meet any lady or ladies during the evening." What I then told you, I know, and you may rest assured was truth however clouded with circumstances which might lead you to a different supposition. You may attribute the effect to "accident, sympathy" or just what you please, it alters not the original cause of action. I feel an happy consciousness of my innocence of the charges you alledged against me (such as imposing on the club &c) which consciousness alone, could support me when absent from a Society, whose pleasures I once eagerly sought, as eagerly wished to deserve, as richly enjoyed.

I think your treatment to me was unkind, severe and illiberal. With pleasure, I can appeal to my own bosom in the calm hour of reflection and retirement, and declare such treatment unmerited.

I write not Gentlemen under the influence of passion and resentment, but give you sentiments dictated by reflection and approved by reason and my conscience. I wish you to consider the affair as relating only to the club.

These circumstances Gentlemen must excuse my absence this ev'ning.

I should be happy to wait on you at my chamber next Thursday evening, where I propose to take my leave of the club and thereby render your happiness secure.

Adieu! may you be united, may you be happy.

Adieu.   S.P.

The Answer

Sir   Newbury-Port. June 5th. 1788

The formal and ceremonious manner in which you have been pleased to address the members of the club, constrains me to adopt a stile, which to a Class-mate and an intimate, I cannot but use with reluctance.

The charges of unkindness, of severity and *illiberality,* which your letter contains, were considered by Stacey and Thompson, so far as they respected them, as unmerited. To me alone, we supposed they could in any manner be applicable. That my observations upon the Subject were severe, I freely acknowledge, since, whatever the truth might be, the occurrence, was not of sufficient importance, to me to justify the strength of my expressions: they might therefore bear the appearance, of unkindness, but if unkindness consists in the intention, I can sincerely declare, that nothing was more foreign to my heart. But Sir I am not conscious that even my treatment of you, could be justly charged with illiberality. For the repeated instances of equivocation in your conduct upon the same subject, which you have acknowledged, might I conceive excuse my doubting the truth of assertions, which upon similar occasions you had always made with equal seriousness; if however you still consider yourself as injured, I am ready to make any acknowledgment which you may think your honour can require. At the same time I would submit to your consideration, whether your leaving thus abruptly a society which among our acquaintance is generally known to exist, might not excite their curiosity; and whether if the occasion of your quitting us, should accidentally transpire, it might not be productive of consequences equally mortifying to us all; as, to every impartial person the original cause of separation must appear trifling and puerile.

Your proposal "that the affair may be considered as relating only to the club," I am perswaded, you, will acknowledge upon further reflection, to be impracticable. For if the injury which you have received is sufficiently great to induce you to dissolve your connection, with a Society "whose pleasures you once eagerly sought, as eagerly wished to deserve, as richly enjoyed" how can you upon all other occasions, retain that friendship and confidence, from which alone those pleasures were derived. I trust you will suffer these considerations to have their weight in your mind, and as you say you write not "under the influence of passion and resentment," I hope you will be induced to drop your present intentions, and not give us reason at every subsequent meeting to regret the loss of one of the original members of the institution.

If however, you should persist in your present sentiments, we must decline waiting on you at your lodgings, as the meeting would necessarily be attended with a great degree of that restraint, an exemption from which is one of those charms whence we derive our greatest enjoyments. As Pickman expects to be absent the week after next he has desired us to call next Thursday evening at his lodgings. There we shall be happy to see you: to renew over a friendly glass the social intercourse which has thus

413

unfortunately been interrupted, and to bury in oblivion a dissen-
tion which we sincerely hope may never be revived.

J. Q. A.

¹ None of the original correspondence copied in the entries for this and the following
day has been found.
² JQA indicates in his line-a-day entry that he took a walk between his club meeting
and letter-writing (D/JQA/13, Adams Papers, Microfilms, Reel No. 16).

6TH.

In the forenoon I sent my letter to Putnam, and in about an
hour received the following reply which crowns the whole. It is
inserted to complete the Story, and because it shows the characteristic consistency of the person.

My dear friend   Newbury-Port June 6–88

The idea of my past follies and imprudences affords me Sensations inexpressibly disagreeable. Had I reflected with an eye of
impartiality, on my conduct, I am confident I never should have
charged you with illiberality. No, my friend, I confess I have had
so many proofs of your candour and openness that I blush to
have ever insinuated an Idea, so different from that which on reflection I find to be the real sentiment of my heart. O how fickle
and weak must be that mind, which sees only the favourable side
of a question wherein self is a party. I trust your candour to bury
this, together with the unhappy cause of all.

You will be pleased for a moment to put yourself in my situation. You must conceive that with the Sentiments I last evening
entertained, I must have been unhappy, had I been present. This
must excuse my addressing you in the manner I did. I think
Thomson and Stacey were equally concerned with you; —'tis
true they did not say so much as you did, but they *assented* to *all*
you advanced. At the time I proposed leaving the Club, I was
sensible, I deprived myself of a source of choicest pleasure—but
when I reflected that pleasure was to arise at your expence—I
could not persuade myself to make the purchase at so great a
price—I will call at Pickman's as you request—May more than
egyptian darkness intercept from light the unfortunate event—
May we once more taste the joys of sociability—Bacchus I am
sure will lend his assistance—May we renew our friendship
over the pipe of peace and banish discord far away.

Believe me dear John to be your real friend.   S. P.

414

These Letters shall be without a comment, as in my opinion they speak enough of themselves.

In the evening I was walking with Thompson; as we were passing before Mr. J. Tracy's, he invited us in: we pass'd the evening there; it was club night; and there were eight or ten such smoakers that we were almost suffocated. The evening however was agreeable; and after supper I completed my walk before I returned home.

7TH.

Mr. Parsons came home from Boston this evening; where he has been attending at the general court; but he brought no news for me. I went with Pickman up to Sawyer's tavern and drank tea there. This walk is very agreeable, and employs the evening well.

8TH.

Mr. Webster[1] from Salisbury preached for us this day: a venerable old gentleman who has been subject to many misfortunes, and whose countenance is expressive of the sensibility which has so often been wounded.

I took a long walk in the evening with Stacey; a young fellow who has been very imprudent; but whose disposition is I believe very good.

[1] Rev. Samuel Webster, minister of the West Parish, Salisbury (Sibley-Shipton, *Harvard Graduates,* 10:250–259).

9TH.

Mr. Parsons had so much information to give every one who came into the office this day that, we could not attend much to the regular course of our reading. I took a long lonely walk in the evening, as I often do at present; and I find the practice advantageous both to my health and spirits.[1]

[1] In his line-a-day entry, JQA notes that the weather was cold (D/JQA/13, Adams Papers, Microfilms, Reel No. 16).

10TH.

Stroll'd a mile or two with Pickman: he has the appearance of a true and faithful Lover, and acknowledges that he takes but very little satisfaction in this Town: he proposes spending but a few weeks more here, and then to open an office in Salem.

As I came home I stopp'd and past an hour at Mrs. Hooper's.

11TH.

I walk'd this evening with Stacey. The weather was very beautiful, and we proposed to form a party for a Serenade, as soon as may be convenient.

12TH.

Townsend arrived in town this forenoon: I called at Mrs. Hooper's to see him immediately after dinner: he looks better than he was when he left this Town; but his situation still appears to me to be critical. Club met at Pickman's. Putnam appeared rather sober. Townsend was obliged to retire just before Sun-set. Farnham too was not in the highest Spirits, for Mr. Prout marries Miss S. Jenkins this evening. At nine we separated and at ten met again at my room. We sallied out at about eleven, and serenaded the Ladies in Town till between three and four in the morning.

13TH.

Townsend, and one or two more of my friends dined with me this day. He went in the afternoon to see Mrs. Emery, and found there, a Miss Taylor who came there last evening from Boston: she was going to Exeter, and as Townsend was going to take a ride; he proposed to go in company with her as far as the ferry. This Miss Taylor is handsome, and remarkably sociable; and although she has been in a declining State of health, for more than a year past, and came very lately from Halifax, to Boston merely to recruit her strength, yet by some unaccountable deception she looks in the finest bloom of Health. It seems indeed to be an uncommon felicity attending many young Ladies at this day, that they can enjoy all the benefits of ill health without, being much afflicted, with its cruel pains.

We accompanied the Lady to Amesbury; and after seeing her into the boat took our leave. Returning home we stopp'd and drank tea with Mrs. Atkins. Mrs. Bass and Mr. Atkins had just arrived from Dunstable. I pass'd the evening with Townsend at

Mrs. Hooper's; but came home quite early, as I was somewhat fatigued by the last night's expedition.

14TH.

Finished reading in Wood's Institutes; a book which has been rendered almost useless by the publication of Blackstone's commentaries. Dined with Mr. Parsons. Took a long walk in the afternoon, and pass'd the evening with Townsend at Mrs. Hooper's. Pickman went to Salem this morning.

15TH.

Mr. Allen preach'd; and as usual delivered a good Sermon, in a very bad manner. After meeting; I went up to Mr. J. Tracy's; I found Townsend there, and rode a few miles with him. We return'd and drank tea at Mrs. Atkins's. Townsend's health not permitting him to be out after Sun-set, we came home early, and I was with him all the evening.

16TH.

Townsend intended to have set away this morning; to go to Medfield; but the weather was so chilly and disagreeable that he thought it would be best to wait another day. Thompson and I dined and pass'd a great part of the day with him. I was again disappointed upon the arrival of the stage, as I have been so often heretofore; by hearing no news from Boston.

I began upon Bacon's pleas and pleadings; a subject which demands great attention.

17TH.

Townsend left Town this morning, but as the wind soon got easterly, I imagine he did not go far. Mr. Parsons went over to Ipswich where the Supreme Court are this week in Session. In the beginning of the evening the weather cleared up, and I took a long solitary walk. I had turn'd round, and was coming home, when I heard a horse coming upon full galop and somebody called me by name. I stopped and found it was Stacey, who congratulated me upon my father's arrival. He came from Ipswich on purpose to give me the Information. Just as I had pass'd by Mr. Tracy's, one of his Servants gave me a Letter,[1] with a re-

417

quest that I would go down to his House: I went accordingly, and
found Mr. Hichborn there; the Letter was from Mr. Thaxter,[2]
and contained the same joyful tidings that Stacey had brought
me. It seems Judge Sullivan left Boston this day at about twelve
o'clock; and when he came away Callahan was coming up the
Harbour: after passing an hour at Mr. Tracy's I came home, with
a light heart; but not wholly without fears that this information
like that of a similar nature which has been given me three or
four times within a month past, should be founded upon a mistake of one vessel for another.[3]

[1] Letter not found.
[2] Not found.
[3] In his line-a-day entry, JQA mentions Putnam's name between references to his
walk and to Mr. Tracy (D/JQA/13, Adams Papers, Microfilms, Reel No. 16).

18TH.

I went to the Office in the forenoon; but found myself incapa-
citated to do any thing, and therefore lost the morning in conversation. Just before two I went with trembling hope to the post
office: and as I went into the door my heart almost failed me: but
I was soon made happy by a letter from my brother Tom,[1] which
confirms the arrival of my Parents. In the afternoon I did
nothing more than prepare to go to Boston in the Stage to-morrow morning. I called in the evening at Mrs. Hooper's, and at Mr.
Carter's, to take their commands.[2]

[1] Letter not found.
[2] In his line-a-day entry, JQA refers to a walk with Thompson before making his
visits (D/JQA/13, Adams Papers, Microfilms, Reel No. 16).

19TH.

The Stage was full from Portsmouth and consequently I could
not obtain a seat. I could not think of waiting till Saturday with a
chance of being again disappointed. So I sent forward my little
trunk by the Stage, and engaged a horse; at about ten in the forenoon, I left Town, and arrived at Ipswich just before noon. The
Supreme Court are sitting there, and I went to the Court house
where I saw a number of my friends: among others my classmate Kendall who is going to the Ohio in a short Time. I found
likewise at Ipswich a number of the young Ladies from Newbury-Port, who to be sure were gallanted by their fathers. It was

near four o'clock when I left Ipswich; and Pickman at the same time returned to Salem. It was so late when we got there that I could not think of reaching Boston this night, and I therefore accepted of Pickman's invitation to lodge in town. He went with me to Mr. Derby's; but the young Ladies were not at home, so that I had not the pleasure of being introduced to his Dulcinea. Learned, who is upon the study of physic in this town, pass'd the evening with us.

20TH.

I was up early in the morning, and mounted my horse at about seven. It was ten when I got into Boston. I went to Mr. Smith's, and found my father was gone to Braintree but my Mamma was at the Governor's: I immediately went there and enjoy'd all the satisfaction that can arise from the meeting so near and dear a friend after a long absence. We dined at Deacon Storer's. Old Mrs. Edwards was there (v. Vol 2. p. 27.)[1] and Dr. Waterhouse, &c. Between five and six we set out for Braintree. As I was already somewhat fatigued, my Cousin Cranch gave me up his seat in the Chaise with my Mamma, and took my horse. At about eight we got to Mr. Cranch's, and there my Satisfaction and pleasures were again renew'd at finding my father in good health. And here I must stop for the present.

[1] See entry for 11 Aug. 1786 (above).

21ST.

The weather was very warm. I went down to my uncle Quincy's, and from thence on the shore. One lighter arrived in the afternoon, with part of the goods and furniture, and the other is expected to-morrow.

22D.

Parson Wibird preached in his usual dull unanimated strain. Of late indeed he has lost it is said his only claim to merit by declining wholly to change with the neighbouring ministers. After meeting this evening, I went with W. Cranch down to Mrs. Quincy's and drank tea. Mrs. Quincy of Boston[1] was there, and very agreeable: I had never been in company with her before.

[1] Abigail Phillips Quincy (1745–1798), wife of Josiah Quincy, "The Patriot."

23D.

A second lighter came up this day with things from the ship. We were very busy in unpacking during the whole day. A bed was set up in the house in which I lodg'd, but we have done sufficient to make a great deal of work before we get at rights. There is yet a great deal to be done to the house. When I came from Newbury-Port, I intended to have studied as much here as I should have done there; but I begin to suspect that I shall find it utterly impossible. At least I have given up all thoughts of doing any thing in that way for the present.

24TH.

This day we got so far in order as to make a home of the house. I dined at my uncle Cranch's. The remainder of the packages are expected to-morrow; but those that are already here, are not all unpack'd. Much damage was done on the voyage.[1]

[1] JQA writes, in his line-a-day entry, "Folks got down to the house. I ⟨*lodg'*⟩dined out" (D/JQA/13, Adams Papers, Microfilms, Reel No. 16).

25TH.

This afternoon Mr. and Mrs. Shaw came in from Haverhill; they found us still in great disorder: we began this day to unpack the books; though we have at present no room to stow them in, properly. They were moist and some what mouldy, but not injured at all.

26TH.

We all dined at Mr. Cranch's. Charles came from Cambridge to spend a day or two with us. I continued this whole day quite industriously, to unpack, and place the books, yet did not get half through with the business. There are a great many books which I wish very much to peruse, but I have not the time at present, and must certainly for some years be separated from them.

27TH.

The day was spent like the preceding ones. There was some company here in the afternoon.[1] I give as much of the little leisure time I have, as I can conveniently to some lectures upon History and general Policy a new publication of Dr. Priestley,[2] whose literary powers may be truly called athletic. There are several other late performances, which I am desirous of reading, but more particularly Mr. Gibbon's continuation of his History of the decline and fall of the roman Empire: which is not however, yet completed.[3]

[1] JQA adds, in his line-a-day entry, "Folks from my uncle's" (D/JQA/13, Adams Papers, Microfilms, Reel No. 16).

[2] Joseph Priestley, *Lectures on History, and General Policy; To Which is Prefixed,* *An Essay on a Course of Liberal Education for Civil and Active Life,* Birmingham, England, 1788 (MQA).

[3] The final three volumes were published in 1788 (DNB).

28TH.

Mrs. Welch and Betsey Smith came from Boston this morning; we all went to Weymouth and dined at Doctor Tufts's. In the afternoon I went over to Mr. Norton's house; where in my Infancy I have spent many days, which I scarcely remember even as a distant dream; but before this day I had not been in the house these nine years.[1] As I returned from Weymouth I was overtaken by the rain, and stop'd at Mr. Cranch's; but it did not abate, and I went home in the midst of it.

[1] Jacob Norton, the minister at Weymouth, was living in the parsonage previously occupied by JQA's grandfather, Rev. William Smith.

29TH.

I attended at meeting and heard Mr. Wibird. The weather was rather dull and somewhat sultry. I am still undetermined whether to return this week to Newbury-Port, or wait till after Commencement: I believe however I shall determine upon the latter.

30TH.

Mr. and Mrs. Shaw return'd to Haverhill this morning: and this day I finished unpacking the books; which however must continue for some time in great disorder.[1]

¹ At the bottom of JQA's line-a-day entries for June in D/JQA/13, he has written a phrase in shorthand, followed, on the line below, by the date "June 17." The inscription is JQA's earliest recorded use of John Byrom's shorthand system, antedating other shorthand specimens in his papers by twenty years, and the first of about a half-dozen examples he entered into this Diary before the end of the year. Byrom's characters here are rendered "year on the 25th August." The significance of either date to JQA is not known to the editors. In 1794, while en route to his diplomatic post in the Netherlands, JQA mentioned having once attempted to learn shorthand, "but soon gave over the pursuit; not having a very high opinion of the utility of the art, and being very early weary of the labour to acquire it." He briefly resumed his study of it, but abandoned it until the following decade (Thomas Molineux, *An Introduction to Byrom's Universal English Short-Hand*, 5th edn., London, 1821; JQA, Diary, 3 Oct. 1794).

TUESDAY JULY 1ST. 1788.

It was nine o'clock before I could get away from Braintree this morning, and I arrived at the Colleges just before the exhibition began. A Latin Oration was spoken by Kirkland and was very well. The Forensic between Palmer and Waterman was tolerable, but I forget the subject. The english Dialogue between Thacher and Gray was well spoken, but rather stiff. The greek Dialogue between the youngest Sullivan and my brother Tom, was quite short and not the worse for that. The English Oration was by Blake; the subject agriculture. It was in my opinion very flimsy and superficial: but as we came out I heard a young fellow, who had something of the appearance of a would-be fop, exclaim "upon my soul Blake has given us one of the *genteelest* Orations I every heard." In former days, gentility with respect to composition, consisted in bad spelling and bad grammar, under which sense the description would not be wholly unjust. But what the expression means at this day I know not; and therefore its singularity was what I chiefly remarked. I was agreeably surprized to meet my friend Thompson here; but saw him only for a few minutes. I went down and dined at Judge Dana's. Mr. Ben. Ellery was there; an uncle to Mrs. Dana; a rich old gentleman; and somewhat singular in his character. In the afternoon I called at Mr. Wigglesworth's, and past an hour agreeably with them. I went to Mr. Gannett's; and at about seven in the evening called at the President's. He was not at home, and as I knew not what to do with myself for the remainder of the evening, I thought I might as well go home; I immediately went to Bradish's, mounted my horse, and after nine arrived safe in Braintree; somewhat fatigued with my day's work; but well satisfied with my jaunt.

12. A VIEW OF BOSTON TAKEN ON THE ROAD TO DORCHESTER, 1776

See pages xiii–xiv

2D.

The weather was extremely warm. I amused myself part of the day in reading, and part in shooting. The cherry trees which are quite full at present, are so inviting to the birds that, there is very good sport with little trouble.

3D.

Between nine and ten I went with my father from Braintree. We got into Cambridge at about twelve. After stopping a few minutes at College, we first went down and called upon Judge Trowbridge:[1] He is very old; and although active for his years, yet the depradations of time are conspicuous upon him. We dined at Mr. Dana's. Mr. and Mrs. Channing from Rhode Island, were there; they are agreeable. In the afternoon we first called at the Presidents, and drank tea there: from thence we went to Mr. Gerry's and past the evening: we found Mrs. Warren there, and were in the midst of antifederalism: but quite in good humour. My father had promised to take a lodging, at Judge Dana's; but at Mr. Gerry's invitation I past the night at his house.

[1] Edmund Trowbridge, loyalist and former judge of the pre-Revolutionary Massachusetts Superior Court of Judicature, and uncle of Francis Dana (Sibley-Shipton, *Harvard Graduates*, 8:507–520; 15:204).

4TH.

We left Cambridge by nine o'clock, and got into Boston in the midst of the bustle. We went immediately to Brackett's tavern. After dressing, I walk'd out; and met with a number of my very good friends. At about eleven we went to the old South meeting house, and heard Mr. Otis deliver an Oration.[1] The composition and the delivery were much superior even to my expectations, which were somewhat sangwine. It was greatly superior in my opinion to that which he delivered when he took his second degree; the only public performance, that I had heard before from him. I saw my good friend Bridge for a few minutes only: he told me he expected to be at Newbury-Port in about three weeks from this. I likewise met with Townsend as I was going out of the Church; and we went together to the old brick; to hear General Hull's Oration to the Cincinnati;[2] it appeared to me rather indifferent; and the effect upon me was the greater from the involuntary comparison with that which I had just heard. However I found afterwards there were many persons who thought or pretended to think this Oration better both in matter and manner than the other: and they have certainly a right to enjoy their opinions: I dined at Deacon Storer's. Parson Wibird was there and some other company. In the afternoon I walk'd up on the common, to see the military parade, which was not however so spirited as at the last anniversary: but in the middle of the afternoon, the news arrived that Virginia had acceded to the federal Constitution, and immediately the bells were set to ringing, and the guns to firing again, without any mercy, and continued all the remainder of the afternoon. In the evening a number of young fellows paraded round the streets with candles lighted in their hands, and a drum before them, not much to their own credit or to the honour of the day; but they did no damage. I spent part of the evening with several of my classmates; but not finding Bridge, I returned early, and took my lodging at Brackett's.

¹ Harrison Gray Otis, *An Oration Delivered July 4, 1788 . . .*, Boston, 1788.
² William Hull, *An Oration Delivered to the Society of the Cincinnati . . . July 4, 1788*, Boston, 1788.

5TH.

We called this morning at Dr. Welch's, and at Mr. Guild's; but left town at about ten o'clock: It was almost one when we got to Braintree. I amused myself as I could in the afternoon: Mrs. Warren,¹ with her son Harry stop'd here this night on their way to Plymouth; to which place General Warren has removed back, after living about eight years at Milton. He was formerly a very popular man, but of late years he has thought himself neglected by the People; his mind has been soured, and he became discontented, and querulous: he has been charged with using his influence in favour of Tender acts and paper money; and it has even been very confidently asserted, that he secretly favoured the insurrections and rebellion of the winter before last. Whether his conduct has been misrepresented or not, is a point that must for the present remain undetermined. But he has certainly given some reason for suspicion by his imprudence; and when in a time of rebellion a man openly censures the conduct in general, and almost every individual act of an administration, an impartial public will always judge, that such a man cannot be greatly opposed to a party who are attacking the same measures.

Mrs. Warren however positively declared there was no truth in those allegations, and was very confident, that they were nothing more than the suggestions of the general's enemies, whose malignity, was unaccountable, but whose utmost spite and envy could not disturb his happiness

> "For all the distant din this world can keep
> Rolls o'er his grotto and but sooths his sleep."

[1] Mercy Otis Warren, historian and dramatist, wife of James Warren. The Adamses and Warrens had maintained a close friendship for many years.

6TH.

The weather was rather disagreeable in the morning, and Mrs. Warren was disposed to stay and pass the Sunday with us. But her Son was so anxious to get home, that she finally determined to go; and they went away at about nine. I attended at meeting, and heard Parson Wibird dose over a couple of Sermons. There is none of my time that I regret more than that I spend in hearing him: were it not for the propriety of attending public worship abstracted from all considerations of improvement or entertainment, I should seldom enter within the walls of that house while he continues to slumber there.

7TH.

W. Cranch went to Boston this morning; and I suppose, I shall have but very little of his company for the Future, as he is to be fixed henceforth for some time to his office. I amused myself as I have done for several days past, in diverse manners. In the evening my two brothers arrived from Cambridge; having obtained leave to be absent till friday when the scholars will all be dismiss'd.

8TH.

I past the greater part of the day in gunning,[1] with my brothers. The weather was as it has been for several days past extremely warm; and the fruits of the earth at present greatly require heat.

[1] "Shooting robins" (D/JQA/13, Adams Papers, Microfilms, Reel No. 16).

9TH.

Doctor Leonard[1] came here in the morning: this gentleman came as a passenger with Callahan. He underwent a violent prosecution two or three years ago in England, for endeavouring to come to America with some models of manufacturing machines. But after being two years in prison he was released and immediately resumed his original intentions; but he is now come over without his models; and he rather purposes at present to practice in his original profession as a physician and surgeon.

I bath'd in the Sea, this afternoon; the first time I have done so this Summer; indeed it is rather troublesome here, on account of insects which are almost innumerable.[2]

[1] William Leonard practiced medicine in Newburyport and later in Ohio (S. P. Hildreth, "Biographical Sketches of the Early Physicians of Marietta, Ohio," *NEHGR*, 3:137–138 [April 1849]; same, 5:357 [July 1851]).

[2] In his line-a-day entry JQA adds, between notes on Leonard and bathing, that he "Read a little" (D/JQA/13, Adams Papers, Microfilms, Reel No. 16).

10TH.

George Warren came over from Milton this forenoon, and paid us a visit. He opened an office in Milton last winter, and has done as much business, as a lawyer generally does for the first six months after he begins; but the prospects are far from being encouraging. When I am in spirits this circumstance strikes me only as an incentive to more strenuous exertions: and at such times I feel such a resolution to overcome difficulties, that I seem already in a fair way of acquiring reputation and property. My father says, that when he was a student, he heard, an old lawyer tell the present Judge Sewall, who was then a student likewise, "that he never knew a lawyer that studied, who did not grow rich." The observation made an impression, and his own experience has confirmed it.[1]

[1] JQA adds, in his line-a-day entry: "Rather idle. Time lost" (D/JQA/13, Adams Papers, Microfilms, Reel No. 16).

11TH.

This day completes my twenty first year; It emancipates me from the yoke of paternal authority which I never felt, and places me upon my own feet, which have not strength enough to support me. I continue therefore still in a state of dependence.

One third of the period of my professional studies has also now elapsed; and two years more will settle me, should life and health continue; in a situation where all my expectations are to center. I feel sometimes a strong desire to know what my circumstances will be in seven years from this: but I must acknowledge, I believe my happiness would rather be injured than improved by the information.[1]

[1] In his line-a-day entry, JQA adds: "Mr. Cranch. Shooting" (D/JQA/13, Adams Papers, Microfilms, Reel No. 16).

12TH.

In the diverse amusements of reading, of shooting birds, and playing upon our flutes we past the present day.[1] The weather is and has for a fortnight past been such that fatiguing occupations cannot be attended to: I read very little; and that of a light kind which does not greatly engage the mind; and as for writing, I have so much abandoned it that I have not written three pages since I left Newbury-Port. My brothers are much in the same way.

[1] JQA mentions "Priestley on history. Bathing" in his line-a-day entry (D/JQA/13, Adams Papers, Microfilms, Reel No. 16).

13TH.

Weather still extremely warm. I heard Parson Wibird. Mr. Q. Thaxter was at meeting in the forenoon; and went and dined with us. In the afternoon, Madam, went down to my Uncle Quincy's, and I drank tea with my brothers at my Uncle Adams's. And we bath'd at the creek in the evening.[1]

[1] JQA notes, in his line-a-day entry, "Parson Wibird all day," presumably referring to his attendance at meeting in the morning and afternoon (D/JQA/13, Adams Papers, Microfilms, Reel No. 16).

14TH.

Ben Beale came from Taunton this morning; he did not stop, but promised to come and see us ere long. When I came in from shooting, which still continues to be my sport and my occupation, I found a Parson West[1] here, an old gentleman, who was three years in college with my father, and at that time very intimate with him. He is very sociable and very sensible. He spent the day here, and passes the night likewise. He keeps late hours and entertained me with conversation upon language, till between twelve and one o'clock. Doctor Leonard left us this morning, after having past almost a week with us. He appears to be a very clever well disposed man; but possessing no great learning nor even much information.

¹ Samuel West, Harvard 1754, minister of the First Congregational Society, New Bedford, for whom JA had a life-long "strong affection" (Sibley-Shipton, *Harvard Graduates*, 13:501–510; JA, *Diary and Autobiography*, 3:261).

15TH.

Mr. West went away this morning; My Father and my brother Charles, went to Boston; whence they will proceed to-morrow to Cambridge. Beale came here this forenoon, and took a dinner with us. He is studying law, with Mr. Barnes at Taunton, but spends much of his time at home. Mr. Wibird pass'd the afternoon and evening here. Dr. Tufts called here on his way to Boston, and my brother Tom went to Cambridge this afternoon; for my own part, I preferred waiting till to-morrow morning. And I have finally determined to return here after Commencement, at least for a day or two.

16TH.

Commencement day. I mounted my horse, somewhat early, and arrived at Cambridge by nine o'clock. The first Salutation I received as I was going into the College yard was "repent: for the kingdom of Heaven is at hand." It was a crazy man; but without any great share of enthusiasm, for that sentence was the only thing he said; and he repeated it every two or three minutes during the whole forenoon: and I could not help reflecting with pleasure upon the happy liberality of sentiment, which prevails so much that a man of this kind, so far from attracting the notice of the executive power, could not even draw a crowd around him. I saw my Classmates in abundance; there were more than thirty of us here. At about eleven we went to the meeting house; and I got a seat in the foremost gallery, next to Townsend. The procession soon came on, and the president after making a prayer, and informing the audience it was the desire of the overseers and corporation that there might be no "clapping applause," called For the Salutatory Oration, which was spoken by Phillips, and was pretty well delivered. An English poem, on the prospects of America, by Dodge, was not without its merit; but would not bear comparison with that spoken last Commencement by Harris. The order in which the other performances came on was as follows.

A forensic disputation upon this question. Whether the balance would be in favour of our existence were there no state but the present. By Sanders and Tappan.

A greek Conference upon the evil effects of avarice, and of prodigality, upon Society. By Gardner and Jackson.

A forensic disputation. Whether a republic is more secure of the continuance of its liberties, where the officers in the higher branches of government are elected for several years, than when they are annually elected? By Gordon and Lincoln.

An English conference. Whether a large emigration from Europe into the United States of America, would upon the whole be for the real advantage of the States. By Adams 2d. and Cabot.

An English Oration. By Abbot.

The syllogistics were omitted, and these performances were finished by two o'clock. I went and dined at Judge Dana's, and at about four returned to the meeting house. An English Oration was delivered by Mr. Ware upon the effects of religion, upon civil government and Society. It was an excellent Oration, and notwithstanding the president's Caution in the morning, there was something like a clap; which proceeded chiefly I imagine from the Students that were present. The president with his peculiar elegance of expression said "I am sorry that the desires of the Corporation and Overseers should be infringed upon," and proceeded to give the degrees. There was a new ceremony, of giving a degree of bachelor in physic. Two young fellows by the name of Hall and Fleet received these diplomas, and even the president in giving them seemed to have the awkwardness of novelty about him. A valedictory Oration was spoken by Mr. Allyne, and the president made a concluding prayer, which concluded the public ceremonies of the day. I forgot to observe that after the forenoon performances were finished, the governor got up, addressed the president who was likewise standing, by the title of "reverend and learned Sir," and made a long speech in which he blest his Stars for being born in a land of Liberty and Science &c. Some people thought his performance was equal to any in the course of the day; but opinions on that subject were divided. It was prepared before hand, though it bore ample testimony of the genius and learning which the young gentlemen had display'd.

> "Wherein all prophets far out went he
> Though former days produced a plenty.
> For any man, with half an eye
> What stands before him can espy,
> But optics sharp it needs, I ween
> To see what is not to be seen."[1]

To return. After we came out of the meeting house I stroll'd about for some time, greeting one friend and another as I met them. I went with Forbes and Little, and drank tea at Dr. Wigglesworth's. I returned to College, and spent the evening in diverse places. I finally found young Phillips, and took a supper with him at his chamber where I found also a number of his classmates. I retired at about eleven o'clock having enjoy'd the day very highly; but my spirits had been so much raised that I could get but little sleep.

[1] John Trumbull, *McFingal*, Phila., 1775, p. 3 (lines 65–70).

17TH.

The young gentlemen who graduated yesterday were.

Benjamin Abbot	Charles Jackson
Solomon Adams	Abner Lincoln
Thomas Adams	Henry Phelps
Thomas Bancroft	John Phillips
Oliver Barron	James Prescott
Stephen Baxter	Daniel Clarke Sanders
Joseph Brigham	William Sawyer
Joseph Cabot	Amos Tappan
George Caryl	John Dexter Treadwell
Edward Clarke	Charles Turner
Oliver Dodge	Nathan Underwood
James Gardner	Samuel West
Adam Gordon	Robert Wier
William Hill	

Jacob Kimbal's name is inserted in the Theses and Catalogue but he could not obtain his degree being unable to pay his bills.

This morning Mr. Andrews called me at College, before six o'clock, and we soon departed together towards Braintree where we arrived at about nine. Mr. Andrews breakfasted with us, and then proceeded to Hingham. My Spirits were so much exalted yesterday, that a contrary effect seems this day to take place; the bow-string by being too much distended cannot regain its usual position without an intermediate relaxation; the weather was sultry and I felt much fatigued.

18TH.

Upon the warmest day we have had this Summer I was obliged to go to Boston, upon a hard trotting horse; with the Sun blazing in my face all the way. I do not know that I ever suffered more, from the heat. And when I got into Boston I was obliged to bustle about almost all the day. I had to call three times at Mr. Green's Store before I could get the payment for a bill of exchange, which I think is a very irregular manner for a merchant to transact business. I got the money however in the afternoon. I dined at Mr. Dawes's. He was not at home himelf; but Mrs. Dawes is a charming woman. She is handsome, but there is an amiable sweetness in her countenance and manners, far more pleasing, than the most perfect beauty could be without it. W. Cranch accompanied me in all my excursions. We went together on the top of Beacon hill; and greatly enjoyed the fine prospect, and the refreshing breeze. At about seven o'clock the wind got round, and it grew quite cool. I mounted, and rode about a quarter of an hour in the rain, after which I had a tolerable ride, and got home, by nine o'clock. I had taken some letters from the post-office, which were from my Sister at New York.[1]

[1] Possibly AA2 to JQA, 8 June (Adams Papers); and AA2 to AA, 15–22 June, in AA2, *Jour. and Corr.*, 2:80–84.

19TH.

I was considerably fatigued by my jaunt of yesterday, but made out however to read something, in the course of the day; and in the slow progress which I have made since I came to Braintree, I have at length got through the volume of Doctor Priestley upon history and general policy, which I take to be an excellent work; I shall take as early an opportunity as possible to peruse it again.

20TH.

I tarried at home this forenoon, in order to write a Letter to my Sister.[1] In the afternoon I attended at meeting.[2] Went up to Mr. Cranch's after meeting and pass'd an hour there. I took my leave of them, and went home to prepare for returning to Newbury-Port. I know not that I ever left Braintree with so much regret. I have past my time most agreeably here these five weeks, and have had almost all my nearest connexions and dearest friends about me: but otherwise, almost all the Time has been lost to me, and I must return to those pursuits which are to be the support of my future Life. In the winter I hope, to spend some weeks here, and then I shall endeavour to join the utile dulci.

[1] Letter not found.
[2] "Heard Parson Wibird" (D/JQA/13, Adams Papers, Microfilms, Reel No. 16).

21ST.

This morning I left Braintree in company with my brother Tom, who was going to Haverhill; and in order to have company, so great a part of the way, I determined to go there with him. We stopp'd a short time at Cambridge, and I went to Dr. Rand's to take a Letter from Miss Newhall, as I had promised her at Commencement. She was gone out but had left the Letter. We dined in Wilmington, and got to Haverhill between seven and eight o'clock.[1] In Woburn, we saw young Bartlett who had thoughts some time since, of opening an office in Braintree, but got discouraged there and finally determined upon Woburn, where from the appearance of the place, I should doubt somewhat of his succeeding very much; but in the present state of the profession, there can be but little choice of place for a young man.

[1] JQA adds, in his line-a-day entry, a reference to Mr. Shaw, at whose house he presumably stayed (D/JQA/13, Adams Papers, Microfilms, Reel No. 16).

22D.

I went to see Leonard White this forenoon. His father has been unwell for some days past. His complaints are of a lethargic nature, and his habit is such, that such disorders must probably prove in the end fatal to him. He now sleeps as much as half his time, and is consequently half dead. I went to see Mrs. Bartlett, and saw Mr. S. Blodget there: his brother Caleb, and young Mr.

Breck I met with yesterday on the road from Boston; at the tavern, and they came forward before us. I pass'd the afternoon at Mr. Thaxter's, and the evening at Mr. Shaw's.

23D.

I had almost promised Mr. Thaxter to wait till the afternoon; but as there was an appearance of a probability that the weather would be disagreeable, I thought it would be safest to come home before dinner. My Brother Tom, rode with me about four miles to the ferry. I got to my lodgings between twelve and one. I called at Dr. Kilham's shop: and there received an invitation from Mr. Marquand to dine with him. There was some company there; but persons with whom I had no acquaintance. I called at the office in the afternoon: and returned to Mr. Marquand's to tea. In the evening, I went and delivered to Miss Coats the letter which Miss Newhall left for her, and came home quite early.

24TH.

I returned, and once more took my seat in the office: but did little this forenoon. Thompson was unwell, and did not attend. I went with Putnam to club at Little's; there were only three of us. Thompson being indisposed, and Stacey out of town. I was this day inform'd that Pickman has lain aside all thoughts of practising Law, and has already opened a Store in Boston. The determination was rather sudden; for it is but a fortnight, since he was sworn in to Court at Salem; where he then intended to open an office immediately. But he never was fond of the profession, and while he was studying with us I suspected, that he would never do much business as a lawyer.

25TH.

Mr. Andrews came to town last night, and called to see us at the office this forenoon. They have engaged him to preach here at Mr. Carey's for six Sundays and will probably employ him longer still. I returned this day to Bacon's pleas and pleading, which I left when I went to Braintree. But could not proceed with great advantage, as I left my extract book,[1] in a small trunk which was to come this day in the stage; but has somehow failed. I shall make some alterations for the future in my plan of study:

I shall not confine myself so closely and exclusively to the law; but shall devote some part of the day to studies of a lighter and more entertaining kind.

¹ Not found.

26TH.

I went to pay a visit to Mrs. Hooper: but disappointed her by having no news from her son Jo, who is now with Mr. Townsend. Took a long walk quite alone.

We have a new boarder at my lodgings; a Mr. Romain, a frenchman; who came, a few days after I went from here last. I have not seen him yet: as he went on a fishing party the day that I came home; and is not yet returned.

27TH.

Mr. Andrews preached for us this day; and was somewhat longer than usual to the great *satisfaction* of some people who cannot easily be *contented*. Mr. Spring, and Mr. Murray, both had a third meeting in the evening; it was occasional at Mr. Murray's, but Mr. Spring is determined henceforth to make a practice of giving a lecture on Sundays; besides, one in the evening, on Thursdays. As Mr. Carey's parish may now be considered as vacant, an opportunity presents to attract some of those who belong there. The spiritual welfare of the individuals may charitably be supposed the only motive which Mr. Spring will acknowledge even to himself. But says the duke de la Rochefoucault, (who was as fully convinced of the depravity of the human heart as Mr. Spring, and who was much better acquainted with it.) "l'esprit est toujours la dupe du coeur." The head is ever the dupe of the heart. And when the passions assume the form of principle, the disguise will be discovered by every body else sooner than by the man who is directed by them. Mr. Spring's interest will be promoted should he make converts, for his parish is small and poor: his vanity will be flattered, by bringing people over to his opinion; and when in addition to this, his imagination fondly perswades him, that his cause is likewise the cause of God, it is not to be wondered that he can reconcile himself to contradictions, and that his practice is openly at variance with his theory, which condemns the use of means for bringing sinners to repentance.

28TH.

I finished reading Bacon's pleas and pleading: but the subject is so knotty that I must at some future period, read this over once or twice more. I began a third time upon Blackstone, a book which a lawyer cannot possibly read too much. In the evening I walk'd into Newbury with Stacey. I have been engaged for some days upon a matter which takes all my leisure time: it is in writing a piece for the 5th. of September. The Society at Cambridge, have ordered me to speak on that day; and I shall obey, if I can possibly attend.

29TH.

After spending the day as usual, I walk'd with Stacey and Putnam. After going some way into Newbury we return'd, and walk'd upon a sort of a terrass in high Street.[1] We there saw a number of young Ladies who seemed to expect to be accosted; and some of whom finally sat down on the grass, perhaps to see if that would not call our attention to them; but we were really inexorable: notwithstanding Miss Bradbury was there: indeed it has been observed that Putnam has of late wholly altered his conduct towards her; and there have been many speculations concerning the cause or the causes of this difference. Some of these young Ladies were so much piqued at our apparent neglect of them that they revenged themselves with proper Spirit by laughing loud at us as we past by them: and what punishment could possibly be more severe than the ridicule of a young Lady?

[1] Presumably at the "Frog pond" (D/JQA/13, Adams Papers, Microfilms, Reel No. 16).

30TH.

This afternoon Mr. Cutler called at our office, and perswaded me to ride with him up to Mr. Brown's farm; where we found a number of young Ladies. The afternoon was tolerably insipid: we drank tea there; and afterwards escorted the Ladies. I rode with Miss Jones, and left her at Captain Fletcher's. I afterwards returned there, but she was already gone. There was a very brilliant northern light in the evening.

Mr. Cutler is one of the most complaisant persons with whom I am acquainted. The ladies employ him upon almost every occasion; and yet behave to him in such a manner as does not express a sense of obligations received. They even slight and disregard him for performing those services by which he renders himself useful to them. There are problems in the female character, which are not easily solved.

31ST.

I amuse myself in reading Junius's letters; which though the factious productions of a partizan, contain many excellent observations upon men and manners.

We met this evening at Putnam's. Thompson left us to go to Lecture![1]

[1] Below JQA's line-a-day entry for 31 July in D/JQA/13, he has written in Byrom's shorthand method "year August 28th," the significance of which is unknown to the editors, but may be related to his earlier notation in Byrom's shorthand. See entry for 30 June, note 1 (above).

FRIDAY AUGUST 1ST. 1788.

The day was spent in the usual uninteresting manner: indeed it may be generally observed that the more advantageously the day is employed for myself; the less I have to say at the close of it.[1] I walk'd in the evening with Stacey till after nine o'clock.

[1] JQA notes, in his line-a-day entry, Blackstone's *Commentaries,* which he presumably read this day (D/JQA/13, Adams Papers, Microfilms, Reel No. 16).

2D.

Mr. Farnham proposed to me this morning to join a party, which was formed to go in the afternoon to the grove; a romantic spot, where the young people are fond of visiting. I declined however: and they finally gave up the scheme, as they were informed the proprietor of the land had some objections. I have been this week tolerably industrious.

3D.

I heard Mr. Andrews preach. About as long as he was last Sunday. I think he is gaining ground in the parish. And am in hopes that he may be finally settled, without much opposition. Which would greatly disappoint some flaming zealots, who like all zealots justify unworthy means by the sanctity of the end.

I walk'd in the beginning of the evening with Stacey: and afterwards called at Mrs. Hooper's. Betsey gratified her temper by the most unlimited severity upon a number of young Ladies who usually associate together. There appears by her conversation to be some peculiar enmity against them: her mother always reproves her, and always follows her example. There appears a singular pleasure in observing the trifling and silly conduct of that circle; and thus throughout Society, the follies of one, always contribute to the gratification of many others.

4TH.

Blackstone still furnishes me with employment for my forenoon hours; and I this day took up the fourth volume of Hume's History, which I was reading when I last went from here. This author's manifest partiality in favour of the Stuarts, his unceasing labours to palliate their faults, and his blindness to their crimes, must be overlook'd or forgiven in favor of the great entertainment which he affords.

I pass'd the evening with Thompson, at Mr. Carter's. The Conversation was not uncommonly interesting, though the old gentleman, is always agreeable to me. Betsey Smith of Boston was there and has been with them for several weeks.

5TH.

This forenoon A Doctor Young came to our office, for a writ against a number of insurgents. It seems he was a volunteer in the service of government, the winter before last; and being upon a party against several of them received a ball in his knee, which has made him a cripple for Life. He brought an action against them some time since at Worcester, but his jury were one half of them insurgents, who were for giving him no damages, and the other half thought he should have a thousand or fifteen hundred pounds, they could not agree: upon which he discontinued his action, and is now determined to bring one forward in this County, where he hopes to find a more impartial jury. The cause will, I doubt not, be very interesting, and Mr. Parsons will exert himself.

I walk'd in the evening with Stacey.

6TH.

Putnam went last week to Danvers, and return'd this forenoon. He brought me a Letter, which came from Townsend,[1] enclosing one for Mrs. Hooper. Amory it seems has suddenly determined to open an office in Salem; and has already put his
determination into execution. He had concluded to take a trip,
either to Georgia, or Carolina; but upon being informed that
Pickman had altered his scheme; he thought it would be best to
try his fortune first in this part of the Country. I went in the evening with Thompson, up to Mrs. Atkins's. I told them that
Townsend was coming here next week. Becca said she hoped he
would make himself welcome by bringing Jo. Hooper with him:
it was conjectured while Townsend lived in this Town, that he
had a partiality for this lady. He frequented the house very
much; and there appears now a coolness in them bordering upon
the resentment of disappointment. Mrs. Atkins said that a man
must generally be a good judge of his own compositions, and
ask'd me if I was of that opinion; I was not and endeavoured to
avoid answering directly; but she would not suffer it; and I was
finally obliged to agree, to the truth of her observation; protes-
tando to myself that it was only from complaisance to a Lady,
that I agreed; which will always excuse a little self-denying as
Hudibras calls it.

¹ Letter not found.

7TH.

Thompson did not attend this day at the Office. Phillips called
to see us this afternoon. He has been to Portsmouth, and is now
upon his return to Boston: he expects to read law in Mr. Dawes's
office. I walk'd into Newbury this evening with Stacey. The evenings grow long to my great regret. At present I can employ the
evening from dusk till nine o'clock in walking; and as I am not
over fond of visiting, this is the most agreeable, as well as to me
the most useful method of spending my Time. I am not upon familiar terms in one house in Town; and upon the cold formality
of ceremony, with which all my visits must be accompanied, I
confess I wish not to be extensively acquainted.

8TH.

We met this evening at my lodgings, as we have changed the evening in order to accommodate Thompson who wishes to attend Mr. Spring's lectures. This young fellow, who is possessed of most violent passions which he with great difficulty can command, and of unbounded ambition, which he conceals perhaps even to himself has been seduced into that bigoted, illiberal system of religion which by professing vainly, to follow purely the dictates of the bible, in reality contradicts the whole doctrine of the new testament, and destroys all the boundaries between good and evil, between right and wrong. But like all the followers of that sect, his practice is at open variance with his theory. When I observe into what inconsistent absurdities those persons run, who make speculative, metaphysical religion a matter of importance, I am fully determined never to puzzle myself in the mazes of religious discussion, to content myself with practising the dictates of God and reason; so far as I can judge for myself; and resign myself into the arms of a being whose tender mercies are over all his works.[1]

[1] To this account JQA adds, in his line-a-day entry, "Walk'd after nine. Journal" (D/JQA/13, Adams Papers, Microfilms, Reel No. 16).

9TH.

Thompson went to see Miss Roberts at Newtown. I cannot read with so much satisfaction for some days past, as I usually do, as my eyes are very troublesome. Walk'd in the evening, but quite alone: I finished a day or two since, my performance for the 5th. of next month;[1] and am now very closely engaged in a matter which has been accumulating upon me these two months.

[1] According to JQA's draft copy of the Phi Beta Kappa speech, he had completed it on 6 Aug.

10TH.

Mr. Kimball supplied the place of Mr. Andrews this day. I observed none of Captn. Coombs's family were at meeting, and heard in the afternoon that his Daughter Polly, had left this world; and I trust for a better, this morning; after an illness of four or five months. In the afternoon I went to Mr. Spring's, meeting and heard a Mr. Story[1] preach there hammering away in the true stile upon predestination and free-will. None but an atheist he said could doubt of the former; and no man that had common sense of the latter. He endeavoured to soften his system as much as possible; hoping thereby, I suppose, that he might be employ'd in the other parish.

I walk'd with Stacey and Romain, in the evening. We met Amory who was returning from Cape Ann with Miss Fletcher. After he had carried her home, he went at about 9 in the evening with Stacey to Ipswich.

[1] Probably Isaac Story, minister of the Second Congregational Church of Marblehead (James McLachlan, *Princetonians, 1748–1768: A Biographical Dictionary*, Princeton, 1976, p. 655–657).

11TH.

Thompson watch'd last evening;[1] in consequence of which he felt not much disposed to study closely this day, and was but little at the office. Walk'd in the evening with Putnam.

[1] For protection against fires and other disorders, the town of Newburyport required the services of two night watchmen, chosen by the constables from a list of all able-bodied townsmen (Currier, *Newburyport*, 2:46).

12TH.

I called in the afternoon for about half an hour, at the office. Attended Miss Coombs's funeral. It was very long. I walk'd with Putnam. As we were returning we accosted Miss Jones and Miss Fletcher; and waited on them home. After which we went to see Townsend Who came in town this forenoon; we past an hour or two there and afterwards walk'd till between nine and ten. Townsends cough, still hangs upon him; and although he fansies himself essentially better, his situation appears to me more dangerous, than it did four months ago. His spirits however are as brisk and lively as they ever were; and he talks as much as ever; which I believe is rather injurious to him.

My Time flies from me with the rapidity of a whirlwind. Every hour is precious, and every moment unemployed becomes a subject of regret. This afternoon has been lost to me; unless the view of the object before me, be turned to some profit; though even that by showing more forcibly the brevity and uncertainty of Life, should rather condemn me, for neglecting to improve every minute to the best purposes.

441

13TH.

Mrs. Emery who has been very ill these four or five weeks, died last night, leaving to the wide world two orphan children, who three years ago had the fairest prospects of sharing a fortune of ten thousand pounds sterling; but who in consequence of Mr. Tracy's misfortunes, are now almost destitute of support.

I walk'd in the evening with Stacey and Little. Stacey left us. We met Putnam walking with some young Ladies. I joined them, and pass'd the remainder of the evening at Mr. Frazier's. These young Misses have assumed an importance rather above their years, and to the trifling conduct and conversation of childhood, unite the punctilious formality of riper years. I receive not much satisfaction in their company, and as they are handsome, I had rather look at them for five minutes than be with them five hours. Putnam is not so difficult to please. He can conform to their manners, and enter into all their debates: he is consequently a favourite.

14TH.

This was a day of humiliation and prayer at Mr. Carey's: on account of his sickness; and to implore the assistance of providence in choosing a colleague to supply his place. Mr. Webster of Salisbury preached in the forenoon; and performed very well. But Dr. Tucker in the afternoon was very interesting and pathetic; in showing how good and pleasant a thing it is for brethren to dwell together in unity. I attended Mrs. Emery's funeral. Mr. Andrews made the prayer; and performed even better than was expected. I passed part of the evening with Townsend; called at Mr. Tufts's, to see Mrs. Shaw; but she was gone out. Mr. Shaw called to see me in the morning. They came in town last night.

15TH.

I called in at Mr. Tufts's to see Mrs. Shaw this morning. I found old Mr. Carter there. Geneological as usual. I dined at his house, with my friends from Haverhill. He asked me to return to tea: I excused myself. He said that *tippling* business would be going on, every afternoon at six o'clock; if I would call there, I should be welcome. I returned to the Office but felt so much dissipated, that I could not attend with much application. We met this evening at Stacey's lodgings. Townsend went away just before Sun-set. *Lincoln*[1] a classmate of Thompson's, pass'd the evening with us. Though a young preacher, he is not so rigid in his principles as many others are. In the close of the evening we took a walk.

[1] Rev. Henry Lincoln, minister at Falmouth, Mass. (*History of the Town of Hingham*, 4 vols. in 3, Hingham, 1893, 2:467).

16TH.

Dined with Townsend, in company with Mr. Andrews, and Thompson. After dinner we took a ride: went down to Mr. N. Tracy's, but he was not at home. On the road we met the governor, who was coming into Town. We went to Mrs. Atkins's. She was in fine spirits and consequently very good company. We were however obliged to come away early as the weather was rather disagreeable. I spent the evening at Mr. Hooper's. Mr. Cutler was there. We stroll'd about, an hour or more after we came away.

The week has disappeared in a very singular manner; some thing or other has taken me from my studies every day; and at the close of the week I regret the Time lost without being able to repair it. This is not the first time that I have experienced this effect since I came into this Town, and I greatly fear it will not be the last.

17TH.

Mr. Andrews preach'd for us; this forenoon he was lengthy in his prayer upon the late misfortunes in the several families. In his Sermon he likewise touched upon the subject, in recommending to us, so to number our days, that we might apply our hearts unto wisdom. I past the evening with Townsend. There fell a considerable quantity of rain, in the course of the last night, and of this day. And it will be very useful, as the fruits of the ground were languishing for want of moisture.

18TH.

This morning I perceived a deal of stirring in the Streets; and was finally informed that the governor was reviewing the troops of this Town; after which a number of officers, and other gentlemen escorted his excellency to Haverhill; where he intends to dine; and then I suppose he means to show himself some where else. I passed the day at the Office. And the evening, at home in writing; I intended to have taken my usual exercice; but upon leaving the office, I found it was raining, and it continued all the evening. I amused myself tolerably well at home. I have indeed had for some time past almost as much business to do at my lodgings as at the office; but I hope to be gradually relieved.

19TH.

Several of the gentlemen who accompanied the governor, yesterday to Haverhill, went on to Salem with him, and did not return till this evening. I was with Townsend.[1]

[1] JQA's line-a-day entry for this day reads: "Stacey return'd. Rain. Walk with Putnam. Townsend" (D/JQA/13, Adams Papers, Microfilms, Reel No. 16).

20TH.

I was walking with Putnam in one of the Streets in Town, this evening, when we heard a strange noise in a house, and a number of people standing round it. We went up to the window and heard a man exhorting as they call it. That is calling upon God, in every tone of voice, and repeating a number of texts of scripture, incoherently huddled together, so as to make an unintelligible jumble of nonsense, which they think is a proper method of seeking the Lord.[1]

[1] JQA adds in his line-a-day entry, "Busy doing nothing" (D/JQA/13, Adams Papers, Microfilms, Reel No. 16).

21ST.

Upon Stacey's invitation I went with him and Putnam, and two young lads by the name of Greenough, to Mr. Greenleaf's; where we had something like a concert of music. The house was soon filled with people; it seemed as if there was nobody within five miles that had ever heard the sound of a violin before. Some of the young Ladies thought it would be pretty to join with their voices in the music; and the concert thenceforth became both vocal and instrumental. I was fatigued by ten o'clock; and could blow no more: and finding that Stacey and Putnam had got so much engaged, with a lovely songstress, (or one that might be lovely) as shew no prospect of an intention to quit, I came off and left them at about eleven o'clock.

22D.

We assembled this evening at Thompson's. Mr. Greenleaf called in and past an hour with us. He was apprehensive that we were disgusted with the crowd last evening; but we undeceived him. He talk'd about the war; for he was an officer in our army.

> "And little of this great world can he speak
> More than pertains to feats of broils and battle."[1]

Putnam has not yet got over his trick of leaving us to join the young Ladies; but this evening he acknowledged, he was going to Mr. Frazier's. We likewise walk'd in the evening, and stroll'd about till ten o'clock.

[1] *Othello,* Act I, scene iii, lines 86–87.

23D.

Dined at Thompson's, with Mr. Andrews and Townsend. In the afternoon I took a ride with Little to Haverhill. I endeavoured to persuade him to go with me the week after next to Cambridge; but my labour was in vain. We had a very smart thunder shower, while we were on the road, but it was very soon over.

[24 AUGUST – 2 SEPTEMBER]

Here, this journal very abruptly breaks off. I had long doubted whether the utility attending the method which I have pursued were adequate to the time I have devoted to it. But an indisposition, which for two months has prevented me from writing has finally turned the wavering scale.

I will not however immediately drop all memorials of my transactions; but the remainder of this volume will probably contain a space of time as long as that recorded already in more than two vols. and an half.[1]

[1] This entry appears immediately after the previous one. Handwriting and the lighter ink suggest that it and the entries for 23 Aug. and 3 Sept. were probably written at the same time. After this entry, with scattered exceptions, the only Diary entries for the remainder of the year come from line-a-day memoranda in D/JQA/13. The exceptions, from D/JQA/12, are 3, 4, 5, 7, 10, 12, 13, 14, 20, 24, 27, 30 Sept. and 1, 2, 3, 7, 14 Oct.

24.

Parson Dutch preach'd. L. White and Mr. Thaxter.

25TH.

Return'd from Haverhill. Somewhat interrupted.

26TH.

Office business. Takes from reading. Dined with Mr. Parsons.

27.

Mr. Parsons went to Boston. Wrote. Mr. Cabot &c.

28.

Walk'd with Stacey. Curious conversation. Greenough's.

29.

Funeral. Mr. Atkins. Met in the evening at Putnams.

30.

Rain. Little past the evening with me.

31.

Heard Mr. Prince. Mr. Marquand's. Mr. Jackson's. Religious tattoo.[1]

[1] At the bottom of the page of line-a-day entries for Aug. 1788, but not necessarily referring to the date of 31 Aug., appears the following note: "Memorandum: Stacey borrow'd book, for Ipswich."

SEPTEMBER 1. 1788.

Rain. Pass'd the evening with Stacey.

2.

Finished Hume and Blackstone. Little &c.

WEDNESDAY SEPTEMBER 3D.

I went over the river with Stacey and Romain upon a shooting party. We had tolerable success. It was very windy; and with a heavy boat and only one oar, we had some difficulty to get across the river. Bridge arrived this day in town. I proposed to him to go with me to-morrow: and he has partly promised to accept my proposal. I this evening informed Mrs. Leathers of my intention to change my lodgings.

THURSDAY SEPTEMBER 4TH.

Left Newbury-Port this morning with Bridge: we dined at Putnam's in Danvers. Very indifferent entertainment. After mistaking our road, and going to Winisimet ferry, we finally got to Cambridge a little before 9 o'clock. Lodg'd at Bradish's.

FRIDAY SEPTEMBER 5TH.

The assembly at the anniversary of the Φ.B.K. was more numerous than I have known it. There were near forty members present, among whom were two from Dartmouth college. Lincoln, who was to have been one of the speakers obtained leave to be excused on account of ill health. The governor, happening to be here with the admiral, and some other officers of the french squadron, now in Boston harbour, honoured us with his presence; as did all the college officers.

I spoke the oration which is hereto annexed,[1] after which we retired to the butler's chamber: the french Consul, who had likewise attended came there to compliment me &c. After doing what business was necessary, we all went down to Warland's and dined together; and the festive board crowned the enjoyments of friendship.

An Oration.

Spoken, at the request of the ΦBK Society

at Cambridge, September 5th. 1788.

Among the various objects which attract the attention of a youth about to enter upon the scenes of active Life, a view of the prospects before him, and of the Fortunes which expectation leads him to imagine will attend him affords one of the most fruitful sources of contemplation. From an anticipation of futurity, and from the recollection of the past, we chiefly derive the variety of mental enjoyment; and at an early period of life, as

447

we are necessarily precluded in a great measure from the satisfaction arising from the one, the mind naturally recurs more frequently and with a firmer confidence to the other. It must however be acknowledged that we are often prone to view the distant objects through the deceptive medium of fansy, or of the passions.

Should a concurrence of agreeable circumstances, lead us to the contemplation of this subject, at a time when the spirits are elated by the temporary impulsion of successful satisfaction, we soar rapidly upon the wings of a flattering imagination, and soon lose ourselves bewildered amidst the magnificent objects with which we have adorned the road around us. Unmindful of the precarious tenure by which all human enjoyments are held, we behold Fortune and Fame emulously striving to invest us in the possession of all the blessings which they can impart, and in the ardor of juvenile exultation eastern opulence is scarcely competent to the satisfaction of our avarice, eastern grandeur to that of our ambition. But should some untoward event occur, to awaken us from these fantastic dreams, we descend with rapidity from the visionary elevation, and sink as far beneath the level of rational probability, as we had before been raised above it. The path of life becomes rugged with thorns: a thousand obstacles apparently stand before us, and the approach to the seats of happiness, like that to the garden of the Hesperides seems under the perpetual custody of fiery dragons. We dwell with involuntary terror upon the ideas of the malice, the treachery and envy which we expect from our fellow mortals untill we are ready to imagine that our Life is to be a state of continual warfare with the whole human race. The baseless fabric of our hopes vanishes like the phantom of a fairy tale, and the mind oppressed by the contemplation of these gloomy objects is almost ready to settle in a state of sullen despondency.

I presume your own feelings, my worthy friends, will testify that this representation can scarcely be charged with exaggeration: and yet, why on the one hand, should we ever indulge ourselves in expectations which never can be realized; why on the other, anticipate evils, which can surely never come too late.

Egregiously indeed should we deceive ourselves were we to imagine that in the course of a life of ease and contentment, we could obtain the enjoyments of riches or of honour. It is by a combination of indefatigable industry and rigid oeconomy that great wealth is acquired; for when we have done all that can depend upon ourselves, when we have laboured without intermission, and been sparing even to parsimony, still we frequently experience that "bread is not always to the wise nor yet riches to men of understanding." Great honours we must remember are the reward of great exertions. The reputation of a Statesman or a Warrior is generally proportioned to the distresses from which he relieved or attempted to relieve his country; and the defeats of Thrasymene and Cannae are monuments erected to the fame of the elder Scipio, no less glorious than the victory of Zama.

When we contemplate the atchievements of the numerous train of heroes whose names, through the successive revolutions of four hundred years, adorn the annals of the roman republic our bosoms are animated with an ardent desire to emulate their virtues. We admire the undaunted fortitude with which every danger was braved, we admire the invincible resolution and perseverance, with which every difficulty was overcome, in the defence of their country: and when these virtues are recommended by such illustrious examples, the most exalted minds will fervently wish for opportunities to display those qualities which command the admiration of mankind. But when we consider, that those atchievements could never have been performed had not their Country during the same period been engaged in a perpetual struggle to maintain her very existence against her hostile and surrounding neighbours; when we reflect upon the dreadful calamities which the republic underwent, and how often she was brought to the brink of destruction, the rude and imperious calls of ambition must yield to the soft, persuasive eloquence of humanity, and a sentiment of real patriotism, must forbid us from pursuing the painful preeminence.

But if we should carefully avoid a delusion which by promising unreal advantages exposes us to the mortification of disappointment, how much more reason have we to shun another, which by threatening future distresses, embitters the present moment with the reality of woe. If we can circumscribe our desires within rational bounds; if we can be contented with a situation which affords the most essential enjoyments, we may safely conclude ourselves in a great measure, independent of external circumstances. There is a certain station in life, which if well filled will entitle us to the respect and esteem of our fellow citizens, without holding us up exposed to the envenomed shafts of rancorous envy. The rewards of Reason are proportioned rather to the improvement than to the magnitude of the trust; and in her impartial eye we may presume that the man whose usefulness is confined only by the limits of his opportunities to serve his fellow mortals, is no less meritorious than the founder of an empire or the discoveror of a world.—Such is the Divine, whose paternal labours are calculated to instruct, to enlighten and to improve the minds of the flock committed to his charge: whose periodical precepts teach the importance of the great duties of morality and religion, and whose exemplary sanctity of manners endears the virtues which from the sacred desk he earnestly recommends.—Such is the patriotic merchant whose industrious activity is exerted to promote the public interest in connexion with his own, and who by encouraging the agriculture and manufactures of his Country, enlarges the sphere of her beneficial commerce, and liberates her from the humiliating shackles of european dependency.—Such is the lawyer, who, disdaining the base and servile arts of chicanery and intrigue, uniformly exerts his learning and his talents in the cause of injured innocence and of truth.—And such is the humane physician, whose skill and benevolence are directed to the alleviation of the complicated miseries with which humanity is burthened; who, called to the assistance of human nature in all the variety of physical distress, administers not only the restoring preparation to the languishing body; but the balm of consolation to the wounded mind.

The combined advantages of utility and respectability, are not however confined to these professions. In a free country where honour consists not in idleness, the farmer, the mechanic, and the tradesman maintain the dignity due to their station, and become active constituent parts of the political body.

As the regulation of our conduct must in some measure, depend upon the sentiments which we form in the anticipation of our future appearance in life, it may be of some importance to lay a restraint upon the freedom of a wanton imagination, and to view ourselves seated for life, in one of these intermediate stations where removed "Far from the madding crowd's ignoble strife"[2] we may spend our days with happiness to ourselves, and with usefulness to our fellow mortals. If notwithstanding all our precautions we are destined to become the sport of adverse Fortune, and to undergo evils against which no human prudence can guard, at least the cruel stings of disappointed ambition will not add a poignancy to our woes. If on the other hand the blind capricious deity should bestow upon us unexpected favours, we shall be better enabled to improve the advantages which she may offer; to follow her with cautious steps, and to stop without disgrace wherever she may show a disposition to forsake us.

There is indeed one form under which Ambition assumes not merely the form, but with it all the amiable attractions and all the conscious dignity of Virtue. It is in the desire to appear conspicuous in the walks of literature and Science. An ambition, which to the members of the institution, at whose request I appear in this place, which to the sons of Harvard in general, must present itself under an aspect peculiarly engaging. Its gratification depends, not upon the destruction, but upon the improvement of mankind. The trophies erected to the Muses are not upon plains drenched in human gore, but in the hearts of the virtuous and the wise: and although the vulgar of mankind will always bestow more liberal applause upon their destroyers than upon their benefactors, yet the generous and humane will ever esteem the passage through the portico of Science, to be the most honourable avenue to the temple of Fame.

The situation of an infant country is necessarily unfavourable to an extensive encouragement of literary genius: the equality and mediocrity of fortunes renders an active profession necessary for the support of every individual: even those who are the most attached to the pursuits of Literature can view them only as a secondary object: in the ordinary course of human transactions the noblest faculties of the mind must droop and languish for want of culture and improvement.

> "Full many a flower be born to blush unseen
> And waste its sweetness on the desart air."

We find accordingly, that previous to the late revolution, America had produced so few men of great eminence, that European philosophers of no small note, arguing from this single fact, which is otherwise so well accounted for, have ventured to affirm, that Nature, like a partial step-mother had distributed her favours very unequally between the inhabitants of the two hemispheres: that a smaller portion of the etherial spirit had been allotted to man, on this than on the other side of the atlantic; and in the presumptuous pride of human reason, they have been almost tempted to deny us the honours of the species, and to assign us a station among the inferior animals of creation. This humiliating theory is ere this well exploded. The late revolution has brought forth american characters in arts and arms whose reputation is limited only by the boundaries of the civilized world: one of our most illustrious countrymen has successfully combated the insulting system in all its connections: and his performance[3] carries an internal evidence in favour of his opinions; as unanswerable, as the arguments and the facts which he adduces.

It becomes then incumbent upon the rising generation to maintain in all its lustre the splendid reputation which our country has acquired. To you therefore who are conscious of possessing the divine spark of transcendent genius, suffer me to express my ardent desire, that you may cherish the generous flame: that, in the various departments of Philosophy and History; of Oratory and Poetry, you may extract from this blooming garden of Science, such fragrant sweets, as shall hereafter diffuse their salutary influence throughout this extensive continent: that you may live to enjoy the fruits of a reputation founded upon your extensive usefulness to mankind; and that, after treading honourably the theatre of human life, when the scene shall close, and the curtain drop, you may be dismissed from the stage of action, with the unbounded plaudits of a grateful and admiring universe.

We separated early in the afternoon, and I went and paid a visit at Dr. Waterhouse's, and at Mr. Williams's. I went to Boston; where Bridge left me; and I took up my brother Tom. We met my classmate Tom Chandler, who just came from Hallifax: we got to Braintree between 7 and 8 o'clock, where I found Mr. Parsons, who pass'd the evening with us but lodg'd at Mr. Woodward's.

[1] Two other contemporary MS copies of JQA's Phi Beta Kappa speech are in the Adams Papers. These include his draft copy, dated 24 July–6 Aug., and a loose copy, presumably made from the draft. Excluding the one exception noted below, these two copies contain only minor stylistic changes from the Diary copy (M/JQA/46, Adams Papers, Microfilms, Reel No. 241; "An Oration," originally microfilmed under the date [1786–1787]).

[2] This and the next quotation are from Thomas Gray, "Elegy written in a Country Churchyard."

[3] At this point JQA made the following notation: "Notes upon Virginia, by Thomas Jefferson Esqr." The whole passage at the end of this paragraph, beginning with "one of our most illustrious countrymen," was added to the speech after JQA wrote his draft copy.

6.

Saltmarsh. Read. Mr. Cranch's.

SUNDAY SEPTEMBER 7TH. 1788.

The Marquis to Sainneville, commander of the french Squadron now in the harbour, and the Chevalier Maccarty de Martegues captain of the Achille, dined here to day. Several other officers were detained by the badness of the weather.[1]

[1] In his line-a-day entry, JQA mentions "Meeting, forenoon" (D/JQA/13, Adams Papers, Microfilms, Reel No. 16).

8.

Company afternoon. Angier.

9.

Went over to Milton.

WEDNESDAY SEPTEMBER 10TH.

The Governor with the Captains of the french vessells, the french Consul, and some other gentlemen dined with us.

11.

Mrs. Smith and Louisa. W. Cranch.

FRIDAY SEPTEMBER 12TH.

I left Braintree to return to Newbury-Port. Found Bridge in Boston. Dined at Mr. Smith's. We left Boston at about five o'clock and rode ten miles; to Newhall's tavern; where we lodge.

SATURDAY SEPTR. 12TH. [*i.e.* 13TH].

Breakfasted in Salem: saw Amory and Learned. Dined at Ipswich. We got to Newbury-Port, at about five. We lodge this night at Mrs. Hooper's.

SUNDAY SEPTR. 13TH. [*i.e.* 14TH].

I did not sleep a wink the whole night. My nerves are in a very disagreeable state of irritation. I attended meeting all day at Dr.

Tucker's, with Bridge. I called in the evening at Mr. N. Carter's, and at Mr. Tufts's to deliver letters. At Mr. Tufts's I saw Mr. Shaw, who, I find preached for Mr. Andrews this day. I retired early, and went to bed, but could get no sleep. After laying about three hours, I got up and went over to Dr. Swett, and requested him to supply me with an opiate, which he did; it gradually composed my nerves, and gave me a few hours of sleep.[1]

[1] This is the first of several references during the fall of 1788 to JQA's uncertain state of health. David Musto has argued that he was in a depressed state of mind, owing to the pressure that his family was placing on him to distinguish himself (to perpetuate the "family myth") and to his own worries about his future in an overcrowded legal profession. Musto's explanation for the resolution of these difficulties, which apparently occurred only months later, is largely undocumented ("The Youth of John Quincy Adams," Amer. Philos. Soc., *Procs.*, 113:269–282 [Aug. 1969]).

15.

Sleepless. Could do no business.

16.

Strolling about all day. Idle.

17.

Can neither read nor write.

18.

Training. Unwell out of spirits. Foster.

19.

Spent my time in visiting &c.

SATURDAY SEPTEMBER 20TH.

I have had three or four sleepless nights this weeks, and for the little rest I have enjoyed I have been indebted to soporific draughts. I dined this day with Mr. Parsons with Bridge and with Foster who took his station in the office on Thursday. This afternoon I mounted a horse and went to Haverhill where I am determined to spend a few days, and see if I cannot recruit my health. I found H. Lincoln here.

21.

Meeting afternoon. L. W. Mr. Thaxter.

22.

H. Lincoln. Dined with Mr. T. Mr. B's.

23.

Lincoln went home. Dr. Price's Sermons.

WEDNESDAY SEPTEMBER 24TH.

Lincoln went yesterday for Hingham; I went with Mr. and Mrs. Shaw to Andover. There was a large company at Mr. Symmes's; and after dinner we had a lecture, the Sermon was intolerably long. Singing remarkably good. We got back to Haverhill just after Sun-set. My Brother Charles with Daniel Russell arrived here this evening. Charles obtained leave to come and see me. Mr. Thaxter and his Lady pass'd part of the evening here.

25.

Mr. Noyes. Afternoon with White.

26.

Dined with Mr. Thaxter. Genl. Lincoln.

SATURDAY SEPTEMBER 27TH.

Another tedious sleepless night. Charles and Russell returned to Cambridge. I dined at Mr. White's. And in the afternoon got a little sleep which greatly refreshed my drooping spirits. Mr. French was here in the evening.

28.

Meeting Forenoon. Mr. Marsh. L. White.

29.

Tea at Mr. Adams's.

TUESDAY SEPTEMBER 30TH.

The weather was not very favourable, but, as the court of common pleas was to sit this week in Newbury-Port, I concluded to return there. When I got home, I found Bridge unwell. Nothing done at court but preparatory business this day. I retired early to bed.

WEDNESDAY OCTOBER 1ST. 1788.

"Oh gentle sleep
Nature's soft Nurse, how have I frighted thee
That thou no more wilt weigh mine eye lids down
And steep my senses in forgetfulness."[1]

In the present situation of my health I cannot possibly attend at all to study, and this circumstance with some others has determined me to spend some weeks, perhaps some months at Braintree. I spoke for a place in the stage which goes to Boston to-morrow. No business of consequence done at Court this day. Pass'd part of the evening at Mr. Jackson's.

[1] *Henry IV, Part II,* Act III, scene i, lines 5–8.

THURSDAY OCTOBER 2D.

I took my seat in the stage, in Company with a Lady who came from Portsmouth, and Mr. Vaughan, a brother of the gentlemen with whom I was acquainted in London. It was seven in the evening before we got to Boston. I went to Mr. Smith's; we pass'd part of the evening and lodged at Dr. Welch's. Lodg'd at Mr. Smith's.

FRIDAY OCTOBER 3D.

W. Cranch came into Boston with my father, who coming upon business which will detain him in town this night, gave me an opportunity to get to Braintree. I came home in company with my cousin.

4.

My father came home.

5.

Weymouth at meeting. Dr. Tufts's.

6.

Rode over to Milton in the afternoon.

TUESDAY OCTOBER 7TH.

Mr. Murray[1] the preacher who came from England with my father, came this day to pay him a visit, with his Lady whom he has lately married. He appears to be a man of an easy temper, and an ingenious mind, though not highly improved by learning. His wife is agreeable, though she appears a little tinctured with what the french call le precieux.

[1] Rev. John Murray, minister of the Church of Christ in Gloucester, Mass., and the founder of Universalism in America (JA, *Diary and Autobiography,* 3:216).

8.

Went over to Hingham.

9.

Charles and Otis were here. Got up shelves.

10.

Slept none. Went to Weymouth.

11.

Medicine. Voltaire's works.

12.

At home all day. But dull somewhat. Rode.

13.

Went to Milton. Put up books.

TUESDAY OCTOBER 14TH.

My occupations have been very regular, and similar for a week past. Last Thursday night I again experienced a total want of sleep. By the help however of medecine and of constant exercice I think I am in a way to recover. This evening, my[1]

[1] This entry, incomplete at the bottom of the page, is the last in D/JQA/12 until 6 Sept. 1789. In JQA's line-a-day entry, he adds: "Charles and Tom. Mr. and Mrs. Shaw" (D/JQA/13, Adams Papers, Microfilms, Reel No. 16).

15.

Company to dine. Mr. B. &c.

16.

Dr. Tufts &c. Mr. Shaw went to Hghm.

17.

Fine weather. Gunning with Tom. Townsend.

18.

Madam and Tom went to Boston. Violent Thunder.

19.

Meeting to hear Mr. Wibird. W. Cranch. And[rews?].

20.

Cranch went to Boston. Rain.

21.

Variable weather. Gibbon's history.

22.

Rode my horse. Andrews went towards Nby Pt.

23.

Mr. Russell's and returned at Night.

24.

Gunning in the morning with Charles. Tired.

25.

Mr. Thaxter. Mr. and Mrs. Smith. Mr. Shaw.

26.

Heard Mr. Shaw. Cranch and Phillips.

27.

Splendid parade.[1] Much company.

[1] Several regiments of troops from Boston were reviewed by Gov. Hancock and other dignitaries at Braintree (*Massachusetts Centinel*, 29 Oct.).

28.

Company gone. Went to Mr. Cranch's.

29.

Went with Tom to Cambridge. Returned.

30.

Mr. A. went to Boston. Charles to Cambridge.

31.

Mr. A. returned. Company at dinner. Mr. and Mrs. Storer. C. Storer &c.

NOVEMBER 1. 1788.

Rode as usual; and read Gibbon &c.

2.

General Knox dined with us. P. M.[1]

[1] After "P.M." follows in shorthand "no meeting."

3.

Cicero de Senectute.[1] Getting well.

[1] Cicero's *Cato Major de Senectute,* or *Essay on Old Age.*

4.

Went to Boston with Mrs. Cranch. Returned.

5.

W. Cranch came from Boston. Fine weather.

6.

Evening at Mrs. Quincy's. Parson Wiberd.[1]

[1] The entry concludes with shorthand for "no feeling."

7.

Mr. and Mrs. A went to Boston. Dined at Mr. Cranch's.

8.

Quite lonesome. Mrs. C. came home.

9.

Parson Wibird dined at Mr. C's. Folks came home.

10.

Madam preparing for New York.[1]

[1] AA was planning to visit AA2 (AA2, *Jour. and Corr.,* 2:105).

11.

Rain all day. Cleared up in the evening.

12.

Went to Boston. Mrs. A. N. York. Lodgd at Camb.

13.

Returned to Braintree in the forenoon.

14.

Justinian's Inst.[1] Foster's Cr. Law. Gibbon &c.

[1] Justinian's *Institutes,* a textbook of Roman law and a foundation of continental law, originally issued by Justinian I in 533.

15.

Cold Weather. Dr. Tufts this evening.

16.

Mr. Norton. He dined with us.

17.

Went to Milton. Chilly weather looks like snow.

18.

Rode as usual. Read a variety at home.

19.

My health happily recovered. Rain; part of the day.

20.

Went to Mr. Cranch's. Mrs. C. gone to Boston.

21.

Letter from Mamma. Hartford. Fed. Senators.[1]

[1] Probably AA to JA, 16 Nov. (Adams Papers). In this letter, written from Hartford, AA makes reference to the elections of federal senators in Massachusetts and Connecticut.

22.

Went to Boston. Return'd with W. Cranch.

23.

Mr. Everett of Dorchester: dined with us.

24.

Very warm; rainy, disagreeable weather.

25.

Charles came home from Cambridge.

26.

Wm. Cranch was here. Rode to Milton.

27.

Thanksgiving day. Dull weather.

28.

Bad night. Dined at My Uncle Adams's.

29.

Snow. Charles could not go to Cambridge.

30.

Mr. Wibird preach'd. Charles dined at Mr. C.'s.

DECEMBER 1. 1788.

Charles return'd to Cambridge.

2.

Winslow Warren. Rode in the afternoon.

3.

Gibbon 5th. vol. 4th. gone which I much regret.

4.

Very cold. At Mr. Cranch's. Dr. Fogg. Mr. Thayer.

5.

Wm Cranch came from Boston. Heard from N. York.[1]

[1] Presumably the letter written by AA to JA between 16 Nov. and 3 Dec., not found (JA to AA, 2 Dec., AA to JA, 3 Dec., Adams Papers).

6.

Went to Milton with Wm. Cranch. He dined with us.

7.

Mr. Cranch's after meeting. Mr. C. quite unwell.

8.

Left Braintree. Went as far as Wilmington. Rain.

9.

Went to Haverhill. Wet through.

10.

Got to Newbury-Port. Ordination.[1] Dancing.

[1] John Andrews, JQA's frequent companion, was ordained associate minister of the First Religious Society of Newburyport, to assist the ailing Rev. Thomas Cary (Currier, *Newburyport*, 1:253).

11.

Dined with Mr. Tufts. Not very bright. Dr. Swett's.

12.

Company chiefly gone. *Russell.* Rode with Thompson. Dancing again.

13.

Put my horse at Tappan's. Eve with Dr. Kilham.

14.

Heard Mr. Ware. Preach'd admirably. D. Atkins.

15.

Attended the office. Read a little. Mr. Jackson's.

16.

Mr. Parsons &c went to Salem Court. Miss Coats.

17.

Snow storm. Went to Salem. Supp'd at Amory's.

18.

Attended court. Sat late. Lodg'd with Mr. Atkins.

19.

Dined with Amory. Went to the ball.

20.

Cold weather. Came home with Bridge. Sleepy.

21.

Heard Mr. Andrews, preach. *Bouscaren.* Mr. Carter.

22.

Very cold weather. Evening in the office.

23.

Cold continues. Eve at Judge Greenleaf's.

24.

Went to Haverhill. Colder than ever.

25.

Mr. Thaxter's. Miss Hazen. Eve at Mr. Bartlett's.

26.

Return'd to N. Port. Wrote in the Eve.

27.

Dined at Judge Greenleaf's. Foster came home.

28.

Parson Allen preached. Snow storm.

29.

Thompson got home. Court at Mr. Atkins's.

30.

Eve at Dr. Sawyer's. Mr. Boyd.—a youth.

31.

Eve with Foster at Mr. Jackson's, He was out.

Chronology

Chronology

JOHN QUINCY ADAMS, 1767–1788

1767

July 11: Born in Braintree on the Adams farm at the foot of Penn's Hill.

1775

July 17: With his mother (AA) witnesses the Battle of Bunker Hill from Penn's Hill.

1778

Feb.–April: Sails with his father (JA) from Mount Wollaston aboard the frigate *Boston,* to Bordeaux; thence travels to Paris where JA serves as one of the three United States commissioners.

April 14: Enters M. Le Coeur's Academy at Passy, near Paris.

1779

March–June: With JA, leaves Passy and awaits passage to America at Nantes, Lorient, and St. Nazaire.

June 17–Aug. 2: Sails from Lorient to Boston aboard the French frigate *La Sensible.*

Nov. 12: Begins his Diary.

Nov. 13–Dec. 8: Leaves Boston aboard *La Sensible* for France with his father, his brother Charles (CA), John Thaxter Jr., and Francis Dana. The congress had named JA to negotiate peace and commercial treaties with Great Britain. The frigate makes port at El Ferrol, Spain.

Dec. 26: The Adams party begins its overland journey to France across northern Spain.

1780

Feb. 9: Arrives in Paris.

Feb. 10: Attends M. Pechigny's school at Passy with CA.

July 27–Aug. 10: With CA, accompanies father to the Netherlands, JA's purpose being to negotiate a loan for the United States.

Aug. 30: With CA, becomes a boarding student at the Latin School on the Singel, in Amsterdam.

Nov. 10: Leaves the school with CA after JA's dispute with the preceptor.

Dec. 18: Goes with CA and John Thaxter Jr. to Leyden, where all three matriculate at the university during the following month.

1781

June 9: Travels to Amsterdam with his father.

July 7: Leaves Amsterdam for Russia with Francis Dana.

July 25: Arrives in Berlin.

Aug. 27: Arrives in St. Petersburg, where he serves as secretary and interpreter to Dana, appointed to seek Russian diplomatic recognition of the United States.

1782

March 9–10: Visits Oranienbaum and Peterhoff, near St. Petersburg.

July 10–11: Attends the Grand Duke's annual ball at Peterhoff.

Oct. 30: Leaves St. Petersburg for The Hague by way of the northern overland route through Finland.

Nov. 22: Arrives in Stockholm, where he remains until 31 December.

1783

Jan. 1–25: Travels from Stockholm to Göteborg.

Feb. 15: Arrives in Copenhagen, remaining there until 5 March.

March 10: Enters Hamburg and stays there until 5 April.

April 21: Arrives at The Hague, where he continues Latin and Greek studies with C. W. F. Dumas until JA's return from Paris in July.

Aug.–Sept: Serves as his father's secretary in Paris, where JA and his fellow commissioners on 3 Sept. sign the Definitive Treaty with Great Britain.

Sept. 22–Oct. 20: Lodges with JA at Thomas Barclay's house at Auteuil, near Paris.

Oct. 20: Leaves with JA for England on vacation, spent largely in London with short visits to Oxford and Bath.

1784

Jan. 2: Leaves London for The Hague with JA, who seeks a second Dutch loan to save American credit.

May 14: Journeys to London to await the uncertain arrival of his mother and sister (AA2). Remains for more than one month before returning to The Hague alone.

July 30: Is reunited with AA and AA2 in London.

Aug. 8: Joined by JA, the Adams family travels to France, arriving in Paris on 13 August.

Aug. 17: The Adamses establish their residence in Auteuil, while JA serves as a joint commissioner to negotiate treaties with European powers.

1785

May 12: Leaves Paris en route to America to attend Harvard.

May 21: Sails from Lorient on the *Courier de l'Amérique.*

July 17: Arrives in New York.

Aug. 13: Leaves for Boston after a month in the company of members of the congress and New York society.

Aug. 26: Arrives in Boston.

Aug. 31: Is advised by President Joseph Willard to wait until the spring to enter Harvard.

Sept. 7: Arrives at Haverhill to begin intensive study of Latin and Greek under the tutelage of his uncle, the Reverend John Shaw.

1786

March 15: Examined and admitted to Harvard as a junior sophister.

May 29: Becomes a member of the "A.B." Club.

June 12: Gives his first speech before the "A.B." Club on the topic "Nothing is so difficult, but it may be overcome by industry."

June 21: Elected to Phi Beta Kappa.

July 6: Delivers his first speech before the Harvard chapter of Phi Beta Kappa on the question "Whether civil discord is advantageous to society."

Sept. 26: Takes part in a forensic dispute at the Harvard Exhibition on the question "Whether inequality among citizens be necessary to the preservation of liberty of the whole."

1787

April 10: At the Harvard Exhibition partakes in a conference on the comparative utility of law, physic, and divinity.

July 18: Gives English oration at his commencement on the topic "Upon the Importance and Necessity of Public Faith, to the Well-Being of a Community," which becomes his first published work when it appears in the *Columbian Magazine* in September.

Sept. 8: Begins his legal studies in Newburyport in the office of Theophilus Parsons.

1788

June 20–30: Greets his parents on their return from Europe and assists the move into the new family residence, the Vassall-Borland house in Braintree.

Sept. 5: Gives the annual Phi Beta Kappa Oration at Cambridge on the topic of young men's ambition.

NOTE ON THE INDEX

This Index covers volumes 1 and 2 of the *Diary of John Quincy Adams* in accordance with Adams Papers practice of providing an index at the end of each published unit.

Every index is designed in some measure to supplement the annotation. The compilers have tried to furnish the correct spellings of proper names, to supply forenames for persons who appear in the text only with surnames, to indicate places of residence and occupations of persons whose forenames are either unknown or not known with certainty, and finally to distinguish by dates persons with identical or nearly identical names. Markedly variant spellings of proper names have been cross-referenced to what are believed to be their most nearly standard forms, and the variant forms found in the MSS are parenthetically recorded following the standard spellings. Undoubtedly the index contains mistakes and incomplete identifications; the editors would warmly welcome corrections of mistakes of this kind, and indeed of every kind, from users who can put them straight.

Wives' names, with a few exceptions for special reasons, follow their husbands' names. *See*-references under maiden names are used for members of the Adams and collateral families and for women mentioned in the text who married subsequently but before 31 December 1788.

Adams' Harvard acquaintances are identified by class year: e.g. (H.C. 1787).

Under major place names (e.g. Boston, Paris) there are appended separate gatherings of "Buildings, landmarks, streets, &c.," the items in which are arranged alphabetically rather than in order of their appearance (as other subentries are throughout the Index).

The index was compiled in the Adams Papers editorial office.

Index

Index

Index

Index

494

The *Diary of John Quincy Adams* was composed by Progressive Typographers. Rudolph Ruzicka's *Fairfield Medium,* with several variant characters designed expressly for *The Adams Papers,* is used throughout. The text is set in the eleven-point size, and the lines are spaced one and one-half points. The printing and binding are by the Murray Printing Company. The paper, made by the Mohawk Paper Company, is a grade named *Superfine.* The books were originally designed by P. J. Conkwright and Burton L. Stratton.